Using
the World Wide Web

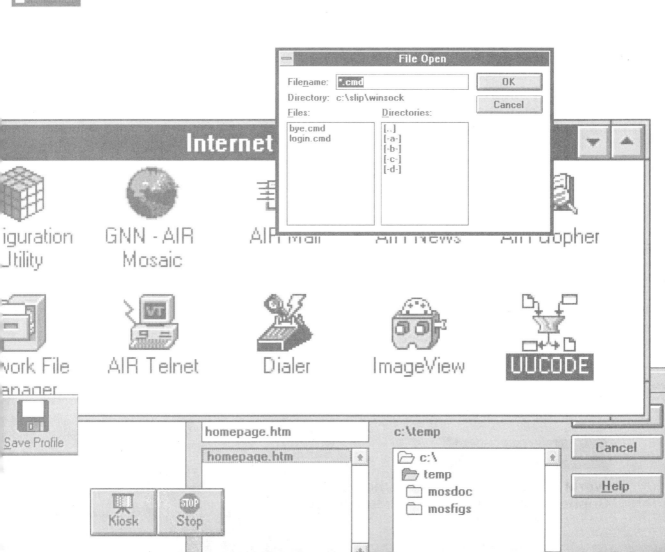

Using
the World Wide Web

Bill Eager

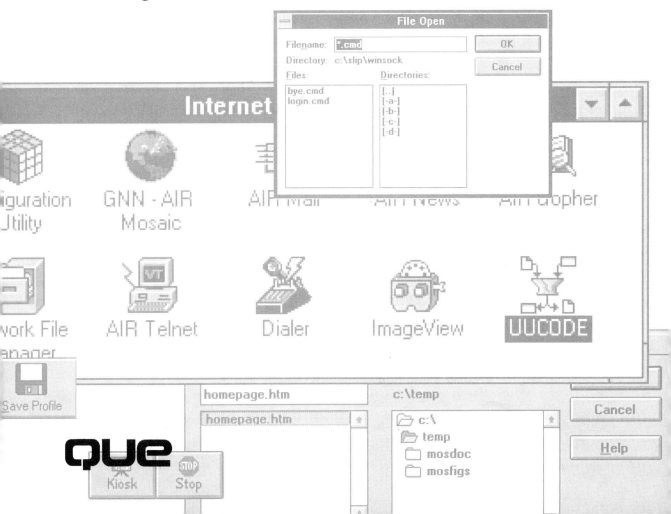

que

Using the World Wide Web

Copyright © 1994 by Que® Corporation

Library of Congress Catalog No.: 94-68827

ISBN: 0-7897-0016-6

97 96 95   6 5 4 3 2

Interpretation of the printing code: the rightmost double-digit number is the year of the book's printing; the rightmost single-digit number, the number of the book's printing. For example, a printing code of 94-1 shows that the first printing of the book occurred in 1994.

Publisher: David P. Ewing

Associate Publisher: Corinne Walls

Publishing Director: Brad R. Koch

Managing Editor: Michael Cunningham

Product Marketing Manager: Greg Wiegand

Dedication

I dedicate this book to a few dear friends: Dan Lu, who showed me how to retrieve games from a mainframe when computer programs were stored on "ticker tape"; Dave Barker, whose fascination with technology frequently has a social bent; Klaus Stadler, who knows how to make computers solve problems; and Ed Simmons, who likes to push the envelope with computers. They have shown me that electronic communications can be fun, socially relevant, practical, and always challenging.

Credits

Publishing Manager
Jim Minatel

Acquisitions Editor
Cheryl Willoughby

Production Editor
Heather Kaufman

Editors
Kelli M. Brooks
Noelle Gasco
Theresa Mathias

Technical Editors
Jeff Bankston
Paul McIntyre
Tobin Anthony

Figure Specialist
Cari Ohm

Book Designer
Paula Carroll

Cover Designer
Dan Armstrong

Production Team
Steve Adams
Karen Gregor
Aren Howell
Daryl Kessler
Debbie Kincaid
Elizabeth Lewis
Erika Millen
Steph Mineart
G. Alan Palmore
Beth Rago
Kaylene Riemen
Michael Thomas
Suzanne Tully
Jody York

Indexer
Rebecca Mayfield

Editorial Assistant
Andrea Duvall

Acquisitions Assistant
Ruth Slates

Composed in *Stone Serif* and *MCPdigital* by Que Corporation

About the Author

Bill Eager lives in Conifer, Colorado. With more than 12 years of communications technology experience, Mr. Eager designs, writes, and speaks about electronic communications. While Manager for the Corporate Communications Department at BASF Corporation, Mr. Eager proposed and helped develop a computer-based system that distributes hypertext-based multimedia information to thousands of employees at sites across the country. Mr. Eager has been an editor of several national trade magazines, including *ComSat Technology* and *Communications Technology*. His book *The Information Payoff* by Prentice Hall details how companies use network-based communication to improve productivity, enhance training, and become more competitive, and *The Information Superhighway Illustrated* by Que combines text and colorful artwork in an easy-to-understand overview of the technology and applications of the Information Superhighway. Mr. Eager is President of the Colorado Chapter of the International Interactive Communications Society. In addition to computers, Bill enjoys photography, hiking, and skiing. Bill can be reached electronically at eager@sosi.com.

Acknowledgments

A book like this is the result of the efforts of many different people who contribute and combine a variety of creative skills. I would first like to thank the many professionals at Que who make books like this possible, including Brad Koch, Publishing Director, who had the insight to develop this timely book; Jim Minatel, Publishing Manager, who managed the project and constantly strives to ensure that readers, like you, get a book that offers comprehensive coverage of a subject, has useful and accurate information, and is fun to read and use; and Heather Kaufman, Kelli Brooks, Noelle Gasco, Theresa Mathias, and Cheryl Willoughby, who all provided advice and input on the manuscript, making it better with each query.

Very special thanks go to Harry and Ione Teff, Terry Smith, and Mark Kimbrel, who helped travel through the Web, research information, explore home pages and links, and develop and write copy. Spry, Inc. was kind enough to provide an evaluation copy of its Internet/Web package Internet In A Box, which includes Air Mosaic. In addition to helping with our review of the features of this client, the software proved to be an excellent interface for Web exploration. Rocky Mountain Internet, Inc. helped out by providing SLIP connections for research of this book. A final note of thanks to the thousands of Web authors who invest a tremendous amount of time and energy to create exciting, multimedia-filled Web pages about subjects they clearly love.

Trademarks

All terms mentioned in this book that are known to be trademarks or service marks have been appropriately capitalized. Que Corporation cannot attest to the accuracy of this information. Use of a term in this book should not be regarded as affecting the validity of any trademark or service mark.

Disclaimer

The publisher and author of *Using the World Wide Web* make no direct or implied endorsement of any of the companies, services, or products listed herein, nor do they warranty the accuracy of the resource listings or the information contained in the listings.

Contents at a Glance

Contents

7 Business on the Web   177

8 Computer Resources   209

9 Education on the WWW   249

10 Government Resources   293

11 Health and Medicine 325

15 Publications: News, Periodicals, and Books   429

16 Science Resources   457

B Other Versions of Mosaic for Macintosh   591

Introduction

The Internet—the global network of networks, referred to by users as simply The Net—continues to receive tremendous publicity. Magazines, newspapers, television networks, and radio stations all produce stories about the Internet. In a two-week period, *BusinessWeek* featured a cover story called "The Information Revolution: How Digital Technology Is Changing the Way We Work and Live," and the cover of *Time* magazine pronounced, "The Strange New World of the Internet: Battles on the Frontiers of Cyberspace." Editors at *U.S. News and World Report*, NBC, and National Public Radio (NPR) receive electronic-mail messages from Internet users.

The technology and applications of the Internet now extend beyond the realm of computer techies and industry trade publications. The Internet receives this extensive attention because it is an exciting communications medium, business tool, and commercial outlet, much as television and radio were 50 and 75 years ago, respectively. Now, with its simple interface and multimedia applications, the World Wide Web makes the Internet accessible to millions of people who previously stayed away because of the difficult technical command language and the dull visual appearance of the system.

One indication that the Internet has evolved from technical experiment to widespread acceptance is the fact that jokes are beginning to surface. Some of the more than 20 million Internet users have posted suggestions for new books about the Internet, including the following:

- *The Internet User's Guide to Internet User Guides*

- *Confessions of an Internet Guide Reader*

- *The Lost Guides of the Internet*

- *A Guide To Getting Coffee on the Internet*

The suggestions, of course, poke fun at the phenomenal growth of books and guides about the Internet. Some bookstores devote entire sections to the subject. Why are publishers and authors madly creating new titles for the Internet?

It Keeps on Growing

Historically, the Internet has doubled in size every 10 months for the past 6 years. This growth occurs in both the physical aspects of the Net—the host computers and the connections between computers—as well as the number of people who use the system. In 1985, the Internet had about 1,961 host computers, or *nodes*. These mainframes, minicomputers, and microcomputers can provide access to the services of the Internet to hundreds of thousands of people. Today, the number of hosts exceeds 3 million.

Two years ago, the Internet was used exclusively by scientists, academics, and students as a vehicle for sharing information about work and research projects. Today, all demographic groups use the Internet: lawyers, teachers, homeowners, business professionals, and so on. The number of users continues to increase at the phenomenal rate of 2 million new logins each month—the equivalent of 4 new users every minute.

The Internet is not only growing in terms of size, but also expanding in terms of the types of services that are available. The application that was responsible for the initial growth of the Internet is electronic mail, known as *e-mail*. E-mail represents a cost-effective mechanism for people to share messages and send files to friends and colleagues around the world. Two other popular Internet applications exist. File-transfer protocol (FTP) enables users to download files and even software programs from computers around the world; and Telnet enables users to log in to remote computers and to run programs. The Internet also has applications, including the World Wide Web, that search for information. Understanding how these applications work makes using the Internet easier.

Most people want to use technology to accomplish a task: provide entertainment, retrieve information, or assist with research. They don't want to spend time and energy making the technology work. Telephones, radios, and television sets use standard, user-friendly technology; you push keys to operate the telephone, turn a dial on the radio, and press buttons on a remote-control for the television. People want the Internet to be just as simple to use as these common household communication devices.

Until recently, however, both connecting to and using the Internet were complex processes. There were several reasons for this.

■ Rather than being created by a commercial foundation, the system was born from a U.S.-government-sponsored research program.

■ Many types of computers can connect to the Internet, ranging from 286-based PCs to Pentium machines, Macintoshes, and terminals. These computers can use a variety of connections and connection speeds. Users can have dial-in, SLIP, or PPP accounts or direct access lines; and communication speeds range from 2,400 bytes per second to 1.544MB (megabytes) per second.

■ Many software programs—running under UNIX, DOS, Windows, and Macintosh, for example—are used as interfaces to the resources of the Internet and the World Wide Web.

Today, national and local service providers eliminate many of these choices and technical obstacles by offering services that include connection and installation of interface programs. Also, the new software programs and interfaces are extremely easy-to-use, with point-and-click operation and simple icons that represent functions, such as searching.

The World Wide Web: A New Paradigm

The ultimate in user-friendly interfaces is the World Wide Web, also called WWW, W3, or the Web. The WWW is part of the Internet; globally, it represents all the computers (*servers*) that offer users access to hypermedia-based information and documentation. Hypermedia enables users to navigate the Internet, moving with point-and-click ease from one location or one document to another. The Web eliminates unfriendly computer commands. In addition, the resources of the WWW include graphic images, photographs, audio, and full-motion video—elements that make locating and using information fun and useful.

The WWW is an interactive medium. Unlike television, the Web doesn't make you wait for a predetermined schedule to get the information you want, and programming is not defined by a small group of producers. When you use the resources of the Web, you are in control. You decide what you want and when you want it.

This empowerment extends to the creation of information. In the 1400s, the Gutenberg press gave a kick-start to the widespread distribution of knowledge through print material such as books and newsletters. A modern-day version of the printing press is a WWW/Internet resource known appropriately as "Project Gutenberg." This is a computer database that consists of the full text of more than 100 public domain books ranging from titles by Charles Dickens to Mark Twain. You can either read these famous works on-line, or download them to your computer to view at your leisure.

Indeed, the WWW enables anyone who has a computer and the proper Internet connection to be a multimedia publisher. In a few minutes, you can create a message or a document that the entire world can access. When you travel the WWW, you'll find electronic books, magazines, and journals. Authors live and write in countries around the world.

Combining global connectivity and individual empowerment, the Internet and WWW represent a form of electronic democracy. No single government, organization, company, or person controls the technical infrastructure, the computer systems, the applications, or the information that comprise this electronic communications system. The democratic nature of the Internet and WWW are exemplified by the tremendous variety of information that is available—everything from technical studies of astrophysics to reports on rock-and-roll bands. Information and messages fly from country to country in seconds. The speed of information delivery promotes political democracy as uncensored, unpackaged news and information moves freely around the world.

Reports, personal messages, and fund-raising requests were sent through the Internet during the Chinese military crackdown in Tiananmen Square, the 1991 coup attempt in the Soviet Union, and the recent war in Croatia. The widespread dissemination of information is not limited to personal correspondence. For example, the complete text of the North American Free Trade Agreement (NAFTA) is maintained as a WWW document by *The Tech*, MIT's oldest newspaper. In addition, the news-service company VOGON operates a Web server that provides *UK News*, a compilation of hypertext-based stories received from the BBC; and *The San Francisco Chronicle* and *The San Francisco Examiner* maintain Web computers that enable users to access news articles.

Finding the Needle in the Haystack

Because it is easy to use, combines multiple forms of media, and provides access to unlimited information, the Web contributes to the explosive growth of the Internet. The most widely used Web interface is Mosaic, a free, public-domain software program partly developed under a U.S.-government grant.

In a six-month period, more than two million people downloaded Mosaic from the host computer at the National Center for Supercomputer Applications (NCSA) site.

Universities, government agencies, companies, and individual users are fervently developing hypermedia documents and starting W3 servers. This volume of development creates a good news/bad news situation. The good news is that every subject known to man can be found through the Web. The bad news is that navigating that mountain of information is more difficult.

One of the best-selling national periodicals is *TV Guide*, a publication that informs viewers what programs are available and lists air time and channel location. With the growth of cable television, *TV Guide* and other publications cater to people who don't want to spend an hour to locate a good 30-minute television program.

If 40 channels of television programming create confusion, imagine how difficult it is to locate a specific topic, service, resource, or company on a global computer system with three million hosts. Also, although radio and broadcast-television programming are free, you have to pay monthly or hourly charges to wander through the resources of the World Wide Web.

This Book Is a Guide

Despite the jokes about new Internet publications, this book firmly stands as a guide. It is a guide that provides an overview of the principal applications of the Internet and the World Wide Web. It is a guide to the various connections and interfaces that provide access to the Web. It is a guide that provides a basic tutorial on procedures for writing home pages—the starting point for each of the resources on the WWW—and multimedia documents for publication on the Web.

Chapters 1 and 2 ("The Internet" and "The World Wide Web") of this book teach you the techniques and terminology you need to know to navigate successfully through the Internet and the World Wide Web. There is also useful information about the history, current applications, and trends that will shape the way we communicate today, and in the future. Chapter 3, "Connecting to the WWW," provides both reviews and in-depth explanations of the most popular WWW browsers—the software programs that are the interface to exploration and use of the Web. Chapter 4, "How to Create a WWW Home Page," gives you a lesson on how to develop a home page of your own. You learn how to write HTML (HyperText Markup Language), the computer programming language for the WWW. This will allow you to create electronic pointers to all your favorite Web resources and store them in a multimedia document that you can load each time you want to use the WWW.

The remaining 75 percent of the book (chapters 5 through 18) consists of reviews and listings of the multitude of resources now available on WWW servers around the world. Broken down by subject area, the listings give you the URL (Uniform Resource Locator) address for home pages of each Web resource. In addition to a brief review of the resource highlighting the information and the links to other resources and multimedia, each chapter includes figures that depict many of the home pages. Chapters also offer detailed descriptions of the most popular Web resources for a specific category. For example, in the chapter on science resources, there is a comprehensive review of NASA's home page, which offers connections to hundreds of scientific, educational, and space-related organizations and multimedia documents.

With its point-and-click interfaces, the Web encourages exploration. One link quickly leads to a new area or topic. The listings in this book facilitate exploration as they provide a starting point for jumping into the vast resources of the World Wide Web. Enjoy—and don't worry about getting lost. Home is only a click away.

Conventions Used in This Book

The conventions used in this book have been established to help you learn to use Web software quickly and easily and to help you locate the Web resources that you want.

The book uses several type enhancements to indicate special text. The URL addresses of Web sites appear in **bold**. (Don't worry if you don't know what a URL is; see the explanation in chapter 2, "The World Wide Web.") Boldface also is used for other electronic addresses, such as FTP sites and e-mail. Text that you need to type appears in `special type`.

Chapter 1

The Internet

Science Fiction Becomes Science Fact

As the 21st century looms closer, many of the social and technological predictions of science-fiction writers, including Jules Verne, H.G. Wells, Robert
Heinlein, Arthur C. Clarke, and Isaac Asimov, seem uncannily accurate.
People have been to the moon, explored the surface of distant planets, and
created robots. Communication technology frequently is woven into sci-fi
stories. Flash Gordon, Buck Rogers, Doctor Who, and the crew of the Starship
Enterprise all use advanced communication technology, including wireless
communication devices, video conferencing equipment, computer-based
multimedia information systems, and virtual-reality devices. The public and
commercial companies no longer view these scenarios as being far-fetched
daydreams, but consider them to be glimpses into the not-too-distant future.
In this context, the technology and the ideas for the Information Superhighway emerged.

In a speech to the Academy of Television Arts and Sciences, Vice President
Al Gore described the potential impact of a comprehensive communications
system. Such a system will reach every classroom, library, and hospital in the
country, Gore said, serving as an "information superhighway that can save
lives, create jobs, and give every American, young and old, the chance for the
best education available to anyone, anywhere."

To turn these ambitious goals into reality, the Clinton administration and
Congress are forging legislation that will create a National Information Infrastructure (NII). The NII will develop from the integration of hardware, software, connections, and skills that make it possible to connect people with
each other and with an array of services and information resources. The NII
represents an interconnection of computer networks, telecommunications

services, and applications. This system has the potential to improve significantly the way that people communicate and the way that people locate and use information in their jobs and daily lives.

Because the NII is so closely related to economic development, President Bill Clinton established an Advisory Council on the National Information Infrastructure (NII) to provide information on matters related to the development of the NII to Secretary of Commerce Ron Brown. Brown notes, "There's going to be a fundamental change in the way we work, the way we learn, the way we communicate. Knowing how the Industrial Revolution permanently altered American life, we can only begin to imagine how we will be transformed by becoming an information society."

Predictions are that the NII can

- Enhance U.S. manufacturing competitiveness

- Increase the speed and efficiency of electronic commerce and business-to-business communication to promote economic growth

- Improve health-care delivery and control costs

- Promote the development and accessibility of quality education and lifelong learning

- Make the nation more effective at environmental monitoring

- Sustain the role of libraries as mechanisms to provide equal access to information

- Provide government services to the public in a fast and efficient manner

To prove that there is more than theoretical rhetoric behind these concepts, the Information Infrastructure task force maintains an Internet Gopher server that contains reports and documents about the NII. Use your Gopher to connect, or Telnet to **iitf.doc.gov** and login as Gopher. Correspondingly, the White House distributes information on many subjects via the Internet; to receive this information, simply send an electronic-mail message that includes only the words "send info" to **publications@whitehouse.gov**. And if you have a question that demands an answer from the top, you can send electronic mail directly to President Clinton or Vice President Gore; their Internet addresses are **president@whitehouse.gov** and **vice.president@whitehouse.gov.** Although your mail probably won't be answered personally by the President or Vice President, you should receive an answer from an aide.

The Foundation of the Information Superhighway

The Internet encompasses both the U.S. National Information Infrastructure and a global Information Superhighway. An affiliation of tens of thousands of private, academic, and government-supported networks of computers and communication links, the Internet connects some 30 million users in more than 80 countries. Businesses, hospitals, colleges, libraries, and homes have links to the Internet. Technically, the pathways that connect these different end users are confusing—messages or files that travel between Dallas and Tokyo may never take the same route twice. For users, the value of the Internet is in two main functions: the Internet provides rapid, seamless communication among millions of locations, and it makes locating information easy.

We live in a world in which speed and convenience have become the norm. Twenty-four-hour-a-day banking, shopping, and travel are commonplace. Communication and information have a natural place in a world that emphasizes instant gratification and nonstop access.

As the economies of nations around the world become increasingly interdependent, speed of information delivery becomes a valuable competitive tool. Information about stock prices, pending mergers, and new products travels rapidly. A decade ago, businesses could remain competitive even if correspondence took a week; three years ago, however, overnight delivery became standard; and today, same-day delivery is often expected. The Internet is the ultimate in convenient same-day delivery service—a message can travel 10,000 miles in a few seconds, and users don't need to concern themselves with area codes, foreign exchanges, or time zones.

The Internet affects all aspects of society, including commerce, health, education, and interpersonal communication. Many of the visionary goals of the NII are already being realized by organizations, companies, and people who push the envelope with respect to the development and application of the Internet. The following sections provide examples of a variety of futuristic uses of the Internet.

Computers and Commuters Unite

San Diego commuters log in to the Internet to get a snapshot view of real-time traffic information: freeway speeds, accident reports, and construction activity. Updated every minute, the information is available both as a graphical display superimposed on a map of the San Diego freeway and as a text-based listing for users who don't have the Internet's World Wide Web graphical interfaces.

The California Department of Transportation (Caltrans) and the S-Cubed Division of Maxwell Laboratories, a San Diego-based high-technology research and development company, underwrite this public service as a pilot project. By connecting the traffic information available on Caltrans San Diego Traffic Management Center's traffic-control computers with Maxwell's computing network, freeway status is available instantly. Caltrans has approximately 200 instrumented freeway locations in San Diego, providing a complete and instantaneous picture of the county freeway system, including current vehicle speeds for each freeway lane and per-hour vehicle counts for the lanes and ramps at all instrumented San Diego freeway locations. Computer users with Internet access can display this information before leaving their homes in the morning or offices in the evening.

The system not only helps individual commuters, but also has a positive effect on traffic patterns as people adjust their routes and drive times according to the information that is available.

Using the capabilities of World Wide Web, the system incorporates clickable links that display maps of each instrumented interchange. The graphical display shows areas of slow or congested traffic in red and yellow; clear areas appear in green. Additional Web pages contain daily listings of planned construction and maintenance road closures and a current display of the traffic-incident log that reports the status of accidents. The information also is available in ASCII text format for Internet users who don't use the World Wide Web.

The same information could be displayed on kiosks at airports, sporting-event centers, and other locations where people may want to inquire about traffic conditions before getting on the road. In the future, wireless data-communication networks will deliver traffic information directly to cars.

A Newsstand in Your Computer

Based in Washington, D.C., The Electronic Newsstand provides Internet users with current articles from leading periodicals, including *BusinessWeek, The Economist, The New Yorker, Inc., Vibe,* and *Discover.* The Electronic Newsstand carries more than 90 titles and receives more than 40,000 "visitors" every day. The Newsstand also develops Business Information Centers that enable corporations to place information about their products and services on the Internet. (Lufthansa Airlines and Ford's Lincoln-Mercury division have set up on-line business centers.) In the past year, the Newsstand has been accessed 3 million times from more than 75,000 host sites.

Medical Students and Doctors Benefit from On-Line Images

With a $1 million federal grant, researchers at the University of Colorado Health Sciences Center have created a database of the human body. The Visible Human Project (VHP), sponsored by the National Library of Medicine, involves scanning, x-raying, freezing, slicing, and photographing cross sections of male and female bodies.

Each body produces approximately 1,800 one-millimeter cross sections, with an image resolution 16 times better than that provided produced by a video camera. Individual images are stacked to create three-dimensional depictions. The information is digitized and stored in a database so that it can be retrieved via the Internet.

Designed specifically for medical applications, the database requires users to have special accounts, passwords, and documentation. VHP will help train medical students, educate patients about medical conditions, help medical personnel diagnose diseases, and assist in planning treatments such as radiation and surgery.

Educators Get Answers and Ideas Electronically

The academic community has contributed significantly to the resources that are available on the Internet. Teachers and students use the Internet for help with tasks ranging from writing reports to developing lesson plans.

Established in 1966, the Educational Resources Information Center (ERIC) provides users rapid access to an extensive body of education-related literature. The U.S. Department of Education's Office of Educational Research and Improvement supports ERIC. With six subject-specific clearinghouses and three support components, ERIC helps educators with research, reference, and referral services; computer searches; and document reproduction.

ERIC can be accessed in a number of different ways. For example, if you use Gopher to connect to **cwis.usc.edu**, the University of Southern California's Gopher, you'll find a number of pointers to ERIC information (URL address **gopher://cwis.usc.edu/**).

AskERIC is an Internet-based question-and-answer service. When educators refer questions to AskERIC, staff members use the resources of the Internet to locate information and deliver it electronically within two days. The AskERIC electronic library stores files of material that include lesson plans, government information, and resource guides. Every week, 15,000 people use AskERIC.

Network Evolution: From Government Research to Global Information System

The Internet was conceived in 1969, when the Advanced Research Projects Agency (ARPA, a Department of Defense organization) funded research of computer networking. The research focused on creating a packet-switched network—a system in which information (messages or files) is broken into small packets that move independently through various networks and switches until they reach their destinations and are reassembled.

This computer networking research encompassed several objectives. The U.S. military objective was to create a national communications system that would be impervious to attacks by other countries (primarily the former Soviet Union). The new system, known as ARPANET, promised to maintain communication integrity in the event of a national emergency. In the ARPANET system, information moved randomly through many networks and systems rather than traveling over one line and through a central switching point or hub. Earlier in this chapter, it was stated that information traveling between Dallas and Tokyo would never travel the same route twice—this is a legacy of ARPANET's security-consciousness.

For the academic community, ARPANET was an ideal system for geographically separated researchers, who could send information to one another and share the computing power of multiple computers.

In 1975, the Defense Communications Agency gained administrative control of ARPANET. The mission of the agency was to facilitate the communications needs of the Department of Defense. Traffic on the network continued to increase rapidly. Most users, however, were not military personnel but researchers who used the network extensively to send electronic mail and transfer files to colleagues. Because of this dual application, ARPANET split into two networks: ARPANET continued to serve the needs of the academic community, while MILNET focused on the needs of the military. Information could be shared between these two networks. The interconnection between the research-oriented ARPANET and the application-oriented MILNET became known as the DARPA Internet (Defense Advanced Research Projects Agency), eventually shortened to the Internet.

Access to ARPANET remained limited to universities conducting defense research and to defense contractors. New networks, such as BITNET (the Because It's Time Network) and CSNET (the Computer Science Network) provided nationwide networking to other academic and research organizations. These networks initially were not part of the Internet, but over time, connections were made to the Internet to facilitate the exchange of information.

In 1986, the National Science Foundation (NSF) made a significant contribution to the expansion of the Internet when it developed a network to connect researchers across the country to several supercomputer centers. These centers included the following:

- Cornell National Supercomputer Facility, Cornell University, Cornell, New York

- John von Neumann National Supercomputer Center, Princeton, New Jersey

- National Center for Supercomputing Applications (NCSA), University of Illinois, Champaign, Illinois

- Pittsburgh Supercomputer Center, Pittsburgh, Pennsylvania

- San Diego Supercomputer Center, University of California, San Diego, California

- Scientific Computing Division of the National Center for Atmospheric Research, Boulder, Colorado

The high-speed networks that connect NSF supercomputers form a communications backbone known as the NSFNET—the foundation for the U.S. segment of the Internet. The transmission lines of this backbone include telephone, fiber-optic, microwave, and satellite links. These transmission lines are data superhighways that carry traffic long distances at high speeds. Data travels from the backbone to mid-level networks, which route the data through their own systems. Finally, data travels to users: individual users who connect through service providers; and business, government, and academic users who connect through local-area networks.

Originally configured with 56Kbps (kilobits per second) transmission lines, the NSFNET backbone was upgraded in 1989 with T1 lines capable of transmission speeds of 1.5 megabits per second (Mbps). In 1992, the backbone was again upgraded, this time to T3 lines that provide 45-Mbps speed. Soon, the backbone will be upgraded to gigabyte speeds. These high-speed lines make possible the rapid transmission of tremendous volumes of information. At

45 Mbps, 10 copies of *War and Peace* could travel through the network in about one second. The extra capacity, or *bandwidth*, will support new applications for the Internet (such as transmission of real-time video) and will better serve the increasing number of users.

The NSFNET continues to expand. Today, more than 80 countries have host computers and networks that connect to the network. With more than 1 million users, Canada has the second-largest Internet infrastructure in the world. The largest Canadian network is CA*net, which is similar to the NSFNET. CA*net provides global networking to Canada's education and research communities. Each province has a network that connects to CA*net, which in turn connects to NSFNET via high-speed links to Cornell, Princeton, and the University of Washington. Other countries that have major commitments to global interconnectivity include France, Germany, the United Kingdom, Australia, and Japan. Each of these countries operates more than 1,000 networks that connect to the Internet and the NSFNET. Table 1.1 lists the number of networks by country.

Table 1.1	NSFNET Networks by Country (Total networks: 34,051)	
Code	**Country**	**Networks**
DZ	Algeria	3
AU	Australia	1,215
AT	Austria	230
BE	Belgium	107
BR	Brazil	152
BG	Bulgaria	3
CA	Canada	1,540
CL	Chile	58
CN	China	4
CO	Colombia	2
CR	Costa Rica	4
HR	Croatia	20
CY	Cyprus	24

Code	Country	Networks
CZ	Czech Republic	304
DK	Denmark	31
EC	Ecuador	85
EG	Egypt	7
EE	Estonia	54
FJ	Fiji	1
FI	Finland	384
FR	France	1,539
DE	Germany	1,458
GH	Ghana	1
GR	Greece	61
GU	Guam	4
HK	Hong Kong	61
HU	Hungary	144
IS	Iceland	31
IN	India	6
ID	Indonesia	48
IE	Ireland	143
IL	Israel	146
IT	Italy	436
JM	Jamaica	11
JP	Japan	1,462
KZ	Kazakhstan	1
KE	Kenya	1
KW	Kuwait	6
LV	Latvia	3
LB	Lebanon	1

The Internet

(continues)

Table 1.1 Continued		
Code	**Country**	**Networks**
LI	Liechtenstein	3
LT	Lithuania	1
LU	Luxembourg	26
MO	Macau	1
MY	Malaysia	1
MX	Mexico	73
NL	Netherlands	279
NZ	New Zealand	267
NI	Nicaragua	1
NO	Norway	198
PA	Panama	1
PE	Peru	1
PH	Philippines	42
PL	Poland	128
PT	Portugal	88
PR	Puerto Rico	5
RO	Romania	14
RU	Russian Federation	206
SG	Singapore	55
SK	Slovakia	26
SI	Slovenia	34
ZA	South Africa	208
KR	South Korea	229
ES	Spain	248
LK	Sri Lanka	1

Code	Country	Networks
SZ	Swaziland	1
SE	Sweden	224
CH	Switzerland	276
TW	Taiwan	407
TH	Thailand	46
TN	Tunisia	13
TR	Turkey	72
UA	Ukraine	20
AE	United Arab Emirates	2
GB	United Kingdom	1,342
US	United States	19,689
UY	Uruguay	1
VE	Venezuela	7
VI	Virgin Islands	2

This list was up-to-date as of July 1994.

Open for Business: Transition from Academic Research to Commercial Business

The major costs of running the NSFNET are shared in a cooperative arrangement by the National Science Foundation, universities, national labs, and high-technology corporations. The NSF spends approximately $24 million annually to operate the backbone. As more users join the NSFNET portion of the Internet, the NSF winds up subsidizing traffic that is not related to its research mission—one reason why the government is getting out of the networking business, in terms of both funding and operation.

Commercial companies are stepping in to fund research, connections, operation, and new applications of the Internet. Soon, most of the financing will be in the hands of the communications industry, end users, and service and information providers. Naturally, commercial firms want to use the Internet as a for-profit business system.

Two factors led to significant commercial application of the Internet:

- First, the NSF lifted many rules that banned commercial applications on the NSFNET. Originally, the NSF established an Acceptable Use Policy (AUP) to govern the types of information that could be transported over the federally- and publicly-funded NSFNET. Use of the system by for-profit organizations and use for private or personal business was prohibited.

   The policy did not, however, specifically ban use of the system to provide technical support; so, for example, on-line documentation about computer products was not prohibited. This loophole soon was exploited, and after a series of government rulings, the NSF lifted most restrictions against commercial applications in 1991.

- The NSFNET represents an increasingly smaller portion of the Internet as commercial, private, and regional networks and gateways connect to the Internet. Commercial traffic now can be sent over the Internet without ever using the NSFNET segment of the system.

Commercial firms view the Internet as a terrific vehicle for business development, direct marketing, product sales, and customer support. The potential customer base exceeds the population of 49 of the 50 states, and a demographic profile of users shows upscale, computer-literate people who don't mind using electronic communications to make purchasing decisions.

Internet shopping malls and department stores develop faster than their real-world counterparts. The economic advantages include low overhead, 24-hour-a-day service, and rapid revision of catalog information. Today, you can use the Internet to purchase thousands of products and services, ranging from books (Telnet to **books.com** for an on-line listing of 240,000 titles) to fresh flowers (Absolutely Fresh Flowers, URL address **http//www.cts.com/~flowers**) to automobiles (Rood's Nissan/Volvo, URL address **http://www.dealernet.com**) to quotes on home mortgages (URL address **http://www.internet-is.com/myers/**).

Fig. 1.1
The home page of
Absolutely Fresh
Flowers, one of the
many businesses
that do business as
easily over the
Internet as over
the phone.

The Internet Shopping Network (URL address **http://shop.internet.net**) is a WWW server that offers more than 75,000 computer hardware and software products that can be purchased on-line. The products of over 800 vendors are shipped the same day from nine warehouses throughout the United States. On-line reviews and downloadable demos provide more information about the products.

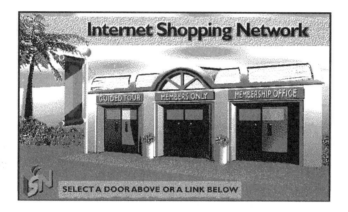

Fig. 1.2
Quick and easy
shopping for
computer products
is now possible on
the World Wide
Web.

The most ambitious project devoted to using the Internet for commercial purposes is CommerceNet, a consortium of approximately 40 Silicon Valley companies. Initial participants include computer-systems makers, subsystem suppliers, service providers, semiconductor manufacturers, financial institutions, and information providers. Any organization or company that offers or seeks on-line information or services can join CommerceNet.

The federal government has awarded $6 million to the development of CommerceNet; member companies and state and local governments have added another $6 million. The funds help to create everything from electronic directories of services to purchasing, accounting, delivery, and security systems for electronic funds transactions. Initially, CommerceNet will serve the needs of businesses and customers in California; service is expected to extend around the world in less than two years.

When CommerceNet is complete, users will have access to electronic directories that list international businesses. Users will be able to retrieve detailed product information from potential suppliers of a wide range of products and services; price comparisons will be available, and products can be ordered on-line.

For companies, CommerceNet is a mechanism that can create a competitive advantage as it helps bring products to market rapidly. Managers and employees can share design and data files with colleagues in other departments—and even in other countries—to enhance product development, manufacturing, sales, and marketing.

For more information on CommerceNet, send e-mail to **info@commerce.net**.

The Language of the Internet: TCP/IP

Computers and humans have one common trait: both use complex languages for communication. When two people who speak different languages (say, French and Japanese) need to share information, they can use an interpreter to translate, or they can use a third language (such as English) that both of them understand.

With some 30 million users on-line, the Internet connects computers that use very different operating systems or languages: UNIX, DOS, Macintosh, and so on. To facilitate communication among all these systems, the Internet uses a third language: *TCP/IP*, or Transmission Control Protocol/Internet protocol. Created in the 1970s, TCP/IP was part of DARPA's research on connecting different types of networks and computers. Because public funds were used to develop TCP/IP, the standards are nonproprietary—that is, no one has exclusive rights to their use. Furthermore, TCP/IP is hardware- and software-independent, so that any type of computer can connect to the Internet and share information with any other computer.

Functionally, TCP/IP breaks messages, documents, and files into small packets that move rapidly through the networks of the Internet toward their destination. Each packet contains from 1 to 1,500 characters, including the addresses of the sending and receiving computers. These packets can travel independently of one another from one computer to another by any route or at any speed.

As an analogy, consider a 500-piece jigsaw puzzle. You assemble the puzzle, much the way that you would construct a letter or create a database file; then you number each piece of the puzzle (1 to 500), insert each piece into an envelope, and mail all 500 envelopes to a friend who lives across the country. Because of handling methods at the post office, the envelopes may travel in different planes or trucks that take different routes to your friend's home. When your friend gets the envelopes, he can put the puzzle together by looking at the numbers that you placed on the pieces. If an envelope gets lost, your friend can call and say, "I don't have piece number 42. Could you send another one?" This process is similar to the process of sending information over the Internet.

Internet packets move through transmission lines—the roadways of the network. As packets move through the network, they travel through routers, which are the switches of the system. At the intersections of networks, routers decide the best pathway (or route) for packets to take. Routers possess information that helps them evaluate network traffic and the distance to the next computer, so that they can move information to its destination efficiently. If a packet becomes lost or corrupted en route, the receiving computer keeps requesting retransmission until the packet arrives intact.

After packets reach their destination, the computer removes source- and destination-address information and reassembles the packets to create the original message or file. Packets frequently arrive out of sequence because they travel through many different pathways. However, sequencing information embedded in the packets reconstructs the complete message or file, like the numbered puzzle pieces help reconstruct the puzzle. With small packets of data traveling over the best routes, the traffic load is distributed over the entire network. This packet-switching method helps data move through the Internet efficiently and keeps any part of the system from being overburdened.

Addresses on the Internet: The Domain Name System

To be able to send or receive information via the Internet, you must have an electronic address. The Internet uses a method known as the Domain Name System (DNS) to assign addresses to computers and to people. An address for an Internet host computer can be represented both by a series of numbers and by a plain-English name. The numbers and the name represent the same address. Computers use the numerical address to route data through the Internet. The plain-English names are simply a convenience for people who can remember names with greater ease than they can numbers.

The Domain Name System has a three-part hierarchy:

user name	@	host.subdomain (first-level domain)
1	2	3

Part 1 represents the user's name. Part 2 literally means *at*. Part 3 is the address of the host on which a person (or his mailbox) can be located.

Part 3, which represents the address of the host computer, also consists of three elements:

host	subdomain	first-level domain
1	2	3

Part 1 is the name of the computer. Part 2 represents one or more subdomains. Part 3 is the first-level domain.

Subdomains help you find the location of a person who works in a large organization that has many divisions or departments. For example, Frank Thompson may work in the biology department of the science school at the University of California, and his Internet address could be **Thompson@bio.sci.ucal.edu**.

The first-level domain (the right-most part of the host computer's address) provides an indication about the type of company or organization to which the computer belongs. In the United States, six first-level domains are possible. The following table lists these domains.

Code	Organization Type
edu	Educational or research institution
gov	Government, nonmilitary
mil	Military
com	Commercial entity
net	A network support company
org	Other organizations

The numeric Internet Protocol (IP) address is equivalent to the plain-English address; this address, however, is a series of numbers, and the order of information is reversed. For example, the plain-English name for a college computer is **library.dartmouth.edu**. The name suggests that this computer provides library information, that it resides at Dartmouth, and that the institution to which it belongs is an educational institution. By the way, this host enables users to search for text in several on-line works, such as Dante's *Divine Comedy*. The less-user-friendly IP address of this computer is **129.170.16.11**.

When you send a command that tells your computer (or your local host) to connect with or send information to another computer, the system first must find that computer in a directory, much as you use a phone book for a particular city to locate a friend's telephone number. To accomplish this task, the Domain Name System coordinates a global system of distributed databases that contain both the plain-English and numeric IP addresses of Internet computers. Computers called *name servers* house these databases of addresses.

The name servers translate the plain-English address that is so easy for you to remember and type into the numerical IP addresses that computers prefer. When you transmit a message or begin the process of linking with a remote computer, your local Internet host accesses a name server and translates the plain-English address to its corresponding IP address before beginning the routing process. To ensure proper connection and delivery of messages, the IP address accompanies data packets on their journey through the Internet.

Three Essential Applications: E-Mail, Telnet, and FTP

For users, the value of connection to the Internet resides not in the physical networks or the technology that makes the system work, but in the applications that enable people to perform tasks. TCP/IP protocols support three essential applications: transmitting and receiving electronic mail, logging in to remote computers (Telnet), and transferring files and programs from one computer to another (FTP).

Electronic Mail

Electronic mail, known as *e-mail*, is the application that ignited the growth of the Internet in the 1970s. Today, e-mail remains an extremely popular application. Because e-mail is a fast, economical, and easy-to-use method of sending information, many people include their Internet addresses on their business cards.

Fig. 1.3

A sample of how electronic mail works. The program, called Eudora, is available for Windows and Mac computers.

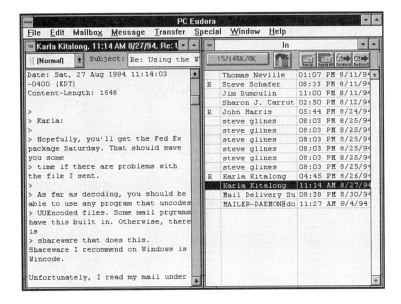

Using high-speed modems and transmission lines, electronic mail travels around the world in a matter of seconds. Advanced features in e-mail programs provide

- automatic sorting, which helps eliminate unwanted junk mail

- the ability to copy and forward mail to other people, eliminating the need to write or send multiple copies

- a mechanism to attach files (such as spreadsheets) directly to the mail message

- a means of sending a message simultaneously to thousands of people through electronic mail lists

E-mail also is cost-effective. A 100KB ASCII text file is equivalent to approximately 20,000 words, or 70 pages of printed text. If you use a 9600-bits-per-second (bps) modem, it takes less than three minutes to send a file from Chicago to Miami or London. The cost of sending this file electronically ranges from a few cents to a dollar, depending on the fee structure of your service provider or commercial on-line service. In contrast, fees of $3 to $6 are customary for standard postal delivery, while overnight delivery costs $10 to $20. The latest modem technology, called V.Fast, uses standard phone lines and operates at an incredible 28,800 bps.

Electronic mail is becoming a pervasive tool as telecommunications standards ensure that messages can be received on many different types of networks, and computers and new gateways enable people who use commercial on-line services to communicate with people who have Internet addresses. In 1984, the Consultative Committee for International Telephony and Telegraphy, or CCITT—now the ITU Telecommunications Standardization Sector (TSS), a worldwide telecommunications-standards organization—began to address the issue of compatibility by developing international technical standards for e-mail. Known as X.400, these standards describe requirements that vendors and organizations must use to connect different messaging systems. The X.400 standard enables organizations and users to send and receive many types of dissimilar data, such as e-mail messages, binary files, images, and fax and TELEX transmissions.

A second set of standards, known as X.500, defines a global directory standard. Like an international electronic phone book, X.500 makes it easy to locate people who have e-mail addresses and eliminates the need for users to have more then one identification name across different e-mail systems. Special mail computers, known as X.500 servers or white pages, maintain libraries of electronic phone books, which contain information about all the people in one company or organization. The National Aeronautics and Space Administration, for example, provides an X.500 directory that includes names, addresses, telephone numbers, and e-mail addresses for people who work at NASA centers. You can search these electronic directories to find specific people.

Because of the Internet's global connectivity and enormous user base, many commercial on-line services, electronic bulletin boards (BBSs), and public and private networks connect to the Internet, enabling e-mail to reach even more people. With 2.5 million subscribers, CompuServe represents a significant population of users who can send and receive messages from the Internet, and one million America Online subscribers also can link to the Internet. In addition, in the United States alone, there are about 45,000 public electronic bulletin-board systems, many of which provide access to Internet e-mail. AT&T, IBM (through Advantis), MCI, and Sprint all provide commercial electronic services that include the capability to send and receive mail from the Internet. Many private companies also have gateways that enable employees to send e-mail through the Internet. As these different organizations and networks link to the Internet, e-mail becomes an extremely attractive alternative to regular hard-copy mail or fax transmission.

Two steps are necessary to transmit mail between these networks and the Internet. First, because the Internet doesn't support 8-bit, or *binary*, text, such as the files produced by word processors or drawing packages, messages must be converted to ASCII (7-bit) format before transmission. Many e-mail programs are designed to perform the conversions "automatically," but this is not always the case. The user may have to process files before sending them through the Internet. Second, proper address information is required to get from one system to another. To get a message from CompuServe to the Internet, for example, a user must use the format **INTERNET:userid@organization.domain**; to get from the Internet to CompuServe, the address format is **userid@compuserve.com**. It can take between 15 minutes and 48 hours for a message to travel between networks.

Telnet

Telnet is an application that uses the TCP/IP protocols to link your computer with one of hundreds of thousands of remote hosts. When a communications link occurs, your PC acts like a terminal connected to the remote host, and you can execute commands that run software programs on the remote computer. Telnet provides access to many computers that offer public services, such as electronic library catalogs, information databases, and educational programs.

After connecting with the remote computer, you enter a login ID and password to use the computer. Because it is unlikely that you will have an account on the host computer, public service computer systems usually allow you to log in with a special ID such as guest or newuser. The system may allow you to become a registered user, however. For example, NASA's SpaceLink computer asks for registration information and then provides a user login ID and password for future connections.

When Telnet sessions begin, a public access remote computer usually displays a menu-based navigational system or other instructions to help you move through the resources on the computer. Remote hosts sometimes operate shell environments that enable you to access specific services or programs but prohibit access to secure areas of the system.

The Telnet address connects you to a port that starts the program automatically. Sometimes you must specify a particular port; for example, the University of Michigan operates a Weather Underground application that provides information on current weather conditions as well as forecasts for all portions of the United States. The Telnet address is **downwind.sprl.umich.edu 3000**. This address connects you directly to port 3000, the port on the computer that initiates the weather program.

File Transfers (FTP)

Besides receiving electronic messages and connecting to remote computers, you can use the Internet to access files that reside on remote computers and transfer them directly to your computer. This capability is particularly useful when you don't want to spend much on-line time scanning through a large text file; when using the file requires special tools, such as a graphics viewer; or when you simply want to have a copy of the file, such as a shareware accounting program.

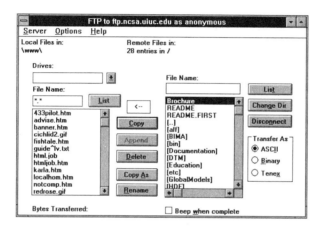

Fig. 1.4
Using a Microsoft Windows-based FTP client (top) to transfer files from an anonymous FTP site on the Internet back to a local computer. The bottom screen shows the same procedure in Fetch on a Mac.

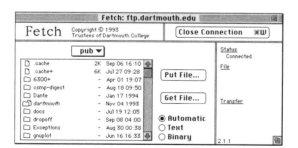

Files can be documents, digital images, sound files, or programs. File transfer protocol (FTP) is the application that enables you to send and receive files between distant computers. To use FTP, you connect to a remote computer (host) the way that you do with Telnet. Again, the computer asks for log-in information. Computers that maintain public archives of files allow strangers log in with the ID anonymous or FTP. The log-in password is your Internet address.

When you are on-line, your computer becomes a *client* that sends commands to the remote computer, which is referred to as a *server*. Commands tell the computer to perform tasks, such as change directories, list files, or send files. By using these commands, you can browse the directories of public access computers to find files that may be of interest or to locate the specific file that you want to use. Using FTP to browse for files can be difficult because FTP doesn't allow you to look at a file's contents. Therefore, file names and extensions provide the best indication of what a file might contain. But they might be misleading.

A file with the name diamond.txt, for example, could be a document that contains information about the precious gem. But it could just as easily be a short story about baseball. If you know generally what information resides on a particular computer, you will have a better idea about the information in individual files. Often, the best way to locate information that is of interest to you is to conduct a search for specific files (searches are discussed in "How to Locate Information in Cyberspace," later in this chapter). Another way to locate specific files is through references in World Wide Web pages or mailing lists, a friend's referral, or an Internet information directory. When you have the file name, you can retrieve that file rapidly.

When you retrieve—or *download*—a file from a remote computer, that file will be sent in either of two formats: ASCII or binary. An *ASCII file* is a file that contains textual information; a *binary file* could be a program, an image, or a spreadsheet. To retrieve a file, you must know its format, because you send a command to the server to switch from ASCII to binary transfer mode before transmission. Binary file transfers perform error checking, which makes them slower but more reliable than ASCII transfers.

> **Caution**
>
> Sometimes downloaded files (especially programs) are infected with viruses. You should use a virus scanning program before running downloaded files.

Electronic-mail, Telnet, and file-transfer protocol are the Big Three tools that transform the Internet from an enormous system of computers, wires, and gateways to a functional information-management resource. Electronic mail helps you save time and money in correspondence; Telnet opens new doors to information and services; and FTP enables you to bring useful files and programs directly into your computer.

Getting the News with Newsgroups

Although it may not fit the scientific definition of life, the Internet is a living entity. More than any other communications medium, the Internet represents communication *among* people. Electronic newsgroups, also known as *netnews*, represent a significant vehicle for global interpersonal communications. Need to find out what type of flowers grow well at high altitudes? Want to share some favorite scuba-diving locations? Need tips about what clothes to bring on a trip to Indonesia? Have an urge to discuss the latest proposal for health care? Newsgroups are an ideal place to do these things. Newsgroups are global forums in which people with common interests share information, discuss topics, and ask questions.

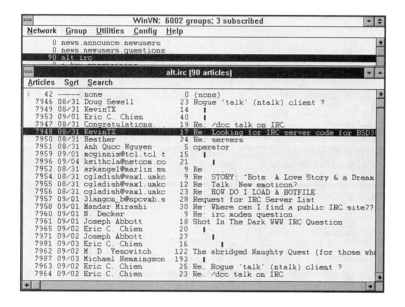

Fig. 1.5
Reading netnews with WinVN, a Windows-based news reader.

The network newsgroups are distributed via Usenet, a global network of computers. (You can access Usenet without an Internet connection; for example, America Online subscribers can receive netnews, and some local BBSs also carry partial Usenet feeds.) Almost all Internet users take advantage of Usenet information, which moves across and between the Internet and other private networks. Usenet has approximately 3 million participants, and every day, thousands of new messages appear on more than 6,000 different newsgroups.

A *newsgroup* is a database of messages focused on one subject. You view these messages by using a *news reader*, an application program that commonly is supplied by the Internet service provider and that resides either on your computer or on the local computer to which you link to access the Internet. Borrowing publishing terminology, newsgroup messages are called *articles*, and articles are open-ended. For example, someone in Egypt may post a message about cat behavior. A cat lover in Florida reads the message and adds a new message that talks about the effect of hot weather on cats. Next, a veterinarian in Australia provides some useful tips about cat care...and the stream goes on.

Technically, Usenet employs a procedure called *store and forward*, in which one host distributes a copy of the newsgroup messages to other hosts, which in turn feed the copy to additional hosts. In a very short time, the articles are transmitted to hosts around the world.

The name of a newsgroup describes the subject on which the articles focus. One newsgroup, for example, is called alt.politics.usa.constitution. It doesn't take much imagination to realize that this newsgroup focuses on politics in relation to the U.S. Constitution. For purposes of identification, newsgroups are organized in a hierarchy that identifies the information that can be found in articles. Newsgroup names contain several subcategories, separated by periods. The broad, top-level category name is on the left side; the most specific identification category is on the right. The following table lists the major top-level categories for newsgroups.

Top-Level Category	Description
alt	alternative system
biz	business
comp	computer-related
k12	education (kindergarten through 12th grade)
misc	miscellaneous
rec	recreation
sci	science
soc	social issues
talk	controversial subjects

Just as you sign up to receive a magazine or newspaper, you subscribe to specific newsgroups. Unlike their hard-copy counterparts, though, newsgroups charge no fee, and you can cancel your subscription at any time.

After you subscribe to a newsgroup, the daily messages are stored for viewing on the local computer on which you access the Internet. Typically, Usenet sites store only current or recent newsgroup messages; it wouldn't take long to fill a computer with newsgroup messages if they were kept forever. When you post a question or suggestion that relates to the topic of the newsgroup, people around the world see your message, but there is no way to determine exactly how many people will read and respond to your message. As people interact, discuss, and argue about topics, newsgroups take on a life of their own.

How to Locate Information in Cyberspace

The tremendous volume of information available on the Internet simultaneously represents exciting opportunities for discovering new information resources and daunting challenges in locating what you need. If you were to download 100 files every day for the next 10 years, you would accumulate fewer than 20 percent of the files that are publicly available today. Fortunately, several Internet applications are available that help you sort through the universe of electronic information.

Computers can search electronic data rapidly to locate word patterns, which can represent the names of specific files and documents or index references to information that resides in files. A file named hiking.doc, for example, may turn up in a search of files that contain the word *hiking*. The same search would find a file called everest.doc that was indexed under the word *hiking*.

Archie, Gopher, Veronica, and WAIS, described in the following sections, are tools that you can use to locate files on the Internet by subjects, titles, locations, and keywords.

Archie

A system called Archie maintains a database of file names that reside on approximately 1,500 host computers. This database is distributed to about 40 Archie servers located around the world, in Australia, Italy, Germany, South Korea, Sweden, and the United States. Daily, each Archie server searches a specific region of the world to get updates on files. Then, once a month, the Archie servers share their databases. This process ensures that each Archie server has a complete, updated database of all file names. The database also contains address information that identifies where the files reside.

A common way to perform an Archie search is to Telnet to a nearby Archie computer and log in with the ID archie. (No password is necessary.) You can search the Archie database by *keyword*—a word that describes what the file is about—or by file type. An Archie search produces a list of files that match your search criteria, the names of the FTP sites that contain these files, and the subdirectories in which the files reside. You then can use FTP to connect to appropriate sites and download the files that you want.

Gopher

Archie is a good tool for locating files, but it is not user-friendly. You must remember several rather cryptic search commands to narrow your searches, and after you get the result of a search, you still have to go through a second step to download the file. Developed at the University of Minnesota (home of the Golden Gophers sports teams), Gopher is a simple Internet-searching tool. Gopher, like Archie, is a software application that resides on a host computer; the Internet has more than 5,000 Gopher servers. You use Gopher to search and navigate through the Internet by making menu-based choices.

Gopher menus have a hierarchical structure. You begin with a main menu that offers a broad category listing. Figure 1.6 shows a Gopher main menu at the University of Minnesota (**consultant.micro.umn.edu**).

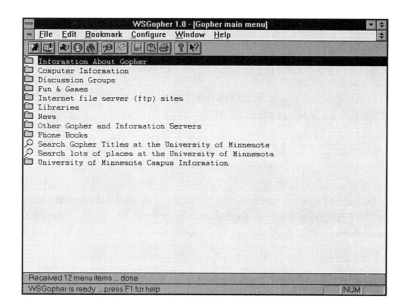

Fig. 1.6
The main Gopher
menu at the
University of
Minnesota, where
Gopher was
invented. Gopher
is shown in
Windows (top)
and on a Mac
(bottom).

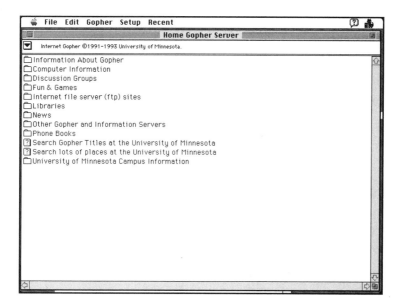

You move through this menu by using simple keyboard techniques: pressing
the up-arrow key, the down-arrow key, or the space bar, or typing a number).
One of several things may happen when you choose a menu item:

- A new menu appears, providing a further breakdown of the subject area.

- The text of a document appears.

- A connection is made to a different Internet computer, which may display new Gopher menus.

A forward slash (/) after a Gopher listing means that another menu is connected to this link. If no forward slash is used, you connect to a resource (file) by choosing the menu item. Gopher takes you directly to the computer where the file for which you are looking resides; you don't have to quit and then use FTP to download the file to your computer. If the file is a text-based document, you can look at the file on-line to make sure that it is what you want before you download it.

Veronica

Moving through Gopher menus is a bit like visiting a new city without a map and weaving your way from street to street. If you're looking for adventure, this technique can be great fun. If your goal is to visit all the five-star restaurants in town, however, it would be more effective to have a list of those establishments and their addresses. The same is true with Gopher. It is impossible to know whether all the information you need about the topic *cooking* resides on the Gopher to which you have linked, and visiting all 5,000 Gopher sites for complete research of the subject would take an enormous amount of time.

Like Archie, Veronica (Very Easy Rodent-Oriented Netwide Index to Computerized Archives) is a searching mechanism. However, while Archie enables you to search FTP sites, Veronica is designed to search all of the menus at Gopher sites around the world by using keywords; the system accomplishes this task by maintaining a database of Gopher menus.

While Archie scans FTP sites, Veronica regularly visits Gopher servers worldwide (twice a week), scans the menus, and creates a comprehensive index. Veronica indexes approximately 10 million items. You access the Veronica system from a Gopher menu, usually moving into it from a broad-topic menu item. For instance, if you were using the menu shown in figure 1.7, you would see the following item:

8. Other Gopher and Information Servers/

When you choose an option such as this, a new menu appears, often listing several Veronica servers. Because all these servers—in theory at least—

maintain the same database information, all of them should provide the same result in a search. To minimize the load on the Internet, always try using the server that is closest to your location. The following menu items might appear on a Gopher.

1. Search gopherspace by veronica at PSINet <?>

2. Search gopherspace by veronica at SUNET <?>

When you choose a Veronica server, a fill-in search box appears, similar to the one shown in figure 1.8. Enter your search criteria in the box. When the search is complete, a new Gopher-like menu appears. This menu matches your search criteria and lists many selections that contain your search word. As is the case with Gopher, when you choose one of these menu items, you jump directly to the server or resource to which the item points.

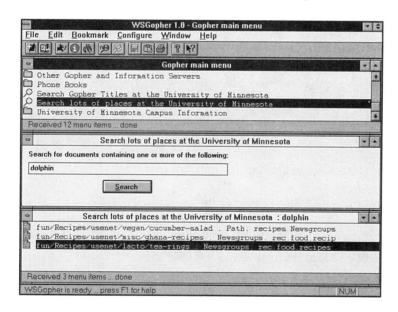

Fig. 1.7
A sample Veronica search, using the word "dolphin" as a keyword.

In the sample search box shown in figure 1.7, the user is searching for information on dolphins. By using the singular, dolphin, she ensures that the search will pick up all references on the Gopher system.

WAIS

The results of Archie, Gopher, and Veronica searches depend on how accurately a file name or menu selection describes what you are looking for. Suppose that you want to perform a search to locate information about the movie star Cary Grant. You use the search term Grant. An Archie search generates some likely candidates, including one named grant.gif. You FTP to the server, download the binary graphic file, load the file into a graphic viewer, and obtain a stunning photograph of Ulysses S. Grant, the 18th president of the United States.

You skip Gopher and move directly to a Veronica search. Now you get a list of other unlikely candidates, including *Grant, Library and Research Resources* and *Grant William T Foundation*. It would be difficult to get files that focus on Cary Grant—and almost impossible to get a reference to a file about the Alfred Hitchcock movie *North by Northwest*, in which Grant played the lead role.

Here is where the WAIS system (short for Wide Area Information Servers) may prove to be helpful. WAIS looks for information that resides in individual files or documents. WAIS also relies on an index, created by administrators at various WAIS sites, that describes the contents of files. Indexed files are collected in databases of related topics. For example, one WAIS location may house a collection of titles on the subject of films. The great advantage of using WAIS is that individual files may contain hundreds of referenced index words; in fact, every word in a text file is usually indexed.

One way to access a WAIS server is to go through a Gopher menu. For example, from the Gopher screen shown in figure 1.7, you might select

   8. Other Gopher and Information Servers/

The resulting menu might look like the menu shown in figure 1.8.

Look for a menu item such as the following:

   6. WAIS Based Information/

When you access WAIS, you see a list of databases. Choose a database, enter search commands, and then receive a list of files or documents that meet your criteria.

WAIS prioritizes the results of a search. Files that contain more occurrences of the search word or phrase appear at the top of a display list. Prioritization is based on a score; files or directories that contain the most matching words, or *hits*, receive a score of 1,000; files that contain fewer hits get rankings below 1,000. For example, if you search the WAIS database ANU-Philippine-Studies.src by using the keyword medicine, the first file, *Local government units and health-service delivery in Ilocos*, will have more references to medicine than following listings do.

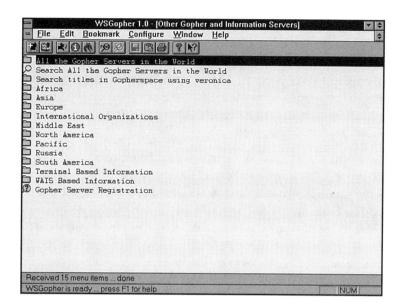

Fig. 1.8
A sample menu of
Other Gopher and
Information
Servers.

WAIS indexes can point to files that contain data other than text. For example, a database of images of dogs could be keyword-indexed, and a search
for greyhound could produce digital images of greyhounds.

Moving into the Future

Keeping up with the pace at which the Internet expands and changes is difficult. Clearly, growth changes the ways in which governments, companies,
and individual users manage and use the system. In the United States, communication and computer companies play a significant role in the development of communication lines and computer hardware to run the system.
Software developers and information providers create new applications and
electronic libraries, and businesses advertise and sell products.

Most of these changes are positive—the system is becoming easier to use and
provides more and more useful information and services. These changes are
unlikely to destroy the hallmark of the Internet: global communication. As
more countries, companies, and individual users connect, the opportunities
to communicate with colleagues, make new friends, locate information, and
keep up with news will increase. Many concepts that the NII initiative envisions will become a reality as the Internet continues to enhance education,
create new business opportunities, and improve interpersonal communications.

It is highly possible that use of the Internet will produce results that were not foreseen when the system was developed. The environment, for example, may benefit from an increase in the use of electronic communications. Annually, 22 million tons of paper are consumed in the United States for business and personal communications. If a significant portion of this communication occurs electronically, the reduction in paper production, distribution, and disposal may result in less pollution.

New users continue to flock to the Internet as the process of sending, locating, and retrieving information becomes as simple as turning on a television set. Archie, Gopher, Veronica, and WAIS all help users make the best use of their on-line time, but it is the World Wide Web, a relative newcomer to the world of Internet navigational tools, that opens the vast resources of the Internet to a wave of new users. The next chapter highlights the specific features and capabilities of the World Wide Web.

Chapter 2

The World Wide Web

World Wide Web is a simple, catchy phrase that contains tremendous meaning. Activities that occur around the globe affect the lives of millions of people. In the realm of finance, stock-market activity in Europe, the Far East, or South America directly affects financial institutions and economies around the world. Environmental activities also interconnect. A volcanic explosion in the United States emits debris that affects weather in China; and man-made disasters, such as oil spills and nuclear accidents, don't stop at the borders of the countries in which they occur.

The notion of an integrated world has evolved in this century. R. Buckminster Fuller, the inventor of the geodesic dome, referred to the world as Spaceship Earth, a single entity in which the relationship between ecological forces is always delicate. In the 1960s, Marshall McLuhan, then director of the Center for Culture and Technology at the University of Toronto, spoke and wrote about the concept of a global village: a world in which electronic media enable people of all nations to share their thoughts and experiences.

Communication technology facilitates global connectivity, and the World Wide Web provides a functional means for people around the world to locate information and share knowledge. The World Wide Web is:

- An Internet-based navigational system

- An information distribution and management system

- A dynamic format for mass and personal communications

The Web links the many resources that exist on the Internet. For users, the Web is easier to use and more exciting than the other Internet navigation systems: Archie, Gopher, and WAIS. This is because the Web seamlessly integrates different forms of information: still images, text, audio, and video. When you use the World Wide Web, you jump effortlessly among locations (the thousands of computer hosts), system applications (FTP and Telnet), and information formats (files and documents).

The multimedia aspects of the Web transform use of the Internet from a clerical operation into an exciting voyage. You become an adventurer as you jump from topic to topic and place to place. Leap to Canada to join Canadian Broadcasting Corporation Radio's "Quirks and Quarks," an acclaimed science program that covers topics including ozone updates, DNA fingerprinting, and chimpanzees that diagnose and treat themselves. Click an icon, and you can listen to a 10-minute broadcast in which endocrinologist Dr. Jerilyn Prior of the Department of Medicine at the University of British Columbia explains why giving women estrogen helps slow bone loss from osteoporosis.

Alternatively, you can jump to a NASA computer and view photographs of Jupiter that show fragments of the comet Shoemaker-Levy 9 smashing into the planet's atmosphere. These amazing images were transmitted from the Hubble Space Telescope to NASA and then shipped around the world via the Internet and WWW. This live coverage of an event that occurred some 390 million miles from Earth created enough excitement that one of NASA's computers received more than 90,000 inquiries in a single day. The NASA home page, URL address **http://hypatia.gsfc.nasa.gov/ NASA_homepage.html**, is shown in figure 2.1.

Fig. 2.1
NASA's home page, from which you can jump to a wealth of information about the U.S. Space Program.

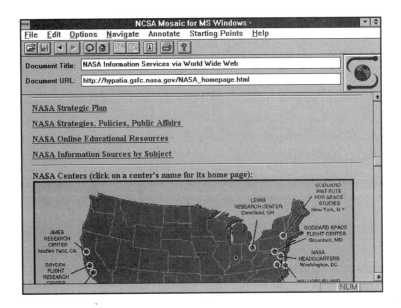

The images on the Web are not all about scientific subjects; you can just as easily get pictures of music great Muddy Waters, the Eiffel Tower, or rare Chinese art. If you'd rather sit back for entertainment, connect with the Web server at the Massachusetts Institute of Technology lab for computer science, whose Telemedia, Networks, and Systems Group stores video clips from the Indiana Jones movies, *Star Trek*, CNN Headline News, and "The Nightly Business Report."

This is just a small sample of the type of multimedia information available via the Web. The Web is a constantly changing repository of information that can help people learn about subjects ranging from medical break-throughs to scientific exploration and business news. The Web is knowledge that organizations, companies, and individual users passionately develop and format to share with other people. The Web is global, interactive, multimedia communications.

Where Did the Web Come From?

The Web began at the European Particle Physics Laboratory, known as CERN, an organization comprised of European high-energy-physics researchers. Funded jointly by the 12-nation European Community, CERN is a meeting place for physicists from around the world who collaborate on complex phys-ics, engineering, and information-handling projects. The facility straddles the Swiss–French border near Geneva, Switzerland.

In 1989, CERN physicist Tim Berners-Lee proposed the concept of the Web as a system for transferring ideas and research among scientists in the high-energy-physics community. Effective communication was critical for this group of scientists located around the world. The proposal defined a simple system that would use *hypertext*—a way of presenting and relating informa-tion that uses links rather than linear sequences—to transmit documents and other communications over computer networks. Initially, the system was not intended to transmit images or to include sound or video.

By the end of 1990, the first Web software was introduced on Steven Job's NeXT computer system. The NeXT software provided the capability to view and transmit hypertext documents over the Internet and enabled users to edit hypertext documents. Demonstrations of this system were presented to CERN committees and attendees at the Hypertext '91 conference. Over the next few years, the Web system expanded rapidly.

II

The World Wide Web

Amazing as it is that the Internet doubles in size every 10 months, the Web grows even faster—at an annual rate of 3,000 percent. In 1993, fewer than 100 Web servers existed; today, the Web has more than 10,000 servers (see figs. 2.2 and 2.3).

Fig. 2.2
World Wide Web
server growth
trend.

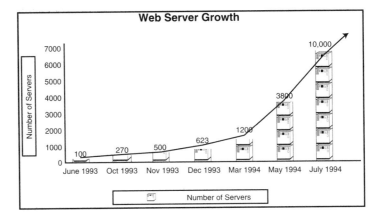

Hypertext and Hypermedia Concepts

When we sleep, dreams carry us effortlessly from one location or subject to the next. Images, sounds, and scenes move quickly and sometimes irrationally in an unending stream-of-consciousness pattern. This process is similar to navigating through information on the World Wide Web. The computer-based information programs that make WWW navigation possible are hypertext and hypermedia.

Hypertext, a subset of hypermedia, refers specifically to computer-based documents in which readers move from one place in a document to another or between documents in a nonlinear or nonsequential manner. This means that you don't access information in a traditional beginning-to-end fashion. With a book, for example, you normally begin reading at page one and move page by page, chapter by chapter to the end. In a nonlinear computer document, you move randomly through the document. Words, phrases, and icons in the document become links that enable you to jump at will to a new location in the document or even to a new document.

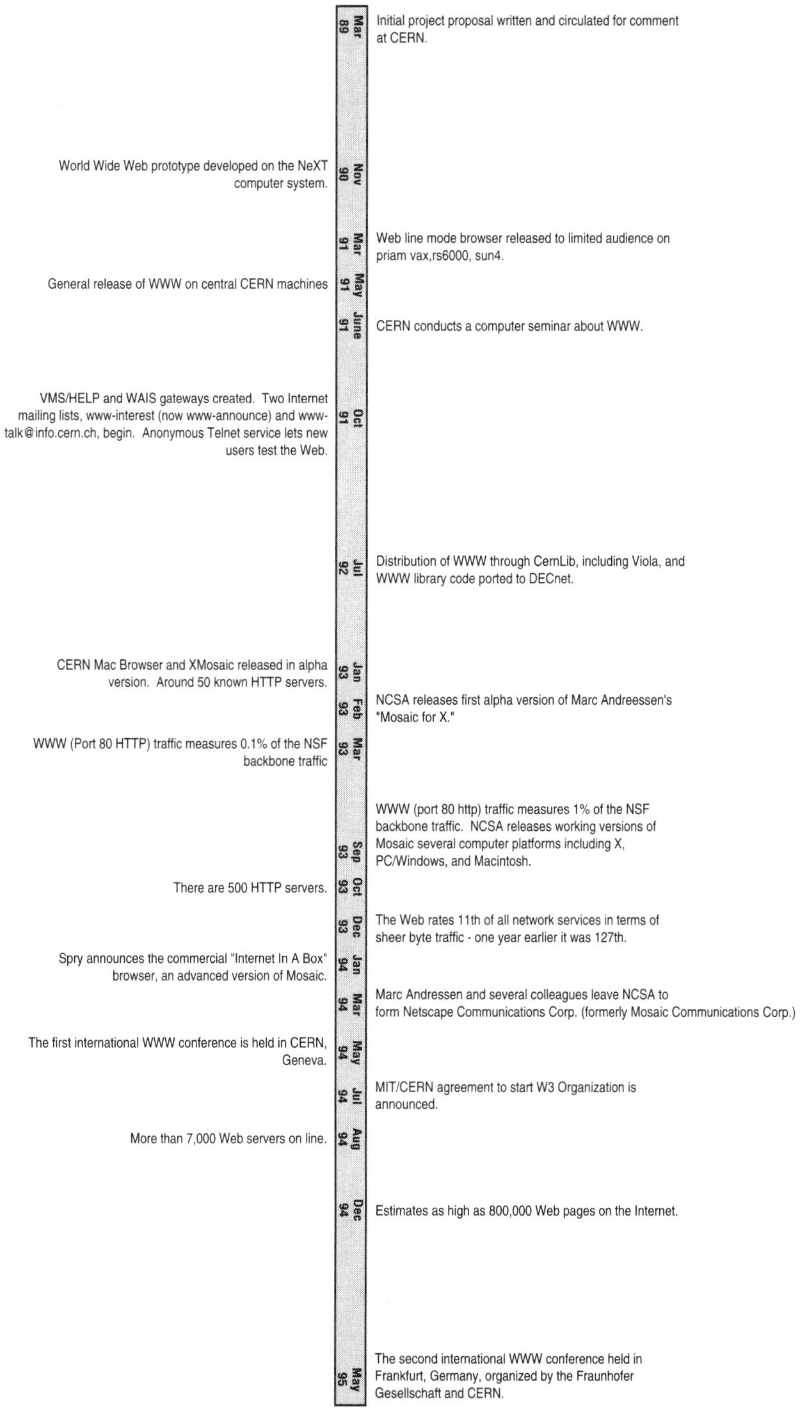

Fig. 2.3
WWW Timeline.
Important events
in the brief life of
the Web.

Mar 89	Initial project proposal written and circulated for comment at CERN.
Nov 90	World Wide Web prototype developed on the NeXT computer system.
Mar 91	Web line mode browser released to limited audience on priam vax, rs6000, sun4.
May 91	General release of WWW on central CERN machines
June 91	CERN conducts a computer seminar about WWW.
Oct 91	VMS/HELP and WAIS gateways created. Two Internet mailing lists, www-interest (now www-announce) and www-talk@info.cern.ch, begin. Anonymous Telnet service lets new users test the Web.
Jul 92	Distribution of WWW through CernLib, including Viola, and WWW library code ported to DECnet.
Jan 93	CERN Mac Browser and XMosaic released in alpha version. Around 50 known HTTP servers.
Feb 93	NCSA releases first alpha version of Marc Andreessen's "Mosaic for X."
Mar 93	WWW (Port 80 HTTP) traffic measures 0.1% of the NSF backbone traffic
Sep 93	WWW (port 80 http) traffic measures 1% of the NSF backbone traffic. NCSA releases working versions of Mosaic several computer platforms including X, PC/Windows, and Macintosh.
Oct 93	There are 500 HTTP servers.
Dec 93	The Web rates 11th of all network services in terms of sheer byte traffic - one year earlier it was 127th.
Jan 94	Spry announces the commercial "Internet In A Box" browser, an advanced version of Mosaic.
Mar 94	Marc Andressen and several colleagues leave NCSA to form Netscape Communications Corp. (formerly Mosaic Communications Corp.)
May 94	The first international WWW conference is held in CERN, Geneva.
Jul 94	MIT/CERN agreement to start W3 Organization is announced.
Aug 94	More than 7,000 Web servers on line.
Dec 94	Estimates as high as 800,000 Web pages on the Internet.
May 95	The second international WWW conference held in Frankfurt, Germany, organized by the Fraunhofer Gesellschaft and CERN.

II

The World Wide Web

Hypertext has several advantages over normal text:

- Hypertext eases navigation in very large documents. Northern Telecom, the world's leading supplier of digital telecommunications switching equipment, provides customers this type of electronic documentation for telecommunications switches. Because the hard-copy, multivolume manuals can exceed 100,000 pages, it is much easier for readers to click a subject and instantly hop to that topic in the hypertext document than to locate the right volume and find the proper page in the hard-copy version of the manual.

- Besides providing speed of use, hypertext helps readers explore new ideas and locate additional sources of information as they jump from place to place. For example, an article about the Civil War might mention Abraham Lincoln, whose name links to a biography that in turn links to a guidebook on Illinois.

- Hypertext brings depth—a type of third dimension—to the written word. Readers become explorers and make navigational decisions about the topics that they want to investigate. Hypertext enables users—not documents or computer-system administrators—to decide exactly what information is most important at any moment.

Hypermedia is a natural extension of hypertext. In hypermedia, links connect to visuals such as graphics or photographs, audio messages, or video, as well as to text. Hypermedia brings documents to life, and the personal computer becomes a multimedia device that can have far more appeal and impact than radio or television. An electronic auto-repair manual, for example, could have a section that describes how to adjust a carburetor. Click an icon, and a short movie shows the proper procedure. Later, the text may say, "Adjust until it sounds smooth." You don't know what smooth sounds like, so you click an audio link that plays a recording of a smoothly running carburetor.

The home page of the U.S. Geological Survey (USGS) WWW server (**http:// info.er.usgs.gov/**) provides an excellent example of the electronic combination of different media. The page opens with several Graphic Interchange Format (GIF) images of covers of USGS literature. These images link to additional menus for USGS activities. The home page also contains an icon that links to an audio welcome message and another icon that links to a short MPEG video featuring Dane County, Wisconsin.

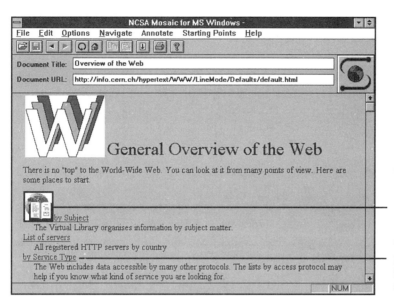

Fig. 2.4
A sample Web page, showing graphical and textual hypertext links.

A graphical hypertext link is an image with a box around it. If you have a color screen, the box will be blue.

Textual links are underlined. On colored screens, the links are usually colored blue and underlined.

The resources of the Internet and World Wide Web are vast. More than 2 million document files are available on the Internet, and more than 7,000 Web host computers support interactive hypermedia information. The Web is a distributed system—its bits and pieces are located on different Web servers worldwide, each of which utilizes electronic pointers, or links, to connect information and resources on other Web servers. As a result, you can leap among documents and media sources located on thousands of computers in more than 80 countries.

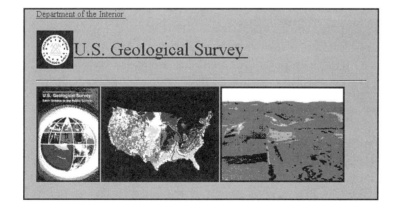

Fig. 2.5
USGS home page, showing effective use of different types of media.

II

The World Wide Web

WWW links can point to non-media-based information. A link can open an FTP site or begin an information search with the Gopher system. Traveling through the Web gives new meaning to the term *channel surfing*. When you surf your television set, you flip channels because you're not happy with the programs that appear. When you surf the Web, you change channels every few seconds, and you click because every link opens new avenues for exploration.

The documents and information on the Web frequently are linked by different authors. The process is similar to placing a footnote in a document; the footnote can automatically open the resource to which it refers. Hypermedia authors use a special software language known as HyperText Markup Language (HTML) to create hypertext and hypermedia links. Chapter 4, "How to Create a WWW Home Page," highlights the application of this language and the creation of hypermedia.

Hypertext and hypermedia are the engines that make it possible to maneuver easily through the immense resources available on Web servers. They facilitate the seamless connection of different types of information—text, visuals, audio, and video—in a type of electronic dreaming.

What Happens When You Connect to the Web?

The computers that maintain Web information are Web servers. Using the HyperText Transport Protocol (HTTP), these servers enable you to access hypertext and hypermedia information on your computer (known as a *client*), which sends requests to the server.

A significant difference exists between what occurs when you connect to a remote computer with file-transfer protocol and with a Web browser such as Mosaic. With FTP, the connection to the remote computer is continuous. You open a line and continue to use the connection until you finish; and while you are on-line, nobody else can use the connection.

Mosaic and other Web browsers, on the other hand, are *stateless* programs—that is, they open a connection to a remote computer, retrieve the initial information, and then quickly close the connection. The connection briefly reopens when more information needs to be transmitted to your computer, or when you click a link that in turn requests more information from the server. Because the connection with a remote host occurs for only a fraction of a second, the process minimizes the effect on the limited resources of the Internet.

The first information that you get from a remote Web server is known as a *home page*. The home page is an initial interface to a series of other documents, files, and resources that reside on that computer or on other Web servers around the world. The concept of the home page extends to your own computer. You can create and save a personal home page that has links to the resources and servers on the Web. Chapter 4 explains this process.

The links in Web documents use hidden addresses to connect with the resources to which they point. For example, a Web document about the speed of light may include the phrase "Einstein was a great scientist," with the name *Einstein* highlighted to indicate a link, possibly to a picture of Einstein. The address of the digital photograph, however, is encoded and invisible.

These hidden addresses, called Uniform Resource Locators (or URLs for short), can represent a link to almost every document, file, and service on the Internet. If you know the URL address for a document or a server, you can enter the address in a browser and jump to that resource. Following is the URL address for an interactive dinosaur exhibit located on a server at Honolulu Community College:

http://www.hcc.hawaii.edu/dinos/dinos.1.html

Following is a URL address that connects with space-physics information stored at the National Space Science Data Center:

telnet://NODIS@nssdca.gsfc.nasa.gov/

The first portion of the URL address, on the left side of the colon, refers to the method of access for retrieving the resource. Notice that the dinosaur exhibit is an HTTP resource and that the space-physics address indicates a Telnet connection. The information between the first set of double forward slashes (//) and the next single forward slash (/) refers to the specific computer host on which the information resides and to which your connection will go. The remaining portion of the address details the path on the computer to the specific resource that you want. You type a URL as a single, unbroken line (no spaces).

Just as the Domain Name System uses a plain-English phrase to reference a numerical sequence, the URL address can be referenced as an easy-to-remember name. Thus, **http://nearnet.gnn.com/wic/med.11.html** can be referenced as CancerNet (the NCI International Cancer Information Center).

II

The World Wide Web

Obviously, it is much easier to remember a plain-English name for a Web resource. Mosaic and other Web browsers, however, require the URL address to make a connection, because your local Internet host computer initially must look up the address of the computer to which you are trying to connect. The good news is that after you enter or save a URL address and its plain-English equivalent, you can simply click the name during future sessions.

Key WWW Developments: A Recipe for Success

In addition to the tremendous contributions of CERN, Tim Berners-Lee, and the other people involved with the creation of the Web, several factors played a role in the phenomenal growth of the WWW. The expansion of the Internet as a global communications network set the stage for the application of a system that links resources all over the world. Two software developments also are responsible for igniting the explosion of the Web. The first development is the interactive hypertext, hypermedia, and multimedia software that enables people who are not computer geniuses to write multimedia software and presentations, and to create links between different files and media sources. The second development is a series of software interface programs that help users navigate the links of the Web.

Today, multimedia technology is in offices and living rooms around the world. Businesses quickly embraced the concept of multimedia for employee training (usually, with stand-alone computer-based training stations) and for the distribution of electronic documents. Using their own private computer networks, companies can send electronic news, phone directories, manuals, and product information to employees around the world. Divisions, departments, and work groups share data, status reports, and details about specific projects. Hypertext software links this information.

Interactive information kiosks and CD-ROM applications enhance consumer awareness of multimedia. More than 5,000 CD-ROM titles currently are available.

Sponsored by Interval Research Corporation, the Electric Carnival is a traveling road show of interactive digital multimedia. The Carnival tours with the Lollapalooza concerts and shows hundreds of thousands of concertgoers, mostly people in their 20s, how to create and send poems, art, and music via the Internet.

The Internet represents functional anarchy—a multitude of networks that successfully connect but don't have one designated owner or oversight organization. The Web is a close cousin because no single person, company, or organization owns the Web; it is a distributed system with millions of users and, potentially, an equal number of document/multimedia authors who can become information providers to the world in a few keystrokes. Authors are holders of Ph.D. degrees, students from grade-school age through college, marketing professionals, lawyers, musicians, gardeners, and so on—all types of people.

When multimedia information moves into this enormous computer network, a universally accessible database of knowledge begins to form. So many people contribute to the electronic warehouse that the database contains all sorts of information and knowledge. The applications of this global database range from entertainment to education to business communication. The Web links this smorgasbord-like collection of human thought.

An initial challenge arose, however: How do you navigate these endless links easily? The solution was the development of software interfaces known as *browsers* that make using the Web a simple and exciting experience.

The first Web browsers were text-based programs whose simple keyboard commands enabled users to follow the links of the Web. The browsers can operate at modem speeds of 2,400 bps (bits per second) and up; they don't require direct-access connections to the Internet (such as SLIP or PPP); and they remain easy-to-use interfaces to the Web. These browsers do not, however, enable users to access the most exciting aspect of the Web: multimedia.

The National Center for Supercomputing Applications (NCSA) helps the scientific-research community by developing and distributing non-proprietary software and by investigating new technologies that may be transferred to the private sector for commercial application. Beginning in 1991, Marc Andreessen and a team of programmers at NCSA known as the Software Design Group used NSF funds to write a program has become the de facto graphical-interface browser for the Web: Mosaic.

Mosaic was one of the first browsers; it continues to be a free, public-domain program, and there is nothing quite as enticing in the world of computers as free software. Mosaic is available at many FTP host computers on the Internet. In the six months following its September 1993 release, more than 2 million people downloaded Mosaic from the NCSA host computer in Champaign, Illinois. Mosaic is discussed in more detail in chapter 3. For full details, check out Que's *Using Mosaic*.

Who Uses the Web?

Millions of people use the Internet and the Web. What are the demographics of the people who use these resources? Stanford Research Institute (SRI International) compiles statistics about use of the Internet and the World Wide Web. A comparison of hosts at government, research, education, and corporate Web sites shows that the people who use the Web are similar to the people who use the Internet, with an emphasis on users in the educational sector.

Table 2.1 breaks down Web use by domain and compares use to the approximate percentage of Internet hosts that these domains maintain.

Table 2.1 Breakdown of Organizational Use of the WWW		
Domain	**% of Web Traffic**	**% of Internet Hosts**
U.S. educational	49	27
U.S. commercial	20	26
U.S. government	9	6
Other countries and domains	22	41

*Statistics available by anonymous FTP from **nic.merit.edu**.*

In early 1994, James Pitkow and Mimi Recker of the Georgia Institute of Technology conducted a survey to identify traits of Web users. (As the Web evolves, becoming more accessible to a broader cross section of the world's population, these demographics are likely to change.) The 1,300 responses to the study indicate the following facts about Web users:

- 56 percent are between the ages of 21 and 30.

- 94 percent are male.

- 69 percent are located in North America.

- 45 percent are professionals, and 22 percent are graduate students.

The Future of the Web

If no single entity controls the Internet or the Web, how will the system develop to address the concerns and requirements of new users (such as companies that want to conduct commercial business on the system)? Who will ensure the realization of the one inherent goal of the Web: to provide a system that any person, using any type of computer, can use to access the resources of the Web? The W3 Organization (W3O) is one group that focuses on these important issues.

CERN and the Laboratory for Computer Science at the Massachusetts Institute of Technology (MIT) are the founding W3O member organizations. MIT operates several research groups that tie into the Web, including the Media Lab and the Artificial Intelligence Lab. Before W3O, CERN was the only organization that played a significant role in the ongoing definition of the Web.

Although it is based at two sites, the W3O intends to arrange with other institutes and sites to provide centers of excellence and local contact points. In Europe, W3O aims to establish a contact point in each country.

W3O's initial focus will be the development of new international data entry and retrieval standards for the Web, which are expected to make it much easier to find information. Since the Web is becoming like one huge electronic library, standard ways to catalog will improve the accessibility of information on the Web. Evolving from existing Web standards, these standards will supply a common architecture for use by commercial developers of browser software. The standards also will ensure that software created by different companies will be compatible.

For global commercial application of the Web, W3O will address issues related to security, privacy, and electronic transfers of funds. Funding for this project will come from the U.S. government, the European Union, and various international companies. Although it is not itself a standards organization, W3O works with developers and researchers to create awareness of the implications of converging and emerging technologies. Specific areas of technical and operational development include the following:

- Name and address syntax and semantics: Universal Identifiers

- Network transfer protocols: HyperText Transfer Protocol (HTTP)

- Data formats for hypertext and hypermedia: HyperText Markup Language (HTML)

- Encoding methods for compression and security

- Protocols for billing and for the transfer of legally binding documents

- Protocols that enhance the functions of the Web (proxy servers, caching, replication, and optimal request routing)

■ The use of alternative high-speed-network technology, such as Asynchronous Transfer Mode (ATM)

Robots on the Web

Even with browsers and guidebooks, quickly getting all the information you want on one subject through the Web remains a challenge. To make this task easier, research is being done on electronic robots called *knowbots*: computer programs that search the Web for you. You tell the knowbot exactly what you are looking for, and it weaves its way through the networks and host computers to find the information or resources that meet your needs.

For commercial applications, a knowbot can do price-comparison shopping. The knowbot first searches for all vendors that carry a specific product; it then accumulates specific details about the product, checks prices, and brings back a report to help you make your purchasing decision.

Knowbot companies face some technical challenges, however, including issues related to the security of individual computers (a knowbot could spread a computer virus) and system traffic (millions of knowbots weaving through the network could really slow traffic)

Some first-generation knowbots already are running around on the Internet and the Web. Alternately known as web crawlers and digital agents, these software applications look for and report on information related to Web servers and information resources. MIT's Matthew Gray developed a program named The World Wide Web Wanderer. This program travels through links in the Web to find the number of sites that provide specific information and the quantity of hypertext documents that are available.

The WebCrawler is another knowbot. Developed by Brian Pinkerton at the University of Washington, the WebCrawler program focuses on accumulating information about the specific documents that reside on Web servers. The program creates indices of the documents that it locates on the Web, and it enables users to keyword-search these indices.

Functionally, the WebCrawler begins with a set of one or more documents; it then locates the outbound links in the document and visits those links. The WebCrawler database compiles a list of all these documents, visited and unvisited, and establishes an index based on the content of visited documents. Each document link points to a specific host that, if visited, lists pointers to other documents. The program uses CERN's Web library to locate the necessary URL and then retrieves the document to the database in which it indexes.

The WebCrawler typically operates with 5 to 10 knowbots simultaneously. Figure 2.3 shows the mechanics of the WebCrawler process. Refer to Chapter 3, "Connecting to the WWW," for more information on using WebCrawler.

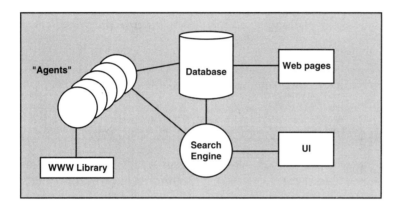

Fig. 2.6
A schematic diagram of the WebCrawler process. The UI, or user interface, is your window into the process. The search engine employs agents to comb the databases and libraries on the Web, eventually compiling a collection of relevant Web pages for your perusal.

In the WebCrawler home page, Pinkerton notes:

> The WebCrawler tries hard to be a good citizen. Its main approach involves the order in which it searches the Web. Some web robots have been known to operate in a depth-first fashion, retrieving file after file from a single site. This kind of traversal is bad. The WebCrawler searches the Web in a breadth-first fashion. When building its index of the Web, the WebCrawler will access a site at most a few times a day.

Finding What You Want on the Web

Like Gopher and WAIS, the Web is a tool that helps you locate information. The Web is similar to both WAIS and Gopher because it is a client-server information system that runs over the Internet. One important distinction exists, however: the Web delivers all information (documents, menus, and indexes) as hypertext and hypermedia.

You can travel through the Web in two ways: click and then follow a link, or send a search to the Web server to which you link. The search option is part of a Web document; this option appears as a search box in which you enter your search term and then click a search button. Not every Web document or server includes the searching function.

Not only does the Web deliver all information in a standard format, but almost every information system on the Internet can be represented in a Web document. This arrangement means that you can use the Web to access Gopher and WAIS information, as well as menus and files from Telnet or FTP sessions, and that you can use the Web to perform a WAIS index or Gopher search. Through the Web, WAIS databases are searchable documents, and the WAIS hit list that you receive after a search is a hypertext document that contains links to the documents that were found. Gopher menus on the Web are lists of items containing icons that link to other Gopher resources

When you use a Web browser to initiate a Telnet session or to retrieve files with FTP, you again get this same visually easy-to-use interface that makes the Web an all-encompassing Internet navigator.

Is the Web Electronic Nirvana?

With all these capabilities, the Web may seem to be perfect. A downside exists, however. One disadvantage is that multimedia information—pictures, graphics, and sound—consumes a tremendous amount of digital space. If you have a modem with less than 14.4 Kbps speed, transmitting this information to your computer will take an intolerable amount of time.

In addition, many people who write Web documents are not professional multimedia developers. As a result, many documents with which you connect contain with as many as 20 graphic images, and you can't access any of the links on the home page until all the graphics download to your computer.

As with Gopher or WAIS, a link can connect you to a resource that doesn't meet your needs. Web users rely on document and server authors to update their information. When these authors don't update their material, you can link to information that is out-of-date or the link might point to an off-line server.

Although these complications become frustrating at times, they are a small price to pay for access to the knowledge databases of humankind.

WWW Reference Information

A variety of governmental, educational, and private institutions participate in the development of the World Wide Web and provide information about it. Information is also readily available through mail lists and newsgroups. Here are a few sources of information to get you started.

Government Entities, Organizations, and Companies

National Center for Supercomputing Applications (NCSA)

152 Computing Applications Building
605 East Springfield Avenue
Champaign, IL 61820
217-244-0072

With your WWW client (Lynx, Mosaic, or WWW) use URL address
http://www.ncsa.uiuc.edu.

The Internet Network Information Center (InterNIC)

InterNIC makes current documentation on the NSFNET available via a mail
server, by anonymous FTP, Gopher, WAIS, and the World Wide Web.

InterNIC Information Services

P. O. Box 85608
San Diego, California 92186-9784
Phone: 800-444-4345 or 619-455-4600
FAX: 619-455-4640
Electronic mail: **refdesk@is.internic.net**

With your WWW client (Lynx, Mosaic, or WWW) use URL address
http://ds.internic.net/.

CERN

Swiss site:

European Laboratory for High Energy Physics
H - 1211 Geneva 23 (Switzerland)

French site:

Organisation Europeenne pour la Recherche Nucleaire
F - 01631 CERN Cedex (France)
Central telephone exchange: +41 22 767 6111

With Your WWW client (Lynx, Mosaic, or WWW), use URL address **http://
info.cern.ch** or try CERN's W3 project page at **http://info.cern.ch/
hypertext/WWW/TheProject.html,** where you'll find information
about WEb software, servers, conferences, protocols, and source code.

II

The World Wide Web

World Wide Web Consortium

The MIT World Wide Web Consortium is managed by the Laboratory for Computer Science at the Massachusetts Institute of Technology (MIT). It has been established in support of the CERN-MIT W30 initiative.

545 Technology Square
Cambridge, MA 02139
617-253-5851

With your WWW clients (Lynx, Mosaic, or WWW), use URL address **http://www.lcs.mit.edu/.**

Enterprise Integration Technologies

459 Hamilton Avenue
Palo Alto, CA 94301
Information: (415) 617-8000
Fax: (415) 617-8019
World-Wide Web: **http://www.eit.com/**

Web-Specific Newsgroups

alt.hypertext

A news group that focuses on hypertext.

cern.sting

Discussion about software engineering issues at CERN.

comp.infosystems.www.users

A forum for discussion of WWW client software and use in contacting various Internet information sources. New user and client setup questions, client bug reports, resource-discovery information on how to locate information on the Web that can't be found by the means detailed in the FAQ, and comparison between client packages are some of the acceptable topics for this group.

comp.infosystems.www.providers

A forum for discussion of WWW server software. Topics include server design, setup questions, server bug reports, security issues, and HTML page design.

comp.infosystems.www.misc

A forum for general discussion of WWW related topics not covered by the other newsgroups, including discussions of the Web's future, politics regarding changes in the structure, and protocols of the Web that affect both clients and servers.

comp.text.sgml

Standard Generalized Markup Language (SGML) technical discussion. HTML, the Hypertext Markup Language used by the World Wide Web, is a subset of SGML, so this newsgroup might be of interest.

Web Mailing Lists

A robot-like computer program called a list server maintains W3 mailing lists and enables documents to be retrieved on request. You subscribe to the W3 mailing lists by sending e-mail to the robot.

Address your mail to:

```
listserv@info.cern.ch
```

Leave the subject line blank. On the first line of the e-mail message, type the following:

```
subscribe www-announce your name
```

For example, if your name is Angela Douglas, the first line of your subscription request would read

```
subscribe www-announce Angela Douglas
```

There's no need to include your e-mail address in the subscription request. The robot picks up your address from the e-mail address. If you have problems or questions that you would like a person to answer, include them in an e-mail message to **www-request@info.cern.ch**.

www-announce

For individuals with an interest in the Web, its progress, new data sources, and software releases.

www-html

Provides technical discussions of the HyperText Markup Language (HTML) and HTMLPlus designs.

www-proxy

Technical discussion about Web proxies, caching, and future directions.

www-talk

Technical discussion for individuals or institutions developing Web software.

www-rdb

Discussion of using gateways to integrate relational databases into the Web.

Chapter 3

Connecting to the World Wide Web

The World Wide Web system is your gateway to the millions of documents and hundreds of thousands of multimedia resources on the computer servers that are on the Internet. Although Web servers are specifically designed to offer the hypermedia and hyperlinks that make Web information so easy to navigate and fun to use, you can also travel from a Web site to a Gopher server or begin a Telnet session. To use the World Wide Web, you must either connect with a computer that speaks the Internet's TCP/IP language (overviewed in chapter 1, "The Internet") or link to one that does.

Large businesses, educational organizations, and government agencies normally purchase a direct—or *dedicated*—Internet connection. A dedicated connection enables these organizations to operate a computer that speaks the TCP/IP language, letting users link directly to other Internet hosts. Dedicated connections use high-speed lines, 56 Kbps to 1.544 Mbps, and provide full-time access. These features make this type of connection attractive to organizations with many employees or students who need to use the Internet.

In fact, the number of users allowed to connect through a dedicated line has no specified limit. Thus, a business or university might have a computer in each department linked to the Internet through a local network. High-speed access is important for applications such as scientific research projects or business communications (video conferencing); these require extremely fast transmissions of large amounts of data. A full-time connection has two benefits: It makes it easy for people in an organization to use the Internet and it enables companies, schools, and government agencies to make their computers WWW servers. Dedicated connections are great, but annual fees can exceed $10,000.

Individuals who want to connect to the Internet/WWW usually don't need dedicated access. As a home-based user, your modem links your PC to a service provider's computer, known as a *local host*. A local host contains application software that uses the TCP/IP protocols to communicate directly with other Internet host computers. This type of access is appropriately known as a *dial-up account*.

Defining Account Types

There are three main types of dial-up accounts. One is *dial-up terminal emulation,* where your computer acts as a "dumb" terminal that connects to the local host (you choose a terminal emulation protocol in your communications software). Terminal emulation requires minimal software investment, perhaps none at all. In this type of dial-up account, the local host manages all the Internet activity—including file and document storage.

A second type of dial-up account, sometimes called *client software access*, places client software on your computer. Some Internet functions, such as accessing electronic mail and newsgroups, can then be done directly on your computer. The Internet provider normally supplies client software as a part of the service and a graphical environment may also be included, which makes the Internet much friendlier and easier to use.

The third type of account is *dial-up IP*, a variation on a direct connection. With dial-up IP, your computer becomes a physical part of the Internet—it receives a host name and an Internet Protocol (IP) address. You still contract for access with a service provider, but when you connect to their computer you transmit TCP/IP packets between machines. While your connection remains open, your PC is on the Net.

To communicate directly with other Internet computers, you load a software program that lets your computer use the TCP/IP language. There are two choices: *SLIP* (Serial Line Internet Protocol) and *PPP* (Point-to-Point Protocol). Besides being low-cost alternatives to direct access, SLIP and PPP provide full peer access to the Internet. As a result, you can load and run software programs that reside on other Internet computers. You don't need to shuttle files between the local host and your PC; other PCs in a small local network can connect through your PC to the Internet and you can use all the functions of a WWW multimedia browser.

SLIP and PPP are serial protocols you use in situations where two computers and their modems connect by a telephone circuit. SLIP, sometimes called

"Serial Line IP," was developed first. SLIP doesn't provide error correction or data compression, but it works well for home and small business applications. To address SLIP's error-correcting weakness, Point-to-Point Protocol (PPP) was developed as an Internet standard. PPP checks incoming data and asks the sending computer to retransmit when it detects an error in an IP packet. Modern modems, which use advanced error correction schemes, can be utilized very effectively with SLIP. A v.32bis modem not only provides advanced error correction (such as MNP-5 or LAP-M) but also has effective data compression, which increases the perceived throughput.

Because you connect directly to the Internet when you use SLIP or PPP, you need an *Internet Protocol (IP) address*. Your Internet access provider assigns this address each time you start a dial-up session. You can receive a permanent IP address, which is necessary if you have a registered host name. You also need a modem with a minimum speed of 9600bps (14.4 Kbps is desirable) when you use a SLIP or PPP connection.

The benefits of SLIP/PPP connectivity for individual users are:

1. Relatively low connection costs, usually a per-hour fee, and you only pay for what you use.

2. You have direct access to the resources of the Internet (you are ON the net).

3. You can use WWW browsers with their graphical interfaces.

4. You can directly transfer files from other remote hosts (servers) to your computer.

5. SLIP/PPP dial-up connections are available from many commercial Internet service providers—nationally, in your state, and locally.

The benefits of dedicated connectivity for businesses and organizations are:

1. File and information transfers with dedicated lines (speeds that range from 56 Kbps to T1—1.54 Mbps) take much less time than with other types of connectivity.

2. A multiple number of users, students in a classroom or business people in an office setting, can simultaneously share one dedicated line.

3. Dedicated connections make it easy for companies or educational institutions to operate servers that are available to other Internet users 24 hours a day. As a result, they can start up a Web server to offer information to the outside world.

III

Connecting to the Web

Computer Hardware and Software Requirements

Good news! The costs for high-powered personal computers continue to decline. You can buy hard drives with storage capacity between 350 and 600MB for less than $1 per megabyte. RAM memory chips are also inexpensive, going for less than $50 per megabyte. Simultaneously, computer processor speeds continue to increase.

But where there is good news, there is also bad. To use the sophisticated, memory-eating WWW browsers, and to have access to the multimedia resources of the Web, you need a powerful PC. For example, Mosaic software files take up more than 5MB of hard disk space. And to run under Windows, the application requires at least a 386DX machine with 4MB RAM; anything less and the application simply won't work. In the Macintosh environment, Mosaic on the Mac (2.0.0 Alpha 6) requires 1.3MB of disk storage, and prefers 3MB of memory, although it will run in as little as 2MB.

The multimedia information you link with or download also consumes digital space. The home pages on the WWW often contain many graphic images that temporarily download to RAM, and multimedia information takes even more space. For example, digital photographs (commonly in JPEG file format) can exceed 150KB, and a 10-second audio clip will require about 3MB of space. Beyond the issue of memory, you must have software and hardware that can run the multimedia information on the Web. Audio files, for example, require a digital-to-analog conversion chip, which you get with an audio card.

But don't throw away your one-year-old computer just yet. You can use WWW browsers that don't require as much system memory and jump from one Web server to another without downloading every multimedia file. Consider a television analogy. There are a few people who still own small black-and-white television sets and don't subscribe to cable. There are other people who own room-size, interactive color televisions and subscribe to every movie channel available. All these people can turn on their sets and watch *NBC Nightly News*. Like television, the Web is a form of media and it requires certain hardware configurations to take full advantage of the resources.

There are three different types of WWW browsers. Each offers specific features and functionality, and each has different hardware and software requirements (see tables 3.1 and 3.2).

■ *Line mode browser.* Provides WWW access to anyone with a "dumb" terminal. It operates as a general-purpose retrieval tool.

■ *Full screen browser.* A hypertext browser for systems using terminal emulation (usually VT100 or VT102). It uses the full screen, arrow keys, and highlighting.

■ *Multimedia browser.* A hypertext and hypermedia browser with a full graphical interface.

Table 3.1 Minimum Hardware

Type Connection/ Browser	Mac	PC
Terminal emulation/ line mode	MAC 1MB memory, 2400 baud modem	80286 1MB memory, 2400 baud modem
Client software/full screen browser	MAC 1MB memory, 2400 baud modem	80286 1MB memory, 2400 baud modem
SLIP or PPP/multimedia browser	MAC 4MB memory, 14.4 modem, hard disk, color monitor	80386DX 4MB memory, 14.4 modem, hard disk, color monitor

Table 3.2 Minimum Software

Type Connection/ Browser	Mac	PC
Terminal emulation/ line browser	MAC OS Communications software	DOS or MS Windows Communications software
Client software/full screen browser	MAC OS Communications software	DOS or MS Windows Communications software
SLIP or PPP/multimedia browser	MAC System 7, MacTCP 2.0.2 (or later) Mosaic, MACHTTP, etc.	MS Windows 3.1 enhanced, 1.1 compliant winsock.dll, Mosaic, Cello, etc.

III

Connecting to the Web

Read, Listen, and Watch: Multimedia Is Here

Everyone has experienced multimedia. On any given day we exercise all our senses to process a variety of information. Much of it is packaged in different forms: text and pictures in the morning newspaper, the highway billboards, and the reports we read at work; music and news on the radio; and video and graphics on the television. Computer technology enhances the utility of multimedia. You can convert all kinds of information to digital data and place it on computer hard drives and media (floppy disks and CD-ROMs). You can rapidly search and access this digital information—deciding what information you want and when you want it.

> **Note**
>
> The public domain (free) browsers such as NCSA Mosaic and Cello require that you also download and install special viewer software/drivers to see images or play movies. The Multimedia Viewer chart at the end of this section details the Internet sites, directories, and files where you can use "anonymous" FTP to acquire public domain and shareware multimedia viewers. If you don't want to deal with this aspect of getting multimedia on your PC, you might consider purchasing one of the commercial browsers that have viewers bundled in their packages.

Graphics Galore: Images on the Web

If you enjoy thumbing through illustrated books or watching slide shows, you'll love the digital image resources on the Web. Perhaps you're a history buff. Take a trip to the University of Georgia Library's server and examine a collection of photographs that chronicle the various Work Progress Administration (WPA) projects that were built in Georgia, including streets, airports, and schools. Fascinated by the world of insects? The Gillette Entomology Club at Colorado State University offers a large collection of insect slides for sale—take a peek at slide #281: a close-up of *Vanessa cardui* (painted lady butterfly). The On-Line Images from the History of Medicine service provides access to nearly 60,000 color and black-and-white images including a photograph of a Greek vase from the 4th century B.C. that shows a bandaging scene and a picture of Abraham Lincoln visiting soldiers' graves at Bull Run.

You encounter two types of images on the WWW. First, there are images directly embedded in the various Web home pages and documents. These inline images appear when you link to those documents (through the URL address). One example is the graphic icon or seal that many universities include at the top of their home page. You can see these inline images, but you can't manipulate them or store them on your computer.

Two image file formats, GIF (Graphical Interchange Format) and XBM (X Bitmap), display inline images in Web home pages and documents. GIF (pronounced "jif") was introduced by CompuServe in 1987 as a medium for exchanging pictures over their commercial service. GIF files can hold images with up to 256 distinct colors, from a palette of about 16 million.

GIF files are compressed to save space and transmission time. When you connect to a home page (load a URL address into your browser), the WWW document begins to transmit to your computer. You should note that your computer and the remote host don't have an exclusive, uninterrupted link. After all, it would waste valuable transmission line time to have your computer linked to a remote host in Japan while your PC processes a graphic image or you go to the kitchen for a glass of water. Normally, your computer (the client) and the remote server communicate several times before an entire home page appears. If there is more than one inline GIF or XBM image, they are downloaded to your PC individually and then decoded or decompressed.

The second type of Web image that you will encounter is one that you request to view or download to your PC. Housed in a database, these images are usually in a graphic file format that provides higher image resolution than GIF or XBM, such as JPEG. The JPEG (Joint Photographic Experts Group) format is an industry standard for compressing 24-bit and 8-bit color and gray image files. GIF images take up less space than JPEG images, but they only represent 8-bit, 256 colors, whereas JPEG supports 16.7 million colors, 24-bit images. The NCSA operates a Web site with a Mosaic Demo Home Page. On it you will find a small image of Vice President Al Gore. When you click on this small image, a JPEG file is transmitted to your computer and JPEG viewer as in figure 3.1.

There are at least 15 different graphic file formats, and each requires the use of image display software. *Image display software*—known as viewer software—processes and presents images on your monitor. The public domain browsers, Cello and Mosaic, display inline images in home pages, but don't have built-in viewers for display of other types of graphic file formats, notably JPEG.

III

Connecting to the Web

Fig. 3.1
This is a JPEG image of Vice President Al Gore available on the home page of the NCSA Mosaic Demo and viewed with ImageView in Air Mosaic.

You must, therefore, install and load a graphics viewer, either a commercial product or a shareware or freeware viewer to see, manipulate, and store these images. On MacMosiac, once you click on and download an image file, Mosaic automatically launches the appropriate viewer application (such as Sparkle or JPEGview), but you must have these programs resident on the computer. There are also public domain and shareware viewers, such as Lview for IBM, available on the Net, and the commercial browsers, such as Internet In A Box, have viewers bundled with their browser.

Table 3.3 Some Graphic Image Formats	
File Type	**Description**
GIF	Graphics Interchange Format (bit-mapped)
JPEG	Joint Photographic Experts Group
PCX	Bit-mapped file format
PICT	Macintosh image format
PostScript—Encapsulated PostScript	Intermediate print format
TIFF	Tagged image file format
XBM (X Windows Bitmap)	UNIX bitmap image

Table 3.4 NCSA Recommended Drivers		
Media Type	**Mac**	**PC**
GIF/JPEG images	JPEGView	Lview
PostScript files	Ghostview	
TIFF images	Gif Converter	Lview

Graphics and photographs add spice to computer-based information; unfortunately, it can take a long time to download and process images. Some WWW home pages take more than two minutes to appear—even at 14.4 Kbps. To prevent temporary insanity—when you might want to throw your keyboard through the monitor—multimedia Web browsers do have options that let you disable the presentation of images. This speeds up your journey through the Web so that when you come across a description of an image that sounds particularly appealing, you can enable the image display feature.

Let's Hear It: How to Enable Sound

The simplest way to listen to sounds (audio files) on the WWW is to purchase a computer that meets standards for multimedia PCs. The Multimedia PC Marketing Council (which consisted of Microsoft and other leading hardware and software companies) published a standard—the Multimedia PC (MPC) Standard—for future developments in PC-based multimedia. The standard was founded on the Windows graphical user interface enhanced with multimedia software components and programming tools. The first version of this standard set a minimum configuration for hardware manufacturers based on the 80286 PC with sound, image, and file storage. An upgraded version of the standard focuses on the 80386SX PC. Basic PCs typically have a single, small mono speaker that emits sounds ranging from barely audible to adequate volume levels. The more recent 80486 and Pentium-based IBM-compatible computers go beyond these initial standards. All models of Mac can record and play back sound; the IIfx, IIcx, IIci, and newer models have built-in stereo speakers, while earlier models have built-in mono speakers.

Sound cards play, record, or generate sounds of any kind, including speech, music, and sound effects. With an MPC-compatible PC and appropriate driver software, you will be able to travel through the Web and listen to a jazz session, a volcanic eruption, or a debate on taxes. MPC computers require sound cards with specific requirements.

Table 3.5 MPC Sound Card Requirements

External Connections	Input and output
Microphone	Built-in amplifier
Speakers/headphones	Synthesizer
Stereo system	Stereo channels
MIDI devices	8-bit DAC/ADC (16-bit recommended)
CD-ROM drive	22.05 KHz sampling rate (44.1 KHz recommended)

Table 3.6 Common Audio Formats

File Type	Description
UNIX au	UNIX audio file format
WAV	Waveform audio

Table 3.7 NCSA Recommended Drivers

Media Type	Mac	PC
AU sounds	SoundMachine	WHAM

Note

PCs that do meet the MPC standard can play sound. Here is what you do to set up a PC that has a speaker but doesn't have a sound board. The PC speaker driver for basic PC speakers was developed by Microsoft and is available at no charge to licensed users of Windows 3.1. Download the file SPEAK.EXE from the URL address **<http://www.ncsa.uiuc.edu/SDG/Software/WinMosaic/speak.html>** or FTP to **ftp.ncsa.uiuc.edu** directory Mosaic/Windows/viewers/ file SPEAK.EXE (21,236).

Other file archives can be searched using WWW browsers or search software. SPEAK.EXE is a self-extracting file. From within DOS, place the SPEAK.EXE in a new directory, and type speak at the DOS prompt. Extraction will produce a SPEAKER.DRV file. Do not place it in a separate directory from OEMSETUP.INF.

Lights, Camera, Action: How to Enable Movies

In the 1930s and 40s, audiences could watch the latest news events in movie theaters that played News Reels. In the 1950s, 60s, and 70s, television crews traveled all over the world to capture current events and bring them back home. In the 1980s, with the invention and wide distribution of video camcorders, individuals who captured interesting and newsworthy events could get their footage broadcast. Now, at the turn of the century, the Internet opens a vast avenue for video (news, entertainment, commercials, etc.) that individuals and companies record and place on the WWW. By completely bypassing the traditional outlets for video—broadcast and cable companies—the Web promises to deliver a tremendous amount of specialized video information that we would not otherwise be able to access. And because it is "on-demand" video, we can watch when our own schedule permits. One example of WWW video, for a very small target audience, is a QuickTime movie (on a server at Stanford) that shows people hang gliding from ridges and mountains in California.

You can get digital video movies through WWW browsers—using MPEG (Motion Picture Experts Group) and QuickTime file formats—although download time may be excessive when using SLIP/PPP dial-up connections. Regardless, expect a comparatively short playback time (for example, 5-minute download at 14.4 Kbps for a 10-second video clip). These frustrating time factors will become less of a problem as larger bandwidth and faster modems become available. Like image and sound files, special movie viewer software plays the movies.

Mac Mosaic systems can play MPEG movies by using the viewer Sparkle or QuickTime movies by using SimplePlayer from Apple. QuickTime, an extension in the Mac environment that works with System 6.0.x or 7.x, enables you to record and play back digital video. PC Mosaic uses MPEGPLAY to view MPEG movie files. You can retrieve the Sparkle QuickTime/MPEG viewer for Macintosh and QuickTime viewers for Microsoft Windows from the URL address **http://cougar.stanford.edu:7878/MoviePage.html**. NCSA recommends a set of viewers for image, audio, and video display.

Table 3.8 Video Formats	
Format	**Description**
AVI	Video for Windows
MPEG (Motion Picture Experts Group)	Standard for compressed video
QuickTime	Apple Computer's cross-platform movie format

III

Connecting to the Web

Table 3.9 NCSA Recommended Drivers		
Media Type	**Mac**	**PC**
QuickTime movies	SimplePlayer	QuickTime or Media Player
MPEG Movies	Sparkle	MPEGPLAY

Following is a list of viewers that you can use to view graphics, photographs, and movies and listen to sounds that are available on the Web. Most of these are shareware/freeware products. The list includes viewers that NCSA recommends for use with NCSA Mosaic, however, they may also work well with other Web browsers—you may have to experiment a bit. The NSCA FTP site is very popular and is frequently busy. If you can't get through, you may want to check out some of the other Web sites that contain viewer shareware. These are listed in chapter 8, "Computer Resources," in the sections "Internet and World Wide Web Resources" and "Personal Computers and PC Software."

To use the viewers on the Windows platform, you may have to either configure the software from the program menu or add a statement to the browser (Mosaic, Cello, etc.) .ini file to let it know the directory the viewer resides in. Specific configuration instructions come with many of the viewers in a *readme* text file. The NSCA Web site **http://www.ncsa.uiuc.edu** also has information about viewer installation.

Windows-Based Multimedia Viewers

■ Lview

Description: This is a freeware GIF/JPEG viewer.

FTP site: **ftp.ncsa.uiuc.edu**

Directory: /Mosaic/Windows/viewers

File: lview31.zip

File size: 224,269

■ MPEGPLAY

Description: A shareware MPEG movie viewer.

FTP site: **ftp.ncsa.uiuc.edu**

Directory: /Mosaic/Windows/viewers

File: mpegw32e.zip

File size: 921,020

- PC speaker driver

  Description: For basic PC speakers, available at no charge to licensed users of Windows 3.1.

  FTP site: **ftp.ncsa.uiuc.edu**

  Directory: Mosaic/Windows/viewers

  File: speak.exe

  File size: 21,236

- QuickTime

  Description: Video player from Chinese University in Hong Kong.

  FTP site: **ftp.cuhk**

  Directory: /pub/mov/

  File: qtw11.zip

  File size: 325,867

- Wham

  Description: Waveform Hold and Modify Version 1.31, freeware plays .au and .aiff sound files for systems with Windows-supported sound cards.

  FTP site: **ftp.ncsa.uiuc.edu**

  Directory: /Mosaic/Windows/viewers

  File: wham131.zip

  File size: 138,130

Macintosh-Based Multimedia Viewers

NCSA Mosaic for Macintosh will view the majority of files available by itself, but some images, movies, and sounds require additional viewer software. All of the following programs, except SimplePlayer, are either freeware or shareware. They are available using anonymous FTP (login anonymous) from **sumex-aim.stanford.edu** or **mac.archive.umich.edu**.

- JPEGView

  Description: Viewer for GIF and JPEG images.

  FTP site: **ftp.ncsa.uiuc.edu**

  Directory: /info-mac/Graphic/Utility

  File: jpeg-view-30.hqx

- GIFConverter

  Description: Displays TIFF images.

- QuickTime movies/SimplePlayer

  Description: QuickTime is Apple Computer's cross-platform movie file format. NCSA Mosaic supports QuickTime movies on the Macintosh, Microsoft Windows 3.1, and plans to support it on Silicon Graphics platform—it is copyrighted and not public domain. SimplePlayer is a copyrighted application that Apple Computer Inc. creates and distributes. It can be redistributed only by organizations with a distribution license. NCSA bundles SimplePlayer with NCSA Mosaic and you can download it with NCSA Mosaic from the directory Mac/Mosaic/Apple on NCSA's anonymous FTP server (**ftp.ncsa.uiuc.edu**).

- Sparkle

  Description: PlaysMPEG movies.

  FTP site: **sumex-aim.stanford.edu**

  Directory: /info-mac/Graphic/Utility

  File: sparkle-16.hqx

- UlawPla1.0b

  Description: Plays AU file format sounds.

  FTP site: **mac.archive.umich.edu**

  Directory: /mac/sound/soundutil/

  File: ulaw1.4.cpt.hqx

- GhostView

  Description: PostScript file format viewer.

  FTP site: **ftp.nisc.sri.com**

  Directory: /outgoing/adrain

  File: macGS

Text-Based Web Browsers

The following sections examine several software programs that help you navigate through the World Wide Web. These applications use the client/server technique to bring information from a remote computer into your PC. They are known as clients, navigators, or browsers. Multimedia browsers (Mosaic, Cello, etc.) install and become a client on your PC. The overview of each browser will give you a good understanding of the major functions and operational procedures. You can obtain more details from the reference sites and documents that are mentioned.

Dumb Terminal Connection

The most inexpensive way to access the WWW is to use a line mode browser. The CERN Line Mode Browser was the first browser developed for the Web. A UNIX-based server, this simple WWW browser works with any terminal and provides access for people who use PCs or Macs that emulate a dumb terminal (communication software programs provide selections for terminal emulation).

The Line Mode Browser (see example of display in fig. 3.2) allows you to find information by following references or searching for keywords. It uses HTML hypertext links and lets you follow a link to display text. Reference numbers help you navigate through a page—enter a number and press Enter to follow a link. To try this WWW interface, Telnet to **telnet.W3.org,** and log in as WWW if asked for a user name.

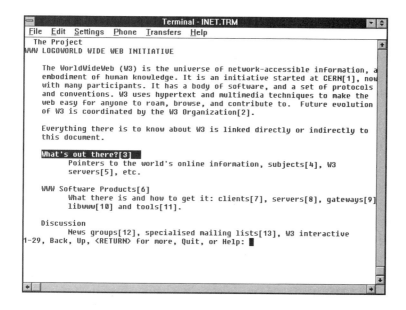

Fig. 3.2
This figure illustrates the Line Mode Browser interface. Links to other documents appear as numbers in the text.

III

Connecting to the Web

Table 3.10 Line Mode Browser Commands	
Function Command	**Description**
Help, ?	Provides a list of available commands depending on the context, the version number of the WWW program, and the hypertext address (or UDI) of the document you are reading.
<Return>	Displays the next page (if any) of the current document.
Top, Bottom	Goes to the top or bottom of the current document.
Up, Down	Scrolls up or down one page in the current document.
Load a Document <number>	Follows the corresponding reference number from the currently displayed document.
Back	Returns to the document you were reading before.
Next, Previous	Goes to the next or previous document in the list of pointers.
Go <address>	Goes to the document represented by the hypertext address.
Home	Goes back to the first document you were reading.
Find, Keywords <keywords>	Queries the current index with keywords (separated by blanks).
Recall	Gives a numbered list of the documents you have visited.
Quit, Exit	Leaves the application.

Text-Only Connection (Terminal Emulation)

Lynx is a WWW browser that fills a niche between line mode browsers and multimedia browsers. Lynx was designed by Lou Montulli, Charles Rezac, and Michael Grobe of Academic Computing Services at the University of Kansas, as part of an effort to build a campus-wide information system. Initial efforts produced a user-friendly hypertext interface for multi-user systems that were UNIX- and VMS-based. Lynx evolved from its initial hypertext language to the current use of HTML. One limitation to Lynx is that it only allows the use of keyboard cursors to display information.

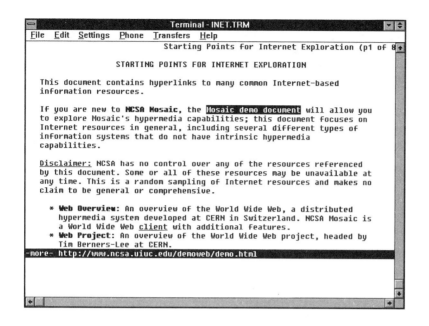

Fig. 3.3
With the Lynx browser, the connections to other resources appear as highlighted text. Here, Lynx is being used with the Terminal program of Microsoft Windows.

You can use Lynx from dial-up access, a dedicated connection, or Telnet. PCs and Macs need to run VT100 terminal emulation for presentation. When you start Lynx, it opens a default file—or home page—usually selected by your Internet service provider. When Lynx displays WWW documents, the connections to other resources display as highlighted text. You use simple keyboard commands to navigate through documents with Lynx. For example, to select a particular link on the screen, press the up-arrow or down-arrow key until a link highlights, and then press the right-arrow or return key to view the new information. Lynx keeps a list of each file you visit, known as a *history list*. The Backspace or Delete key displays the history list and enables you to recall any of those documents.

Table 3.11	Summary of Key Commands for Lynx	
Key	**Action**
\	View the original source of an HTML document.
/	Activate searching within a document. Search type depends upon options set by the system administrator.
? or H	On-line help. A list of help topics is provided.
Ctrl-L	Refresh or wipe screen to remove or correct errors from operating system.

(continues)

Table 3.11	**Continued**
Key	**Action**
Ctrl-W	Refresh or wipe screen to remove or correct errors from operating system.
Ctrl-R	Used to reload the current file being viewed.
\<delete\>	Display the history list—a list of documents accessed.
\<space\>	Next page.
=	Shows information about the current document and the currently selected link if there is one. Displays the file, URL, title, owner, and type.
a	Bookmark. You will be asked to: Save D)ocument or L)ink to bookmark file or C)ancel? (d,l,c). Answer "d" to save a link to the document you are currently viewing or "l" to save the link that is currently selected on the page. Selecting "c" will cancel without saving anything to your bookmark file.
c	Used to mail a message to the owner of the current document— if the author has specified ownership. If no ownership is specified then comments are disabled. The system will prompt you for information. End the message with a single "." on a line.
d	Download a file. Lynx will transfer the file into a temporary location and present the user with a list of options. The only default option is "save file to disk," which is disabled if Lynx is running in anonymous mode.
e	Edit a file. The type editor spawned depends upon which editor is configured.
g	View a URL. A prompt will be displayed asking you to enter the URL you wish to view.
i	Presents an index of documents.
m	Returns you to the starting document.
o	Opens the Lynx options menu. Used for configuring Lynx.
p	Print options. A menu of print options will be displayed.
q	Quit Lynx.
s	Activate searching. The "s" option lets you search index documents from an index server.
v	View a list of saved bookmarks. While viewing the bookmark list you may select a bookmark as you would any other link.
z	Halts the connect or data transfer process. Lynx supports completely interruptible I/O processes. If any data was transferred before the interrupt, it will be displayed.

Mosaic

The Mosaic browser is a cross-platform application, which means there are versions for PC (running Windows), Macintosh, Amiga, and UNIX-based systems. In the network environment of the Internet, Mosaic is a *client*—an application program that runs on a desktop computer and sends out requests for information that come back to your computer. NCSA's Mosaic is a freeware program that you can load and use at no charge. NCSA (The National Center for Supercomputing Applications) was established in February, 1985, with a National Science Foundation (NSF) grant. The NCSA continues to play a major role in the development of the WWW with Mosaic, which is produced and maintained by the Software Development Group (SDG).

> **Note**
>
> There are also several versions of Mosaic from commercial companies. These third-party products are discussed in appendix A, "Other Versions of Mosaic for Windows," and appendix B, "Other Versions of Mosaic for Mac."

As a cross-platform tool, Mosaic provides a means to transmit information between different hardware, software, and information systems. Some Mosaic functions—like e-mail—have an identical look and feel on different platforms, making it easy for users to exchange information. This type of cross-platform compatibility is significant, yet difficult to achieve. The fax machine, for example, emerged as an effective tool for cross-platform document compatibility because other efforts to standardize documents didn't work. Besides documents, Mosaic operates as a cross-platform tool in the presentation of sound, graphics, and video. The capability to present multimedia information with a graphical user interface (GUI) distinguishes Mosaic from the less versatile line and full-screen browsers. A good Web starting point for information on Mosaic is the NCSA home page (see fig. 3.4).

> **Note**
>
> This chapter is going to present the major features of Mosaic and some details on how to use them. However, a complete discussion of Mosaic is beyond the scope of this chapter. For a comprehensive discussion of Mosaic and how to use all of its features, see *Using Mosaic* from Que.

III

Connecting to the Web

Fig. 3.4
WWW home page for the National Center for Supercomputing Applications (NCSA) using the NCSA Mosaic program.

Major Mosaic Features

NCSA Mosaic continually upgrades with new features. NCSA creates the software in three typical versions: Alpha, Beta, and Official. The Alpha version incorporates new features and helps identify program bugs, the Beta version fixes the bugs, and the Official release theoretically resolves all bug problems. You can download Mosaic in various stages of development. The first Official release, Mosaic 1.0, was in November of 1993. By September of 1994, NCSA had Alpha v2.0 alpha 7. New information about the Mosaic releases, answers to questions, and documentation can be found by connecting to the NCSA Web server, URL address **http://www.ncsa.uiuc.edu**, and examining the NCSA Software Tools documents.

There are different versions of NCSA Mosaic for different computer platforms. Thus, there is a version for the PC, Macintosh, and UNIX platforms. Each version has slightly different operating features and visual appearances. For the Windows platform, all Mosaic versions after 2.0 alpha 2 require Win32s or a 32-bit version of Windows, such as NT. Win32s enables you to run 32-bit Windows applications under Windows 3.1, Windows 3.11, and Windows for Workgroups. Win32s is a beta product developed by Microsoft and is distributed at no charge to licensed Windows users.

Win32s is available via Microsoft's anonymous FTP server **ftp.microsoft.com** and you can find Win32s115a.Zip in the /developer/ DEVTOOLS/WIN32SDK directory. NCSA maintains a copy of the latest release on their FTP server **ftp.ncsa.uiuc.edu** directory /Mosaic/Windows/ win32s.zip.

Supports Existing System and Application Interfaces
Mosaic has many features that support full, interactive access to multimedia information. It operates with the popular graphical interfaces used by Mac, PC, and UNIX systems. This gives the application familiarity and makes it easy to share information between Mosaic and other applications.

Displays Visual Elements In Documents
Mosaic can display hypertext and hypermedia documents with a variety of font attributes, including bold, italic, and strikethrough. Within a document

(such as a home page), Mosaic can display visual layout elements such as paragraphs, bullet lists, headings, and hypermedia links. Additionally, characters can be displayed in foreign languages (it is not uncommon to link to a WWW server in another country and find documents written in a foreign language). These type attribute, layout, and language functions make WWW documents fun to view and read. Hypermedia links, also known as anchors or hyperlinks, display as highlighted words or graphics. When you click on a hyperlink, you jump to the resource.

Presents Graphics, Sounds, and Movies

Mosaic must use an audio driver or sound card to play sound files. Movies are in popular formats such as MPEG and QuickTime. Interactive graphics in GIF (Graphics Interchange Format) and XBM (X BitMap) are also supported. XBM is a black-and-white format, and GIF displays up to 256 distinct colors.

Supports Interactive Forms

Mosaic supports interactive electronic *forms*, which allow you to directly interact with information providers using the Forms function. For example, when you connect with a WWW searching mechanism (such as the WebCrawler), you can enter specific keywords into a text box to start a search. Or, if you connect with a business that sells products, you can enter your address and billing information to complete an order. A variety of basic form elements include fields, check boxes, and radio buttons. The capabilities and even reliability (security) of the forms features are dependent upon the version of Mosaic you use.

Navigates Documents and Media

At startup, Mosaic displays a *home page*. Home pages can be personalized to an individual, company or institution, or another WWW home page can be selected. A personalized home page can contain links to your favorite Web sites. As you travel through the Web, Mosaic maintains a history of the places you visit. This history feature, which is actually a list of the URLs you've been to, allows you to jump back to (reload) one of the sites you have visited during your session.

Tip
If you want to learn how to create your own Web home page, read chapter 4, "How to Create a WWW Home Page."

Mosaic for Windows

NCSA has created the Mosaic for Windows client software, a Web browser that more than 2 million people have downloaded. NCSA maintains an on-line hypertext NCSA Mosaic for Windows Users Guide. The address to access

III

Connecting to the Web

this guide is **http://www.ncsa.uiuc.edu/SDG/Software/WinMosaic/ Docs/WMosTOC.html** and you can download the guide by going to the FTP address **ftp://ftp.ncsa.uiuc.edu/Mosaic/Windows/Documents/ mosdocA5.zip**.

How to Get Mosaic Software

If you have access to the Internet, these directions will help you get the necessary Mosaic software for a PC or Macintosh system from NCSA at the University of Illinois at Urbana-Champaign. The Mosaic software is available from NCSA without charge, but be aware that some applications that work with Mosaic (viewers, for example) may be shareware that require registration and payment of a license fee.

Tip

Que's *Using Mosaic* provides comprehensive instructions on the installation and use of Mosaic (for both PC and Macintosh).

Download the Mosaic software, decompress it, and follow standard Microsoft Windows or Macintosh instructions to set up the Mosaic icon on your system. You can find the Mosaic software on the NCSA computer. FTP to **ftp.ncsa.uiuc.edu**. The Mosaic software for Windows is in subdirectory **/PC/Windows** with the file name **Mosaic**; the latest 32-bit Windows Mosaic is in subdirectory **/Web/Mosaic/Windows/** file name **wmos20a7.zip**; and for Macintosh you want to access the program by moving to subdirectory **/Mac** and again downloading **Mosaic.**

Installing and Setting Up Mosaic

To access resources on the Web, you must have a direct connection to the Internet, or you must have the capability to establish a dial-up SLIP or PPP connection to a system with a direct Internet connection. These options are discussed earlier in this chapter.

In addition to the connectivity and the hardware configurations for your computer system that have already been discussed, NCSA Mosaic for Windows also requires a WinSock 1.1-compliant *Windows Sockets* library (WinSock DLL or winsock.dll). Windows sockets is a Windows program in dynamic link library (DLL) form that acts as a "behind-the-scenes" interface between the TCP/IP connection and different Windows applications, such as Mosaic and Cello. You use the WinSock program to initiate your connection to the Internet and begin a Web session.

Trumpet Winsock is a shareware product written by Peter Tattam, which you can get by FTP to **ftp.utas.edu.au**. Go to subdirectory **/pc/trumpet/ winsock/** and the file name is twsk10a.zip. This compressed file contains all the files you need. Begin by reading the file install.doc (Word for Windows 2.0) or install.txt (text format). If you use commercial TCP/IP networking software, you must obtain the winsock.dll from the vendor, such as Spry, Novell, or Microsoft.

How to Configure the MOSAIC.INI File for Windows

Before you run Mosaic, you should make a few changes to its configuration. Configuring Mosaic involves several steps, beginning with modification of the MOSAIC.INI file.

1. Copy the MOSAIC.INI file from its current directory to your \WINDOWS directory. Keep your original MOSAIC.INI. This is a text file that appears each time you update Mosaic. It should be examined for changes and selectively updated to the \WINDOWS directory.

2. Using a standard editor, such as Notepad, install the configuration changes in the \WINDOWS\MOSAIC.INI file. The key changes to consider on an initial installation are adding the home page status and adding the home page URL.

Other changes, such as inserting hot lists and other URLs or inserting updates from NCSA, can be made later. This is also a good time to make sure the MOSAIC.INI file has the proper references (path, extension, and so on) to any media viewers you may be installing.

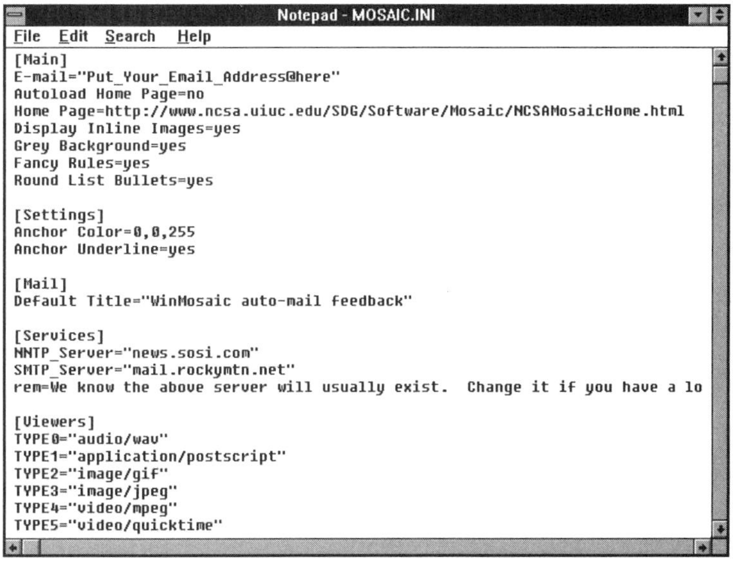

Fig. 3.5
You can use Notepad to modify the MOSAIC.INI file to customize features and add viewers.

III

Connecting to the Web

Starting Mosaic

Your first step in beginning a Mosaic session on the Web is to initiate your SLIP/PPP connection by starting your TCP/IP program (such as Trumpet Winsock) and logging onto the Internet. Login can be accomplished automatically if you have developed a login command script. Figures 3.6–3.8 illustrate the sequence as follows:

1. Open the program and choose **D**ialler on the main menu.

2. Click on **E**dit Scripts and open the login.cmd file. Make any adjustments to your connection, such as adding or changing the phone number that you dial for access and your login name and password.

3. After this has been done you only need to select **D**ialler, then **L**ogin to start an automatic login.

After the connection is established, double-click the Mosaic icon to start the program. The options you choose in configuration determine which home page displays first. If you choose a home page on your local system or one from the Web, the home page should load quickly.

Fig. 3.6
From the Dialler menu on Trumpet Winsock, you can select Edit scripts to establish your preferences for dialing into your service provider. After the settings are established, simply choose Login from the Dialler menu to automatically connect to the Internet.

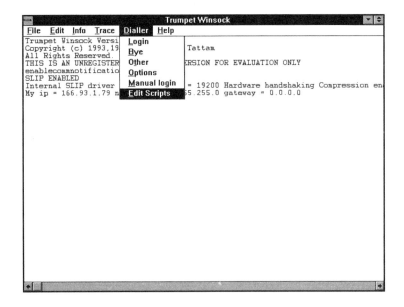

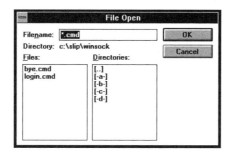

Fig. 3.7
This dialog box appears after you select **E**dit Scripts. Login.cmd is the file that contains the script for connecting to your service provider.

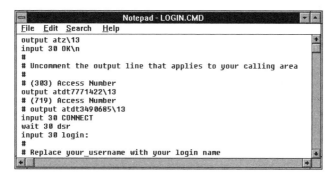

Fig. 3.8
Notepad is the default editor, where you can change your access phone number, login name, and password.

A Quick Look at the Mosaic Screen

Before you get started using Mosaic, it is useful to have a quick overview of the various parts of the screen. A typical Mosaic screen is shown in figure 3.9.

The following is a brief description of these parts:

■ *Toolbar.* The buttons on the toolbar substitute for menu commands. From left to right the buttons are Open URL, Save, Navigate Back, Navigate Forward, Reload, Home, Copy, Paste, Find, Print, and About NCSA Mosaic.

> **Note**
>
> As of this writing, the most current version of NCSA Mosaic—2.06a—has not yet implemented the Save, Copy, or Paste functions, so these buttons are always dimmed.

■ *Document title.* This is the name of the currently loaded Web document.

■ *Document URL.* This is the address of the currently loaded Web document.

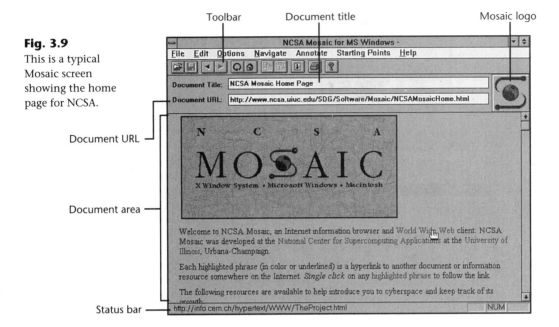

Fig. 3.9
This is a typical Mosaic screen showing the home page for NCSA.

Toolbar · Document title · Mosaic logo · Document URL · Document area · Status bar

■ *Mosaic logo.* This logo changes while documents are being retrieved.

■ *Document area.* This main part of the screen is where you see the Web documents you load.

■ *Status bar.* Various message are shown here. These will be discussed as needed.

Navigating to Other Pages

Once you have Mosaic running, you have many ways to move to any home page on the Web. The next few sections show you the most common methods for navigating.

Tip
If the pointer doesn't change to a hand when it's over a hyperlink, open the **O**ptions menu and choose Change Cursor over Anchors so that this option is checked in the menu.

Jumping to a Hyperlink

Jumping to a hyperlink is probably the simplest and most common way to navigate Web pages with Mosaic. Hyperlinks are shown in a different color or underlined text. All you have to do is click on the link and Mosaic loads the file and displays the new page or loads the media, such as a JPEG image. When the mouse pointer is touching a hyperlink, it becomes a hand. Also, look at the status bar at the bottom of the screen. The left side of the bar shows the address for the link that the pointer is over.

Note

Watch the Mosaic logo (the globe) at the upper right edge of the page while a file loads. The globe should spin and small yellow indicators should move across the blue curves by the globe. As long as this is happening, the page is still loading. Also, watch the status bar at the bottom of the screen. It will describe what action Mosaic is taking, what file is loading, and other messages. If it looks as if the page has loaded but you can't scroll in it, Mosaic may not be done loading part of the page or images that are off-screen.

Tip
If the URL address doesn't display in the status bar, open the **O**ptions menu and choose Show Anchor URLs so that this option is checked in the menu.

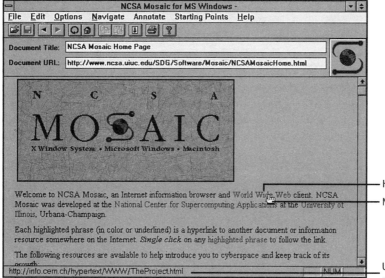

Fig. 3.10
The hyperlink that the mouse pointer is touching is the page you will go to if you click here. Its address is shown at the bottom of the screen.

Hyperlink

Mouse pointer changed to hand

URL Address for hyperlink mouse pointer is touching

Hyperlinks don't have to be text, they may also be graphics. Clicking on a linked graphic will also jump you to the linked page.

Note

If you click on a hyperlink for a multimedia file (graphic, movie, text, or audio clip) instead of a home page, Mosaic will open a viewer or player for that type of file after it is loaded.

Jumping to a Page by Using Its URL Address

Another common way to navigate is to type in the URL address. This is a very useful way to navigate the Web by using this book because all the pages reviewed and listed here give the URL address. To jump directly to a specific home page or document with a given URL, follow these steps:

1. Open the **F**ile menu and choose **O**pen URL. The dialog box shown in figure 3.11 opens.

Fig. 3.11

Use this dialog box to jump to a home page by typing its URL.

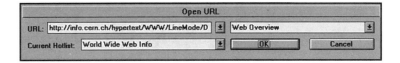

2. Double-click in the URL text box. This selects the entire address that is shown.

3. Type the URL address for the page you want to jump to. Be sure to type in the URL exactly as given, with no spaces before or after the address.

4. Click OK.

Working with Other Internet Servers and Applications

You can use Mosaic to access and use FTP, Telnet, Gopher, and WAIS functions and systems. The process, which is the same for all versions of Mosaic and for all computer platforms, involves entering a specific URL address format. The following information provides specific instructions for using these other valuable Internet applications via Mosaic.

How to Begin a Telnet Session with Mosaic. In order to Telnet with NCSA Mosaic, you need to have a native Windows Telnet product on your system, and you have to define the path to this application in the mosaic.ini file. The last line of the [viewers] section of the mosaic.ini should include a line such as:

```
telnet="c:\path\executable_name.exe"
```

To begin the Telnet session, open a URL using the following format:

```
telnet://machine.name/path/to/desired/directory
```

Mosaic will display a dialog box for your username and password (if required).

How to Initiate an FTP Session with Mosaic. To begin an anonymous FTP session, open the URL with the following format:

```
file://address.of.the.machine/
```

This address command logs you into the root directory of the anonymous FTP site. Log in to a non-anonymous FTP with the following format:

```
file://username@machine/pathname
```

For example, to log into a system as user "tsmith" at the FTP site **ftp.sample.com** and directly go to the /new/pubs directory, you type the URL with this format:

```
file://tsmith@ftp.sample.com/new/pubs
```

Mosaic displays a dialog box that asks you to confirm the username and provide a password.

How to Connect to a Gopher Server with Mosaic. You connect to a Gopher server by using a URL address with the following format:

```
gopher://name of gopher server:port number/ID
```

Here is an example URL address for a Gopher server located at the University of Minnesota:

```
gopher://gopher.micro.umn.edu:70/1
```

Navigation Shortcuts

Once you have been using Mosaic for an hour or two, you will realize that typing a URL is a very mistake-prone way to move on the Web. And once you've discovered a Web page that you want to use frequently, you'll want a way to get back to it quickly. Wouldn't it be nice if you could jump back to any page that you have used previously since you started Mosaic?

Fortunately, Mosaic has built-in features to handle all these needs. Using these shortcuts will save you time (and—if you pay for your Internet connection—money too!) and make your Web sessions more productive.

Using Hot Lists

The hot lists in Mosaic are one of its greatest features. With these you can save the addresses of up to 800 pages. Mosaic saves the page's title and URL address and you can jump directly to this page at any time.

Tip

If you ever get totally lost on the Web and don't know where to go next, or need to get back to your home page for any reason, open the **N**avigate menu and choose Home, or click on the Home icon on the menu bar

III

Connecting to the Web

To add a page to a hot list, follow these steps:

1. Navigate to the page by using any of the navigation techniques described earlier.

2. Open the **F**ile menu and choose **O**pen URL. The dialog box shown in figure 3.12 opens.

Fig 3.12
The Current
Hotlist box with
the list of defined
hot lists dropped
down.

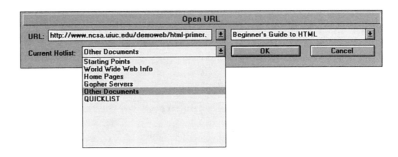

Tip
There is one special hot list called the QUICKLIST. This hot list does not have the 40-item limit and it does not count against your 20-hot list limit.

3. Click on the drop-down arrow on the Current Hotlist text box and select the hot list that you want to add the page to. If you want to add a new hot list, type the name in the Current Hotlist text box.

> **Note**
>
> Mosaic can accommodate up to 20 hot lists. Each hot list can contain up to 40 documents. So, you can have as many as 800 pages in the hot lists. Mosaic comes with a few predefined hot lists, but it's a good idea to make your own (you can arrange your favorite pages by topics). Procedures to add a new hot list are covered later in this section.

4. Click Cancel.

5. Open the **N**avigate menu and choose Add Current to Hot.

This adds the current page to the hot list you chose as your current hot list. Now, to jump to any page in any of the hot lists:

1. Open the **F**ile menu and choose **O**pen URL.

2. Click on the drop-down arrow on the Current Hotlist text box and select the hot list containing the page you want to jump to. Type the name of the hot list in the Current Hotlist text box.

3. Click on the drop-down arrow on the URL text box and select the URL of the page you want to jump to (see fig. 3.13).

or

Click on the drop-down arrow on the text box to the right of the URL text box (this would be the Document Title or Name if the text box had a name) and select the Name of the page you want to jump to (see fig. 3.14).

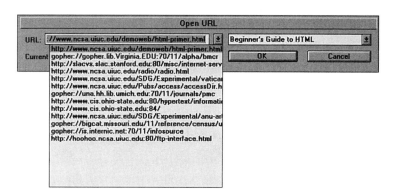

Fig. 3.13
Choosing a document on the hot list by URL.

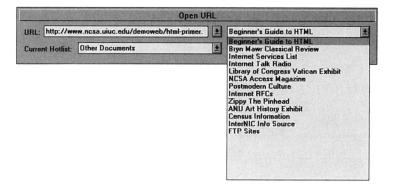

Fig. 3.14
Choosing a document on the hot list by Name.

4. Click OK.

Adding a new hot list is not the most intuitive operation in Mosaic, but it is very useful. Follow these steps carefully.

1. Open the **N**avigate menu and choose Menu Editor. The Personal Menus dialog box shown in figure 3.15 opens.

III

Connecting to the Web

Fig. 3.15
This is where you
create a new hot
list.

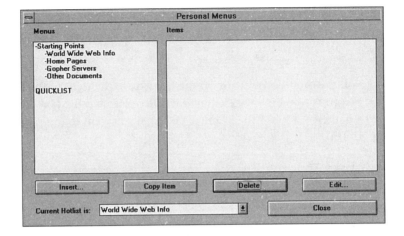

2. Select Starting Points in the menus box.

3. Click on the Insert button. The Add Item dialog box shown in figure 3.16 appears.

4. When this dialog box opens, the current document's URL and name will be in the text boxes and the Document Item radio button will be selected. Select the Menu radio button.

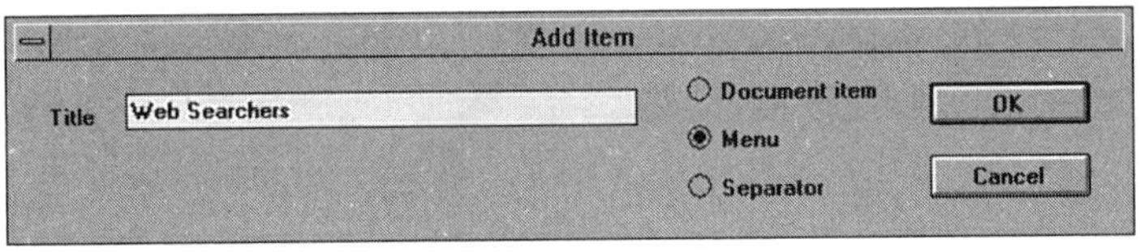

Fig. 3.16
After selecting
the Menu radio
button, the URL
text box is gone,
leaving just the
Title text box.

5. Type the Name of the hot list you want to add, and then click OK.

6. Click Close.

You can now add items to this hot list—just like any other hot list—by using the procedure described earlier. The side effect of adding a hot list is that you also add an item to your Starting Points menu. (This menu is described later in this chapter.)

Using the History List

So you were just looking at a document 10 minutes ago and now you want to go back to it. But you've loaded three other pages since then and you don't remember where this document was. Or an even simpler case is when you jump to a page, realize it's not what you want, and want to jump back to where you were. Mosaic's history list makes either of these easy.

To use the history list, follow these steps:

1. Open the **N**avigate menu and choose History. The NCSA Mosaic-History dialog box shown in figure 3.17 opens.

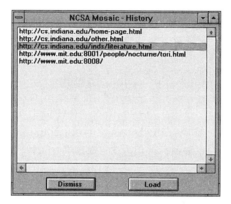

Fig. 3.17
The History dialog shows a list of all the documents you have loaded in this Mosaic session. The first document you loaded (probably your home page) will be at the top of the list and the current document will be at the bottom.

2. Select the document you want to go back to from the list.

3. Click Load or double-click on the address. If you change your mind and don't want to jump to one of these documents, click Dismiss.

Jumping back to the last page you were at is easy. Open the **N**avigate menu and choose Back. This takes you to the previous page. You can also move forward, if you have previously moved back or used the history list to move back. To move forward, open the **N**avigate menu and choose Forward. The other, perhaps easier, method to move back and forward through pages is to click on the left (backward) and right (forward) arrows on the menu bar.

Navigating from the Starting Points

There is one final navigation method worth noting here. The next-to-last option on the Mosaic menu bar is the Starting Points menu, it is based on the hot list called Starting Points. This is a quick way to access your most frequently used Web documents. To use it, all you have to do is open the Starting Points menu and choose a menu option. Many of the options will open submenus and from there you can choose a document to jump to.

The Starting Points menu is easy to personalize, you can add single home pages and entire hot lists. To add a single home page to this menu, add it to the Starting Points hot list by using the steps described earlier (see fig. 3.18).

III

Connecting to the Web

Fig. 3.18
This Starting
Points menu has a
Tori Amos home
page added to it.

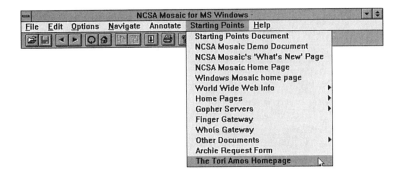

You can also add an entire hot list name. An entire hot list name has an arrow next to it and opens as a submenu of the Starting Points menu. If you
have several items you want to add to the Starting Points menu, this is probably the best way to do it. Adding too many individual items to the Starting
Points menu will make it large and inconvenient to use.

Your hot lists are automatically added to the Starting Points menu when you
create a new hot list—as described in an earlier section. So, to add an entire
hot list submenu to the Starting Points menu, just follow those earlier steps.
Figure 3.19 shows the Starting Points menu with a hot list for searching the
Web added.

Fig. 3.19
This Starting
Points menu has
a Web Searchers
menu added to it.

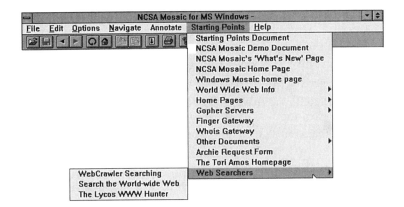

Disabling Graphics

Some Web documents have so many inline images, or a few very large ones,
that they can take several minutes to load on a slow modem connection. To
speed things up, open the **O**ptions menu and choose Display Inline Images.
This removes the check mark next to the option. Now Mosaic does not

request the inline images from the server—a small logo is displayed where the image would have been.

> **Note**
>
> This option does not alter images that you download. Those will download normally and display in your viewer.

Saving a Document to a File

Files (home pages, documents, graphic images) from any URL can be downloaded to your hard drive. There are many useful reasons to do this: You can make the file a local home page (which will load faster) or send the file to another computer, to name a few. You can also save files from Gopher, FTP, and others without viewing them first. To save a file, follow these steps:

1. Open the **O**ptions menu and choose Load To Disk so that it is checked.

2. Once you select Load To Disk, the next time you click on a hyperlink a "Save As" box appears, as shown in figure 3.20.

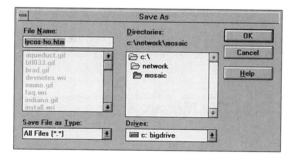

Tip
To download the current URL document, open the **N**avigate menu and choose Reload.

Fig. 3.20
The Save As dialog box should be familiar from other Windows applications.

3. Choose a drive, a directory, and make sure the file name is a legal DOS file name, and then click OK.

4. After you receive the file, open the **O**ptions menu, uncheck the Load to Disk option, and continue with your WWW session.

Printing

> **Note**
>
> Printing is not available in some older versions of Mosaic.

Printing a Mosaic document so that you have a hard copy is straightforward and essentially optionless. To print the current document, open the **F**ile menu and choose **P**rint. Click OK in the Print dialog box.

Mosaic for Macintosh

Macintosh Mosaic is very similar to PC/Windows-based Mosaic. There are, however, a few functional differences. For example, Mac Mosaic Help uses Macintosh Balloon Help—when you aim your mouse at a function, a help balloon automatically appears (if Balloon Help is enabled). To obtain Mac Mosaic, you can FTP to **ftp.ncsa.uiuc.edu** to locate and download the program from directory /Mosaic. Installation involves drag and drop set-up procedures.

System Requirements include having System 7 or later with four or more megabytes of memory. You also need MacTCP 2.0.2 or later (MacTCP 2.0.4 or later is recommended).

Installing, Setting Up, and Starting NCSA Mosaic for Macintosh

If you downloaded NCSA Mosaic from the NCSA FTP server, unStuff and unBinHex the file by using StuffitExpander or another data compression program (e.g. Compact Pro). Now drag the NCSA Mosaic icon onto your hard disk.

A Quick Look at the Mosaic Screen

Before you get started using Mosaic, it is useful to have a quick overview of the various parts of the screen. A typical Mac Mosaic screen is shown in figure 3.21.

The following is a brief description of these parts.

- *Toolbar*. The buttons and information boxes on the toolbar help you perform functions quickly and see information that tells you where you are. From left to right the buttons are Navigate Back, Navigate Forward, Home, History, and Search.

- *Document title*. This is the name of the currently loaded Web document.

- *Document URL*. This is the address of the currently loaded Web document.

- *Mosaic logo*. This logo changes while documents are being retrieved.

Mosaic logo Toolbar   Document title   Document URL

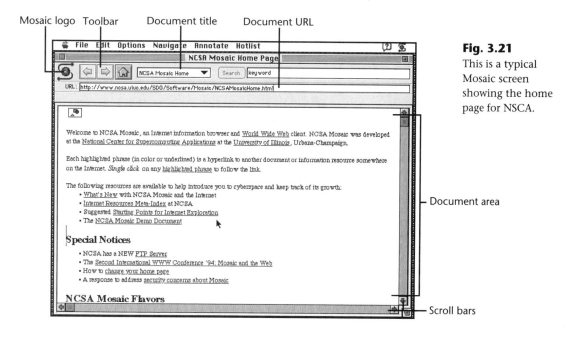

Fig. 3.21
This is a typical
Mosaic screen
showing the home
page for NSCA.

Document area

Scroll bars

- *Document area.* This main part of the screen is where you see the Web documents you load.

- *Scroll bars.* The scroll bars on the side and bottom of the page help you move through a loaded document.

How to Configure Mosaic for Macintosh

Choose Preferences from the Options menu to start configuration. Here is a brief overview of the procedures and options for establishing the various preferences (see fig. 3.22).

1. The home page data determines which home page will be displayed when you start Mosaic. The home page URL address can be the one supplied from NCSA, your own personal home page, or another page from the Web. The address for a NSCA Mac home page is **http://www.ncsa/uiuc.edu/SDG/Software/MacMosaic/MacMosaicHome.html**.

2. Enter an Internet domain name address for the Newshost and WAIS gateway—these are standard Internet addresses. The Newshost is the address for the server that provides you with newsgroup news. You can use Mosaic as a news reader to read, but not to respond to or add news to the newsgroup postings.

Tip

In addition to the color of links, you can establish a "fade" color feature. As an example, links may be red after you have tried them, and then gradually (over 2 or 3 weeks) they will fade back to blue if you don't visit that site again. As soon as you visit it again, the color changes back to red. This is a nice way to visually see how long it has been since you've visited a site.

III

Connecting to the Web

3. Insert your e-mail address in the E-Mail Address box and your name in the User name box. This information is used to send electronic mail to NCSA developers or any other parties.

4. Mosaic keeps track of the links you use in a document. Anchor colors for links have a default of blue and red. Links start as blue, and then, after you click on a link and view the new media or document, the link to that information changes to red. This feature enables you to quickly glance at a page and determine which links you have tried and which you haven't. You can change the color of these links in the Preferences dialog box.

Fig. 3.22
Use the Prefer-
ences dialog box
(under the
Options menu) to
set up many useful
defaults, such as
your e-mail
address, the color
of links, and the
display variables
(such as fonts) for
HTML documents.

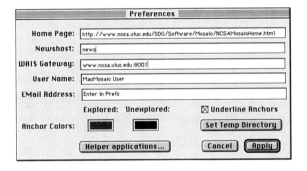

You can complete your configuration of preferences by clicking on the Helper applications button.

1. Click on the Helper applications button to open the Helper Configuration box (see fig. 3.23).

Fig. 3.23
Use the Helper
Configuration
dialog to deter-
mine which
applications will be
used to display or
play files you
download.

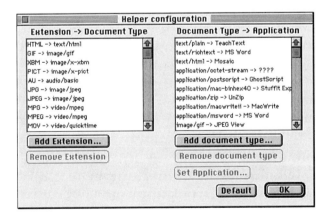

2. At this point, viewer software can be specified for different media types.

3. Use the Styles command to configure how HTML (HyperText Markup Language) will be displayed on your screen.

4. The Auto-Load Images item controls the display of graphic images on retrieved documents. Turning it off may speed up your Mosaic session.

Navigation

When you double-click on the Mosaic icon, Mosaic loads the home page that was configured earlier. To follow a hyperlink, a phrase, or graphic with a default color highlighted in blue, click on it. Mosaic determines the type of media to display, whether it needs a special viewer, and then loads and displays it. Notice that Mosaic lets you view the screen and move the scroll buttons on the right while it continues to load the rest of the media.

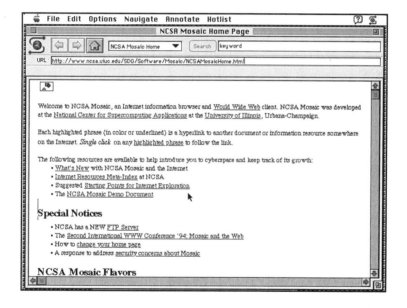

Fig. 3.24
The Mosaic screen has scroll bars on both the bottom and side of the screen that let you reposition and move through Web documents.

You can also use the **N**avigate menu, the icons on the toolbar, and other menu items to further navigate through Mac Mosaic. The **N**avigate menu allows you to go forward or back, reload the current URL, or go to your home page. To go directly to a Web site, follow these procedures:

1. Choose **O**pen URL from the **F**ile menu.

2. Type the URL address of the Web site/page you want to retrieve.

III

Connecting to the Web

3. Now choose **O**pen. Mosaic will go directly to that Web site.

Fig. 3.25
It is easy to load a Web URL address in Mosaic.

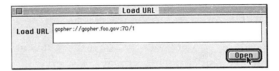

Tip
If you are getting frustrated with the loading time on a document, you can cancel loading by using ⌘+Period. This stops the transfer, but may freeze the Mac for 10–20 seconds while the transfer cancels.

Another method for navigation involves using the history function to move back to sites you have already visited, as shown in the following steps:

1. Click the history list (the text field to the right of the home icon with the downward-pointing arrow). A drop-down list of the documents you have visited in this session appears.

2. You can navigate (or jump) to a URL address by clicking on it.

After you load a document, you can save its URL address for future uses on the hot list by following these steps.

1. First, click Add This Document within the Hotlist menu.

2. You need to save your hot list to use it the next time you use Mosaic. Click on Hotlist Interface-Save under the Hotlist menu to bring up the standard Macintosh File Save dialog box.

Fig. 3.26
Use the options in the **H**otlist menu to create new hot lists and add addresses of your favorite Web sites to hot lists.

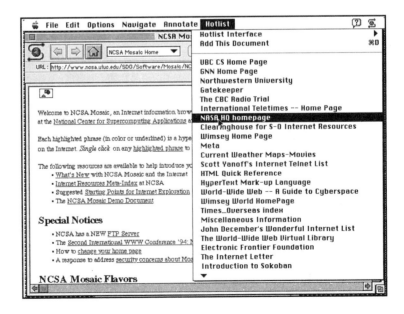

3. Specify the name and location of the hot list. If you want to have Mosaic automatically load this hot list when you start up the application, name it "Hotlist" and save it in the same folder as the Mosaic application.

4. To add, delete, or replace items in your hot list, click **H**otlist Interface-Edit in the Hotlist menu to bring up the dialog box. Entries in the hot list can also be viewed or changed. Using **H**otlist Interface-New in the hot list menu allows you to open a new hot list. You can set up and use several hot lists with Mosaic.

How to Download

There are several ways to save Web document and file information with Mac Mosaic. Figure 3.27 shows the Save dialog box. The following steps outline a few of these different methods.

1. Choose **C**opy from the **E**dit menu to place the current document on the clipboard and make it available to other applications.

or

1. Select text or HTML from the Format dialog box, select the folder, and choose **S**ave. Notice that the HTML saved in this way is not a true copy of the original, it's derived from the document.

> **Caution**
>
> The save feature is not reliable in the version of Mosaic that was available at the time of this writing. It may cause system crashes and the save files may not be usable. Check the current bug list, available from the NCSA site listed earlier, to see if this has been fixed in the version you have.

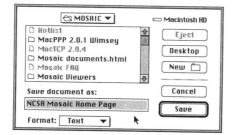

Tip

If you have connected to a Web page that is very large, you may want to search the page for a specific word. Select Find from the Edit menu and enter the keyword "education." ⌘+G enables you to continue to search the page for more instances of the same word.

Fig. 3.27
This is the Document Save dialog box that appears when you save text or files from the Web to your Mac hard drive.

III

Connecting to the Web

Tip
Depending on
your system, you
may not have
enough memory
to run both NCSA
Mosaic and the
external viewers
and view some of
the large multi-
media files that
exist on the Web.
You can, however,
download them
for later viewing.

or

1. To get a true copy of the HTML—one that can be reused—select the document you want to save.

2. Choose **Lo**ad to Disk from the **O**ptions menu.

3. Choose **R**eload from the File menu.

4. Fill out the **F**ile Save dialog when it appears.

or

1. Download files from FTP or Gopher URLs in the same fashion as text pages. After you locate the file, choose **L**oad to Disk from the **O**ptions menu and fill out the **F**ile Save dialog box when it appears.

To print the contents of the current document, choose **P**rint from the **F**ile menu. The standard print dialog appears. Note that the line length of the printed document is determined by the width of the Mosaic window. You may have to resize the window to get it to print properly.

E-mail

E-mail is a convenient way to send mail to developers. To get the mail screen, choose **M**ail Developers on the File menu.

Fig. 3.28
It is easy to send
electronic mail
over the Internet
with Mac Mosaic.

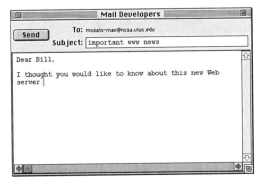

Annotation

> **Caution**
>
> The annotation feature was not working correctly and had been disabled by the developers in the most recent version used to write this book. Again, see the bug list at the NCSA site when you download Mosaic to see if this feature is correctly functioning.

When you identify a document for annotation and want to add personal notes that you can view at a later time, follow these procedures:

1. Open **T**ext on the **A**nnotate main menu and fill in the resulting window. The text line doesn't automatically wrap, so you must hit Return/Enter at the end of each line.

2. When you're done, choose OK to attach the annotation to the current document. It will appear as a URL with a date and time stamp.

3. When you view an annotation, edit its text by choosing **E**dit Annotation in the **A**nnotate menu. This retrieves the original annotation.

4. Once you make changes, choose **Reload** from the **F**ile menu for the edited text to appear. The date and time of the new annotation apply.

5. Delete an annotation by choosing **D**elete Annotation on the **A**nnotate menu.

Help Systems

Mac Mosaic help is provided with on-line documentation using a Balloon menu. It also provides a link to a beginners guide to HTML, a beginners guide to URLs, and access to a FAQ (Frequently Asked Questions) document—you access each of these documents by a URL address at NCSA.

Cello

Cello, like Mosaic, is a free, public-domain WWW browser. The program was developed by The Legal Information Institute (LII) with a grant from the National Center for Automated Information Research. LII distributes legal text electronically through the Internet/Web and on disk in hypertext format.

How to Get Cello Software

These directions will help you retrieve, set up, and use the Cello PC browser for Windows from the Legal Information Institute (LII) at Cornell Law School. Cello software is available from LII without charge, but limits of warranty and license restriction apply. Click **H**elp on the **H**elp menu for further license information. Some components that come with Cello (viewers, for example), may be shareware that require registration and payment of a license fee.

You must have a SLIP or PPP connection and operate in Microsoft Windows environment. Software for Cello includes a set of Cello files with various extensions (DLL, EXE, etc.) that are compatible with SLIP or PPP software. Download the Cello software, decompress it with a program like PKUNZIP, and follow standard Microsoft procedures to set up the Cello icon. The software is available from LII at Cornell. FTP to **ftp.law.cornell.edu**, the program is in subdirectory /pub/LII/Cello/. Read the installation files that come with Cello to ensure that your software environment is compatible.

How to Configure Cello

Configuring Cello involves several steps, including changes that modify the Cello.ini file. Copy the Cello.ini file from its current directory to your Windows directory. Keep your original Cello.ini if possible. This is a text file that contains the Cello configuration data. When doing updates to Cello, use an editor, like Notepad, to examine the Cello.ini file for changes, then selectively update to the WINDOWS directory.

All configuration changes can be done using menus (or edited directly in the Cello.ini file using a standard editor, such as Notepad). The key changes to consider on an initial installation are adding the e-mail address, home page status, home page URL (Universal Resource Locator), news server address, and mail server address.

Fig. 3.29
From the Cello Configure menu, you can adjust specific configuration settings.

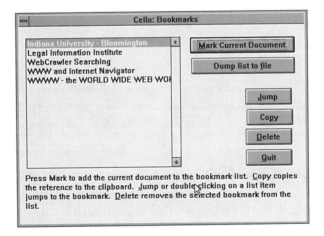

How to Start Cello

As with Mosaic, begin your Web session by connecting to the Internet with a program like Trumpet Winsock. Double-click the Cello icon to start the program. To begin configuration, choose **H**ome Page in **F**iles and Directories of the **C**onfigure Menu. If you want a home page to load when Cello is started, you need to enter the address here. The home page URL address can be your own personal page, or another page from the Internet. If you choose a home page on your local system, or one from your local provider, the home page should load quickly.

A Quick Look at the Cello Screen

Before you get started using Cello, it is useful to have a quick overview of the various parts of the screen. A typical Cello screen is shown in figure 3.30.

The following is a brief description of these parts:

- *Document title.* This is the name of the currently loaded Web document.

- *Document URL.* This is the address of the currently loaded Web document.

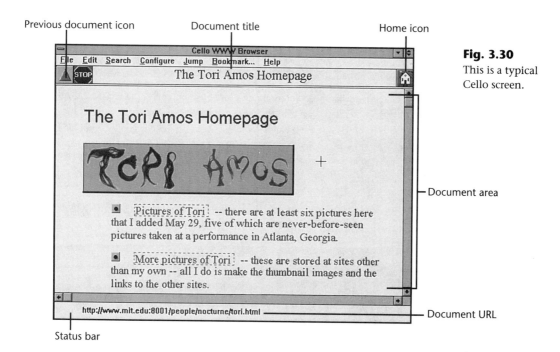

Fig. 3.30
This is a typical Cello screen.

III

Connecting to the Web

- *Document area.* This main part of the screen is where you see the Web documents you load.

- *Status bar.* Various messages are shown here. These will be discussed as needed.

- *Home icon.* This is used to move to your home page, which is discussed later.

- *Previous document icon.* This is used to move to the previous page in the history list, which is discussed later.

Navigating to Other Pages

Once you have Cello running, you can move to any home page on the Web in a number of ways. The next few sections show you the most common methods for navigating.

Jumping to a Hyperlink

Jumping to a hyperlink is probably the simplest and most common way to navigate Web pages with Cello. Hyperlinks are outlined in a box or underlined. All you have to do is click on the link and Cello will load the file and display the page (see fig. 3.31). When the mouse pointer is touching a hyperlink, it becomes an arrow pointing up.

> **Note**
>
> While a file is loading, the pointer changes to a box containing the word NET. As long as the pointer looks like this, the page is still loading. Also, watch the status bar at the bottom of the screen. It will describe what action Cello is taking, what file is loading, and other messages. If it looks as if the page has loaded but you can't scroll in it, Cello may not be done loading the part of the page that is off-screen.

Hyperlinks don't have to be text, they may also be graphics. Clicking on a linked graphic will also jump you to the linked page.

> **Note**
>
> If you click on a hyperlink for a multimedia file (graphic, movie, text, or audio clip) instead of a home page, Cello will open a viewer or player for that type of file after it is loaded. You must, of course, have an appropriate viewer loaded on your computer, and configure Cello to recognize where the viewer is.

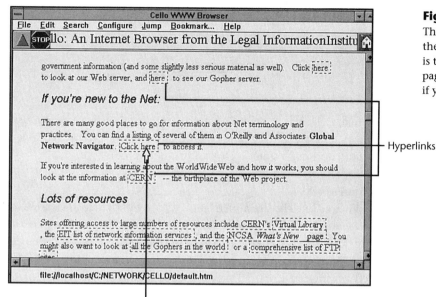

Fig. 3.31
The hyperlink that
the mouse pointer
is touching is the
page you will go to
if you click here.

Mouse pointer changed to up arrow

Jumping to a Page by Using Its URL Address

Another common way to navigate is to type in the URL address. This is a very useful way to navigate the Web using this book because all the pages reviewed and listed here have the URL address given. To jump directly to a specific home page or document with a given URL, follow these steps:

1. Open the **J**ump menu and choose Launch via **U**RL. The dialog box shown in figure 3.32 opens.

2. Type in the URL address for the page you want to jump to. Be sure to type in the URL exactly as given, with no spaces before or after the address.

3. Click OK.

Navigation Shortcuts

Once you have been using Cello for an hour or two, you will realize that typing in a URL is a very mistake-prone way to move on the Web. And once you've discovered a Web page that you want to use frequently, you'll want a way to get back to it quickly. And wouldn't it be nice if you could jump back to any page that you have used previously since you started Cello?

Fig. 3.32
Use this dialog box to jump to a home page by typing its URL.

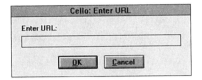

Tip
If you ever get totally lost on the Web and don't know where to go next, or need to get back to your home page for any reason, click the Home icon near the upper right corner of the screen.

Fortunately, Cello has built-in features to handle all of these needs. Using the shortcuts will save you time (and—if you pay for your Internet connection—money too!) and make your Web sessions more productive.

Using Bookmarks

The bookmarks in Cello are a nice feature. Using bookmarks, Cello saves the page's title and URL address. You can then jump directly to this page again at any time during your current session or during future sessions. Also, Cello maintains bookmarks in alphabetical order, which makes it easy to locate a specific Web site.

To bookmark a page:

1. Navigate to the page using any of the navigation techniques described earlier.

2. Choose the **B**ookmark menu. The bookmark dialog box as shown in figure 3.33 appears.

3. Click the **M**ark Current Document button. The dialog box shown in figure 3.34 opens.

4. You can use the name that is given here or change the name. Then click OK. The document will be added to the bookmark list as shown in figure 3.35.

Fig 3.33
The Bookmark dialog box shows any previously defined bookmarks and allows you to add others.

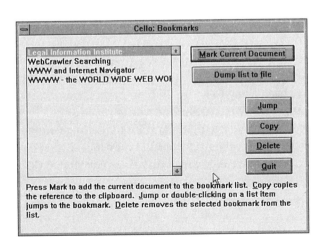

5. Click Quit to close the dialog box and return.

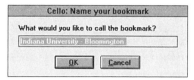

Fig 3.34
Use the name that
is given or enter
any name you
want here.

This marks the current page. Now, to jump to any marked page:

1. Choose the **B**ookmark menu.

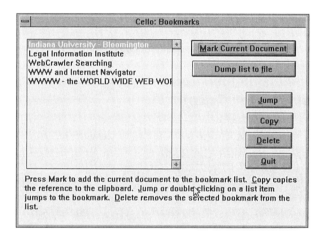

Fig 3.35
The Bookmark
dialog box with
the added
bookmark.

2. Select the name of the document you want to jump to in the bookmark list. Use the scroll bars to scroll the list if needed.

3. Click **J**ump.

Using the History List

So you were just looking at a document 10 minutes ago and now you want to go back to it. But you've loaded 3 other pages since then and don't remember where the page you want to see was. An even simpler case is when you jump to a page, realize it's not what you want, and want to jump back to where you were. Cello's history list makes either of these easy.

To use the history list:

1. Open the **J**ump menu and choose **H**istory. The Cello: History dialog box shown in figure 3.36 opens.

III

Connecting to the Web

2. Select the document you want to go back to from the list.

3. Click **J**ump.

Fig. 3.36
The History dialog shows a list of all the documents you have loaded in this Cello session. The first document you loaded (probably your home page) will be at the bottom of the list and the current document will be at the top.

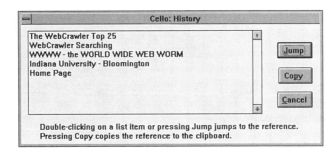

Jumping back to the last page you were at is easy. Click the up arrow near the upper left corner of the screen.

Speed Options for Graphics

Some Web documents have so many inline images, or a few very large ones, that they can take several minutes to load on a slow (modem) connection. To speed things up, open the **C**onfigure menu and choose **G**raphics. Then choose Fetch Automatically to remove the check mark next to it. Now Cello will not request the inline images from the server.

> **Note**
>
> This option does not affect images that you download. Those will download normally and display in your viewer.

The second selection under the Configure menu Graphics option is Dither. Windows does not draw 24-bit graphics on the screen very quickly. You can speed up the process by using dithering. Dithering basically sacrifices accuracy in rendering color in favor of a faster redraw of the display. You should be aware of the fact that most graphics that are not yet stored as 24-bit images will not be affected by this option. You toggle the graphics dithering option on and off just as you do the Fetch Automatically option.

Printing

Printing a Cello document so you have a hard copy is straightforward and essentially optionless. To print the current document, open the **F**ile menu and choose **P**rint. The file will print without further action on your part. A message box will appear, giving you the option to cancel the printing.

Hopefully this chapter has provided both practical advice and specific directions that will have you up and running with your Web browser of choice. You might also want to check out the information that is available in the two appendixes, which highlight some of the commercial WWW clients that are available for both the Windows and Macintosh platforms. The next chapter provides an overview of the process by which you can create, save, and use your own Web home page.

III

Connecting to the Web

Chapter 4

How to Create a WWW Home Page

A *home page* is a place where you begin to explore the resources on the WWW. There are two types of home pages. First, there are the home pages that reside on the Web servers around the world. When you enter a URL (Uniform Resource Locator) address that points to a home page into your multimedia browser (Mosaic, Cello, etc.), you connect with the home page on the remote Web server. For example, when you type in the URL address **http://www.doc.gov/**, you establish a connection to the U.S. Department of Commerce (USDOC) Information server—within seconds the home page for this service appears. The home page is usually a starting point for information about a specific subject or company. The USDOC home page offers hypermedia links to information about business and commerce, as well as links to other government agencies such as the National Institute for Standards and Technology (NIST). When you jump to NIST, the home page for this agency appears. Some USDOC resources that you jump to from this home page are hypertext documents that exist in subdirectories on the server.

The WWW electronic malls illustrate the difference between a home page and other documents. Say you jump to the home page for the Electronic SuperMall (a fictitious mall) that resides on a computer in Wyoming. The SuperMall home page has links to the Rodeo Clothing Store, the Western Music Shop, Rugged Trucks Automotive, and Big Sky Video. Just as you would enter a main door in a real shopping mall, you first enter the home page and then jump to individual stores to shop. The individual "stores" can either be subdocuments on the SuperMall computer, or they can reside on separate computers. Thus, the owner of Big Sky Video can operate a separate WWW computer that simply has a link on the SuperMall home page.

The home pages on WWW servers represent external home pages. A second type of home page, a *local* home page, is a personalized document that you create and maintain on your PC. You develop this document with the same computer language that is used to create home pages on Web servers. A high school music teacher creates a home page that contains links to all the Web's music resources; a travel agent makes a home page full of interesting travel destinations; a stockbroker produces a home page with links to global financial information—and you can develop a home page with links to your favorite Web resources.

You can configure your WWW browser (like Mosaic) to display your home page each time the program loads. If you own a high-speed, dedicated (full-time) Internet connection, you could let the rest of the world jump into your computer and visit your home page. Your computer and Internet connection, however, must be on 24 hours a day. If it is off, people who try to jump to your "server" would get a blank screen or error message.

The rest of this chapter provides step-by-step directions that help you create a home page. The directions refer specifically to the creation of a home page using Microsoft Windows and display of the home page on Mosaic. However, the programming language is common across all computer platforms, and most WWW browsers will load the home page in a similar fashion.

Hypertext Glossary

There are several terms that describe the hypermedia programming language, protocols, and the information components. These terms are basic to the development and use of WWW hypermedia documents.

Home page	The first page of information in a hypermedia document.
Hyperlink	A reference point in a document for linking information, usually stands out with words that are highlighted or underlined.
Hypermedia	A multimedia document that contains and links text, audio, and video.
HTTP	HyperText Transfer Protocol. The protocol used by WWW servers to provide rules for moving information across the Internet.
HTML	HyperText Markup Language. The language that defines the style and information in a WWW hypermedia document.
SGML	Standard Generalized Markup Language. A standard that describes markup languages.
URL	Uniform Resource Locator. An address that identifies and locates multimedia information on the WWW.

HTTP and HTML: The Languages of the WWW

You are about to learn how to be a computer programmer. Don't worry—the creation of a home page is almost as simple as writing a letter.

The WWW uses several protocols to transport and display the multimedia resources that reside on computers around the world. One of them is the *HTTP* (HyperText Transport Protocol). HTTP works with Web servers to provide a client-server environment for the Internet. Normally your PC is the client and the remote Web computer is the server. CERN, the European Laboratory for Particle Physics in Switzerland, proposed the HTTP protocol, along with several other software applications and network standards for the WWW client-server environment. HTTP supports the ability of the Internet to provide access to an enormous quantity of interlinked resources.

The individual multimedia documents on the WWW use a computer programming language, the *HyperText Markup Language* (HTML), to create, format, and identify titles, subheadings, bold, italics, and hyperlinks that enable you to jump between places within a document, on the same computer/server, or to another remote server located somewhere on the Internet. The links can point to any combination of voice, data, graphics, and video—multimedia.

There are several ways to write the HTML code that becomes a document or home page. You can write it from scratch (by using a simple word processor), copy it from another document, or generate it with an HTML authoring program. HTML uses a simple, common text format that allows people who use a variety of computer systems (PC, Mac, UNIX) to create Web documents.

Comparing Web Pages in Different Forms

Before we get into the programming details that make HTML work, looking for a few examples of Web pages in different forms will be useful. By comparing an HTML source document to what you see on-screen in Mosaic or Cello, you should have a better idea of how HTML translates into the hypertext Web documents you browse on-screen.

First, look at the Web page (The Tori Amos home page, URL address **http://www.mit.edu:8001/people/nocturne/tori.html**) shown in Mosaic in figure 4.1 and in Cello in figure 4.2. Notice the similarities between the two views of this same page. They both have the same title and address, they both have the same graphic image, and they both show the same text and hyperlinks.

Fig. 4.1

The Tori Amos home page in Mosaic.

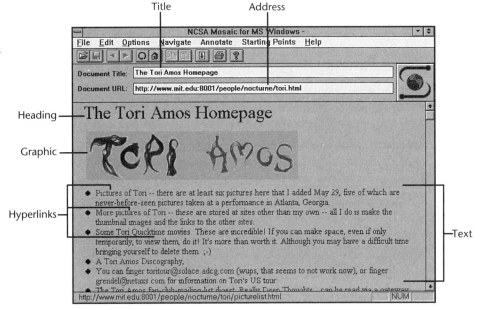

Fig. 4.2

The Tori Amos home page in Cello.

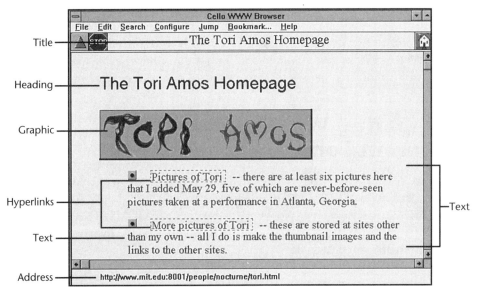

How is it that these two programs can display the same information? They are both reading from the same HTML document. To see what the HTML document for this page looks like, you can view it in Mosaic. To do this, open the **F**ile menu and choose **D**ocument Source. The window shown in figure 4.3 opens. If you look carefully at the areas called out on the figure, you can see which parts of this translate to the hypertext document you see in the normal Mosaic screen shown earlier.

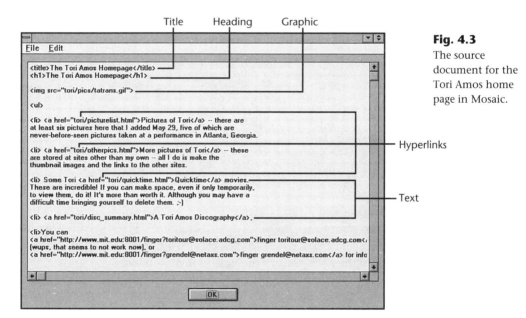

Fig. 4.3
The source document for the Tori Amos home page in Mosaic.

The main difference that you will see is the use of the markup codes in the angle braces < >. These are the codes that HTML uses to define the parts of the home page. Mosaic reads these codes and applies them to what you see on-screen.

Cello works essentially the same way. Open the **E**dit menu and choose View source. A window like the one in figure 4.4 opens.

Note

By default, Cello uses Notepad to view the HTML source. This is a little more difficult to follow than Mosaic's built-in editor. Also, if the HTML document runs too wide, be sure to turn on word wrap in Notepad by opening the **E**dit menu and choosing **W**ord wrap.

Fig. 4.4

The source
document for the
Tori Amos home
page in Cello is
displayed in
Notepad.

Graphic

Hyperlinks

Text

Heading   Title

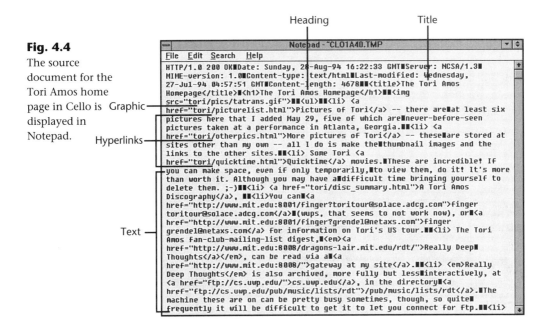

This view in Cello is not as easy to follow but Cello does have one advantage.
If you just want to see the text without any of the markup codes, open the
Edit menu and choose View as **c**lean text. This opens Notepad again and
shows you the document in the form shown in figure 4.5.

Fig. 4.5

The clean text
version of the Tori
Amos home page
in Cello opened in
Notepad.

Title

Heading

Hyperlinks

Text

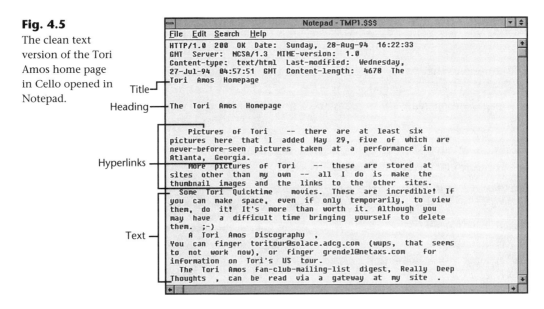

This is useful if you just need to see the text without the distraction of the codes.

Although there are a few HTML codes that identify the size of letters, style (such as italic), and graphic features (such as underlining), much of the control for the visual appearance of text is determined by the configuration choices in your browser. (In Mosaic these font choices are accessed by opening the **O**ptions menu and choosing the Choose Font menu item. In Cello, open the **C**onfigure menu and choose **F**onts. This opens a submenu in Mosaic or Cello where you can set the font for titles, headings, and all the other text parts of documents.)

Programming Your Home Page

This section shows you commands needed to create a single document (home page) from scratch by using simple keyboard commands to write the HTML language in a plain text editor. Here is a simple word of advice: Have patience. If computers can occasionally become frustrating, computer programming can be worse—especially when it doesn't work. Computers and software are extremely picky; one misspelled or misplaced keystroke can prevent a program, here the program for your home page, from working properly. If something doesn't work, go back and make sure that your "code" is written exactly as it is presented here.

> **Note**
>
> Remember, the examples we show in this chapter occasionally show screens from Notepad, a Windows-based text editor. However, you can follow this same basic procedure on a Mac or even a computer running UNIX. Just use a text editor such as Teach Text on the Macintosh or vi (Visual Editor) or emacs (Editor Macros) for UNIX systems to enter HTML commands. One of the terrific aspects of HTML is that it works on all types of computer systems.

To begin creating your HTML home page, the first step is to open your text editor and open a new document.

HTML Basics: Title, Heading, and Text

The most common HTML codes you will use are the title, heading, and paragraph text. The following example shows title, heading, and paragraph tags. *Tags* consist of a left angle bracket (<) followed by the name of the tag and a right angle bracket (>). Usually, there are beginning and ending tags, with a slash (/) just ahead of the name in the ending tag. Paragraphs are one exception. Browsers interpret the tags to determine how to format information and when to start and stop formatting. Within the text on the text file, characters like the carriage return have no effect. The HTML formatting tags determine when a paragraph occurs. The formatting tags in HTML are case insensitive so the term <Title> is the same as <TITLE>.

```
<Title>My Home Page</Title>
<H1>This Is A Level One Heading</H1>
Here is an example of a home page paragraph.<P>
Here is a second paragraph.<P>
```

Note

If a browser doesn't understand an HTML tag, it will ignore it.

Fig. 4.6
Notepad editor
with simple HTML
code for a home
page.

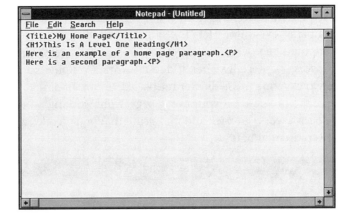

Saving the Document

The next step is to save this home page code in a file that your browser can read. Use the Save command in your editor to save the file. Also, the file must be saved with an extension .htm or .html, which tells Mosaic and other browsers that this is an HTML file.

Give the file a name when saving it and then close the document and exit from your text editor.

Load and Test the Document

It is important to occasionally load and test your home page creations. To do this, follow these steps:

1. Start Mosaic.

> **Note**
>
> You may have to start the SLIP or PPP connection software first (in a typical PC installation, Mosaic needs to have the network software started, but not necessarily connected to the network, to run).

2. With Mosaic running, open the **F**ile menu and choose Open **L**ocal File.

3. A dialog box like the one shown in figure 4.7 appears, which allows you to open your home page file.

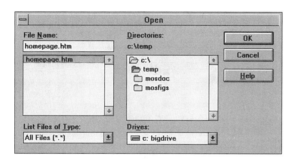

Fig. 4.7
This is the standard Open dialog box for your operating system, Windows or Mac.

4. Select the drive, directory (or folder), and file name for your home page.

5. Click OK to finish the entry and load the new home page.

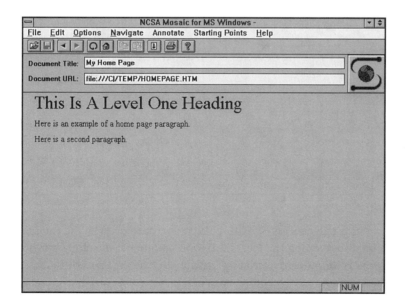

Fig. 4.8
This is your home page in Mosaic. Notice the "file:/// cl" designation at the beginning of the URL. This is how Mosaic identifies local files and drives.

You can do the same thing using another browser. In Cello, the procedure is almost the same:

1. Start Cello.

2. With Cello running, open the **J**ump menu and choose Launch via **U**RL.

3. This displays a dialog box like the one shown in figure 4.9, which you use to open your home page file. Type

   `file://localhost/c:/temp/homepage.htm`

   where `c` is the drive letter, `temp` is the directory, and `homepage.htm` is the file name. `file://localhost/` designates this as a local file for Cello.

Fig. 4.9
This is where you indicate the local file to be opened in Cello.

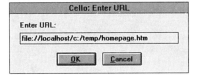

4. Click OK to finish the entry and load the new home page.

Fig. 4.10
This is your home page in Cello. Notice that it is the same as this page in Mosaic, except for font differences.

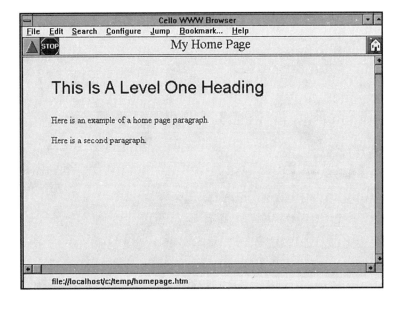

You can repeat this process of editing the home page text, saving the file in a text editor, and opening the local file as you add to and develop your home page. In the Windows environment, be sure to close the text editor after every change so that Mosaic can access the file. This may be the right time to set up your home page as described in the configuration section of the browsers, so that it displays first when you start the browser.

Adding Hyperlinks to Other Web Documents

If you are going to use a document you create as a home page, you need to add some hyperlinks to it so that you can jump to other pages. You can jump to other pages that you create locally (this might be useful if you develop a page that will be accessed by others who use the pages you create) or you can link to pages on other WWW servers. These links, also created in your HTML document, let you click on a word or phrase to connect with other Web resources.

Defining a Hyperlink in the Text Editor

Again, open your text editor and open the HTML document you have created. Now insert a new line of code where you want the hyperlink to appear.

```
<A HREF= "http://www.doc.gov/">U.S. Dept. of Commerce</A>
```

Let's take a look at the parts of this code. In the first set of angle brackets, the A HREF= statement declares that this is a hyperlink address beginning. The URL for the link is contained in quotes.

Following the first ending angle bracket is the name you want to give the link. This name can be the actual name of the document, as it is defined in the document, or it can be any other name you give it. Whatever name you put here, it is linked to the address in the A HREF statement.

Finally, the code ends with the /A code in angle brackets. Figure 4.11 shows this statement in place in the text editor.

You can save the document now to test it or add more hyperlinks or other elements. If you save the document to test it, remember to close the document and exit your editor before trying to test.

If you want to add a hyperlink to a document on your local computer, the code looks like this:

```
<A HREF= "file://localhost/c:/temp/funpage.htm">A Local Home Page
with Some Fun Links</A>
```

Fig 4.11
This Notepad
document has the
HTML code for a
hyperlink to the
U.S. Dept. of
Commerce added.

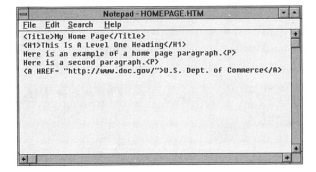

Here, the **file://localhost/c:** part of the hyperlink definition states that this
is a local file and defines the drive to look in. The rest of the statement is
essentially the same as defining a link to a page on another Web site.

> **Note**
>
> Putting hyperlinks on separate lines in your text editor does not place the links on
> separate lines when you load the HTML document. To "force" a new line for your
> links , use the <P> (Paragraph) code.

Checking to See if Your Hyperlinks Work

The next time you start Mosaic and load this page, any new hypertext links
you added to the page should be active (see fig. 4.12).

Fig. 4.12
The document in
Mosaic with the
hyperlinks added.

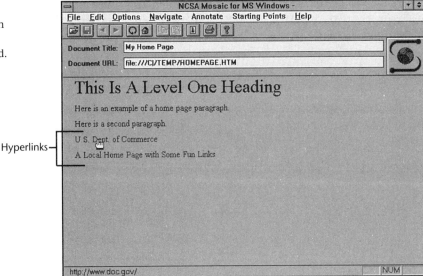

Add a Graphic to Your Home Page

As you have probably seen in the pages on the Web that you have looked at, you can add images to your documents. These images are called *inline* images. The pictures that you see in home pages do not reside in the code for the home page. Instead, the code that you write/type simply tells the browser where to go and find the picture.

The Mosaic browser can view GIF and XBM graphics. To create your own graphic or picture for a home page, you need software that can save or translate images into one of these file formats. If you can't do this, you may be able to download a public domain image from an Internet/Web site to include in your home page.

> **Note**
>
> As with anything on the Web, don't use someone else's copyrighted material (text, images, audio, etc.) in violation of their copyright. Many images that have a copyright are available for purchase. While this seems like common sense, graphic images are often copied on the Web without the rightful owner's permission.

Defining an Inline Image in the Text Editor

Again start the text editor application and load your home page file. Now insert a new line of code where you want the image to appear.

```
<IMG SRC= file:///c¦/temp/money1.gif>
```

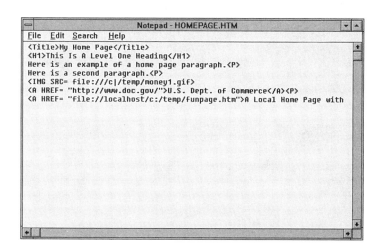

```
Notepad - HOMEPAGE.HTM
File  Edit  Search  Help
<Title>My Home Page</Title>
<H1>This Is A Level One Heading</H1>
Here is an example of a home page paragraph.<P>
Here is a second paragraph.<P>
<IMG SRC= file:///c¦/temp/money1.gif>
<A HREF= "http://www.doc.gov/">U.S. Dept. of Commerce</A><P>
<A HREF= "file://localhost/c:/temp/funpage.htm">A Local Home Page with
```

Fig. 4.13
The image is in the same line as the hyperlink to the Dept. of Commerce.

This places the image money1.gif in the same line as the Department of Commerce hyperlink (since there is not <P> to start a new line after the graphic). Again, you can add links to other graphics or save the file and close the text editor when you're finished.

> **Note**
>
> Keep your inline images small and simple. You don't want too much visual clutter on the page and you don't want to waste time waiting for the image to load.

Testing the Document with the Graphic in Mosaic

The next time you start Mosaic and load this page, any new inline images you added should be visible (see fig. 4.14).

Fig. 4.14
The page now shows the inline image when viewed in Mosaic.

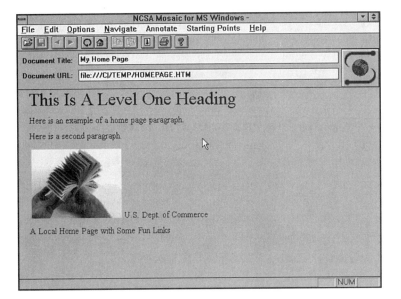

> **Note**
>
> Some browsers don't display graphic images. Home page design should consider that the page will look different when viewed by a line browser, and it also will look different if the Inline Images option is not on.

Other URL Link Commands

The URL is a standard reference for locating information. It can point to exact documents, pages, or paragraphs with pages on the server. It can also point to graphic images, movies, and databases. Besides supporting access to the WWW servers, it allows pointers to other server resources, such as Gopher, FTP (File Transfer Protocol), WAIS (Wide Area Information Server), Telnet, and NNTP (Network News Transfer Protocol). It is important to know how to code URLs (Uniform Resource Locators) when you create home pages or other HTML documents. The URL is written as follows:

scheme://host-domain[port]/path/filename

The address contains three parts.

1. scheme, represents the action or resource you will connect to. In our example, the resource has been a file on your hard disk drive, your home page. Other selections include:

http	(hypertext transfer protocol)
file	(file transfer protocol, FTP)
gopher	(Gopher protocol)
telnet	(open a Telnet session)
wais	(begin a WAIS search)
news	(an Internet news group)
mailto	(send mail)

2. host-domain[port], enter the internet address:port number

3. path/file name, the path to the file

Programs That Help You Create HTML Documents

There are other ways to write HTML source code besides using the Windows NotePad text editor; you can use any text editor or word processor to write HTML documents and home pages. There are also software programs and tools that generate and develop HTML documents; convert documents from plain text format to HTML; and check, edit, and correct HTML. Following is a brief overview of the functions and operations of several of these programs and a listing of URL addresses that will help you retrieve or get information about the programs.

HTML Generators and Converters

RTFTOHTML	Provides translation from RTF to HTML, Mac, and UNIX platform. Information from: **http://info.cern.ch/hypertext/WWW/Tools/ rtftohtml-2.6.html**
GT_HTML.DOT	From Georgia Tech Research Institute, an alpha release of a set of Microsoft Word for Windows macros for HTML document authoring. For information and download: **http://www.gatech.edu/word_html/release.htm**
SoftQuad HoTMetal	A WYSIWYG HTML editor available on PCs and UNIX. A free version and a for-purchase version are available, with different feature levels. HoTMetal simplifies HTML authoring with pick lists for the markup codes and cut and paste for hypertext links. HTML-specific features include knowledge of the HTML DTD and validation of documents, viewing of images, a preview facility for launching Mosaic and other Web browsers, ability to copy and paste URLs into the document, and a publish feature that automatically changes hypertext links from local file references to global URLs. For information: **http://info.cern.ch/hypertext/WWW/Tools/ HoTMetal.html** For information about commercial version of this software, contact Soft Quat Inc. at (800) 387-2777
WPTOHTML	WordPerfect macros that convert from WordPerfect 5.1 for DOS and WordPerfect 6.0 for DOS to HTML. Contact: **hmonroe@us.net** (Hunter Monroe)

HTML Editing Tools

BBEdit HTML	This set of extensions lets you insert HTML tags in your documents so that you can easily edit hypertext documents with Macintosh BBEdit or BBEdit Lite text editors. For information: **http://www.uji.es/bbedit-html-extensions.html**
HTML Assistant	HTML assistant is a Windows text editor with extensions to assist in the creation of HTML. It incorporates a multiple document interface, a user-defined toolbox, facilities that

convert URLs in Cello Bookmark and Mosaic.ini files to HTML text, and functions that test the HTML document with a WWW browser without leaving the editor. For information:

http://info.cern.ch/hypertext/WWW/Tools/html-assistant.html

You can also subscribe to an e-mail newsletter about HTML Assistant and HTML Assistant Pro. It features tips on the software, input from users, lists of WWW sites, and information about upgrades and new releases. Add your name to the list by sending mail to Howard Harawitz at **harawitz@fox.nstn.ns.ca.**

Your e-mail message should have the Subject as "SUBSCRIBE HTML ASSISTANT NEWS" (quotes are not required). Try the freeware version of HTML Assistant available at the FTP site **ftp.cs.dal.cal/htmlasst/**. Start with the short "readme.1st" file for information on the files you need to download. For information on the commercial version, contact Brooklyn Software Works at (902) 835-2600.

Simple HTML Editor	A simple editor for creating HTML documents. Requires Hypercard or Hypercard Player on the Macintosh. For information: **http://info.cern.ch/hypertext/WWW/Tools/ SHE.html**
fix-html.pl	Written in PERL script to legitimize old HTML files into SGML-abiding HTML. For information: **http://info.cern.ch/hypertext/WWW/Tools/ Overview.html**

Advanced HTML

Following are several sources that provide the current HTML languages and protocols, and some "Beginner's Guides" with pointers on writing HTML:

1. A Beginner's Guide to HTML

   http://www.ncsa.uiuc.edu/demoweb/html-primer.html

2. JHU/APL's WWW & HTML Developer's JumpStation—Page 1

   http://oneworld.wa.com/htmldev/devpage/dev-page1.html

3. How to write HTML files

   http://curia.ucc.ie/info/net/htmldoc.html

4. HTML Design Notebook

   http://www.hal.com/~connolly/drafts/html-design.html

5. HTML Documents: A Mosaic Tutorial

   http://fire.clarkson.edu/doc/html/htut.html

6. The World Wide Web Initiative: The Project

   http://info.cern.ch/hypertext/WWW/TheProject.html

Chapter 5

Finding Resources on the World Wide Web

You don't need to create a home page or author hypermedia documents to enjoy the World Wide Web. You can get a thrill and a sense of satisfaction when you connect to a WWW site that has exactly the information you need—perhaps a lesson on how to rewire the electrical outlet that's on the fritz in your basement, a database of bird images that identifies the new feathered friend sitting on your bird feeder, or a lesson plan for a sixth-grade science class that explains how solar energy works. There is a real sense of adventure as you jump from link to link, looking for resources that will make your life a little richer.

For practical purposes, there are two main reasons for using the Web. Either you want to accomplish a specific task—locate information or order a bouquet of flowers—or you simply want to explore the global cyberspace, take a journey, even a mini-vacation. In either case, it helps to have a starting point, a place where you can literally jump in and get started. This section of *Using the World Wide Web* provides listings of the resources on the Web—in all more than 2,000 home pages you can visit and begin the global exploration!

In this chapter, we are going to introduce techniques that will help you search for and locate Web information that is of interest to you. The first technique involves using the resource listings in chapters 6–18 of this book. Using these along with the index, you should be able to find pages on any topic you want. But what if the specific information you need isn't on a page that we list in this book? Then you can search the Web using one of several Web search engines described in this chapter.

Note

You may be wondering why you needed to buy a book listing Web sites if you can simply search the Web itself to find information and resources. The answer is that you'll want to use both of these methods. This book doesn't list every home page—and new ones appear on a regular basis. We have, however, tried to list the best pages that have been around for more than a day or two (things do change fast on the Web). The information on these pages will be a good source of reference, like a phone book or "Yellow Pages," that will point you either directly to the resource you want, or to a very good starting point. Depending upon your service provider's fee structure, you may pay as much as $10 per hour for Web connect time. Weaving your way through thousands of Web home pages can be a very expensive proposition. By helping you quickly get where you want to go, this book will save both time and money.

While valuable, use of the Web searchers does not guarantee that you will find all the pages related to a given topic (you see why later in this chapter), and these searchers are prone to turning up a lot of unrelated topics. (You read about this later, too.)

The Resource Listings

The WWW resources are divided into 13 separate chapters, which represent broad categories, including:

Chapter 6	Arts, Literature, Music, and Entertainment
Chapter 7	Business
Chapter 8	Computers
Chapter 9	Education
Chapter 10	Government
Chapter 11	Health and Medicine
Chapter 12	History and Geography
Chapter 13	International
Chapter 14	Issues, Politics, Religion, and Social Services
Chapter 15	Publications: News, Periodicals, and Books
Chapter 16	Science

Chapter 17   Shopping

Chapter 18   Sports, Hobbies, Games, Travel, and Recreation

The table of contents and index further break down these categories to help you rapidly locate a specific subject—such as interactive art museums or scuba diving.

> **Note**
>
> We have worked to make the index as comprehensive as possible. We've listed every possible occurrence we could find of company names, topics, and subtopics in hope that it would make finding information in this book and on the Web easier.

Each chapter begins with an in-depth review of several of the sites that meet the criteria of the chapter. The reviews discuss the merits of the resources at the site, the multimedia aspects to the site (Are there images or audio samples?), and where the major hyperlinks on the home page take you. For example, chapter 13, "International," has a review of the following home pages:

Gateway to Antarctica

New Zealand

Singapore Online Guide

Japan—Nippon Telephone and Telegraph Corporation

Window-To-Russia

After these reviews, the remainder of the chapter provides shorter summaries of other WWW sites. Here, for example, is one of the listings in the Science chapter under the sub-category Meteorology:

Current Weather Maps and Movies
URL address: **http://rs560.cl.msu.edu/weather**

This weather database receives weather information from around and above the globe including the Department of Meteorology at the University of Edinburgh, Scotland and NASA readings. Maps in this database are updated every hour so that you can view weather patterns as they happen—almost as good as TV weather. In addition to still images, you can view (with the right software) weather movies.

V

Finding Resources

The first line in each listing is either the actual name of the WWW home page, or a description that tells you what you will find there. The second line is the URL (Uniform Resource Locator) address that you need to enter into your browser to get to the site. The paragraph following the URL provides a short overview of the resource.

URL Address Tips

Tip

If pages are loading too slowly, disable inline images (you can always reload the page if you need or want to see an image).

Hopefully, if you are ready to use a resource you already have your WWW browser installed and know how to load it. For both Macintosh and Windows, this is a point-and-click procedure. Once you find a resource that suits your needs or interest you must load the URL address. (This procedure is described in detail in chapter 3 for NCSA Mosaic on Windows and Mac as well as Cello. Appendices A and B cover this for other Windows and Mac WWW clients.) Nine times out of ten you will enter an address and be at your site within seconds. However, there are times when you can't connect. There are a few small rules about URL addresses that will help prevent frustration in this respect.

1. Always make sure you enter the address exactly as it appears. Let's look at a few examples that show where problems can occur.

   URL address:
   http://www.latrobe.edu.au/Glenn/KiteSite/Kites.html

   This is an address for a server that has information about the hobby of kite flying. The address begins with the http://. Notice that there are a few capital letters in the address. You must use uppercase letters if they are indicated. If you don't you won't connect.

   URL address: **http://herald.usask.ca/~maton/bahai.html**

   This is the address of a WWW server that focuses on the Baha'i religion. The character ~ appears frequently in URL addresses. Again, you must have it. This character is the uppercase of the backwards apostrophe, usually found to the left of the number 1 on your keyboard.

   URL address:
   http://ananse.irv.uit.no/trade_law/nav/trade.html

   This address connects you to a server in Norway that contains information about trade law. Notice that there is an underscore between the words trade and law. Make sure you put this in your address.

Tip

Some WWW sites are slower than others as a result of the lines that get you to them. Always try a site that is in your region/country first to see if it has the information you need. This also helps reduce unnecessary burden on the entire Internet/ WWW system.

The number one reason for not connecting to a Web site is misentering the correct address. If you get an error message like "Error Accessing" or "Failed DNS lookup," enter the address a second time. You may have accidentally made a typographical error. Even an extra space in an address like box.ht ml can prevent a connection.

2. Start to enter the URL address at the very beginning of the entry box. This may seem obvious. However, some browsers will not connect if you have a space before the start of the address.

3. If a URL address doesn't work, try a root address. Many home pages actually reside in complex subdirectories on a computer. It is possible that the information has moved to another location on the computer. If you use a long, complex address and it doesn't work, try entering a shorter version of the address. This may connect to a higher directory where you will be able to locate the information you need. For example, the following is the address for an electronic art gallery in New York City:

> URL address:
> **http://www.elpress.com/gallery/homepage.html**

The address tells you that this home page resides on a commercial server (www.elpress.com) that has a special area for the gallery. It is possible that the company also lets other New York City vendors operate Web pages on the computer. So, if the full address doesn't work, try again but eliminate the ending like this:

> URL address: **http://www.elpress.com/gallery**

And if that doesn't work, go one more step to this:

> URL address: **http://www.elpress.com**

It is very likely that you will connect with the commercial company's home page and then be able to find links to the art gallery.

Troubleshooting Troublesome Addresses

You're certain that you entered the correct address and you still can't connect. All the WWW site addresses in this book have been carefully checked for accuracy, but there are a few other things that can prevent a connection.

V

Finding Resources

Tip
WWW documents and servers DO change their addresses; good ones will leave a forwarding address, bad ones just seem to disappear.

■ *The host is busy.* Wait a few minutes (longer if necessary) and try again. By using the "reload" feature you don't have to retype the URL address. With some 30 million plus people using the Internet, it is possible that the WWW server you are trying is busy with other people who are connecting. Or, the lines to the host are overcrowded—like when you try to call home on Christmas day.

■ *The server is down.* The WWW server may be literally unplugged. Sometimes computers are pulled off-line to be repaired or upgraded. Good WWW server owners will either use another computer during downtime, or do repair work during off hours. But, if the server is down, it can take between five minutes to five days before it is back on-line.

Tip

Don't give up on an address. You may not connect for several reasons besides a bad address—for example, the server is down or only allows a certain number of users at one time.

■ *The server/home page has moved.* It is possible for a server to get a new IP address. If this happens, your "old" address will no longer work. It is also possible for someone who maintains a home page to move their home page, and their data, to another WWW computer. Responsible WWW home page owners will "post" a message that you receive when you try the URL. The message tells you the new address, and may have a hyperlink to the new server, which is similar to when you have the phone company place a forwarding message that plays when you move to a new home and get a new phone number. But, like the phone company, the WWW message may not last forever—be sure to write down the new address before it disappears!

■ *The server or home page has died.* Yes, it is possible for a server to completely vanish. You can be pretty confident that NASA will not permanently pull the plug on their WWW computer. However, with the increasing age of commercialism on the Net, it is possible that commercial companies or information providers that host WWW home pages may go out of business. If they do, the server's gone. More likely, however, some of the home pages for small businesses will come and go. After all, if Bill's Barber Shop doesn't get any new business after six months, Bill may decide not to sponsor the interactive haircut database. Likewise, if Joyce is a graduate student at a university and she operates a home page about rocket science, it may disappear when she graduates and no longer maintains the information. These are all worst-case scenarios. Ninety percent of the time you will be able to connect to a WWW site, but it's nice to know why, occasionally, you can't.

Tips for Web Navigation

Here are a few more tips that should make your journey through the Web more enjoyable. Many WWW home pages incorporate a lot of graphic images, often too many. Because the graphics are large files, it takes a long time to load them. The larger the graphic, or the more graphics on a home page, the longer it will be before you can actually use the information or links on the page. Some home pages take in excess of five minutes to load at 14.4 Kbps.

If you start to get bothered by the amount of time it takes to load and then use home pages, turn off the browser feature that lets these images load. In NCSA Mosaic, you can turn the graphics feature on or off by choosing Options, Display Inline Images. In Cello, choose Configure, Graphics, Fetch Automatically. This will save you a tremendous amount of time in fully retrieving a home page. Then, if you find information that is exciting, you can always "Reload" the home page after you turn on the graphics feature.

Another feature on browsers that is worth noting when it comes to Web navigation is the cache. *Cache* (pronounced "cash") is the amount of computer RAM memory that the program sets aside to store information about the home pages or documents you visit during a session. A larger cache means that you can store more of the home page HTML documents in your computer's memory. As a result, you can navigate or jump back to a site you have recently visited because it is still in your computer's memory—you don't actually reload the home page. There are some pros and cons here. A large cache means you can quickly jump back through two, three, or four home pages. The bad news is that an extremely large cache may hinder your computer's functionality—things may simply slow down. So, start with the program's default, and then adjust as necessary.

As you journey through WWW sites, you will find new home pages that you will want to return to. It's easy to think, "Well, I'll be back there in a minute and then I'll write down that address." If you really like a home page, write down the address immediately, or, better yet, add it to the hot list, quick list, or bookmark in your browser. It is very easy to get lost in cyberspace and never find that home page again.

Tip

If you are mysteriously not connecting to any of the resources, it is possible that your TCP/IP connection has been dropped. Depending on your system and software, you may not realize that this has happened (unless you can hear the phone connection disconnect) and your system may, or may not, automatically try to reestablish the connection.

V

Finding Resources

Finding the Elusive Resource: Web Searchers

Tip

If you find a home page you like, put it on your hot list immediately, otherwise you may have a difficult time getting there again.

With more than a 2,000 percent annual increase in the number of WWW sites, the resources available on the Web expand faster than you can possibly visit the sites. There are more than 7,000 WWW servers, hundreds of thousands of hypermedia documents, images, sound, and video files, and millions of subjects. The resources in this book will either get you to the information you need, or to a Web page that has links to that information. However, the time will come when you are looking for something unique or esoteric, such as a tour guide company that will help you climb Mount Everest.

That's when you want to connect with one of the WWW *searchers*. Generally, searchers are computer programs that search the Web on a periodic basis collecting information about new Web documents and servers. Depending on the searcher, the information collected may contain only the name and address of home pages, or it may also include information about the contents of a page, the words in a text-based document, or information about multimedia files. Other searchers don't go out to look for information, but rather ask people who create home pages to send in details of their page. In either case, the information is stored in a database that resides on the searcher's World Wide Web server.

You connect to a searcher just as you do any other WWW resource, by entering the URL address into your browser. When the searcher home page appears, you have an opportunity to enter keywords or phrases to search for resources that meet your needs. It is important to recognize that some browsers (or clients), like recent versions of NCSA Mosaic or Spry's Air Mosaic, support a *forms* feature. Developed by NCSA programmers, forms is a software program/code that allows users to interact by supplying information (or requests for information) to the HTTP-based Web server.

The forms function enables your browser to present fill-in boxes that resemble forms on-screen. The form entry box can be used for several applications. You can enter keywords for a Web searcher search, supply order entry information (such as your credit card number and address) to purchase products on-line via the WWW, or supply comments that you send back to an editor of an electronic publication. Other browsers, like Cello, don't support the forms function. You can, however, still perform keyword searches using the searchers, as most searchers provide a link to an "alternative interface." This interface opens a dialog box in your browser in which you can enter information.

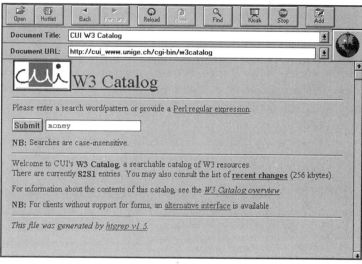

Fig. 5.1
Spry's Air Mosaic uses the Forms interface in a search using the W3 Catalog. Enter your search words in the form box.

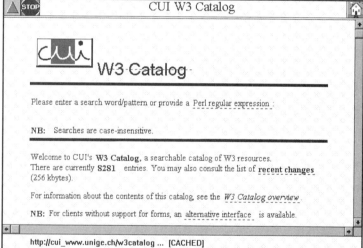

Fig. 5.2
The Cello browser does not use the Forms interface.

The result of a search is a list of Web locations that may contain the information you request, along with hyperlinks that take you directly to those sites. Sometimes the list simply has the name of the home page, at other times it includes a short description of what the site offers.

You can start with a narrow search term, like "climbing" or "Everest." However, it's unlikely this will find much. So, to continue your quest, broaden the search to single words like "mountains" or "adventure." If this doesn't work go even broader to "travel" or "sports." One of these will probably get you to the peak of Everest. There are many Web searchers, and new ones appear all the time. The following sections describe a few of the best Web searchers.

The current generation of Web searchers do have a few flaws, which you will notice fairly quickly. For one, they aren't all updated on a daily or even weekly basis, so you do miss some resources. Perhaps the biggest problem is that they are based on indexes that are created by humans. Unless a home page title or URL address contains a word that fits your search profile, or the creator of the page or document has indexed it with that word, it is possible to miss resources that meet your search criteria *and* get search results that *don't* meet your criteria. For example, there may be a home page that contains links to "Stocks and Bonds" information. If you search for "money," the search could miss this page unless it has been identified with the word "money." Likewise, you will often get erroneous information from a search. For example, a keyword search for "money" produces a home page titled "Web T-Shirts" via one of the searchers. It is possible, although unlikely, that the T-Shirts page offers apparel with images of money.

ALIWEB

URL address: **http://web.nexor.co.uk/aliweb/doc/aliweb.html**

People who maintain a Web home page write descriptions of their services in the HTML file format. This file has a link to their home page. They then tell ALIWEB about the file, which ALIWEB retrieves and combines into a searchable database.

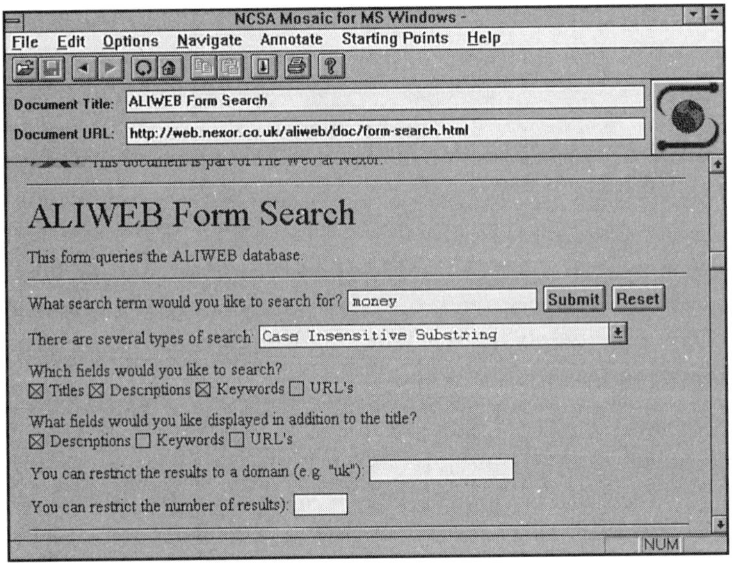

Fig. 5.3
The search input page for ALIWEB. There are several different front ends for ALIWEB, this is only one of them.

CUI Search Catalog

URL address: **http://cui_www.unige.ch/w3catalog**

W3 Catalog is a searchable catalog of resources that is created from a number of manually maintained lists available on the Web. As the site declares, "There is some redundancy amongst the various sources, but a bit of noise seems acceptable to increase your chances of finding what you're looking for." The result of a search is a chronological list of resources that meet your search criteria. Thus, if you do a search in January, the first entries on the list represent sites that came on-line in January and later entries date back to December, November, and so on. Listings also usually include a short paragraph description of the resource and the name of the resource (which is underlined), which is a hyperlink to that resource.

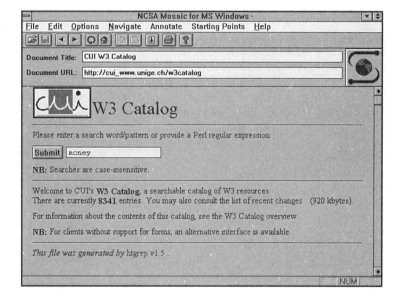

Fig. 5.4
Part of the search results for "money" from W3 Catalog. It continues for several pages.

EINet Galaxy—Search the World Wide Web

URL address: **http://galaxy.einet.net/www/www.html**

This searcher maintains an index that points to Web home pages around the world. When you connect, the home page automatically opens a search dialog box. The result of a search is a name-only hyperlink list of possible resources. The list is prioritized in a fashion similar to a WAIS (Wide Area Information Server) search, with the first entry receiving 1,000 points and the remaining entries getting fewer points. Each entry also indicates the size of the document or home page that you will jump to. This is useful because it tells you how long it will take to load that page.

Fig. 5.5

The search input page for EINet's search.

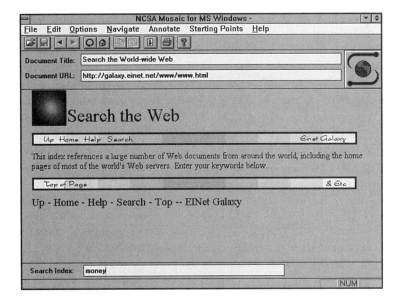

Fig. 5.6

The search results for EINet's search. A succinct list including a priority rating system and size of the documents and files.

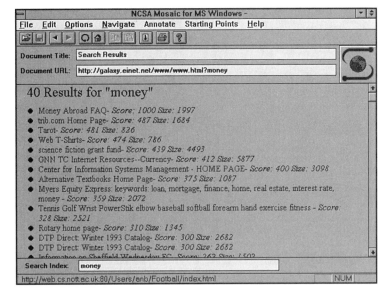

Global Network Academy Meta-Library

URL address:

http://uu-gna.mit.edu:8001/uu-gna/meta-library/index.html

GNA is a non-profit corporation incorporated in Texas. Affiliated with the Usenet University project, it has a long-term goal of creating a fully accredited on-line university. This searcher is one of the information management tools that GNA offers.

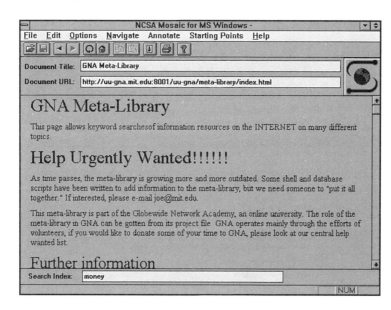

Fig. 5.7
The search input page for Global Network Academy Meta-Library.

Lycos

URL address: **http://fuzine.mt.cs.cmu.edu/mlm/lycos-home.html**

Lycos is a research program that focuses on information retrieval and discovery in the WWW. It uses a "finite memory model of the web to guide intelligent, directed searches for specific information needs." Lycos currently does its retrieval based on abstracts of Web documents.

Fig. 5.8
The search input
page for Lycos.

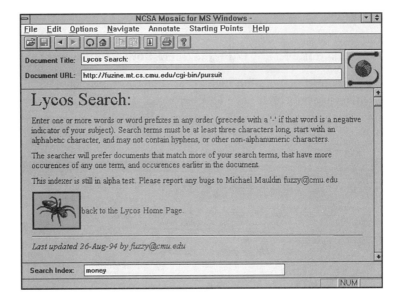

Fig. 5.9
The search results
page for Lycos
includes descrip-
tive text with the
search term
highlighted. It is
several pages
long.

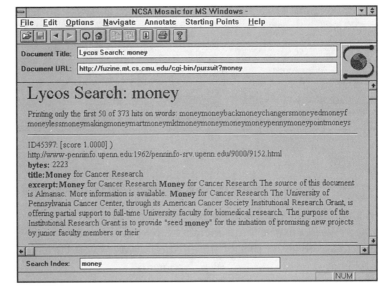

Nomad Gateway

URL address: **http://www.rns.com/cgi-bin/nomad**

This Web resource searching site represents a joint effort between Rockwell
Network Systems and Cal Poly, San Luis Obispo to develop a pool of repli-
cated Web resource locators. The result of your search is a list of single line
entries, each of which is a hyperlink to another Web resource.

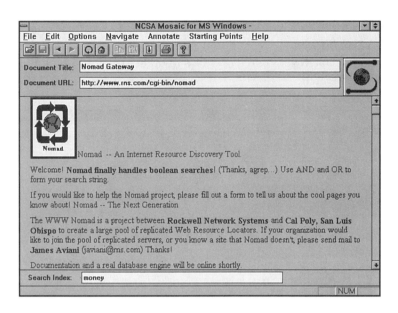

Fig. 5.10
The search input
page for Nomad.

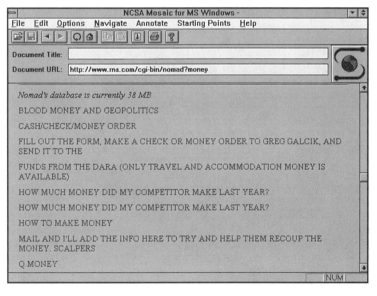

Fig. 5.11
The search results
for Nomad.

Webcrawler Searcher

URL address: **http://www.biotech.washington.edu**

Developed by Brian Pinkerton at the University of Washington, the
WebCrawler program focuses on accumulating information about the specific
documents that reside on Web servers. It creates indices of the documents it
locates on the Web and lets you keyword search these indices. The result of a

search is a list of sites, home pages, and documents that match your criteria. The list is prioritized—the first resource receives a rating of 1,000 and should most closely match your criteria, while a resource farther down on the list is less likely to match.

Fig. 5.12

The search input page for the WebCrawler.

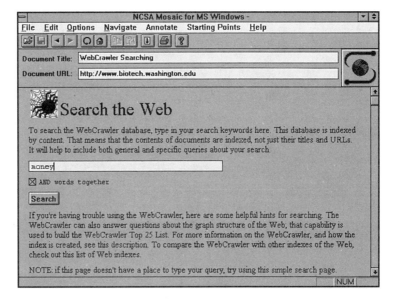

Fig. 5.13

The results of a WebCrawler search provide a priority-based list of hyperlinks to resources.

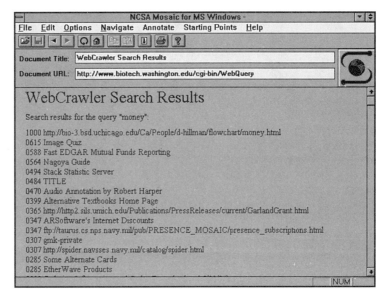

WWWW—The World Wide Web Worm

URL address:

http://www.cs.colorado.edu/home/mcbryan/WWWW.html

This searcher gets used more than 30,000 times every month. The home page tells us, "The Worm is scouring the Web and has found almost all Web resources that are out there. We present the resources in several ways and provide you with search capabilities on this valuable database of over 100,000 multimedia objects."

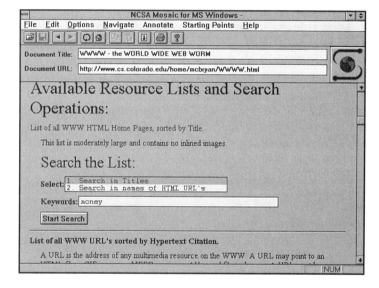

Fig. 5.14
The search input page for the World Wide Web Worm. It offers several types of searches, including a search by home page title and names of URLs.

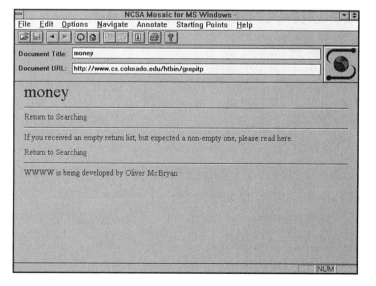

Fig. 5.15
The search results from World Wide Web Worm. For this search, it found no matches.

Yahoo

URL address: **http://adebono.stanford.edu/yahoo**

A comprehensive database of Web sites and pages. There are more than 23,000 entries, which reference different Web resources. The Web pages are organized into subject categories such as art, entertainment, and social sciences, and you can search the entire database for specific keyword matches. According to the statistics (which are available via a link on the home page), the site has had more than 2 1/2 million visits.

Fig. 5.16
Learn where to go on the Web at this site.

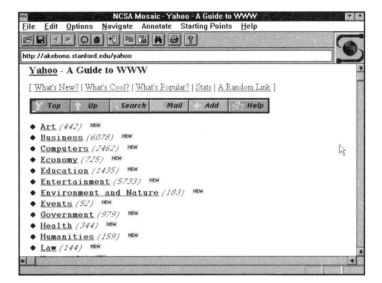

WWW Directories and Index Home Pages

Unlike the searchers, the following WWW home pages are directories and indices of searchers. The directories represent a list of resources that you may find useful, you can cross-reference the subjects and resources in these directories. The indices are pages that have pointers to, or search boxes for, several different Web searchers.

Global News Network Directory

URL address: **http://nearnet.gnn.com/gnn/GNNhome.html**

A directory of the resources compiled by this commercial service, many links are to businesses and companies.

NCSA What's New

URL address:

http://www.ncsa.uiuc.edu/SDG/Software/Mosaic/Docs/archive-whats-new.html

This home page provides a month-by-month, year-by-year list of new WWW resources.

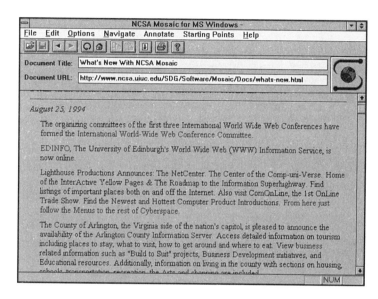

Fig. 5.17
The August 1994 catalog of What's New as of August 25.

W3 Search Engines

URL address: **http://cui_www.unige.ch/meta-index.html**

This is the same computer system that brings you the CUI catalog. Here, the home page presents a list of several different Web searchers. Next to the name of each searcher is a box where you can enter your search phrase and then submit it directly to the searcher. As an alternative, you can click on the name of the searcher and go to its home page.

Web Indexes

URL address:

http://www.biotech.washington.edu/WebCrawler/WebIndexes.html

A page that has hyperlinks to several Web searchers.

V

Finding Resources

World Wide Web Virtual Library

URL address:

http://info.cern.ch/hypertext/DataSources/bySubject/Overview.html

This is a subject catalog that begins with the subject of Aeronautics and ends with Unidentified Flying Objects—but rest assured, not every category relates to outer space.

Fig. 5.18
The main subject listing in the Virtual Library.

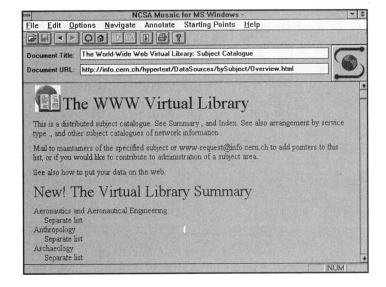

Now get going and enjoy the resources in this book and your exploration of the information, services, and multimedia that the World Wide Web offers.

Chapter 6

Art, Music, and Entertainment

One of the most powerful applications of the World Wide Web is the storage and distribution of multimedia. Artists, musicians, gallery owners, museum curators, and library directors have taken advantage of this aspect of the Web. You can view a painting by Georgia O'Keefe, listen to audio samples of ZZ Top music, or review the schedule for next week's satellite television broadcasts.

Electronic museums represent a new avenue for the public display of art. Now, rather than waiting for museum hours or pushing through crowds to view a masterpiece, you can connect to an electronic museum, like the Frederick R. Weisman Art Museum, and leisurely browse through works of art. If your taste runs more toward current endeavors, visit an exhibition in an on-line New York art gallery (where you can even buy a painting if you see one you like), glance through scripts of Star Trek episodes, or download a collection of songs by the music group Quagmire.

Art is universal. You can appreciate a painting created by a Japanese painter in the 13th century as easily as a print created in the 1950s by an American artist. Art on the Web makes it simple to transcend some of the cultural and linguistic barriers that occur when we try to communicate with people in foreign countries. The diversity of art, music, and entertainment on the Web is tremendous; you can find a resource that will help you develop a research paper on Greek architecture as easily as you can pull up a review of the latest Tom Hanks movie. If you have an interest in Web resources that focus on literature, check out the listings in chapter 15, "Publications, News, Periodicals, and Books," to locate enough electronic text to satisfy the most voracious bookworm.

Collections can be quite large and WWW home pages frequently incorporate search mechanisms that help you locate a specific work of art or information about a specific artist or musician. If your keyword search doesn't produce the results you want, try to broaden the search, say from "New Orleans Jazz" to simply "Jazz." Many of the home pages listed here have links to other art-based WWW resources—so, jump in and have fun.

The broad categories for these resources include:

Art

Dance

Movies

Museums

Music

Publications

Television and radio

Cardiff's Movie Database

URL address: **http://www.msstate.edu/Movies**

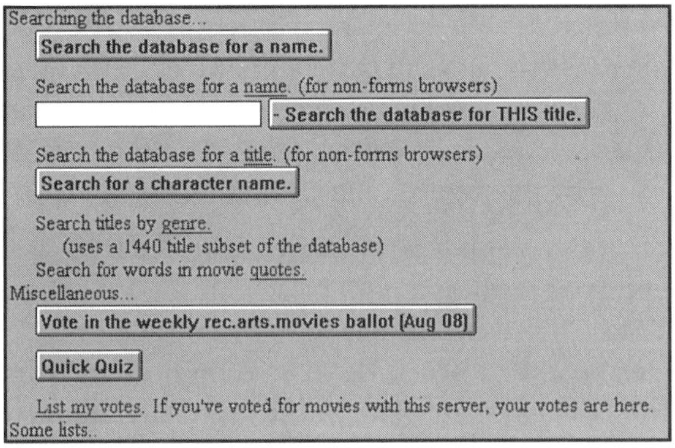

Fig. 6.1
You can search Cardiff's WWW Movie Database to find out about films and the many people that played a role (acting, writing, and directing) in each movie.

Have you ever watched a movie and couldn't remember the name of the actress or actor who had a certain part? Or placed a bet with a friend that you could name the entire cast of *The Maltese Falcon*? Or wondered how many movies Henry Fonda and Paul Newman were in together? If you've ever had any question about a movie regarding plot, characters, actors, actresses, directors, writers, or anything else, this is the home page for you!

A hypertext front-end to the **rec.arts.movies** news group database, this is a wonderful example of interactive information. The home page provides you with a variety of search boxes in which you can enter names of characters, actors, or movie titles to begin your search. The information is vast. The database contains more than 85,000 listings of actors and actresses, some 34,835 titles (including TV series), and 1,500 plot summaries.

As an example of how this works, enter the last name HOLDEN for a name search. This query delivers a list of approximately 35 Holdens (Amy Holden Jones, the writer; David Holden, the writer; Gloria Holden, the actress; and William Holden, the actor). Now click on William Holden to get a list of some 72 films he acted in. You didn't know he was a character in the 1967 film *Casino Royale*? Click on this film name and you get a description of the film that tells you it was a James Bond spoof originally written by Ian Fleming and that many other actors and actresses, including Woody Allen, were in the film.

EXPO Ticket Office

URL address: **http://sunsite.unc.edu/expo/ticket_office.html**

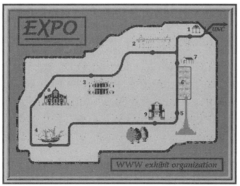

Fig. 6.2
Jump on board an interactive bus tour and visit six interesting pavilions at the EXPO Ticket Office.

This is a WWW must-visit! The home page refers to the EXPO Ticket Office as "the world's most exciting electronic exposition." This isn't far off. From the home page, you can jump onto one of six guided tour buses that take you to one of the six EXPO pavilions (buses leave every few microseconds). Selections include:

The Vatican Exhibit—with precious maps, books, and manuscripts.

Soviet Archive—the first public display of secret Russian records.

1492: An On-Going Voyage—examines the events that settled the "new world."

Dead Sea Scrolls—describes the history and discovery of these artifacts.

Paleontology Exhibit—fossil life from the University of California, Berkeley.

Spalato Exhibit—the history and architecture of this Roman village.

Most of the information and multimedia exhibits have been donated by the Library of Congress. What makes this Web resource unique is the interactive manner in which you move through information. As you move through one of the pavilions, a little icon of footsteps appears to help guide your journey. From the home page, you can jump to an almost three-dimensional map that shows the "location" of the pavilions and includes an audio clip. There is even an EXPO restaurant, Le Cordon Bleu, for the weary traveler. Every day of the week there is a different menu; Wednesday's special is split pea soup with bacon, sorrel, and lettuce. Inline GIF images display your electronic lunch. Have fun!

Traditional Folk Song Database

URL address: **http://web2.xerox.com/digitrad**

This server provides a searchable index of the Digital Traditional Folk Song database. The database contains the lyrics and music for thousands of folk songs, many very esoteric, with some including audio sample files that you can play back. Dick Greenhaus and his friends are credited with developing this collection.

To find a song, you perform a keyword search. Search results bring up a list of songs that either contain or relate to your search word. You click on a song name to retrieve the lyrics. A search using the word "Russian" delivers "It's Sister Jenny's Turn To Throw the Bomb," while a search for the keyword "Spring" produces four songs: "Birds In the Spring," "So Early In the Spring," "Flower Carol," and "Spring Glee." This is a fun and extensive resource—try it out!

The Online Museum of Singapore Art & History

URL address: **http://king.ncb.gov.sg/nhb/museum.html**

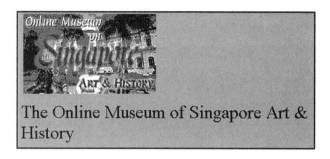

The Online Museum of Singapore Art & History

Fig. 6.3
Travel around the world and back in time when you download images from this on-line collection of historical artwork from the Museum of Singapore.

Art history offers a unique opportunity to appreciate artistic endeavors from another era and a chance to learn about society and life at a particular point in time. The Online Museum of Singapore Art History lets you explore paintings and documents by early Singapore artists. One of the exhibitions is a collection of 19th-century prints of Singapore. When you click on the title for a print, a picture of the artwork appears along with a description of the piece and an overview of the artist. This particular exhibition is quite interesting because many of the prints show you images of Singapore in the early 1800s—so not only do you get to travel halfway around the world to view the artwork, you also travel back in time.

For example, when you select "Plate 5: View from the Mouth of the Singapore River, 1830," you get a wonderful image that shows a view of Singapore from the mouth of the river. You can "look" upstream and see where European merchants used warehouses for their products. View and save the pictures as JPEG files—even start your own personal museum of images in your PC. You can also learn about the artists, engravers, and specific details about each print, such as their size (this one was 31.5 x 23 cm) and where they currently are stored or displayed. Other choices from the main menu include:

Pioneer Artists	Early Singapore artists
Raffles Revisited	A history of the founder of Singapore
Ponts des Art	Explores the influence on area artists who studied in France
From Ritual to Romance	An exhibition of paintings inspired by Bali

VI

Entertainment

Star Trek: The Next Generation

URL address:

http://www.ee.surrey.ac.uk/Personal/STTNG/index.html

Fig. 6.4
Connect with this
Star Trek Web site
to find out
whether Klingons
really like
humans.

It is the year 2364 and the phrase, "Beam Me Up" transmits across the galaxy. This WWW server is located in the UK, where, despite its non prime-time slot, ST:TNG (the abbreviation for Star Trek: The Next Generation) often came in as one of the top 10 rated shows for BBC2, sometimes the highest-rated show on the channel. The home page has so many links you won't have time to visit the Holosuite. There is information about the cast, guest roles, descriptions of all major alien species (even the nasty Borgs), episode summaries, and movie rumors. A trivia section will keep you busy with facts like Professor Steven Hawking (the famous physicist) is the only person to ever appear "as himself" in the show. Here is one example of an episode summary:

"Peak Performance"

"A simulated war game turns deadly when the crew is ambushed by a Ferengi battleship. With the Enterprise crippled in the attack, Picard must try to get Riker, Geordi, and the others back on board."

Art

Art on the Web includes all the forms that exist in the "real world." There are paintings, sculpture, and photography. The listings in this section are broken down into resources for study, research, and resources, which includes databases of historical art, mailing lists, and so on: Artists, which are displays of the works of individual artist; Sculpture, the 3D world of art; Exhibits and Galleries, where there are both temporary and permanent collections; and Photography, both color and black-and-white images.

Art Study, Research, and Resources

African Art: Aesthetics and Meaning

URL address: **http://www.lib.virginia.edu/dic/African.html**

An electronic exhibition catalog sponsored by the Bayly Art Museum and the University of Virginia, Charlottesville, Virginia. A nice introduction and exhibition of African art with links to elements of the African aesthetic, the exhibition, and a detailed bibliography.

Architecture—ANU Art History

URL address: **http://rubens.anu.edu.au**

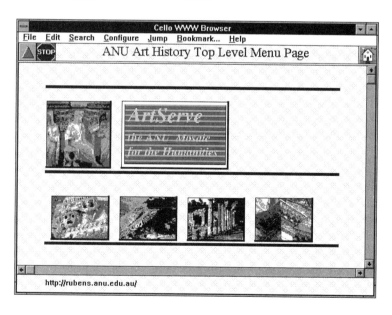

Fig. 6.5

This Web server has links to 2,800 images, many of which are classical architecture and sculptures.

VI

Entertainment

This Web server offers a variety of art-history images. There are two image databases you can access from the main page. One includes 2,800 images and associated descriptions about the history of printmaking from the 15th century to the end of the 19th century. A second collection includes images that focus on the classical architecture of the Mediterranean. For the prints collection, users can choose between menus that provide inline images and ones that don't. The server is adding an additional 2,500 images of classical architecture and architectural sculpture in this collection. Some main menu selections include database access to prints, print history, the architecture of Islam, a few images of contemporary Hong Kong architecture, a brief illustrated tour of a few of the classical sites in Turkey, and work at the Canberra School of Art.

ArtSource
URL address: **http://www.uky.edu/Artsource/artsourcehome.html**

This is a gathering point for networked resources on art and architecture. The content is diverse and includes pointers to resources around the Net, as well as original materials submitted by librarians, artists, and art historians. You can select discipline-specific resources, general resources, and bibliographies from the home page. There are also links to art journals, image collections, and electronic exhibitions.

Art Topics Mailing Lists
URL address: **http://www.willamette.edu/~jpatters/art-lists.html**

Perhaps you'd rather talk about art than simply look at it. This Web page has a list of more than 100 art-related mailing lists. From the "Ceramic Arts" discussion list to the "Medieval Performing Arts" list, you are sure to find a group of people who share your specific interest in the arts.

Fine Art Forum
URL address:
http://www.msstate.edu/Fineart_Online/art-resources.html

This home page provides a directory of links to different art resources on the Web. The broad categories that you start with include Events, General and Academic Resources, Electronic Art, Galleries and E-journals, and Individual Artists. It is a great place to start your exploration of art on the WWW.

University of Art and Design
URL address: **http://www.uiah.fi/**

The University of Art and Design in Helsinki provides information on The International Symposium on Electronic Art (ISEA) and The International Conference on Color Education.

Artists

Berryhill, Tom—Pictures and Poetry

URL address:

http://wimsey.com/anima/NEXUS/TomStuff/Travelling.html

The on-line hyperbook "Travelling with Light," by Tom Berryhill, is a collection of the artist's poetry and pictures connected through hypertext links. Features include options to browse just the pictures or the poetry, or to just follow the links that bring you through this interesting collection. Also featured are clickable pictures that download into a JPEG viewer for modification by the reader.

Dali, Salvador

URL address: **http://www.eunet.es/spain/images-dali/**

Do you remember the famous melting clocks in Salvador Dali's painting "La Persistenciade la Memoria" (translated "The Persistence of Memory")? This is one of the color images that loads on the home page of this Web server, which is in Spain, homeland to Salvador Dali. If you have your inline images turned on, be prepared for a *long* load time as the home page has numerous GIF images of Dali's work. Even though the small amount of text is in Spanish, you can easily find the images you want—proving that art, like music, transcends the barriers of language.

Di Leo, Belinda

URL address: **http://gort.ucsd.edu/mw/bdl.html**

The paintings in "Ancestry: Religion, Death, and Culture" document the native culture of Central Appalachia. The work portrays the character and spirit of this region of the country. Originally shown as a University of California, San Diego MFA Project, Appalachian artist Belinda Di Leo explores relationships between religion and death.

Jacobsen, John E.

URL address: **http://amanda.physics.wisc.edu/show.html**

"Strange Interactions" is a WWW art show of paintings, drawings, and prints by this artist.

Kandinsky, Wassily (1866–1944)

URL address: **gopher://libra.arch.umich.edu/11/Kandinsky**

This Gopher site contains some text files about modern artist Kandinsky as well as several GIF files that you can view on-line or download.

Sculpture

Research into Artifacts
URL address: **http://brains.race.u-tokyo.ac.jp/RACE.html**

From the University of Tokyo, Japan, this WWW site and its links explore the relationship between art, technology, and the environment. There are links to an artist-in-residence program, images, and descriptions of the professors involved in these efforts.

Sculpture Tour
URL address: **http://loki.ur.utk.edu/sculpture/sculpt.html**

This Web site contains photographs of the pieces included in the 1992-93 Sculpture Tour of the Knoxville campus. In all there are 26 separate pieces of sculpture located on campus. You can jump to GIF images of each piece (the files are 100K+ but resolution is quite good) and learn a little about the artist who created the work.

Zimbabwe Sculpture
URL address:
http://www.ncsa.uiuc.edu:80//www.twi.tudelft.nl/Local/ ShonaSculpture/ShonaSculpture.htm

This home page on stone sculpture from Zimbabwe has information on Shona sculpture and a list of exhibitions on the subject. These pages are expanded as new information becomes available.

Galleries and Exhibits

Access Art
URL address: **http://www.mgainc.com/Art/HomePage.html**

Fig. 6.6
This WWW gallery lets you look at artwork in several different media and categories (such as land-scapes).

This is the home page for a commercial service run by Medium for Global Access, which helps artists and collectors connect electronically. You can access links to artists like William Buffet, Edson Campos, Olivia Deerardinis, Ted Kimer, Jean-Giraud Moebius, and Alberto Vargas. See their work and use an on-screen order form to add art to your collection. One home page link lets you look at art by subject category, such as fantasy or landscape.

(Art)^n Laboratory
URL address: **http://artn.iit.edu**

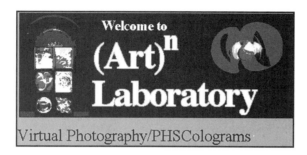

Fig. 6.7
3D will never be
the same again—
this WWW home
page proves you
no longer need
special glasses to
get the illusion of
depth.

In the 1950s it was popular to go to watch a 3D movie where you put on special glasses to get the illusion of depth on the screen. (Art)^n Laboratory is the inventor of PHSColograms (Virtual Photography). These are three-dimensional images that you can view without special 3D glasses. From this home page, you can find out about PHSColograms, the History of (Art)^n Laboratory, and how PHSColograms work. There is a gallery of more than 250 images, drawn from (Art)^n's collaborative works with artists, scientists, and mathematicians.

Electric Gallery
URL address: **http://www.elpress.com/gallery/homepage.html**

You can forget the expenses involved in flying to the Big Apple, renting a limousine and tuxedo, and fighting traffic to visit an exclusive art gallery. Now you can appreciate quality art electronically via the WWW; the Electric Gallery contains an ever-changing collection of paintings.

FineArt Forum Gallery
URL address: **http://www.msstate.edu/Fineart_Online/gallery.html**

To browse through several areas in this electronic gallery, you need a JPEG viewer. The Gallery is constantly being expanded and developed. Some installations include:

Joseph DeLappe—Recent Work

Helaman Ferguson—Mathematics in Stone and Bronze

Celeste Brignac—Photographs

VI

Entertainment

Kaleidospace—Artists and Multimedia
URL address: **http://kspace.com**

Kaleidospace provides a WWW site for the promotion of independent artists, musicians, performers, CD-ROM authors, writers, animators, and filmmakers. Artists provide samples of their work, which Kaleidospace integrates into a multimedia display available via the Internet.

Media West Editions
URL address: **http://www.wimsey.com/Pixel_Pushers**

Media West Editions showcases digital artists for the Pixel Pushers Exhibition of Original Digital Art. Included in the line-up are: Oscar-winning composer and musician, Buffy Sainte-Marie; some of Canada's graphic artists, including Yuri Dojc and Louis Fishauf; Vancouver-based typographer, Stephen Herron; and digital art innovators from the U.S., including Diane Fenster, Jeff Brice, Helen Golden, and Kai Krause.

Ohio State University at Newark
URL address: **http://www.cgrg.ohio-state.edu:80/mkruse/osu.html**

The Ohio State University at Newark Art Gallery has made its exhibition "Roy Lichtenstein Pre-Pop, 1948-1960" available for view via the WWW. The Art Gallery includes over 30 works of the famous American artist, most of which have never been shown to the public. This exhibition provides insight into how the Lichtenstein arrived at his famous Pop Style. The Art Gallery also exhibits local, national, and international artists.

REIFF II Electronic Museum
URL address: **http://www.informatik.rwth-aachen.de/Reiff2**

If you enjoy German art (and can read German), you may enjoy this Web site. The art association "Mehrwert e.V." is on-line. Its staff has established an electronic museum, REIFF II, which is open for all Internet users. The Museum was developed in cooperation with the Department of History of Art, the Center of Computing, and the Department of Computer Science.

Photography

Ansel Adams
URL address: **http://bookweb.cwis.uci.edu:8042/AdamsHome.html**

This site houses an exhibition of photographs by Ansel Adams called "Fiat Lux." You can browse through the digital photographs, which comprise his portrait of the University of California created for the 1968 Centennial celebration.

California Museum of Photography

URL address: **gopher://galaxy.ucr.edu/11/Campus%20Events**

This provides an overview of photo exhibits and schedules for exhibits held at the California Museum of Photography, located at the University of California, in Riverside.

Peoria Art Guild—On-line Juried Art

URL address: **http://www.bradley.edu/exhibit/index.html**

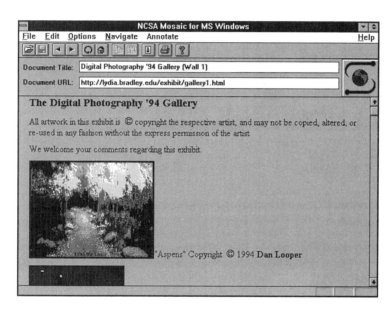

Fig. 6.8
Tour through the galleries in this electronic photo exhibition.

The Peoria Art Guild of Peoria, Illinois, provides this electronic version of their juried exhibition "Digital Photography '94." This exhibit has entries nationwide from photographers whose work involves digital photography. You move from the home page into electronic galleries where inline images of the photographs appear. Click on the inline image to download or display a complete JPEG image of the photograph.

Dance

American Dance Festival

URL address: **http://www.nando.net/adf/adfmain.html**

Established in 1934 in Bennington, Vermont, the American Dance Festival (ADF) encompasses a school with 350 professional and pre-professional dancers. Currently at Duke University in Durham, North Carolina, the ADF has sponsored more than 350 premieres and hosted major American modern dance companies. This resource has a complete schedule of ADF events and activities.

Fig. 6.9
Visit this Web site and learn about the American Dance Festival, which orchestrates and sponsors dance performances across the country.

Dance & Technology
URL address:
http://www.dance.ohio-state.edu/files/Dance_and_Technology/tech-menu.html

This is an Ohio State WWW server that promotes the combination of technology and dance. It provides information that encourages people in dance to investigate the cutting edge applications of dance and technology, including the use of computers with dance performances. There is research, a bibliography, and a listing of "Who Is Doing What & Where."

Global Dance Directory
Internet FTP address: **ftp://ftp.std.com/pub/dance**

This is a Gopher site that has extensive information on global dance resources, including the countries of Brazil, Ireland, Spain, Venezuela, and Yugoslavia. There is also dance clip art, dance steps documents, and access to the rec-arts-dance newsgroup.

International Association of Gay Square Dance Clubs
URL address: **http://molscat.giss.nasa.gov/IAGSDC/.html**

The IAGSDC is an organization of 40 modern western square dancing clubs throughout the U.S. and Canada. Information provided at this site includes details of programs and a convention that attracts more than 1,000 dancers.

Ohio State University, Department of Dance Home Page
URL address: **http://www.dance.ohio-state.edu**

This is a WWW server that focuses on original material related to dance. Topics include dance history, musicians in dance, and dance resources.

UK-Dance
URL address: **http://www.tecc.co.uk/public/tqm/uk-dance/**

This resource includes information and stories on clubs, parties, events, record shops, and radio, with a focus on the underground dance and the music scene in the United Kingdom. It also provides details on an Internet mailing list for people to discuss dance music culture in the U.K.

Movies

Movies Database
URL address: **http://www.cm.cf.ac.uk/Movies**

URL address: **http://ballet.cit.gu.edu.au/Movies/Australia.**

The Web interface to the **rec.arts.movies** database is mirrored in the USA and in Australia. There is information on over 30,000 titles, 75,000 actors and actresses, 6,500 directors, and 7,900 writers. All information can be searched. Whether you're a movie fan or just need answers to movie trivia questions, this is for you.

Movie Reviews
URL address: **http://b62528.student.cwru.edu/reviews/reviews.html**

This WWW home page offers movie reviews. Some movies reviewed here include *Evil Dead, Army of Darkness, Crimewave,* and *Darkman.* It doesn't look like *Mary Poppins* will be reviewed any time soon.

Usenet Postings on Movies
URL address: **http://www.lysator.liu.se/sf_archive/sub/movies.html**

These postings to Usenet focus on science fiction movies. Many reviews are indexed by title.

Wisdom and Lore
URL address: **http://cad.ucla.edu/repository/useful/useful.html**

From UCLA, this is a WWW home page that offers an enormous hodge-podge of information. Much of it is about entertainment, movies, and literature, including things to do in L.A. There's a Kosher restaurant city guide,

VI

Entertainment

hypertext movie information, movie info lists (actors and actresses), movie rating information, and ratings such as the Billboard charts and Nielson TV ratings.

Museums

Frederick R. Weisman Art Museum
URL address: **http://www.micro.umn.edu/weisman/otherArt.html**

Fig. 6.10
This WWW site shows paintings by some of America's most famous 20th-century artists.

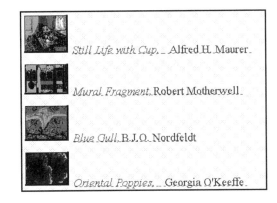

Although it says the museum hours are 10:00 am to 6:00 pm, you can use the WWW to view many of the museum's collections any time, day or night. Small icons of individual paintings are displayed, and when you click on them you can view full-frame images of artwork by the likes of Georgia O'Keefe and Robert Motherwell. GIF and JPEG are choices.

Le WebLouvre
URL address: **http://mistral.enst.fr/~pioch/louvre**

Take a trip to Paris. Start with an inline image of the Pyramid in front of the Louvre. This collection of electronic paintings is maintained by Nicolas Pioch. The server won a "Best of the Web 1994" award in the category of "Best Use of Multiple Media." It should be noted that this server/resource is not officially connected with the Louvre in Paris.

La Trobe University Art Museum
URL address:
http://www.latrobe.edu.au/Glenn/Museum/ArtMuseumHome.html

Fig. 6.11
Look at thumbnails of paintings and sculpture, or download high quality JPEG images.

Located in Australia, this museum hosts a variety of exhibitions including painting and sculpture. Jump from the home page to an overview of the current exhibition where a series of color thumbnails of the artwork are displayed. Then, if you want, you can retrieve a more detailed JPEG image of any work of art. Be prepared for slow load times.

Music Hall

URL address:

http://www.ncsa.uiuc.edu/SDG/Experimental/vatican.exhibit/exhibit/ e-music/Music.html

This Web page is a subset of the Vatican Exhibit, which can be found via the WWW EXPO (described earlier in this chapter). It deserves special mention here because of its unique music resources and because it might be easy to miss otherwise. The focus of this exhibition is on the music of the Renaissance, which was closely tied to the religions and artistic ideals of the 16th century. There are three Music Rooms that you can access via this page. Each room offers a slightly different collection of musical information and artifacts. There are pictures of musical instruments, music scores, and images of singers.

Russian Virtual Exhibits

URL address: **http://www.kiae.su/www/wtr/exhibits.html**

Virtual exhibitions from Russia (by Relcom). You can jump between the Kremlin, the Contemporary Fine Arts Center, the Paleontology Institute, and the Soviet Archives. The Russian WWW servers are all under development, but are worth a visit.

San Francisco Exploratorium

URL address: **http://www.exploratorium.edu**

The San Francisco Exploratorium has a large collection of both art and science exhibits. The focus here is on interactive exhibits that incorporate technology to give the "viewer" a learning experience.

University of Illinois at Urbana-Champaign
URL address:
http://www.ncsa.uiuc.edu/General/UIUC/KrannertArtMuseum/
KrannertArtHome.html

Fig. 6.12
The Krannert Art Museum Web page maintains a diverse collection of Asian, African, and Medieval art, as well as educational resources.

Don't miss this one. Created by the NCSA publications group, the Krannert Art Museum and Kinkead Pavilion have very extensive collections of works, including sculpture, European and American painting, Asian, African, Pre-Columbian, and Medieval art, and Old-World antiques. In addition to viewing works of art, you can jump from the home page to the Education Resource Center, which offers instructional materials and educational workshops.

Music

Music Study, Research, and Resources

American Music Network
URL address: **gopher://tmn.tmn.com:70/00/Artswire/amn/infoamn**

Created to further the appreciation, performance, creation, and study of American music, this home page has links to all historical and contemporary styles. You will also find other information about events, speakers, and important dates in the history of American music.

Batish Institute
URL address: **http://hypatia.ucsc.edu:70/1/RELATED/Batish**

The Batish Institute of Indian Music and Fine Arts maintains this WWW server. The Institute, formed in 1973 by the Batish family, holds classes in vocal and instrumental music and publishes *RagaNet*, an electronic journal about Indian music and art. Pandit Shiv Dayal Batish and his son, Ashwin Batish, create and offer via this Web site material that teaches the theory and practice of Indian music. This is a comprehensive examination of Indian music.

Hyperreal—the Techno/Ambient/Rave Archive
URL address: **http://hyperreal.com**

As the home page states, "There's a lot of stuff here." The stuff includes links to various music archives, mailing lists, publications, and even art-based shareware.

Indiana University Music Library
URL address:
http://www.music.indiana.edu/misc/music_resources.html

This is a great collection of music links that are carefully organized into areas such as academic, geographic, individual artists, and so on.

Mammoth Music Meta-List
URL address:
ftp://ftp.cs.cmu.edu/afs/cs.cmu.edu/user/jdg/www/music.html

This FTP site has lists of lists, giving you access to links about every subject you can think of that pertains to music.

Music References
URL address: **http://freeabel.geom.umn.edu:8000/music.html**

This is a terrific home page for music information; there's everything from links to music lyrics to digital sound clips of The Doors and Pink Floyd.

Rare Groove Charts
URL address: **http://rg.media.mit.edu/RG/charts/top.html**

This Web site shows you ratings charts based on access of song samples, and it lets you make a graph of your top 20 tracks. You fill in the genre, your name, assigned password if you are a DF, the artist, title, and label for each hit.

Usenet Music FAQ's
URL address:
http://www.cis.ohio-state.edu/hypertext/faq/usenet/music/top.html

Boy, there are a lot of questions (and answers) here! Try Q&A on Acappella, Billy Joel, music composition, Deep Purple, percussion drum equipment suppliers, listings of open musical jam sessions, MIDI, and reggae to name a few.

Acoustic

Acoustic Music Server
URL address: **http://kirk.cgrg.ohio-state.edu/Music.html**

There's lots of information on, of course, acoustic music. Hyperlinks include artist overviews: what they've done; profiles—brief bios of acoustic musicians; tour schedules; and audio and video clips.

Blues

Delta Snake Blues News
URL address: **http://www.portal.com/~mojohand/delta_snake.html**

If you like to sing or even learn about The Blues, then stop at this home page. There are fun and heartfelt reviews of new albums such as John Brim's "The Ice Cream Man" on Tone-Cool Records or Roomfull of Blues' "Dance All Night" on Bullseye Blues. Also, there's the Delta Snake Kitchen, which provides recipes like blackened catfish.

Classical

Leeds University
URL address: **http://www.leeds.ac.uk/music.html**

The home page for the Leeds University Department of Music has a lot of links. First, find out about the department and programs in music. Next, search for music information by type, genre, period, artist, or area. Then, learn about Organ Recitals from St. Bartholomew's, Armley, jump to the Opera Schedule Server from the Process Control Department of the Technical University of Budapest, find out about the Oregon Bach Festival, or... well, you get the idea.

Oregon Bach Festival
URL address: **http://jrusby.uoregon.edu/obf/obfhome.html**

This Web site tells you about the annual festival, provides a schedule of events (which run through the summer months), and offers bios of the musicians, conductors, and composers.

Ethnic

Chinese music
URL address: **http://ifcss.org:8001/www/music.html**

When you jump to this home page, you actually FTP to a University of North Carolina computer that brings up a listing of a variety of Chinese music, including Beijing opera, cultural revolution, folk, historical, and modern music. When you jump down to subdirectories, you can download musical files for playback, many of which exceed two megabytes.

Songs of Abayudaya Jews
URL address: **http://www.intac.com/PubService/uganda/music.html**

The Abayudaya music you can listen to was recorded by Kohavim Tikvah, a youth singing group of the Abayudaya congregation. Every week Kohavim Tikvah comes together to sing for the community. Much of the music played by the Abayudaya are versions of American-Jewish songs. The Lecha Dodi and Sh'ma are sung in original Abayudaya tunes, written by Gershom Douglas King, a Jewish man from Britain who visited the community. The audio files are between one and two megabytes.

Rock, Pop, and Alternative

Burnett
URL address:
http://www.cecer.army.mil/~burnett/MDB/musicResources.html

Are you a fan of a musical group? Well, this home page offers links to other Web servers and documents for numerous artists, both older, like the Beatles, and newer, like Alice In Chains.

Communications Research Group
URL address: **http://www.crg.cs.nott.ac.uk**

This server focuses on the music scene in the United Kingdom. It is sponsored by the Department of Computer Science at the University of Nottingham.

Jazz Butcher Conspiracy
URL address: **http://purgatory.ecn.purdue.edu:20002/JBC/jbc.html**

Fig. 6.13
With everything from reviews of releases to info on mailing lists and bootleg recordings, this is a fun WWW music group home page—you'll enjoy the little smoking penguins.

This is hypermedia presentation of information about the Jazz Butcher, an English pop group. Included at this site are albums, lyrics, photos, audio clips, and t-shirt information.

N-FUSION Records
URL address: **http://www.service.com/n-fusion/home.html**

N-FUSION Records was formed by DJ Digit and DJ EFX in conjunction with City Hall Records in San Francisco, California. Their first release was Studio X with Los Kings Del Mambo. The home page has short (30 second) audio clips from a number of recent releases.

On-line Digitized Music
URL address: **http://ftp.luth.se/pub/sounds/songs**

This is the Web site for the San Diego State University sound archives. From Abba to ZZ Top, this server offers a comprehensive index of songs, many with audio sound clips.

Quality In Sound Consortium
URL address:
http://purgatory.ecn.purdue.edu:20002/JBC/quality.html

The Quality In Sound Consortium maintains this site for the British pop group The Jazz Butcher Conspiracy, the Czechoslovakian experimental techno group The Black Eg, and the American group Vergiftung. There are links to photographs, discographies, discussion, and audio.

Underground Music Archive
URL address: **http://sunsite.unc.edu/ianc/index.html**

Information about new, underground bands such as Bedazzled— gothic, epic music from Rob Wyatt and Steve Willet's recording label—and TeenBeat. One group, Quagmire, presents, in it's entirety, a full length music CD available on the World Wide Web—FOR FREE. Don't ask about download time.

Web Wide World of Music
URL address: **http://www.galcit.caltech.edu~ta/music/index.html**

This site may be a tongue twister to pronounce but it is definitely worth a visit for fans of modern music and rock-and-roll. You may want to start with a jump to The Ultimate Band List, a page that contains 746 links to more than 170 bands (wow). There is also band trivia and a forum for interactive discussion of music.

Resources for Musicians

Banjo Tablature Archive

URL address:

http://www.vuw.ac.nz/who/Nathan.Torkington/banjo/tab/home.html

This home page provides you with both original and transcribed tablature for a five-string banjo. The styles range from bluegrass to classical. You may also want to try the Guitar and Bass Tablature at **ftp://ftp.nevada.edu/pub.**

Bottom Line Archive

URL address: **http://syy.oulu.fi/tbl.html**

In this magazine for acoustic and electric bass players, you can jump to compact disc reviews, descriptions of equipment, comments from bass players, and even some GIF pictures.

Drums and Percussion Page

URL address: **http://www.cse.ogi.edu/Drum**

Did you know that a "quinta" is the smallest of the conga drums? If you like any form of percussion, this is a great WWW resource. The home page offers a link to an encyclopedia of percussion, a list of Frequently Asked Questions, a list of percussionists, a Drum mailing list, and a Drum Equipment Suppliers list—and if you get bored a link to drummer jokes.

Guitarland

URL address: **ftp://ftp.netcom.com/pub/jcarson/guitar/gl.html**

When the home page opens with a color photograph of Jimi Hendrix, you know that you've found a resource for guitar lovers. Connections here take you to newsletters, newsgroups, acoustic and classical guitar archives, and even a section on guitar lessons, which ranges from the Basic Blues to the Major Triads.

Clubs and Radio Stations

Alberto's Nightclub

URL address: **http://sunpath.stanford.edu:3007/Albertos.html**

This server offers a taste of Alberto's nightclub in downtown Mountain View, California. You can find out about the live music and shows. Musical styles represented include: Tango, Latin Rock, Reggae, Cajun, Samba, World Beat, Brazilian, African, and Soca.

Anecdote

URL address: **http://anecdote.com**

A club in downtown Ann Arbor, Michigan, the Anecdote serves as an open forum for artists. You can see art and listen to music.

Georgia Tech's Student Radio Station

URL address:
http://www.cc.gatech.edu/gvu/people/Masters/Lisa.Moore/ wrek.html

WREK Atlanta, 91.1 FM, has a WWW home page. WREK offers diverse programming, from rock to blues to jazz. *WREKology* is WREK's quarterly program guide.

Publications

The following electronic publications offer the same variety of articles and images that you find in hard copy publications, however, because they are electronic, you will move through the publication by pointing and clicking with your mouse.

Cambridge University Science Fiction Society

URL address: **http://myrddin.chu.cam.ac.uk/cusfs/ttba**

The magazine of the Cambridge University Science Fiction Society contains fiction, reviews, poetry, and artwork.

Computer Music Journal

URL address:
file://mitpress.mit.edu:/pub/Computer-Music-Journal/CMJ.html

The Computer Music Journal Archive is provided for *Computer Music Journal* readers and the computer music community. It includes a table of contents, abstracts, and editors' notes for several volumes of *CMJ*, including the recent bibliography, discography, and taxonomy of the field, and the list of network resources for music. There are also related documents such as the complete MIDI and AIFF specifications, a reference list, and the text of recent articles.

Cyberkind

URL address: **http://sunsite.unc.edu/shannon/ckind/title.html**

This is a WWW magazine of Net-related fiction, nonfiction, poetry, and art. *Cyberkind* features prose and art submitted by the Internet population. All genres and subjects are included with the condition that there is some connection to the Internet, cyberspace, computers, or the networked world. Features range from articles on writers and the Internet, to computer-related mysteries to hyperlinked poems. There is also a variety of graphic art. Send submissions or queries to **shannon@sunsite.unc.edu**.

Depth Probe E-Zine

URL address:

http://www.lighthouse.com/~ake/DepthProbe/index/home.html

Depth Probe E-Zine is an esoteric collection of movie, book, and modern culture reviews—some interesting, some amusing, and some ridiculous. Check it out.

Quanta

URL address: **http://nearnet.gnn.com/wic/scifi.03.html**

The electronic magazine *Quanta* contains a variety of amateur fiction.

Webster's Weekly

URL address: **http://www.awa.com/w2**

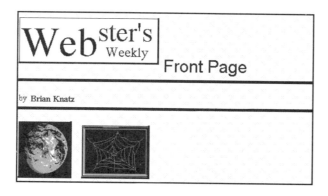

Fig. 6.14
Webster's Weekly is an on-line magazine with articles and images about the arts.

Webster's Weekly—a weekly WWW features magazine on the Web—offers columns on music and movies, politics, psychology, mad rantings, and dangerous toys. The magazine also distributes photographs, poems, cartoons, and a response column.

Mother Jones Magazine

URL address: **http://www.mojones.com/motherjones.html**

This contains on-line current and back issues of *Mother Jones* magazine, and includes an assortment of links to shareware, interactive kiosks, music reviews, and the kitchen sink.

Secular Web
URL address: **http://freethought.tamu.edu**

This includes secular issues including atheism, agnosticism, humanism, and skepticism. The site also offers an archive of free-thought literature called The Freethought Web.

Television and Radio

BBC
URL address: **http://www.bbcnc.org.uk/bbctv/sched.html**

This nine-day schedule for BBC TV and radio programs is categorized into areas such as children's shows, sports, etc. You also can get a daily listing of all TV shows in chronological order.

Big Time Television
URL address: **http://daneel.acns.nwu.edu:8082**

As the home page declares, "Between the Networks and the Web's Edge" this WWW server has lots of interesting information. Areas include The H.P. Lovecraft Image Gallery; Poeticus, the literature page; the Walking Man Project; and the World's Most Dangerous Writing Game.

Doctor Who
URL address: **http://www.phlab.missouri.edu/c621052_www/Dr.Who/**

The archive of Dr. Who programs is maintained at a university in Missouri.

Mystery Science Theatre 3000
URL address:
http://alfred1.u.washington.edu:8080/~roland/mst3k/mst3k.html

If you like Mystery Science Theater, you will love this home page! It contains very complete information on all episodes.

The Prisoner
URL address:
http://itdsrv1.ul.ie/Entertainment/Prisoner/the-prisoner.html

A classic television program from the BBC.

Satellite TV Page

URL address: **http://itre.uncecs.edu/misc/sat.html**

This Web server is a database for information relating to the hobby of satellite television and radio, also known as TVRO. Lists and charts are compiled by Robert Smathers. You can find out about the programs and schedules for satellites that carry radio and TV programs, including specific transponders.

Star Trek—British Starfleet Confederacy and Others

URL address: **http://deeptht.armory.com/~bsc**

The British Starfleet Confederacy is a non-profit organization run by the fans of *Star Trek* for the fans of *Star Trek*. There's information about the British Starfleet Confederacy, The Tardis FTP archive, Star Trek information, Science Fiction Resource Guide, and UK Science Fiction Fandom Archives. Other Star Trek home pages include Brigitte Jellinek's Star Trek resource guide (**http://www.cosy.sbg.ac.at/rec/startrek/index.html**) and the Star Trek Creative Directory (**http://depot.cis.ksu.edu/trek.html**).

Chapter 7

Business on the Web

Business is booming on the Internet and the WWW. One clear sign that the world of business considers this global network to be a useful mechanism for commerce is that businessmen and women now include an Internet address on their business cards. And, if that isn't good enough, DHM Information Management of Redondo Beach, California, will imprint your Internet address on a license plate frame to enable other drivers to find your electronic mailbox.

Thousands of companies now race to get information about their products and services transformed into hypermedia documents that potential customers around the world can access via the WWW. Some of these companies operate their own Web servers, while others contract with a service provider to maintain the information. Generally, companies that put information onto the WWW focus on informational documents more than blatant advertising.

Computer and telecommunications companies have a large presence on the Web. This should not be too surprising when you consider the fact that these companies play a significant role in the development of software, hardware, and infrastructure components that make the Web a reality. Increasingly, however, information, products, and services reach a broad business audience. Web servers at Harvard University, The Kellogg School, and Wharton School of Business provide resources on business education. Other Web resources include home pages in foreign countries that have links to detailed tips and information about doing business with companies in those countries. Some Web servers have up-to-the-minute stock price information, and other servers provide information for entrepreneurs and people who work at home. In other words, whether you own a small, one-person firm or a multinational company, there are resources available on the Web that can help you expand and improve your business.

CommerceNet

URL address: **http://www.commerce.net**

Fig. 7.1
The CommerceNet
home page.
Additional
information can
be accessed by
clicking inside one
of the boxes.

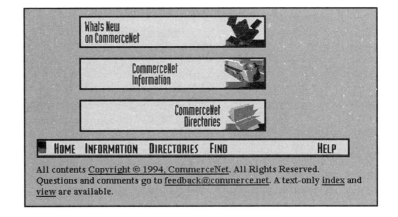

From marketing and selling products to transmitting electronic orders and payments, Silicon Valley-based CommerceNet focuses on the business applications of the WWW. Many of the world's largest companies, including Intel, Apple, Lockheed, Bank of America, and Dun & Bradstreet, have joined the initial phase of CommerceNet to create a virtual storefront. Any size business, from one person to multinational, can join CommerceNet to promote its products and services. From the CommerceNet home page you can jump to a directory of all the companies involved with CommerceNet. If these companies operate Web servers, you can jump directly to them. When Commerce-Net is complete, you will be able to get detailed product information, do on-line price comparisons, and conduct financial transactions electronically.

Half the initial funding for CommerceNet comes from a Federal grant made under the government's "Technology Reinvestment Program" (TRP), which is sponsored by the Defense Department's Advanced Research Projects Agency (ARPA), the National Institute of Standards and Technology (NIST), the National Science Foundation (NSF), and other government agencies. Matching funds come from the State of California and participating companies.

CommerceNet's goal is to make public computer networks such as the Internet "industrial strength" for business use. CommerceNet will address issues including low-cost, high-speed Internet access using newly deployed technology such as Integrated Services Digital Network (ISDN) services and multimedia software. CommerceNet will support a range of commercial network applications such as on-line catalogs, product data exchange, and engineering collaboration. It will also offer outreach services such as technical assistance to small- and medium-size businesses that want to access public networks. CommerceNet is currently testing a system that uses public key cryptography and a version of Mosaic known as Secure Mosaic (**http://south.ncsa.uiuc.edu/security.html**) to ensure the security of financial transactions over the vast Internet. Initially, CommerceNet will serve the needs of businesses and customers in California, but service is expected to extend around the world in less than two years.

The CommerceNet consortium is sponsored by Smart Valley, Inc., a nonprofit organization chartered to create a regional electronic community, and the State of California's Trade and Commerce Agency. Enterprise Integration Technologies, a company that specializes in electronic commerce, is leading the effort. If you want to become an on-line vendor on CommerceNet, you can either place informational pages on-line at the CommerceNet server, or set up a private WWW server and connect it to the CommerceNet. Subscribers who pay an annual fee receive training and are listed in CommerceNet's vendor directory—a logo or listing connects to your server. Sponsors who pay a larger annual fee receive advanced training classes and the opportunity to participate in the governance of the network.

(For more information on CommerceNet, send e-mail to **info@commerce.net**.)

Hong Kong WWW Server

URL address: **http://www.hk.super.net/~rlowe/bizhk/bhhome.html**

Fig. 7.2
On this home page, use the scroll bar to view additional information about doing business in Hong Kong.

This server offers a wealth of information about doing business with Hong Kong, which, as many business people know, is a leading manufacturing and financial center and a gateway to doing business with China. A link to BizHK provides a trade contacts service. This home page matches Hong Kong businesses with potential trading partners worldwide. More information is available by sending e-mail to **rlowe@hk.super.net**.

Via this server, you can access a database of more than 1,000 companies in Hong Kong. You can click alphabetically through the database and find company contacts, financial data, product information, addresses, and phone numbers. Special sections focus on two major areas for business opportunities: the Hotel, Tourism, and Travel industry, and Textiles, Fabrics, and Clothing. The home page also has links to economic statistics that relate to Hong Kong and press releases about business trade, such as an overview of the imports and exports between Hong Kong and the United Kingdom.

The World Bank

URL address: **http://www.worldbank.org**

Fig. 7.3
The World Bank
home page.

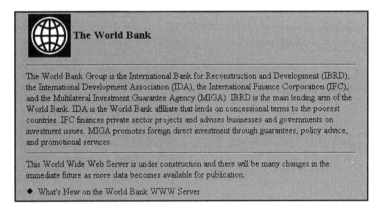

If you need to find out what is going on in international finance or trends in the economies of specific countries, this is the Web server for you! The World Bank Group consists of

- the International Bank for Reconstruction and Development (IBRD), which is the primary lending arm of the World Bank

- the International Development Association (IDA), the World Bank affiliate that lends funds on concessional terms to poor countries

- the International Finance Corporation (IFC), which finances private-sector projects and advises businesses and governments on investment issues, and

- the Multilateral Investment Guarantee Agency (MIGA), which promotes foreign direct investment through guarantees, policy advice, and promotional services.

You can jump from the home page to two areas that contain a wealth of information on the financial status, economic development projects, and social and environmental conditions in countries around the world. Some of the available information is found in books, articles, and documents (many of which are for sale) in the World Bank Publications section. A second area, the World Bank Public Information Center (PIC), maintains a variety of economic reports and environmental data sheets. You can view these reports on-line or download and print one copy. The World Bank maintains copyright on all information. Here are a few examples:

- Privatization and adjustment—Bangladesh

- Public finance reforms in the transition—Bulgaria

- Policies for private sector development—Caribbean countries

- Environment and development: challenges for the future—Indonesia

- Nutrition and national development: issues and options—Morocco

- Social protection during transition and beyond—Russia

ElNet Galaxy

URL address: **http://galaxy.einet.net/galaxy.html**

This is a guide to world-wide information and services. It includes public as well as commercial information and services provided by ElNet customers and affiliates.

The site provides an overview of the latest release of WinWeb, a World Wide Web browser for Microsoft Windows, along with downloading instructions. Similar information is provided for MacWeb, a web browser for Macintosh computers.

EINet Galaxy's most exciting feature from an information-access point of view is its generous collection of links to home pages on a variety of topics. Figure 7.4 shows only a partial listing.

Fig. 7.4

A peek at some of the many sites you can access via EINet Galaxy's home page.

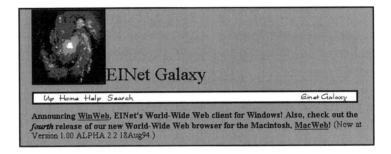

The Business General Resources link takes you to a range of business-related sites, including the Koblas Currency Converter, a comparative chart of currency values that is updated each week.

Apple Computer Home Page

URL address: **http://www.apple.com/**

This server provides links to information about Apple computers, Apple customer support services, the Apple Library of Tomorrow, Code Snippets, Apple-oriented Resources, Internet resources for the Macintosh, a variety of media resources, and much more.

Besides being a comprehensive resource for information about using Apple computers, the site presents the latest business statistics about Apple the corporation. An interesting link takes you to a server at MIT (URL address **http://www.ai.mit.edu/stocks/graph?AAPL**), where you can check out stock market performances on a variety of companies, including Apple. Figure 7.5 shows a sample graph of Apple's ups and downs, as accessed through this link.

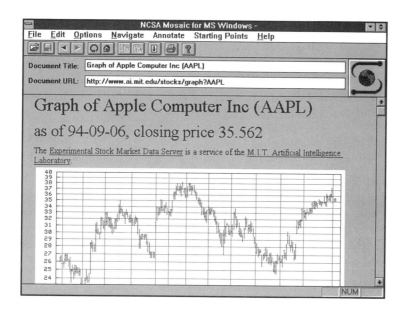

Fig. 7.5
The savvy businessperson needs up-to-date information about a company's earning potential. Now it's available on the Web.

Novell Inc. World Wide Web Homepage

URL address: **http://www.novell.com**

Fig. 7.6
Novell's novel home page, which uses a bookshelf metaphor to point to different categories of information.

Novell's home page makes good use of the WWW's graphic capability. It is just a system designed to help answer questions you have about Novell or its products. But the categories, which include technical support databases, searchable FTP and Gopher archives, an on-line product buyer's guide, and linkage to the Novell European Support Center, are represented by a row of books resting on a bookshelf.

The book metaphor doesn't carry through smoothly to all the links at the site. In fact, most of the links are to plain text files or Gopher servers. But the page demonstrates how navigation of Internet hypertext files can be facilitated when familiar metaphors and motifs are used.

Canadian Airlines International Ltd.

URL address: **http://www.CdnAir.CA**

Fig. 7.7
Query flight times, pricing databases, and more at this home page.

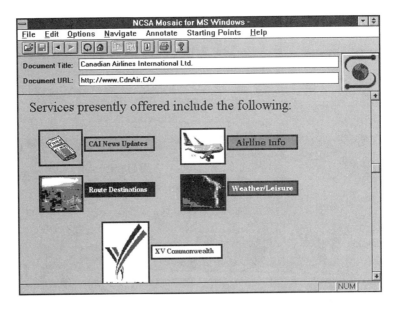

This home page provides service and information about "Canada's premier customer-driven airline." Buttons point to the services presently offered via the home page. These include the ability to query flight arrival and departure databases and to obtain pricing information. News updates as well as weather and leisure information for the traveler are also provided. As shown in the figure, the site also includes clickable route maps of the airline's service areas. Although this site is as yet incomplete, it has the potential to be a very useful and user-friendly information repository.

Business Development and Business Resources

American Business Women's Association
URL address: **http://freenet3.scri.fsu.edu:81/ht-free/abwa.html**

Provides a menu about the association. Items include the mission of the ABWA; officers and contact people; meeting information; and minutes of meetings and club events.

Auction Directory & News
URL address: **http://www.service.com/auction/**

This is the Web site for a magazine that bills itself as a national source of information for thousands of government and major private auctions. The site includes an index to the magazine's announcements of auctions across the U.S.

Translation Service
URL address: **http://www.trib.com/service/braille.html**

Provides contact information for this company in Caspar, Wyoming, that translates text into English Grade II Braille. This is a helpful service for companies wishing to meet the requirements of the Americans with Disabilities Act.

Business Schools
URL address: **http://riskweb.bus.utexas.edu/bschool.html**

This home page provides links to Harvard University, The Kellogg School, Wharton School, and other prestigious business school WWW servers. You find detailed information about business programs and get access to campus-wide on-line phone books and library databases.

Distributed Electronic Telecommunications Archive (DELTA)
URL address: **http://gozer.idbsu.edu/business/nethome.html**

This project is intended to demonstrate how telecommunications and data communications education can be facilitated by sharing teaching and learning materials over the Internet.

GE Corporate Research and Development CE-Toolkit Homepage
URL address: **http://ce-toolkit.crd.ge.com/**

The Concurrent Engineering Toolkit (CE-Toolkit) provides a broad and well-organized collection of resources for implementing manufacturing networks. This site has links to information about services, software, papers, and some related items that are available to you on the WWW.

IBC: Internet Business Center
URL address: **http://tig.com/IBC/index.html**

The Internet Business Center is a WWW server for information specifically related to business use of the Internet.

Fig. 7.8
Learn about business use of the Internet at this page.

Internet Multicasting Service
URL address: **http://www.town.hall.org/**

The Internet Multicasting Service is an NSF- and corporate-funded program that compiles unusual, interesting, and important data. Although the data at this site is ostensibly intended for business use, individuals will find it interesting and useful, too.

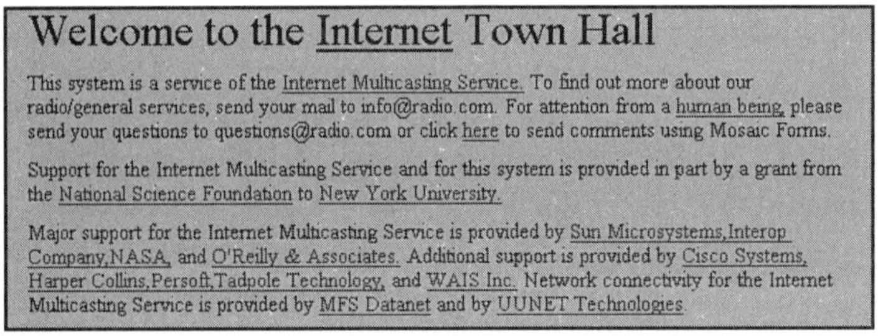

Fig. 7.9
The Internet Multicasting Service home page.

Master-McNeil, Inc.

URL address: **http://www.naming.com/naming.html**

Provides product and corporate naming services to companies worldwide. One section is devoted to information on trademarks, including the full list of international trademark classes and digitized copies of the USPTO trademark application forms.

SURAnet NIC Home Page

URL address: **http://www.sura.net/index.html**

SURAnet is the networking arm of the Southeastern Universities Research Association, Inc., a nonprofit research consortium that serves organizations throughout the Southeast U.S., the Caribbean Basin, and South America. It provides Internet access, and promotes sharing of networked information and computing resources. This Web page briefly describes SURAnet's Network Information Center services.

Technology Board of Trade

URL address: **http://www.tech-board.com/tbot/home.html**

The Technology Board of Trade is a trading place for companies that seek or provide reusable software technology. The Web site has information that will help you and your company define and place a value on intellectual property. There is a link to "Hot Technology," which is recent or cutting-edge software. There are other links that describe technology that is available for licensing as well as tips on how to license technology.

The College of Business Administration

URL address: **http://www.unomaha.edu/docs/business.html**

Located at the University of Nebraska, Omaha, this server provides text-oriented information on the College of Business Administration, which is rated in the top 20 percent of the business schools in the nation.

U.S. Department of Commerce Information Services via World Wide Web

URL address: **http://www.doc.gov/**

This server provides general information on the activities and missions of the Department, contacts and resources within the Department, and links to various department-wide and federal government-wide information services. It also provides links to the Bureau of the Census, National Telecommunications Information Administration (NTIA), National Institute for Standards and Technology (NIST), National Oceanic and Atmospheric Administration (NOAA), and the Patent and Trademark Office (PTO).

Fig. 7.10
From the Department of Commerce page, you can access more government information than you imagined possible.

Welcome to the U.S. Department of Commerce

The official seal of the U.S. Department of Commerce; Secretary Ronald H. Brown; and the main entrance of the Herbert C. Hoover Building in Washington, D.C., headquarters of the U.S. Department of Commerce.

Established on February 14, 1903, to promote American businesses and trade, the U.S. Department of Commerce is the most versatile agency in government. Its broad range of

UniForum WWW Server Home Page
URL address: **http://www.uniforum.org/**

UniForum is a professional consortium, the goal of which is to help individuals and organizations use open systems effectively. The Web site provides a membership roster, conference and seminar schedules, publications and product catalogs, and other information.

United States Patent and Trademark Office (USPTO)
URL address: **http://www.uspto.gov/**

This site includes information about the USPTO's Working Group on Intellectual Property Rights, and provides access to its draft report on the intellectual property implications of the National Information Infrastructure, or Information Superhighway. The server also provides a link to the complete transcripts, prepared remarks, and e-mail comments from the Patent Office's public hearings on software patent protection and lists job openings.

Utah Wired
URL address: **http://www.comnet.com/**

This server provides information about living and doing business in Utah. A new feature, CONNECTions, is an on-line version of the newspaper in Utah that provides information about the computer and information industry within the state. The server also features an "Interesting Link of the Week," which is someone's favorite WWW find.

Companies: Computers and Telecommunications

AT&T Bell Laboratories Research
URL address: **http://www.research.att.com**

Learn how to obtain videotapes of "Live from AT&T Bell Labs" broadcasts and how to access AT&T FTP sites. The site also lists conferences and calls for papers, as well as information or papers on topics such as anonymous credit cards, document marking, multimedia, and the Clipper Chip.

Bellcore Home Page
URL address: **http://www.bellcore.com/**

Bellcore is the communication research arm of Bell. The Web page, which is experimental, provides information about Bellcore products, telecommunications information, and the following information:

- Bellcore's catalog of information products. To access the catalog, login with the userid cat10

- Bellcore TEC Training Catalog

- National ISDN Information

- Bellcore Digest of Technical Information

- MIME (Multipurpose Internet Mail Extensions)—an FTP repository of MIME information

- Telecommunications Industry Forum Information Products Interchange Committee (TCIF/IPI) and S/key authentication system

Berkeley Software Design: Home Page
URL address: **http://www.bsdi.com/**

This server provides information about new features, questions and answers, technical features, and a support summary. The company designs, develops, markets, and supports the BSD/386 operating system.

Bristol Technology
URL address: **http://bristol.com**

Bristol is a developer of graphical user interface development tools. On their Web page, you'll find copies of the company newsletter, pointers to downloadable product demos, a bibliography of published articles about the company, and more. The "What's New" link shares new product information and even personal news about company employees—such as a birth announcement complete with photograph of the new baby.

California Software Incorporated
URL address: **http://www.calsoft.com:80/**

In addition to CalSoft corporate and product information, this server provides links to InterAp Product Information. In describing the company, the page announces, "InterAp is a Microsoft Windows-based suite of Internet applications which clarify for businesses how to approach using the Internet."

Carnation Software
URL address: **file://ftp.netcom.com/pub/carnation/HT.Carn.Home.html**

Carnation Software specializes in connecting Macs to host computers that are running relational databases. The server provides company, product, and ordering information.

Cellular One Home Page
URL address: **http://www.elpress.com:80/cellone/cellone.html**

This server provides links to information about Cellular One's line of cellular telephones, as well as about services, coverage areas, and rate plans and billing.

Commodore Amiga Information Resources
URL address:
http://www.cs.cmu.edu:8001/Web/People/mjw/Computer/Amiga/MainPage.html

Amiga users will appreciate this comprehensive server, which provides information topics such as What's New on This Site, Magazines, Newsletters, Rumors, Hardware, Software, Projects, and User Support. There is a link to A Gallery of Amiga Art, where you'll find Shoemaker-Levy Comet animations, and you'll also appreciate reviews of the Amiga Software/Hardware Archives.

Cygnus Technology Ltd.
URL address: **http://www.cygnus.nb.ca/cygnus/cygnus.html**

Cygnus Technology Ltd. provides a control system used for applications requiring remote intelligence and control. This server supplies information about their products and services, and links to a general telecommunication technology information site sponsored by the same company.

Digital
URL address: **http://www.digital.com/**

This is a suite of servers providing corporate and product information on Digital Equipment Corporation, as well as information on several professional organizations, the Grace Hopper Women In Computing Conference, a gallery of 32 cloud photographs, and more.

Farallon WWW Server
URL address: **http://www.farallon.com/**

Farallon makes networking products that attach personal computers to AppleTalk, TCP/IP, and 10BASE-T networks. This Web site provides information about Farallon's products and services, including Replica, an application for creating and viewing multi-platform on-line documents.

Hitachi, Ltd.
URL address: **http://www.hitachi.co.jp**

Fig. 7.11
The Hitachi home page.

Lots of visuals and graphics here. Topics include labs, products, divisions, what's new, headquarters, and special information. They are also very polite, with an introductory statement that says, "We would appreciate you sparing your time to visit our booth."

HP Business World

URL address: **http://www.wsg.hp.com/wsg/Business/business.html**

The home page says, "This part of the Web provides information and contacts for doing business with HP." Links are to HP dealers and HP sales offices locally and nationally.

IBM

URL address: **http://www.ibm.com/**

This home page looks like a magazine cover, with attractive use of graphics and text. Links are provided to the following IBM departments: Industry Solutions, Products and Services, and Technology.

Fig. 7.12
IBM's home page makes slick use of graphics.

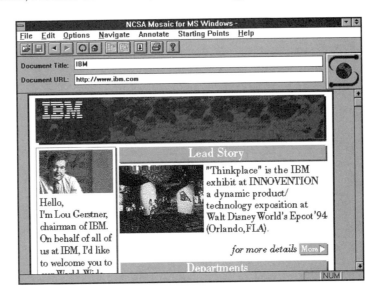

InfoSeek

URL address: **http://www.infoseek.com**

According to its home page, the company's mission is "to deliver products that make it possible for computer users to quickly find information anywhere in the world." You can learn how to get an InfoSeek account, so that you can take advantage of this timely service.

Intel Corporation

URL address: **http://www.intel.com**

This is the Web server for the company that manufactures microprocessors for the vast majority of IBM-compatible PCs. In addition to Intel corporate and product information, you'll find pointers to companies that use Intel chips in their products, to an assortment of other commercial enterprises, and to Web documentation.

Logic-Users Mosaic Page
URL address: **http://web.city.ac.uk:80/~cb170/notator.page.html**

The server, located in the United Kingdom, provides information for users and future users of Emagic software, with an emphasis on Logic (formerly called Notator Logic), but also including Notator SL, SoundSurfer/ SoundDiver, and Logic Audio.

Microsoft
URL address: **http://www.microsoft.com**

The WWW server for the world's largest computer software company includes the usual corporate and product information, public information about research, and job openings.

Micro Star
URL address: **http://www.awa.com/bh/microstar/msclub.html**

Micro Star now offers its Software Club all over the world via the WWW. The Micro Star Software Club, for which a membership fee is charged, allows individuals to receive new, tested, certified virus-free shareware in a variety of categories direct from Micro Star.

NCD Home Page
URL address: **http://www.ncd.com/**

Network Computing Devices, Inc.'s home page offers information about all NCD products, including the three major product lines, NCD X terminals, NCD PC-Xware, and Z-Mail Enterprise-wide Electronic Mail. NCD's sales office locations, white papers, technical support bulletins, new product announcements, press releases, and corporate information are also available on the server.

Pacific Bell Home Page
URL address: **http://www.pacbell.com**

This server explains CalREN, "a $25 million program to stimulate the development of new applications for high-speed data communications services" that "will establish a foundation for broadband services including telemedicine research, diagnosis, and treatment and on-line schools and business partnerships." Other information, including a link to the Pacific Bell Gopher system, is also available.

Quadralay Home Page
URL address: **http://www.quadralay.com/home.html**

The Quadralay Corporation is a designer of a commercialized version of Mosaic. This server provides product and company information and a link to the Quadralay FTP Server. In addition, a link called Austin City Limits makes available "everything you ever wanted to know (and more) about Austin, Texas," and, just for fun, a lighthearted but factual collection of coffee-related information is stored under the heading Caffeine Archive. There's also more, both serious (C++ Forum) and fun (Dilbert). Pay this site a visit.

Fig. 7.13

The Quadralay home page.

Racal-Datacom Corporate Headquarters
URL address: **http://www.racal.com/racal.html**

This home page offers Racal-Datacom product information and announcements, some WWW Data Communications and Networking links and files, and Internet Navigation links.

Robelle WWW Home Page
URL address: **http://www.robelle.com:80/**

Robelle Consulting develops and supports software tools for Hewlett-Packard minicomputers and workstations. Corporate and product information can be found here, as well as Robell and Union Software FTP archives.

RSA Data Security, Inc.'s Home Page
URL address: **http://www.rsa.com/**

RSA is a recognized world leader in cryptography, with millions of copies of its software encryption and authentication installed and in use worldwide. The company's server, characterized at press time as "under development," lists product information, news bulletins, and technical documents, among other topics.

Silicon Graphics' SILICON SURF Home Page
URL address: **http://www.sgi.com/**

This server makes very good use of graphics, as evident in the illustration. You select one of the following:

- Headlines (press release and amp product announcements)

- Surf Shop (catalog of products)

- The Classroom (education)

- Techno Corner (technical information)

- Free Lunch (free software and graphics)

- SGI Investor (info on SGI stock)

- What's New! (what's new in Silicon Surf)

The server also has a unique feature: a counter that tallies the number of people who have accessed the page.

Sony Computer Science Laboratory
URL address: **http://www.csl.sony.co.jp**

The Sony Computer Science Laboratory conducts research relating to computer science and aims toward achieving breakthroughs in computer development. The Web page describes the lab's research environment, its members and their interests, and some of the lab's projects, and has links to other, more general WWW sites.

Sun Microsystems Home Page
URL address: **http://www.sun.com/**

This server makes good use of graphics to provide information about products and services from Sun Microsystems, including current and in-press books, research reports, and other public information.

Sunergy Home Page
URL address: **http://www.sun.com/sunergy/**

The Sunergy program offers satellite television broadcasts, newsletters, and white papers designed to educate members of the computer industry worldwide. The site includes broadcast summaries, the text of printed documents, and transcripts of educational materials originally presented in a variety of electronic media.

T3plus Networking Inc.
URL address: **http://www.t3plus.com**

T3plus Networking supplies T3 and SONET broadband wide-area networking solutions. The server provides corporate and product information, as well as examples of network applications.

Technology Board of Trade
URL address: **http://www.tech-board.com/tbot/**

The Technology Board of Trade, recently acquired by Corporate Software, Incorporated, assists businesses in defining, valuing, and exchanging intellectual property and provides for the transfer of commercial technology. The server lists corporate and product information and links to a database of software technology available for licensing as well as for technology being sought.

The Numerical Algorithms Group Ltd.
URL address: **http://www.nag.co.uk:70/**

The server, located in the United Kingdom, provides non-commercial information about NAG's mathematical and scientific software products and services. Information includes technical reports, availability, user notes, installation notes, demos, and downloadable software. The server is also the home of the Fortran 90 Software Repository.

UniPress Software, Inc.
URL address: **http:/www.unipress.com**

UniPress, a developer and distributor of UNIX software, has designed its server for users to browse their product listings, which range from PC-UNIX connectivity solutions to development tools and applications. Users can also request more information through a form provided on the server. UniPress hosts an on-line t-shirt contest, includes a "rogues' gallery" of company employee photographs, and allows you to link to individual employees' hotlists of favorite Web sites. Spend a little time poking around here. It's fun.

Xerox
URL address: **http://www.xerox.com**

Xerox is one of the companies involved in the development of CommerceNet. This home page links with information about Xerox products and services as well as a listing of Xerox activities on a month-by-month basis.

Companies—General

Automobiles

URL address:
**http://akebono.stanford.edu/yahoo/Economy/Business/
Corporations/Automobiles/Parts/**

Westex Automotive, Inc. is a company that distributes high-quality automotive parts and supplies. The site, although a little confusing to navigate, links you to classified ads and other sources for automotive parts and supplies.

Blacksburg Transit

URL address: **http://www.bev.net/BT/welcome.html**

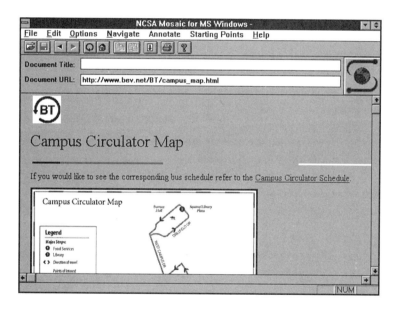

Fig. 7.14
The Blacksburg Transit home page is part of a larger, experimental networked community.

All types of information about this bus line and its schedules, route maps, fares/passes, and transfers is available. It is located in Blacksburg, Virginia, USA, home of the Blacksburg Electronic Village, an experimental networked community.

Bonneville International Corporation

URL address: **http://www.utw.com/bonneville/bonn.html**

Bonneville International provides commercial broadcast and media communications to businesses. Its home page provides corporate information and a link to the Utah Businesses home page.

Lockheed Missiles Company
URL address: **http://www.lmsc.lockheed.com**

Provides information on many of Lockheed's operations, including an artist's rendering of the Hubble Telescope, press releases describing Lockheed's technological successes, and links to other on-line services.

What is Wavefront Technologies?
URL address: **http://wavefront.wti.com/whatis.html**

Wavefront supplies 2D and 3D animation software for creating high-end animation and simulations. Product and corporate information, employees' home pages, newsgroup links, and animations are featured here.

Consulting

Blue Square Inc.
URL address: **http://kaleidoscope.bga.com:80/bs/BS_top.html**

Blue Square EDP Consulting and Marketing currently helps U.S. companies market themselves in the U.S. and Europe. The company's server links to the Global City, where you can browse through directories of products and services offered by clients of Blue Square.

Hundred Acre Consulting
URL address: **http://www.pooh.com/**

Hundred Acre Consulting, located in Nevada, does software engineering and development. Through this server, you can link to GNU on-line documentation and an FTP archive, among other services.

Dainamic Consulting
URL address: **http://www.netpart.com/dai/home.html**

Dainamic Consulting offers overall marketing strategy and management services for high-technology companies. The server provides company information and service descriptions.

Financial

Dun & Bradstreet

URL address: **http://www.corp.dnb.com**

Fig. 7.15
The Dun &
Bradstreet home
page.

A great Web server for locating financial information about companies
and industries and lots of good jumping-off links to other Web financial
resources.

Experimental Stock Market Data

URL address: **http://www.ai.mit.edu:80/stocks.html**

This page provides a link to the latest stock market information. It is updated
daily to reflect the current day's closing information. It consists of general
market news and quotes for selected stocks.

FiNWeb Home Page

URL address: **http://riskweb.bus.utexas.edu/finweb.htm**

FiNWeb bills itself as a financial economics WWW server. It offers links
to economics and finance-related WWW servers. You can locate drafts of
working papers from the National Bureau of Economic Research, jump to
stock market reports, and access thousands of federal, state, and local government WWW sites.

Myers Equity Express
URL address: **http://www.internet-is.com:80/myers/mortform.html**

This service allows you to request a loan interest rate quote via the Internet. You may request a quote for a home loan by filling in as much of the provided form as you care to, by using a point-and-click procedure as shown in the illustration. They respond with a current quote.

Fig. 7.16
Use the Myers Equity Express page to check on home loan rates.

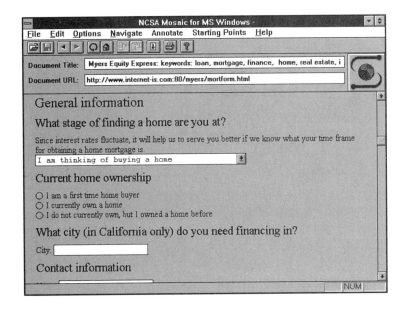

NASDAQ Financial Executive Journal
URL address: **http://www.law.cornell.edu/nasdaq/nasdtoc.html**

Financial Executive Journal is a shared project of the Legal Information Institute at Cornell Law School and The Nasdaq Stock Market. The server provides back issues of the journal for your review.

QuoteCom
URL address: **http://www.quote.com**

QuoteCom provides financial market data to Internet users, both for free and on a subscription basis, if you require more detailed data. This server provides information on the company and its services.

International

E-EUROPE
URL address: **http://freenet3.scri.fsu.edu:81/doc/eebn.doc**

Designed to help persons wanting to do business in Eastern Europe, this server is a text-only collection of files, e-mail addresses, lists of business possibilities, and agencies that can be of assistance.

Interfinance Limited
URL address: **http://intergroup.com/interfinance**

Located in the Netherlands, this company provides advisory and intermediary services in areas of investment banking, real estate, commercial and industrial project loans, and venture capital. The WWW site contains newsletters, statement of policies, and application forms.

Internet Guide to Japan Information Resources (Experimental)
URL address:

http://fuji.stanford.edu/japan_information/japan_information_guide.html

Internet X-Guide to Japan Information, Stanford University's Experimental Guide to Japan Information, represents a first cut at organizing the widely diverse information sources about Japan currently available over the Internet. Major categories of Japan information currently maintained in the X-Guide include the following: Japan Science and Technology Information; Japanese Business, Economic, and Financial Information; U.S.-Japan Relations and Policy; Working, Studying, Traveling and Living in Japan; Japanese Language Computing; Teaching Japanese and About Japan; Internship Opportunities in Japan; Japan Industry and Technology Management Training Program (JITMT) Universities; and a Program Guide.

Japan (via Nippon Telephone & Telegraph server)
URL address: **http://www.ntt.jp**

This server opens doors to a tremendous amount of information on Japanese businesses and documents that help you learn how to do business in Japan. One of the great multimedia aspects is a color map of Japan that has pointers to various companies and institutions. Just click an icon and jump to that resource.

Fig. 7.17
This page sports a clickable map to find information about various companies in Japan.

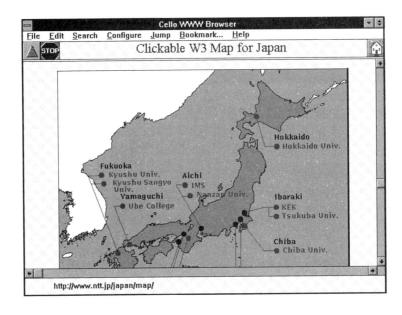

Russian and East European Studies Business and Economics Resources
URL address: **http://www.pitt.edu:80/~cjp/rsecon.html**

The Central Library of the Budapest University of Economics has produced ECONINFORM, an information system that allows you to display information in German, Hungarian, or English. The System contains a bibliographic database of economic special literature and business information, developed on the basis of UNESCO CDS Micro ISIS 2.3 with the cooperation of MTA SZTAKI KFIIR-labor. It is sponsored by the Information Infrastructure Development Programme.

Internet Services

Atlantic's Home Page
URL address: **http://www.atlantic.com/index.html**

This is a server for the Atlantic Computing Technology Corporation, which provides networking/Internet access consulting to Connecticut businesses. Corporate and service information are provided, as well as links to Internet Starting Points, information about living and doing business in Connecticut, and advertisements of Web space for rent.

Canadian Domain Information Server
URL address: **http://www.csi.nb.ca/domain/**

Cybersmith Inc.'s Canadian Domain Information Server lets you use an interactive form to conduct keyword searching to locate information on "the organizations registered in the Canadian portion of the Internet," as their home page puts it.

DataFlux Systems
URL address: **http://www.dataflux.bc.ca/home.html**

Dataflux is an Internet provider in Victoria, British Columbia, Canada. The server provides information about the company and its services. It is a new Web server, clearly still "under construction."

Electric Press, Inc.
URL address: **http://www.elpress.com/homepage.html**

Electric Press will display your information—catalogues, brochures, newsletters—in full-color multimedia format on the WWW. The server provides sample on-line catalogs, newsletters, and brochures, so you can preview the quality of their work.

Enterprise Integration Technologies
URL address: **http://www.eit.com**

Enterprise Integration Technologies is a Palo Alto-based R&D and consulting company that develops software and services to promote commercial use of the Internet. Their home page includes an overview of the company and its services, as well as descriptions of some of their projects.

Evergreen Internet Express
URL address: **http://maple.libre.com:80/evergreen.html**

This company offers Internet and private network management, information source services, and business network consulting and design to clients in Arizona, Nevada, Utah, and other western states. Their server provides company information as well as information about living and doing business in Nevada.

Fnet
URL address: **http://www.fnet.fr**

An association that provides Internet access in France and in Europe. The Web page is, of course, entirely in French, and provides company and technology information, plus pointers to research services.

InteleNet Home Page
URL address: **http://www.intelenet.com/**

This server describes the services offered by InteleNet Consulting Services. The company's areas of expertise include Internet connectivity, support, and maintenance; Network design, installation, support, and maintenance; UNIX systems administration and software development; ISDN design, installation and support, and the maintenance of ISDN-based telecommuting applications.

Internet Business Directory v.0.9 1993 Alice's Restaurant
URL address: **http://ibd.ar.com/IBD/Dolphin_Technologies_Inc.html**

This is the home page of Dolphin Technologies Inc. of Beverly Glen, California, which provides analysis, organization consulting, The Dolphin Kit NeXTSTEP library, and document management services and products. The page links to the Internet Business Directory (URL address **http://ibd.ar.com/**).

Internet Distribution Services
URL address: **http://www.service.com/**

Internet Distribution Services, Inc. provides electronic marketing, publishing, and distribution services on the Internet. You can learn about the company's products, services, and clients, and can link to some of those clients' home pages, through this server.

Kaleidoscope Communications—WWW Information Provider
URL address: **http://kaleidoscope.bga.com/**

They provide international marketing and sales opportunities through the World Wide Web/Internet, as well as news and information concerning the growth and advances in telecommunications, networking, and events of interest to the Internet community. Use the home page to submit a request for more information about the company.

MCSNet Home Page
URL address: **http://www.mcs.net/**

Contains information about Macro Computer Solutions, Inc., owners and operators of the MCSNet Internet Provider in the Chicago area. It has a provision of an automated scanner that is run nightly for subscriber home pages, which appear in the server's domain every night shortly after midnight central time. An "Interesting Places" link points readers to useful Internet resources. An on-line bookstore can also be accessed.

StrategyWeb Pre-Home Page
URL address: **http://fender.onramp.net/~atw_dhw/precom.htm**

You can browse StrategyWeb for information on developing strategic plans, regardless of your business or service area. The Web page is very much under construction, but contains interesting links to information on education, management, and cognitive psychology, among others.

Welcome to XOR Network Engineering, Inc.
URL address: **http://xor.com:80/xor/**

XOR Network Engineering provides Internet services for companies who can't afford to maintain their own Internet connection and services or who choose not to. They also coordinate training and trade show services for clients. Their home page describes these services in detail.

Science and Business

Alberta Research Council
URL address: **http://www.arc.ab.ca:80/**

The Alberta Research Council carries out applied science, engineering, and technology development for the benefit of the province of Alberta. Their home page describes the services they provide, including video and audio clips, presents company news, and links the reader to related Web sites, including the Best of the Web (URL address **http://wings.buffalo.edu/contest/**).

NREL's WWW Server
URL address: **http://www.nrel.gov/**

The National Renewable Energy Laboratory is a national laboratory of the U.S. Department of Energy. Located in Colorado, USA, NREL's server provides information about the laboratory and its research, and about renewable energy research, development, and applications. Other information includes technology transfer of renewable energy research to the private sector; accumulated energy data and resource maps; publications; and business and job opportunities.

Fig. 7.18
The NREL home page.

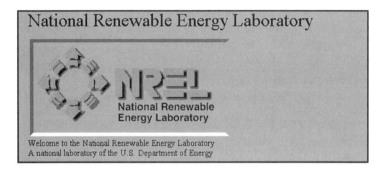

Space Systems, Inc.
URL address:
http://www.commerce.com/global/directory/spacesys.html

Space Systems, Inc., headquartered in Houston, Texas, is the world's largest manufacturer of commercial space vehicles. Corporate and product information about Space Systems, Inc. can be found by linking to the Gopher server through the company's URL, and then selecting spacesys.html from the Gopher menu.

Small Business and Individual Resources

About Home-Based Businesses
URL address: **http://freenet3.scri.fsu.edu:81/ht-free/hbb1.html**

Provides the history of working from home and information about doing it. Through the Tallahassee, Florida, FreeNet, links are provided to topics such as Information About the HBB; Membership in HBB; Meeting Information; Questions/Comments; Featured Business of the Month; The HBB Newsletter, and HBB References.

Corporate Agents, Inc.
URL address: **http://www.corporate.com**

A service to help people form their own corporations or limited liability companies (LLC) over the Internet. You can form a corporation in almost any U.S. state, country, or jurisdiction worldwide and the process takes about 10 minutes. The server also has information on the advantages of incorporation.

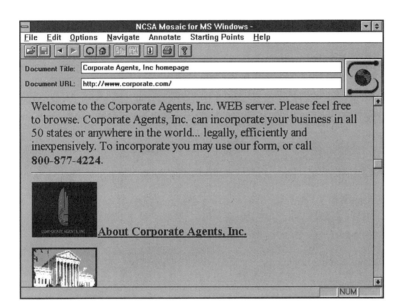

Fig. 7.19
You can incorporate your business by using a form at this server.

Entrepreneurs on the Web
URL address: **http://sashimi.wwa.com/~notime/eotw/EOTW.html**

Provided by No Time Enterprises, this is a server for entrepreneurs. It offers a variety of business information, products, and services of interest to entrepreneurs, including a FAQ document about advertising on the Internet.

Execusoft
URL address: **http://www.utw.com/execusoft/homepge.html**

Execusoft is a high-technology consulting firm that uses its Web page both to advertise its services and to recruit new consultants. The page describes job opportunities in various computer-related projects.

The Company Corporation
URL address: **http://www.service.com/tcc/home.html**

The server gives you information on how you can incorporate your business. It provides links to the company introduction, advises on why it is a good idea to incorporate, explains the four types of corporations and which one is right for you, suggests 16 reasons to incorporate in Delaware, provides basic incorporation costs for all 50 states, and explains additional services The Company Corporation provides.

Westcoast Interchange
URL address: **http://interchange.idc.uvic.ca/**

Fig. 7.20
The Westcoast Interchange home page.

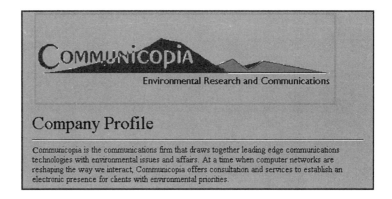

Located in Victoria, British Columbia, Canada, Westcoast Interchange is a startup Internet service business that is initiating a few small ventures. The company is receptive to proposals from others interested in partnering in business via the WWW. It currently offers a free listing service for real estate and links to Communicopia Environmental Research and Communication, an environmental communication firm.

What is the American Risk and Insurance Association (ARIA)?
URL address: **http://riskweb.bus.utexas.edu/whataria.htm**

ARIA is an association of insurance scholars and other insurance and risk management professionals. The server describes the risk management profession and answers questions about risk theory, as well as about meetings, conferences, publications, and educational opportunities available to risk management and insurance professionals.

Chapter 8

Computer Resources

With approximately 80 million computers sitting on office desktops and living-room credenzas across the United States, it is safe to declare that computers are an integral part of our lives and our society. There are almost as many applications for computers as there are vocations and hobbies. Computers help architects design houses, enable musicians to electronically compose and record songs, and allow scientists to create 3D models of DNA—the building blocks of life. It is the application of this technology to specific tasks and industries that makes computers useful to people. The listings in this section portray the diverse applications for computers, and highlight the fact that a tremendous amount of information about these applications exists on the World Wide Web.

The "Educational Resources" and "Personal Computer" sections of this chapter help you locate information and answer questions about the operation of your computer. The use of multimedia, the foundation of the World Wide Web, now stretches into many different fields; the Multimedia listings provide resources that range from software tools to WWW servers that demonstrate multimedia. If you're in the mood for some high-tech reading, visit electronic computer publications for copy that ranges from articles about the industry to science fiction stories. There are listings of organizations, companies, and educational institutions that contribute to the ongoing development of computer hardware, software, and networks—resources valuable to anyone who has an interest in advanced computer technology. The Internet and World Wide Web resource listings provide addresses of home pages that will help you learn more about the Internet and the Web—everything from technical specifications of servers to articles and Frequently Asked Question files about resources and navigational techniques. Here is a breakdown of the categories of computer resources in this chapter:

Computer hardware

Computer software

Educational resources

Graphics, 3D imaging, and virtual reality

Infrastructure and networks

International

Internet and World Wide Web resources

Multimedia

Music

Organizations and Associations

Personal computers and PC software (IBM-compatible, Macintosh)

Publications, magazines, and articles

Research—government agencies

Research—universities

Security

Supercomputing

National Center for Supercomputing Applications (NCSA)

URL address: **http://www.ncsa.uiuc.edu/demoweb/demo.html**

If you want to learn more about the Mosaic WWW browser, update your version of the software, or simply explore interesting Web links, then travel to the server at the National Center for Supercomputing Applications (NCSA)—the same organization that gave birth to Mosaic. This home page provides a fantastic demonstration of the multimedia capabilities of Mosaic and the Web. The page begins with an overview of the history of Mosaic, complete with audio messages. There is a brief explanation of hypermedia, complete with a picture of Vice President Al Gore. The home page also has more than 100 links (with short descriptions) to Web sites around the world.

You can also jump to the NCSA Mosaic home page (URL address **http://www.ncsa.uiuc.edu/SDG/Software/Mosaic/NCSAMosaicHome.html**), which has links that focus on information resources specific to Mosaic. You can find out about the latest developments and features of this browser, such as a version that will ensure security of financial transactions via the Internet.

Another useful link from the home page is to the NCSA "What's New" page (URL address **http://www.ncsa.utuc.edu/SDG/Software/Mosaic/Docs/whats-new.html**). This page offers a chronological listing of new WWW resources. The listings start with the week you connect and date back about three weeks. Each listing includes a brief description and the name of the resource is a hyperlink to that Web server. Here are two examples:

> "The office of USA Vice President, Al Gore, announces *FinanceNet*, providing access to financial management documents and information pertaining to all levels of government: foreign, Federal, state and local."

> "The World's Greatest Rock 'n Roll Band is proud to announce their very own Web Server. They are the *Rolling Stones* and they are now giving you the best place in netland for the real Stones fan to hang out."

In both instances the highlighted text (shown here in italics) represents a link. If these descriptions have piqued your interest, the FinanceNet address is **http://www.financenet.gov**, and you can find the Rolling Stones at **http://www.stones.com/**.

Apple Computers, Inc.

URL address: **http://www.apple.com**

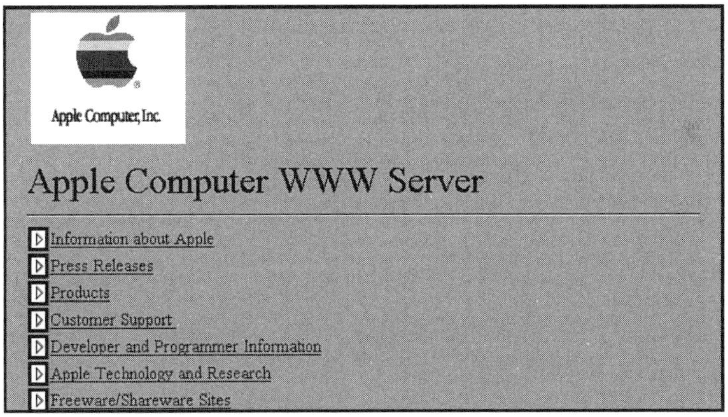

Fig. 8.1
Visit this home page if you own or use an Apple Computer product or service.

Apple Computers continue to develop unique, computer-based products and services. The Apple Newton is a hand-held personal digital assistant (PDA) that manages information and can be used to send electronic mail messages to and from remote locations; the Power PC is a high-speed computer that uses both Macintosh and IBM-compatible files and programs; and E-World is a commercial on-line service similar to CompuServe or America Online.

Perhaps you need to learn how to expand your 4MB PowerBook 150 to 8MB RAM, or you'd like to participate in a local Apple User Group. You can learn about these products and services when you connect to the Apple WWW home page. The main menu offers the following selections:

Information about Apple

Press releases

Products

Customer support

Developer and programmer information

Apple technology and research

Freeware/shareware sites

User groups

Internet resources sponsored by Apple

About 50 percent of these links open hypertext documents that contain other links and informational documents. The other half connect to Gopher menus where you navigate through easy-to-understand subdirectories to get the information you need. The Freeware/shareware sites link offers a list of non-Apple places where you can get free advice and software applications for many different Apple products. Examples include the University of Michigan (**ftp://mac.archive.umich.edu/mac/**); Washington University (**http://www.uwtc.washington.edu/JonWiederspan/MacSupportOnInternet.html**); and University of Iowa (**ftp://newton.uiowa.edu/pub/ Newton Software**).

Do It Yourself—PC Lube and Tune

URL address: **http://pclt.cis.yale.edu/pclt/default.htm**

The PC Lube and Tune (PCLT) home page represents the ultimate in electronic "self-service"—first you learn about a subject, and then you apply that knowledge to suit your needs. PCLT supplies introductions, tutorials, directions, and education on technical subjects for ordinary computer users through hypertext articles. Examples of a few of the articles include:

Introduction to PC Hardware

Introduction to SNA

Introduction to TCP/IP

PC Serial Communications

"Windows on the World" (a project to add Internet software to Windows and OS/2)

InterNIC Provides WWW On-Line Guide

URL address: **http://www.internic.net**

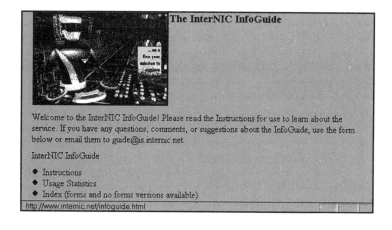

Fig. 8.2
Established by the National Science Foundation, InterNIC offers many resources for people and companies that use the Internet.

If you could only visit one WWW server for information about the Internet, this would be the place to go. The Internet Network Information Center, known simply as InterNIC, was established in January of 1993 by the National Science Foundation and went into operation on April 1, 1993. The InterNIC is a collaborative effort of three organizations that work together to offer a variety of services, which include providing information about how to access and use the Internet, assisting in locating resources, and registering network components for Internet connectivity. The goal of InterNIC is to make network-based information accessible to researchers, educators, and the general public. The term "InterNIC" comes from the cooperative effort between Network Information Centers, or NICs.

From the InterNIC home page, you can access Information Services, provided by General Atomics; Directory and Database Services, provided by AT&T; and Registration Services, provided by Network Solutions, Inc. The Information Services InfoGuide (**http://www.internic.net/infoguide.html**) is an on-line source of information about the Internet, offering pointers to on-line resources, Internet organizations, access providers, usage statistics, basic and advanced user guides, and a hypertext version of the National Science Foundation Network News. There is a simple electronic index, similar to a library card catalog system, where you select an index based on subject, title, and author, and then follow hyptertext links to specific documents, images, sounds, or video. Another source of on-line information are Scout Reports, weekly reports that keep users aware of current network activities and offer reviews of new WWW and Internet resources. The reports contain hyperlinks to the resources mentioned.

ISDN—High Speed On-Ramp to the Digital Highway

URL address: **http://www.pacbell.com/isdn/isdn_home.html**

Pacific Bell and AT&T Network Systems present information on ISDN, Integrated Services Digital Network. ISDN is a high-speed, digital telephone service delivered to businesses and homes over standard copper telephone wires. ISDN offers usage-based pricing, is easy-to-use, and provides high speed data service with voice capability. You can access inline graphics that illustrate how you can use ISDN for Internet access, telecommuting, and video conferencing. Links included in this home page include:

ISDN overview

How to order ISDN to learn more

Receive FREE ISDN e-mail updates

ISDN for Internet access

ISDN for video conferencing

ISDN for telecommuting

Pacific Bell ISDN service options and rates

ISDN-related products and services

Fig. 8.3
The Pacific Bell home page provides an overview of Integrated Services Digital Network for both beginners and advanced computer users.

Try Cutting-Edge Computer Applications at MIT

URL address: **http://tns-www.lcs.mit.edu/tns-www-home.html**

The MIT Laboratory for Computer Science is an inter-department laboratory that focuses on research in computer science and engineering. The Telemedia, Networks, and Systems Group (TNS) is a research group at the MIT Laboratory for Computer Science. The group studies topics in distributed multimedia systems—the hardware, software, and networks that enable multimedia information to travel to computers.

The TNS home page offers hyperlinks that help you navigate the world of computers and computing. For example, you can jump to the WWW Index to Multimedia Information Sources. Another interesting link is to *The National Information Infrastructure: Agenda for Action,* where you can hear a speech by Secretary Brown on the topic of The National Information Infrastructure, and view clips of the video "Toward a National Information Infrastructure."

Fig. 8.4
MIT's Telemedia, Networks, and Systems Group WWW server lets you try some of the cutting-edge applications of computer-network multimedia.

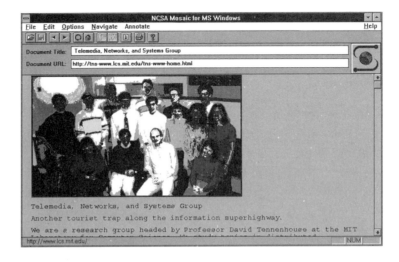

Computer Hardware

People, Services, and Projects
URL address: **file://netcom2.netcom.com/pub/iceman/VC/VC.html**

The Virtual Contractor home page brings together people who need computer services with people who provide these services. Computer contractors submit profiles for listing and review. If you need work done, you can submit requests for work. You can scroll through the current list of contracts and contractors to find ones of interest.

Network Hardware Suppliers List
URL address: **http://www.ai.mit.edu/datawave/hardware.html**

This site has a list of dealers in new and used telecommunications and computer hardware that have been favorably discussed on the Internet. Many of the hardware systems and drivers are for systems running BSDI's UNIX OS.

Telecommunications Products
URL address: **http://www.hello-direct.com/hd/**

This site has descriptions of various telecommunications products, including headsets, teleconferencing units, call controllers, and cellular accessories.

Computer Software

AppleScript at Notre Dame
URL address: **http://www.nd.edu**

The University of Notre Dame WWW server is on-line for general information and includes images, sounds, and AppleScript-based services.

Consensus Development—Collaboration Software
FTP site:

ftp://ftp.netcom.com/pub/consensus/wwwConsensusFrontDoor.html

Consensus Development provides this service, which covers software support for collaboration. This includes *groupware* (defined as software to support collaboration and intentional group processes), decision support, facilitation, electronic democracy, hypertext authoring, on-line documentation, document architecture, shared spaces, virtual organizations, and on-line knowledge management.

Cyberspace Communications Inc.—Computer Conference Software
URL address: **http://www.cyberspace.org**

From Cyberspace Communications Inc., this server contains descriptions of the purpose, ideals, bylaws, and FAQs relating to this system. Information about how to access and use the system is also present. The system provides free access to conference software (PicoSpan) and many other services to the general public.

Genome Software
URL address: **http://www-hgc.lbl.gov/GenomeHome.html**

The Human Genome Center at the Lawrence Berkeley Lab (LBL), in Berkeley, California, provides samples of computer software developed at LBL for use in various Genome studies. For more information about Genome studies, see Chapter 16, "Science Resources," later in this book.

Lumina Decisions Systems, Inc.
URL address: **http://www.lumina.com/lumina/**

Lumina Decision Systems, Inc. of Palo Alto, California, maintains a WWW server that provides information about software for modeling and decision support. Lumina's DEMOS software (Decision Modeling System) is a Macintosh-based, visual environment for creating, analyzing, and communicating probabilistic models for business, risk, and decision analysis.

VIII

Computer Resources

Macintosh Image Software

URL address: **http://bioviz.biol.trinity.edu/**

The Trinity University Biological Imaging and Visualization Lab offers its Web server for general browsing. Located here is an information server about Trinity University and the BioViz lab. There is on-line documentation about the popular Macintosh freeware Image Analysis software, NIH IMAGE, from the National Institute of Health.

Numerical Algorithms Group Ltd.

URL address: **http://www.nag.co.uk:70/**

The Numerical Algorithms Group Ltd. (NAG) WWW server provides (non-commercial) information about NAG's mathematical and scientific software products and services. Information includes technical reports, availability, user notes, installation notes, demos, and downloadable software. The server is also the home of the Fortran 90 Software Repository.

Project GeoSim

URL address: **http://geosim.cs.vt.edu/index.html**

Project GeoSim has a WWW server to distribute Geography Education software, developed by the Departments of Geography and Computer Science at Virginia Tech. The software runs on MS-DOS, Macintosh, and DECstations running X-Windows. The Gopher address **gopher://geosim.cs.vt.edu/1** is also available.

Software Development

URL address: **http://www.center.org/csd/home.html**

Do you develop software? Do need to develop or test on every type of UNIX, PC, Apple Macintosh, pen-based or wireless system, printer, or network available? The Center for Software Development can help you. The Center is a nonprofit organization that promotes the growth of software companies. It acts as a catalyst between areas of the software industry—software developers, hardware and software vendors, and service providers. This Web site has information about the Center and resources to help software developers.

UNIX Index

Gopher address: **gopher://ici.proper.com/77c/unix/.cache**

This is a searchable database of information on the Internet that relates to UNIX. There are many UNIX-related Gopher and WWW servers on the Internet that have interesting information. If you are primarily an e-mail user, there are UNIX mailing lists. Much of the current information is found in Usenet news groups. The UNIX frequently asked questions (FAQs) files, produced in the Usenet news groups, have become repositories for UNIX-related information on the Internet.

Windows (The GUI/Operating System)
URL address: **http://jwd.ping.de**

This server comes from the Windows Programmer's Group, Dortmund. It offers a collection of programming-related tools and is currently in the process of setting up a hypertext-based FAQ for Windows programmers.

Educational Resources

The following resources list general educational resources, such as on-line computer dictionaries and bibliographies of texts devoted to computers. If you have an interest in college and university programs devoted to computer science, check out the resources in Chapter 9, "Education on the WWW," which focus on educational programs in the U.S. and in foreign countries.

CERN—High Energy Physics and The World Wide Web
URL address: **http://info.cern.ch/hypertext**

Visit the home page for the European high energy physics laboratory—the organization that began the World Wide Web and continues to contribute to its development. There are some terrific WWW resources and links here—everything from on-line Web tutorials to searchable indexes of WWW servers.

Computational Science Education Project
URL address: **http://csep1.phy.ornl.gov/csep.html**

This home page provides links to a variety of educational teaching materials for undergraduate and graduate students in computational science and engineering.

Computer Dictionary
URL address: **http://wombat.doc.ic.ac.uk**

This WWW site provides a free on-line dictionary of computing terms. If you want to keep up with all the latest buzzwords, try finding them here. This is a great source of information for browsers who aren't computer experts, but who need to know the "language."

Computer-Mediated Communication
URL address: **http://www.rpi.edu/~decemj/cmc/center.html**

The Computer-Mediated Communication Studies Center serves the needs of researchers, students, teachers, and practitioners interested in computer-mediated communication (CMC)—in plain English, communication that is created and distributed via computer. This Center and Web site help people share information, make contacts, collaborate, and learn about developments and events related to CMC. The home page has links to the *CMC Magazine*, a directory of people interested in the topic (you can add your name and e-mail address), and a list of activities such as conferences and other resources.

Computer Science Bibliography
URL address: **http://www.ira.uka.de/ftp/ira/bibliography/index.html**

This Web site offers a computer science bibliography collection that contains more than 400 bibliographies and 240,000 references to journal articles, conference papers, and technical reports. Subjects include artificial intelligence, databases, neural networks, and parallel processing.

DELTA
URL address: **http://gozer.idbsu.edu/business/nethome.html**

Distributed ELectronic Telecommunications Archive (DELTA) is an archive of information related to teaching and learning about business telecommunications and data communications. This is a good site for higher level educators.

Great Computer Minds
URL address: **http://www.sun.com/sunergy/**

Sun Microsystem's Sunergy program offers satellite television broadcasts, newsletters, and white papers. Sunergy presents the views of people who work in the computer industry.

Help for UNIX Novices
URL address: **http://www.ucs.ed.ac.uk/Unixhelp/TOP_.html**

Unixhelp is an experimental WWW server with helpful information for new users of the UNIX operating system. For anyone wanting to learn the ins and outs of UNIX, this is worth browsing.

IBM Kiosk for Education
URL address: **http://ike.engr.washington.edu/ike.html">**

IKE, the IBM Kiosk for Education, is a free information service for IBM users in the higher education community. IKE offers IBM product information and news, as well as software to download and a bulletin board for exchanging ideas with colleagues.

Jargon File
URL address: **http://web.cnam.fr/bin.html**

An electronic dictionary of computer jargon—the foundation of the book *The New Hacker's Dictionary.*

National Center for Supercomputing Applications (NCSA)
URL address: **http://www.ncsa.uiuc.edu**

This is the address for the NCSA home page. NSCA has been instrumental in the development of the World Wide Web, notably for the creation of the Mosaic browser. There is a tremendous amount of information on Mosaic and the WWW at this site, and numerous links to WWW demos and other servers.

On-line Educational Technology
URL address: **http://ccat.sas.upenn.edu**

Educational Technology Services (ETS) and SAS Computing in the School of Arts & Sciences at The University of Pennsylvania maintain this server. ETS supports the instructional and research computing and technology needs of the School of Arts & Sciences. Incorporated in the server is the CCAT (Center for Computer Analysis of Texts, a sub-unit of ETS) Gopher server, which contains one of the largest on-line text archives in the world. Other areas under development are the digital language lab; an attempt to distribute audio/video materials traditionally delivered in a cassette language lab digitally over the Internet; and the digital slide library, an initiative to make slides for Art History and other courses using images available on the Internet.

ULTRALAB
URL address: **http://ultralab.anglia.ac.uk/**
This is the experimental ULTRALAB server of software and information. ULTRALAB is a learning technology research center, so the server is of particular interest to everyone in the learning/teacher training/educational software fields.

VIII

Computer Resources

Fig. 8.5
The ETS digital language lab distributes audio and video materials that were traditionally delivered in a cassette language lab digitally over the Internet.

Graphics, 3D Imaging, and Virtual Reality

Computer Graphics
URL address: **http://info.mcc.ac.uk/CGU/CGU-intro.html**

The Computer Graphics Unit (CGU) at Manchester College maintains this interesting server. Included here are CGU services, software, research, images, computer graphics, and scientific visualization information. Officially mandated and representative of the CGU.

Computer Graphics
URL address: **http://info.mcc.ac.uk/CGU/ITTI/gravigs.html**

The ITTI Gravigs project produced complete teaching packs on the use of computer graphics and scientific visualization for scientists, engineers, and medics. Some packs have been released; you can read about the pack contents, scope, and prices:

> Standards for Computer Graphics
>
> Color in Computer Graphics
>
> Visualization 1: Graphical Communication
>
> Visualization 2: Graphical Exploration

Computer Graphics at the University of Manchester
URL address: **http://info.mcc.ac.uk/CGU/CGU-intro.html**

The Computer Graphics Unit at The University of Manchester provides computer graphics and scientific visualization services. They are now serving information on the Web, including descriptions of graphical software they have developed (much of which is freely available), and graphics research they are doing (which means lots of pretty pictures and several MPEG movies).

Graphics Bibliography
URL address: **http://kirk.cgrg.ohio-state.edu/SIGBIB.html**

This is a page allowing simple keyword searches of the ACM SIGGRAPH Online Bibliography Database, a collection of over 16,000 unique computer graphics and computational geometry references.

On-line Searchable Map
URL address: **http://www.cica.indiana.edu/**

The Center for Innovative Computer Application (CICA) Web server provides information about CICA, articles and projects by CICA staff, computer graphics, visualization, sonification, high-performance computing, special computing needs, and other areas of interest to CICA. It also contains the Indiana University Bloomington Searchable Campus Map and the Graphical Bloomington Weather Report.

Virology Images and Animation
URL address: **http://www.bocklabs.wisc.edu**

The Institute for Molecular Virology at the University of Wisconsin offers their WWW server, which provides computer-generated images and animations of viruses, topographical maps, digitized electron micrographs of viruses, and tutorial information on selected topics in virology.

Virtual Reality and 3D Computing
URL address: **http://www.dataspace.com/**

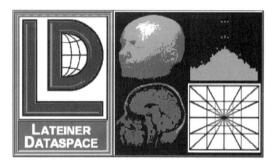

Fig. 8.6
Virtual reality is a computer-created world that enables users to experience events and environments that they can't visit in the real world, such as virtual surgery where doctors can practice surgery on patients that only exist electronically.

Lateiner Dataspace supports this server of information on high-performance 3D computation, including the ARPA proposal done in partnership with Kendall Square Research for a real-time volume rendered virtual reality with real-time physical simulation.

Virtual Reality at Argonne National Laboratory
URL address: **http://www.mcs.anl.gov/NEW/index.html**

The Mathematics and Computer Science Division at the Argonne National Laboratory presents this WWW server. It includes information on Argonne's Mathematics and Computer Science Division, which has the world's largest IBM massively parallel computer (an SP1) and is establishing a CAVE virtual reality environment.

Virtual Reality in the United Kingdom (UK)
URL address: **http://eta.lut.ac.uk/**

This server provides access to the United Kingdom (UK) Virtual Reality Special Interest Group. This application of computers is headed towards the casual user at a rapid pace. If you want to keep up with what's happening in the UK, check this out.

Infrastructure and Networks

AT&T—Computer Networks
URL address: **http://www.research.att.com/**

Fig. 8.7
This AT&T home page has a link to a bibliography of more than 11,000 documents that focus on computer networks.

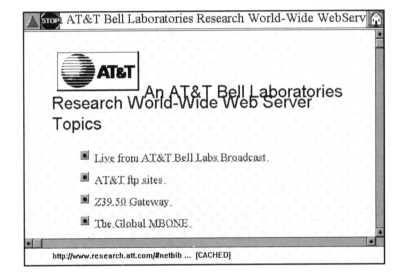

A WWW server at AT&T Bell Laboratories is available. The home page includes a link to a bibliography of about 11,000 entries covering computer networks. About one-third of these have abstracts and some entries have links to PostScript copies of the paper. Another home page link focuses on electronic publishing.

Bell Operating Companies—Modified Final Judgment
Gopher address: **gopher://bell.com**

The Modified Final Judgment (MFJ) Task Force, a committee of the several regional Bell operating companies that works on telecommunications issues in Washington, is now on the Internet via this WWW home page. The MFJ is the ruling that broke up the telephone monopoly.

California PUC

Gopher address: **gopher://brie.berkeley.edu:2234/0/Infra**

The California Public Utilities Commission (CPUC) released "Enhancing California's Competitive Strength: A Strategy for Telecommunications Infrastructure," its report to Governor Pete Wilson. This is a helpful document if you are working with your local public utilities commission to advance telecommunications in your state.

Community Networks

URL address:

http://www.cs.washington.edu/research/community-networks/

This site provides access to information gained from community computer network surveys. If you are performing your own research, this site can provide insight into the work of others. If you are in the process of justifying telecommunications in your area, this information will be very helpful.

Computers in Networks (article)

Gopher site: **gopher://gopher.psg.com**

Information about networking in the developing world, low-cost networking tools, and computer networking in general. This is an article that presents a general overview that will be of interest to anyone who is working with limited resources.

Global Networks

URL address: **http://santafe.edu/**

This site provides information from the Santa Fe Institute about complex systems, including global computer networks. The Santa Fe Institute is known for its approach to complex problems.

High Performance Computing

URL address: **http://www.hpcc.gov/**

The National Coordination Office for High Performance Computing and Communications (NCO/HPCC) server. The server contains a variety of HPCC-related information, including the FY 1994 "Blue Book" titled *High Performance Computing and Communications: Towards a National Information Infrastructure*.

National Telecommunications and Information Administration

Telnet address: **telnet://ntiabbs.ntia.doc.gov**

Information from the National Telecommunications and Information Administration (NTIA-USA). The NTIA is the group responsible for the development of the Information Superhighway in the United States.

Network Conferencing (article)
FTP site: **ftp://nic.merit.edu/documents/rfc/rfc1324.txt**

A discussion on computer network conferencing by D. Reed. Computer network conferencing is an application that some find valuable and others find frustrating. If you want to learn more about this major application of telecommunications hardware and software, check out this site.

Telecommunications and the Environment
URL address: **http://shebute.com:2000/ETT.HTML**

Environmental Technology and Telecommunications, Ltd., provides this WWW site to provide information about energy/efficiency and telecommunications. In environmentally conscious areas, the use of telecommunications can be of major benefit.

USC Network Research
URL address: **http://cwis.usc.edu/**

Fig. 8.8
High speed computer networks enable the use of multimedia applications. The information on the Web site focuses on the issues of these networks.

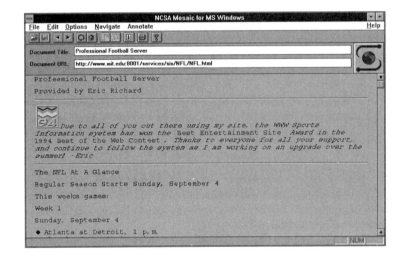

The University of Southern California's (Los Angeles) Computer Networks and Distributed Systems Research Laboratory provides information about high speed network support for multimedia traffic with real time requirements.

U.S. Department of Commerce
URL address: **http://www.doc.gov**

The United States Department of Commerce in Washington, D.C. has a WWW server that provides access to both the National Telecommunications

Information Administration (NTIA) and the National Institute for Standards and Technology (NIST). These two agencies sponsor several initiatives that impact the future of networks and computing in the U.S. You can also jump to the National Information Initiative home page.

Usenet Archives
FTP site: **ftp://lcs.mit.edu/telecom-archives**

This Web site contains Telecomm archive files about telecommunications, from the Usenet group **comp.dcom.telecom**. As with most Usenet archives, some of this information is very valuable, some of it is just fun, and some of it is junk.

International

Canada—Public Works and Government Services Canada
URL address: **http://www.Pwc-Tpc.ca/**

The Experimental Public Works and Government Services Canada (PWGSC) World Wide Web server is now on-line. This server is being developed by members of Government Telecommunications and Informatics Services (GTIS), a special operating agency of PWGSC. They plan to provide the general public and government departments with information on PWGSC services, programs, initiatives, press releases, and documents.

Canada—Victoria FreeNet Information
URL address: **http://freenet.victoria.bc.ca/vifa.html**

The Victoria FreeNet Association's Web server is open to all Internet users. You can access both hypertext/media magazines featuring Canadian titles and a FreeNets and Community Computer Networks home page. If you have an interest in FreeNets, which are essentially electronic towns for local and regional areas, see the FreeNets listings in Chapter 10, "Government Resources."

Croatia
URL address: **http://tjev.tel.etf.hr/zzt/zzt.html**

This is the first WWW link to Croatia. It is the home page of the Telecommunications Department, University of Zagreb. It provides links to currently existing Net resources in Croatia.

France
URL address: **http://arctique.int-evry.fr**

The Web home page for the Institut National des Telecommunications, France, also check out URL address **http://www.enst.fr/index.html**. Telecom Paris is part of a larger institution for graduate-level instruction in telecommunications.

France—INRIA
URL address: **http://zenon.inria.fr:8003**

INRIA is a French research institute. You can access and keyword search a library catalog database of thousands of scientific and technical research reports. The home page also has links to news and info about INRIA and its research activities and services.

Germany—Institute for Open Communikation Systems
URL address: **http://www.fokus.gmd.de/**

This Web site is sponsored by the Institute for Open Communikation Systems FOKUS, an institute of the German National Research Center for Computer Science (GMD). You can find out about research activities that deal with the Open Application and Intercommunications Model (OAI).

Greece—Parallel Processing
URL address: **http://www.hpcl.cti.gr/**

The Athens High Performance Computing Laboratory in Athens, Greece, is a nonprofit organization. The lab and the information available via this home page focus on research and development in High Performance Computing and Networking (HPCN).

Japan—Telecommunications in Japan
URL address: **http://www.crl.go.jp**

Fig. 8.9
Japan's CRL home page has links to a vast amount of technical and application-related information.

The Communications Research Laboratory (CRL) of the Ministry of Posts and Telecommunications is the only national institute responsible for the study of telecommunications technologies, radio science, and radio applications in Japan. As you would expect, Japan has expressed an extremely high degree of interest in telecommunications and this site provides the user with some insight into that country's efforts.

Switzerland—High-End Research in the Alps
URL address: **http://www.idiap.ch/**

IDIAP (Institut Dalle Molle d'Intelligence Artificielle Perceptive) is a publicly funded Swiss research institute located in the canton of Valais. They make this WWW server available to share information on their efforts. Researchers at IDIAP work on computer vision, handwriting recognition, OCR, expert systems, neural networks, optical computing, and speech recognition.

Internet and World Wide Web Resources

CERN
URL address: **http://info.cern.ch/hypertext/WWW/TheProject.html**

Need a Web primer? Researchers at CERN created the Web, and this CERN document provides an overview of the development of the system. A link that explains the background includes an "illustrated talk" complete with viewgraphs you can download and print out. Other link choices include a bibliography of reference material, technical information, WWW newsgroups, and information about getting CERN code for the Web. Another CERN home page—**http://info.cern.ch/hypertext/WWW/LineMode/ Defaults/default.html**—is a great place to get a general overview of the Web's resources. Links break WWW sites into subject categories, servers by country, and "service types," which encompass services such as X.500 mail gateways, FTP, and Telnet sessions.

Charm Net Personal IP Page
URL address: **http://www.charm.net/ppp.html**

This site has lots of information and links to resources about how to obtain connection to the Internet. There are magazine articles, Frequently Asked Questions files, comparisons of SLIP versus PPP connectivity, and, for advanced users, information on establishing an Internet/Web server.

Finding People on the Internet
URL address: **http://alpha.acast.nova.edu/phone.html**

With some 30 million users, it is no small challenge to locate a single Internet user. This home page may help. It offers resources and advice on several Internet search/address systems, including Netfind—search for a user's electronic mail address; Finger—how to identify a user from their e-mail address; Phonebooks—a means of searching organizational directories; X.500—the new standard in global mail directories; and Whois—enables you to look up details about an institution from the domain name.

Global Network Navigator Internet Help Desk
URL address: **http://gnn.interpath.net/gnn/helpdesk/index.html**

Fig. 8.10
This page is a good resource to get answers to some basic Internet questions.

This is a very easy page to navigate. You can do on-line keyword searching to find what you need. Jump to the first link, *Ask The Experts*, which is a weekly advice column hosted by different experts. An example of one Q&A format question fielded by an expert was, "Are Internet and Usenet the same? I hear these names used synonymously." Other home page choices include:

- *Internet Basics.* A variety of help documents and user's guides

- *Resource Guides.* A subject-based hypertext list of resources

- *Internet Tools.* E-mail, FTP, Telnet, Gopher, and more

- *Training.* Resources for Internet training

- *Access Providers.* A list of Internet/WWW service providers

Information on WWW
URL address: **http://www.bsdi.com/server/doc/web-info.html**

This site offers an extensive array of information links, including an overview of the WWW project and hypertext terms and starting points for Internet exploration. To help you learn about getting connected, there is a link to service providers, and for hypertext authors there are guides to the hypertext markup language (HTML) and URL information.

Matrix Information and Directory Services
URL address: **http://www.tic.com**

The resources and information at this site cover the field. There are links from the home page to Frequently Asked Questions and maps and graphs that depict the growth of the Internet and Web. Try the link labeled "About and through WWW, Gopher and Hytelnet" to get a variety of catalogs, indexes, and resources that will help you navigate through either the Web or Internet. Another home page link, "Other Interesting Stuff," brings up interesting choices such as WebWeather and mailing list archives.

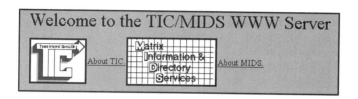

Web Information
URL address: **http://loanstar.tamu.edu/~rjsparks/www.html**

Find out what transpired at the first WWW International conference, get information on different Web browsers, or learn proper etiquette for information providers. There are also tutorials for using Mosaic and WAIS and links to WWW and Internet newsgroups and search engines.

The Best of WWW Contest
URL address: **http://wings.buffalo.edu/contest/**

Brandon Plewe, Assistant Coordinator for Campus-Wide Information Services at the State University of New York at Buffalo, oversees this WWW site, which announces the winners of the "Best of the Web" contest. There are a total of 13 categories, which include "Best Educational Service," "Best Commercial Service," "Best Navigational Aid," "Best Use of Multiple Media," and "Best Document Design." In addition to a brief description of the winners in each category, there are hyperlinks to the various sites that receive the award. There is also a brief highlight and link to honorable mentions and other nominees.

Multimedia

Academic Multimedia
URL address: **http://148.100.176.70:80/prasad.htm**

The Marist College Web site represents a forum for the presentation of the work and research of students and faculty. There is a lot of experimentation, particularly in the use of multimedia technologies—and this home page will tell you about it.

Art and Multimedia

URL address:

http://cui_www.unige.ch/Chloe/OtisCrosswire/index.html

The CROSSWIRE collaborative art collection is available courtesy Simon Gibbs at Centre Universitaire d'Informatique, University of Geneva. CROSSWIRE is a collaborative art project run by the OTIS digital net-gallery.

Artists and Multimedia

URL address: **http://kspace.com**

Kaleidospace provides a WWW site for promotion of independent artists, musicians, performers, CD-ROM authors, writers, animators, and filmmakers. Artists provide samples of their work, which Kaleidospace integrates into a multimedia document available via the Internet. Kaleidospace also provides placement for artists wanting to showcase their work to agents, directors, gallery owners, publishers, record labels, and other industry professionals.

Biological Multimedia

URL address: **http://130.17.2.215/wolf/csuwww.html**

This is a Biological Sciences WWW server for the California State University system in the Department of Biological Sciences at CSU Stanislaus. Its function is to consolidate existing WWW biological sciences teaching and research resources, and to create and distribute original multimedia materials for the teaching of biology.

Boston University Multimedia Communications Laboratory

URL address: **http://spiderman.bu.edu/**

A Web server is up at the Multimedia Communications Laboratory at Boston University. A brief description of current lab projects and some additional information is available. Abstracts of all lab publications and some movies of the lab, the park where lab staffers eat lunch, and the Charles River are on-line.

Down South Multimedia

URL address:

http://sunsite.unc.edu/doug_m/pages/south/center/center.html

The Center for the Study of the American South and SunSITE at UNC-Chapel Hill have set up the American South Internet Resource Center, a multimedia collection of resources for research and information about the South. This site is expanding quickly and welcomes any suggestions for additional links and sources.

Index to Multimedia

URL address:

http://cui_www.unige.ch/OSG/MultimediaInfo/index.html

See the index of multimedia information sources at CUI for a comprehensive overview of multimedia on the Internet. This is a large set of information that includes URL, Gopher, and FTP WWW sites, including several Frequently Asked Questions (FAQ) archives.

Instruction and Multimedia

URL address: **http://library-www.scar.utoronto.ca/**

Bladen Library at Scarborough Campus, University of Toronto, invites people to visit their WWW server, which contains locally authored material by faculty, librarians, staff, and students as well as links to other WWW servers. This server also includes a home page for The Centre for Instructional Technology Development that has information on several projects, as well as links to multimedia and instructional technology information. In addition, it provides a home page for Physical Anthropologists in Canada, with information on their activities.

Irish Multimedia

URL address: **http://www.iscm.ulst.ac.uk/**

The Interactive Systems Centre (ISC) of the University of Ulster opened its WWW server in mid-1994. The server currently contains information about the ISC and a set of links to interactive multimedia research information, which are related to the centre's research activities.

K–12 Multimedia

URL address: **http://www.nbn.com/~branson**

The Stone Soup project is an Internet multimedia cooperative for K–12 educators and students. This project is based in the Branson school, an independent high school in Ross, California.

Fig. 8.12
Appropriately named the "Stone Soup" project, this WWW site offers users images, sounds, and video produced at the Branson school in California.

Medicine and Multimedia
URL address: **http://www.nlm.nih.gov**

The National Library of Medicine offers its Web server, HyperDOC, which includes electronic access to the library's on-line database services (some of which require registered accounts), an interactive multimedia course on the history and uses of the Internet, several multimedia exhibits from the History of Medicine Division (HMD), and a cataloged image collection of nearly 60,000 images.

MIT Synergy Multimedia
URL address: **http://synergy.mit.edu/synhome.html**

The Synergy WWW server provides a variety of links to multimedia and graphics sources. It also allows access to a large collection of GIF images, and plans to include other multimedia formats in the future.

Multimedia Cancer Information
URL address: **http://cancer.med.upenn.edu/**

OncoLink provides multimedia information regarding all aspects of cancer and cancer therapy. This includes childhood and adult cancer, medical oncology, and radiation oncology. The purpose of this server, in alliance with the University of Pennsylvania Medical Center, is to promote cancer research, to educate, and to care for patients with cancer. This WWW server is officially mandated by the Radiation Oncology Department of the University of Pennsylvania Medical Center.

Multimedia Information Sources
URL address: **http://www.clr.toronto.edu:1080/clr.html**

The Centre for Landscape Research (CLR) provides general access to their WWW server. The CLR is the research arm of the Programme in Landscape Architecture at the University of Toronto. It provides a collaborative environment for the exploration of ideas related to the design, planning, and policies of the environment. Its primary focus has been on the utilization of electronic media to foster more informed decision-making. The CLR-WWW provides information about CLR software for interactive and integrating CAD, GIS, remote sensing, multimedia and virtual worlds, teaching, publications, collaborative projects, and more. This site also serves as a major connection and resource for landscape architecture related electronic resources.

Multimedia Museum

URL address: **http://www.informatik.rwth-aachen.de/Reiff2/**

The new art association "Mehrwert e.V." is on-line. Its staff has established an electronic museum, which is open for all Internet users. The Museum was developed in cooperation with the Department of History of Art, the Center of Computing, and the Department of Computer Science at Aachen, Germany.

Multimedia Newsletter (on-line)

URL address: **http://www.hal.csuhayward.edu**

Cal State Hayward's *Mosaic Network News,* a networked multimedia newsletter, includes sample animations. Also included is a tutorial on creating multimedia. This tutorial is about picking a development platform and selecting software tools for development. Other topics include The Delta Project—Distance Learning and Beyond, and Learning about Mosaic.

Multimedia Publishing—NandoNet

URL address: **http://www.nando.net/welcome.html**

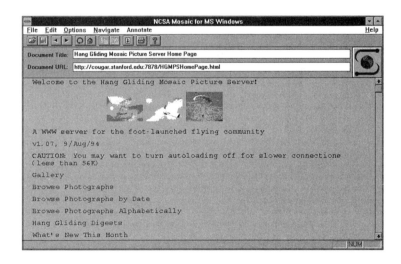

Fig. 8.13
Many of the electronic publications available via the NandoNet home page use multimedia.

The New Media Division of The News and Observer Publishing Co. maintains a World Wide Web server with a variety of publishing pieces that include *The News & Observer* (the daily newspaper for Raleigh, NC, and the Research Triangle), *The Philanthropy Journal, North Carolina Business, The Insider* (daily NC legislative updates), *Cartoons by Duane Powell*, *The North Carolina Discoveries* series (a multimedia joint effort by *The News & Observer*, WTVD [Durham, NC], and WUNC-FM [Chapel Hill, NC]), The American Dance Festival (Durham, NC) schedule and background, Unisphere (a resource for international business ventures), and NandoX (which experiments in new ways to deliver news and information).

Multimedia Tools
URL address:
http://www.cs.cmu.edu:8001/afs/cs.cmu.edu/project/atk-ftp/web/ andrew-home.html

Andrew Consortium at Carnegie Mellon University has a Web home page that focuses on Andrew, an extensible compound document system for UNIX systems running X windows. It includes a multimedia word processor, a program editor, a drawing editor, a table/spreadsheet, a font editor, and a MIME format mail/bulletin board manager. Their Web pages have more detailed descriptions of Andrew, screen snapshots, and links to an FTP archive containing the source code for their release, version 6.2.

Neuroscience Multimedia
URL address: **http://salk.edu/**

NeuroWeb, the server for the program in Neurosciences at UCSD, is open for browsing. Check out the page on the department that has information about the program, as well as faculty abstracts. Also see a fledgling "Virtual Poster Session" where actual scientific posters enter the WWW and multimedia.

Norwegian Mogul Media, Inc.
URL address: **http://www.mogul.no/**

Mogul Media offers information about multimedia, interactive television, media technology, CD-ROM publishing, and Internet services, as well as general information about the company. Information is written in Norwegian. Some articles and information are available in English.

Scripting and Prototyping for Multimedia
URL address: **http://www.cwi.nl/~guido/Python.html**

Python is an object-oriented scripting and prototyping language that some prefer over Perl, TCL, or Scheme. Python, developed in Amsterdam, is free, extensible, and runs on UNIX, DOS, and Mac. The UNIX version has optional X11 and Motif interfaces and considerable multimedia support for SGI and

Sun platforms. All documentation and sources for Python are now available on-line via the World Wide Web, as well as via FTP at FTP site **ftp:// ftp.cwi.nl/pub/python/index.html**.

U.S. Government and Multimedia
URL address: **http://info.arc.com**

Advanced Research Corporation offers a government-related home page on the WWW. Its server provides technical reports and information on the viability of NCSA Mosaic and NCSA HTTPD to meet U.S. government information dissemination requirements. The requirements include interactive documents, multimedia, database applications, and document conversion. The server is available from 1:00 to 4:00 p.m. Eastern Time (U.S.) only.

Music

Alf MIDI
URL address: **http://alf.uib.no/People/midi/midi.html**

The Alf MIDI site has a good WWW home page—the main topic is the MIDI Sample Dump Standard, but it also covers MIDI in general. The site includes documentation, programs, and sound samples.

Computer Music Journal (on-line publication)
WWW file:

file://mitpress.mit.edu:/pub/Computer-Music-Journal/Subscribe.t

The *Computer Music Journal* (CMJ) archive is provided for the computer music community in general. It includes the tables of contents, abstracts, and editor's notes for the several volumes of CMJ including the recent bibliography, discography, and taxonomy of the field, plus the list of network resources for music, a number of useful related documents (such as the full MIDI and AIFF specifications), a lengthy reference list, and the full text of several recent articles, among other data.

Project Gutenberg
FTP site: **ftp://mrcnext.cso.uiuc.edu/etext/NEWUSER.GUT**

Project Gutenberg, a project aimed at providing copyright-cleared electronic texts, now offers computer music MIDI files. The first is Beethoven's Fifth Symphony In C-Minor.

VIII

Computer Resources

Organizations and Associations

FARNET—Networks for Research and Education
FTP site: **ftp://farnet.org/farnet/farnet_info/**

This site provides information about FARNET, a nonprofit corporation. The primary goal of FARNET is to advance the use of computer networks for research and education.

International Computer Science Institute
URL address: **http://http.icsi.berkeley.edu**

ICSI is a computer science research organization affiliated with the Computer Science division of the Electrical Engineering and Computer Science department at U.C. Berkeley. ICSI connects research scientists from all over the world working together with U.C. Berkeley EECS professors and graduate students on a variety of subjects. At the ICSI WWW site, you can locate PostScript technical reports, an interface to the ICSI Gopher server, and information about the Sather and pSather languages.

International Interactive Communications Society (IICS)
URL address: **http://www.iics.org**

The IICS is an international organization that focuses on the development and application (such as education, commerce, and training) of interactive technologies (such as videodisc, CD-ROMs, and on-line communications). This Web site offers information about the organization and about individual chapters located around the world.

International Telecommunications Union
Gopher address: **gopher://info.itu.ch/**

This contains information from the International Telecommunications Union, an agency of the United Nations that attempts to set international standards for telecommunications. Also, check out the URL address **http://keskus.hut.fi** for information about their telecommunications laboratory.

Internet Society
URL address: **http://info.isoc.org/home.html**

The Internet Society is an international organization that represents companies and individuals that focus on the applications and operation of the Internet. Many of the recommendations of the Internet society become the foundation for the development of technologies and policies for the Internet.

Parallel Tools Consortium—Parallel Processing
URL address: **http://www.llnl.gov/ptools/ptools.html**

The Parallel Tools Consortium offers this server to the world. It contains information on not only parallel tools, but also conferences and other parallel programming related issues.

Personal Computers and PC Software (IBM-compatible, Macintosh)

Apple Newton
URL address: **http://www.uth.tmc.edu/newton_info/**

This WWW server provides information about the Apple Newton. It provides some insight into this device and what may be in store for the future of Personal Digital Assistants (PDAs).

IBM
URL address: **http://www.ibm.com/**

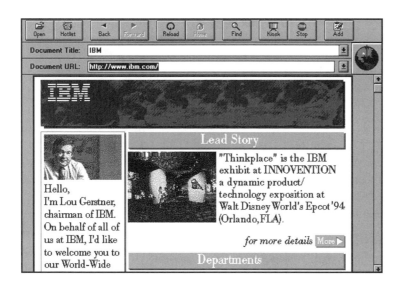

Fig. 8.14
At the home page for "Big Blue" you can listen to a short audio message from IBM chairman Lou Gerstner or jump to an overview of an IBM exhibit at Disney World Epcot Center.

In addition to some fancy graphics and use of multimedia, this WWW server provides links to the following IBM information areas: Industry Solutions, Products and Services, Technology, More Information, News, and About IBM.

Internet Computer Index
URL address: **http://ici.proper.com**

Internet Computer Index (ICI) is an easy-to-use, free service that leads Internet users to all the information available on the Internet relating to PCs, Macintoshes, and UNIX computers. It has a comprehensive listing of FAQ files, FTP sites, Gopher directories, newsgroups, mail lists, and on-line publications. You can keyword search these resources for information about specific topics or products.

Internet Resources for Macintosh
URL address:
http://www.uwtc.washington.edu/ JonWiederspan/ MacSupportOnInternet.html

From the University of Washington, this Web site has pointers to a variety of Macintosh resources. One link, Macintosh Internet Client Software (URL address **http://www.uwtc.washington.edu/Computing/Internet/ UsefulSoftware.html**), provides a review of Macintosh-based software clients for use with the WWW, Gopher sessions, and news readers. All are available via **ftp://ftp.uwtc.washington.edu/pub2/Mac/Network**. The home page also offers a link to a list of Mac e-mail lists and Usenet newsgroups.

Macintosh Index
URL address: **http://ici.proper.com/1/mac**
Gopher address: **gopher://ici.proper.com/77c/mac/.cache**

This is a searchable database of extensive information on the Internet that relates to the Macintosh. There are many Macintosh-related Gopher and WWW servers on the Internet that have interesting information. If you are primarily an e-mail user, you will find many good Macintosh mailing lists. Much of the most current information is found in Usenet news groups for the Macintosh.

Macintosh Information
URL address: **http://www.engr.scarolina.edu/**

The University of South Carolina's College of Engineering WWW server includes Rob's Mac Page, which has comprehensive information on the Macintosh, as well as links to WWW sites.

PC Index
URL address: **http://ici.proper.com/1/pc**

This is a searchable database of extensive information on the Internet that relates to the PC. There are many PC-related Gopher and WWW servers on the Internet that have interesting information. The files produced in the Usenet news groups have become the de facto repositories for PC-related information on the Internet. For more current information, you may find the on-line PC publications of value.

The Well Connected Mac
URL address: **http://rever.nmsu.edu/~elharo/faq/Macintosh.html**

A terrific home page for people who own Macintosh computers. Link to Macintosh Software to get a page with more than 100 other links to Web, Internet, and electronic bulletin board systems that offer commercial, shareware, and freeware products. There are also reviews of Mac hardware and software, mailing lists, newgroups, and vendor information.

Windows World (CSUSM)
URL address: **http://coyote.csusm.edu/cwis/winworld/winworld.html**

Need new Microsoft Windows software? This Web site offers a directory and access to a variety of Windows shareware programs, which you can download. (Remember shareware is NOT freeware—if you use a program you must pay a small fee to the author.) Most of the programs are compressed with the PKZip utility. The directory does list how large the program files are so you know how long it will take to download. Categories include address books, database programs, editors, games, and mail programs.

Publications, Magazines, Radio Programs, and Articles

Computer-Mediated Communication Magazine
URL address: **http://www.rpi.edu/~decemj/cmc/mag/current/toc.html**

Computer-Mediated Communication Magazine (ISSN 1076-027X) is on the Web. *Computer-Mediated Communication Magazine* is distributed for free use from the Computer-Mediated Communication Studies Center.

Cyberkind
URL address: **http://sunsite.unc.edu/shannon/ckind/title.html**

Cyberkind is a World Wide Web magazine of "Net-related fiction, nonfiction, poetry, and art." *Cyberkind* features prose and art submitted by the Internet population. All genres and subjects are included, as long as there is some connection to the Internet, cyberspace, computers, or the networked world in general. The features range from an article on writers and the Internet to a

VIII

Computer Resources

computer-related mystery, to a hyperlinked poem. The magazine also features a variety of graphic art. *Cyberkind* is always looking for submissions of prose, poetry, and art. Send submissions to **shannon@sunsite.unc.edu**.

Ericsson, Inc.
URL address: **http://www.ericsson.nl**

This server contains articles and technical information on various aspects of telecommunications. It will expand in response to reader input. Ericsson is a telecommunications supplier that assists with the mobile telecommunications infrastructure.

Gender Issues (article)
FTP site:
**ftp://alfred.carleton.ca/pub/freenet/93conference
leslie_regan_shade.txt**

"Gender Issues in Computer Networking," by Leslie Regan Shade, is an article that presents some interesting information regarding various gender-related issues with respect to telecommunications and the information age.

GlasNews
URL address: **http://solar.rtd.utk.edu/friends/news/glasnews/
master.html**

GlasNews is an on-line quarterly publication on East-West contacts in communications—including journalism, telecommunications, advertising, and public relations—by Art Pattison Communications Exchange Program, based in Seattle.

INFOMART Magazine
URL address: **http://onramp.net/infomart/infomart.html**

INFOMART is an information and technology showcase in Dallas, Texas. This electronic magazine contains articles for the information systems industry on client/server issues, multimedia, ATM, networking, and other topics. The INFOMART directory offers telephone numbers and gives brief descriptions of INFOMART tenants.

Journal of Computer-Mediated Communication
URL address: **http://www.huji.ac.il/www_jcmc/jcmc.html**

A scholarly publication, *The Journal of Computer-Mediated Communication* (JCMC) is a joint project of the Annenberg School for Communication, University of Southern California, and the Information Systems Division of the School of Business Administration, Hebrew University of Jerusalem.

Macmillan Computer Publishing
URL address: **http://www.mcp.com/**

Find information on the best computer books publishers in the world. Books from Que, SAMS, New Riders, Alpha, Brady, and Hayden are featured here. You can review a sample chapter or table of contents from current books. This site also contains a wealth of reference articles pulled from these leading books to answer your questions about computer software and hardware. You can order any Macmillan Computer Publishing book directly from this Web site. Download software associated with best-selling titles. (This site will become available in December, 1994.)

PowerPC News
URL address: **http://power.globalnews.com/**

PowerPC News is an independent, electronic magazine published every two weeks for users and developers who want news about the IBM/Motorola/Apple microprocessor family and the systems built upon it. The home page contains links to the full text of the magazine.

Social Issues and Cyberspace
URL address: **http://www.ics.uci.edu/~ejw/csr/cyber.html**

The Cyberspace Report, a public affairs radio show aired on KUCI, 88.9 FM in Irvine, California, is now available on-line from the Department of Information and Computer Science at the University of California, Irvine, WWW server. Social issues of computing is the theme of the Cyberspace Report, which features interviews. Currently available shows explore the future of electronic mail, the information infrastructure in Singapore, and the future of communities on the Internet. Notable guests include Dr. Nathaniel Borenstein of Bellcore, Professor John L. King from U.C. Irvine, and Professor Phil Agre from U.C. San Diego.

Telecommunications Electronic Reviews
Gopher address: **gopher://info.lib.uh.edu:70/11/articles/e-journals/lita**

This is an on-line review of telecommunications news and activities. This is a good place to find helpful information for advanced users.

Technical Reports Archive
URL address: **http://cs.indiana.edu/cstr/search**

At this Indiana WWW server, you find the Unified Computer Science Technical Report Index. For people who need fairly heavy technical information, this represents a nice compilation of reports that you can scan.

VIII

Computer Resources

Worldwide Collaborative Multimedia Magazine
URL address: **http://www.trincoll.edu/homepage.html**

The Trincoll Journal is a weekly multimedia magazine run by students at Trinity College in Hartford Connecticut, with all design, programming, contributions, and artwork created by people from around the world, that is available on the Web. This student project demonstrates just what can be done in terms of worldwide collaboration.

Research—Government Agencies

Telecommunications Research
URL address: **http://www-atp.llnl.gov/atp/**

The Advanced Telecommunications Program at the Lawrence Livermore National Labs. If you are serious about investigating telecommunications research, try out this site.

Research—Universities

Carnegie Mellon University—Computer Vision
URL address:
http://www.cs.cmu.edu:8001/afs/cs/project/cil/ftp/html/visio n.html

A WWW home page for Computer Vision is available at Carnegie Mellon University. It includes pointers to 20 research groups' home pages, image archives, and source code related to Robot Vision and Image Processing.

Columbia University
URL address: **http://www.ctr.columbia.edu/**

The Center for Telecommunications Research at Columbia University has just started up its WWW server. It contains pointers to other Columbia University information sources.

Computer-Mediated Communication Studies Center
URL address: **http://www.rpi.edu/~decemj/cmc/center.html**

The center serves the needs of researchers, students, teachers, and practitioners interested in computer-mediated communication. The server provides links to the CMC magazine, people, activities, and resources.

Cornell Theory Center Overview
URL address: **http://www.tc.cornell.edu/ctcIntro.html**

The Cornell Theory Center at Cornell University is one of four National Advanced Scientific Computing Centers supported by the National Science Foundation. From this home page you can find out about research efforts in visualization, vectorization, and parallel processing and investigates highly parallel processing resources for the scientific community.

MIT Demonstrations
URL address: **http://www.lcs.mit.edu/**

The Massachusetts Institute of Technology Laboratory for Computer Science provides this server. It includes an index to pages and demos provided by research groups at the MIT Laboratory for Computer Science.

MIT—Telecommunications Archives
FTP site: **ftp://lcs.mit.edu/telecom-archives**

The telecommunications archive at the Massachusetts Institute of Technology (MIT) site isn't for the casual user, but it contains many items of interest to engineers and developers.

University of Iowa
Gopher address: **gopher://iam41.arcade.uiowa.edu:2270**

The Iowa Comm Gopher server at the University of Iowa features many communications-related resources including journalism, media studies, multimedia, and telecommunications.

The University of Kansas
URL address:
http://kuhttp.cc.ukans.edu/cwis/UDK/KUhome/KUHome.html

The University of Kansas Home Page now provides easy access to locally produced services, including The Electrical Engineering & Computer Science Telecommunications & Information Sciences Laboratory at Nichols Hall (TISL). KU provides this site for information on its work on high speed networks, digital signal processing, simulation of communications systems, and networks. Be sure to check out the other offerings at this university.

University of Michigan College of Engineering
URL address: **http://www.engin.umich.edu/college**

The University of Michigan College of Engineering offers the Computer Aided Engineering Network's WWW server. It contains a considerable amount of on-line documentation, as well as network services such as the face/finger gateway.

VIII

Computer Resources

University of Missouri
URL address: **http://www.cstp.umkc.edu/**

The University of Missouri Computer Science Telecommunications Program provides a variety of valuable computer and computer research information. If you want to be a student or if you want to see "what's happening" there, this is the place to go.

University of Washington—Image Processing
URL address:
http://www.cs.washington.edu/research/metip/metip.html

The University of Washington Department of Computer Science & Engineering has created the Mathematics Experiences Through Image Processing (METIP) home page. The METIP project uses image processing techniques to create tools and activities for middle school students to motivate them in the subject of mathematics.

University of Wisconsin Computer Sciences Department
URL address: **http://www.cs.wisc.edu/~upluse/**

The Undergraduate Projects Laboratory (UPL) of the University of Wisconsin Computer Sciences Department has a home page that highlights the projects and people of the UPL. The UPL is one of the only laboratories of its kind which allows undergraduates from multiple disciplines to have access to UNIX workstations for personal independent programming projects and computer research.

Security

Computer Security
URL address: **http://mls.saic.com**

The Wateridge facility of Science Applications International Corp. (SAIC) makes its WWW Computer Security Web Site available to all who are interested. Dedicated to the many facets of computer security, this site includes documents concerning current SAIC projects, security newsgroups from Usenet, and security information from around the Web.

Cryptography and Computers
URL address: **ftp://rsa.com** (login as anonymous cd pub /ciphertext)

CipherText is a newsletter (available as ASCII text) that covers ongoing issues and technologies of cryptography.

Cryptography, PGP and Your Privacy
URL address: **http://draco.centerline.com:8080/~franl/crypto.html**

You can find volumes of information at this site with links to all types of material about computer privacy and methods of protecting it.

Supercomputing

Alabama Supercomputer Network
URL address: **http://sgisrvr.asc.edu/index.html**

Fig. 8.15
Fast, powerful and expensive—this is the world of supercomputers, which you can explore through the Alabama Supercomputer Network. Don't be shy; there's even an area for K-12 instruction.

If you haven't experienced the world of supercomputing, then you should check out the Alabama Supercomputer Network. This site provides a jump-off point to other WWW servers.

Caltech—Supercomputer Sample
URL address: **http://www.ccsf.caltech.edu/ccsf.html**

The Caltech Concurrent Supercomputing Facilities (CCSF) offers this server that includes CCSF annual reports, postscript manuals for the Intel Paragon parallel supercomputer (PostScript), as well as Xmorphia: an interactive exhibition of pattern formation by a partial differential equation of reaction-diffusion type—is this how the leopard gets its spots?

Florida State University Supercomputing
URL address: **http://www.scri.fsu.edu**

The Supercomputer Computations Research Institute (SCRI) at the Florida State University in Tallahassee, Florida is on-line through WWW. This server contains:

- Information on computing facilities at SCRI, and pictures and descriptions of some of the equipment.

- Recent publication information, and listings of several thousand abstracts from recently published articles.

■ Information about software developed at SCRI that is available on the Internet. Notable projects include SciAn, DQS, and Dmake.

■ Notes on the Tallahassee FreeNet.

Piedmont Supercomputing Center
URL address: **http://services.csp.it/welcome.html**

Fig. 8.16
Find out about supercomputing research and projects in Italy when you connect with the Piedmont Supercomputing Center home page.

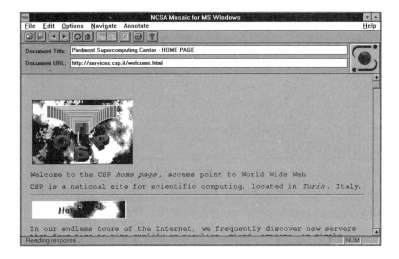

This is a WWW home page at the Centro Supercalcolo Piemonte center, located in Turin, Italy. It is a national site for scientific computing that provides the regional scientific structures, adequate instruments, and computing resources of the most advanced level.

San Diego Supercomputer Center
URL address: **http://www.sdsc.edu/**

The San Diego Supercomputer Center is a national laboratory for computational science and engineering. It promotes research and U.S. economic competitiveness with computational tools. SDSC is affiliated with the University of California, San Diego, which is one of the nation's leading research universities. SDSC features a variety of collaborative research and educational programs, and high-performance computational and visualization tools.

Chapter 9

Education on the WWW

With its origins in academia, the Internet, and now the WWW, offers tremendous resources for educators, students, and people who simply have an interest in learning. The educational resources and topics on the Web are not limited to the world of higher education. Public school districts, elementary, junior, and high schools, and even individual classes continue to develop and operate WWW servers. The home pages of these servers frequently include links to other educational resources as well as information about the individual schools, often a school newspaper.

It is also common to find requests in the school home pages for other schools/classes to send e-mail to begin inter-school electronic communications, where students in different parts of the world can send letters to each other and share their experiences and knowledge. The K–12 resources are vast, ranging from the HungerWeb, a server that has an interactive "hunger quiz" and databases that relate to world hunger, to three-dimensional images and movies of frogs maintained at the Imaging and Distributed Computing Group of Lawrence Berkeley Laboratory.

Do you have an interest in the future of public education programs in the United States? The U.S. Department of Education maintains a server that offers details about Goals 2000, the act designed to help America reach the National Education Goals and help every child realize high academic standards. Offering access to searchable databases containing millions of records, the WWW libraries may help students achieve these goals. Many university and government WWW libraries focus on specific topics, such as agriculture, engineering, literature, or medicine. A search for information may produce text documents, photographs, or movies that you can download and use for future reference.

Universities and colleges continue to have a strong presence on the WWW. The last section of this chapter includes a list of all the WWW addresses for educational institutions in the United States—more than 700 of them!

If you are looking for further educational Web resources, take a look at the listings of WWW interactive museums that are in chapter 6, "Art, Music, and Entertainment," and chapter 16, "Science Resources," and the list of electronic literature and books in chapter 15, "Publications, News, Periodicals, and Books."

The Teacher Education Internet Server

URL address: **http://curry.edschool.virginia.edu/teis**

Fig. 9.1
Explore the Web's educational resources as you click your way through a hypermedia image of a classroom.

This Web site proves that you're never too old to learn. It represents a combined effort between the Society for Technology and Teacher Education, the University of Virginia, and the University of Houston. The entire focus of its resources is the exploration of ways in which the Internet/WWW can benefit global teacher education programs. The home page includes a graphic picture of a schoolroom. The icons in the picture link to the resources. For example, a microscope links to science information, a bookshelf links to reading resources, and the telephone on the wall links to telecom and networking information. If you don't have graphics capability or have difficulty with the image links, there are four hypertext links just beneath the image. These, in turn, open a world of educational resources. The Whole TEIS Gopher opens doors to electronic publications like the Journal of Technology and Teacher Education and Interface, an IBM teacher preparation grant school newsletter, as well as documents for subjects that range from social studies to international education. Other home page links include Special Ed, Math Education, and Reading and Language Arts.

DeweyWeb

URL address: **http://ics.soe.umich.edu**

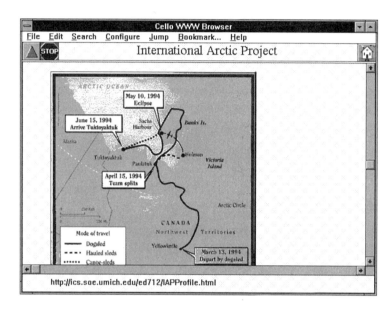

Fig. 9.2
Designed primarily
for K–12 education,
the DeweyWeb
home page provides
access to interactive
exploration about
global political
and scientific
exploration.

This Web server is a Sun Sparcstation 2 located at the University of Michigan
School of Education. It is an experiment that uses the WWW to facilitate
communication between students and classrooms around the world. Links
from the home page include the following highlighted items.

- *The ICS World Forum.* The ICS (Interactive Communications Simulations)
  World Forum is a computer-mediated conference in which 30 schools
  follow the adventures of the International Arctic Project, where explorers
  train for an expedition across the Arctic. The project helps students analyze challenges from different perspectives as they role-play characters
  from many walks of life. Ghandi, William Bennett, Rachel Carson, and
  Pope John Paul II are some of the individuals who have "attended" the
  World Forum.

- *DeweyWeb and the Journey North.* The DeweyWeb was inspired by the
  work of the University of Michigan ICS and the Indiana University
  World School for Adventure Learning. These projects attempt to expand
  the classroom experience with reports from scientists and explorers, as

well as linking distant schools together through telecommunications. The information in the DeweyWeb experiment is closely aligned to the World School's activities, and is therefore called "The Journey North." When you go to the Journey North, you receive the news, issues, and feelings that surround the Arctic Adventure.

Between ICS and the World School, various telecommunications and networking technologies help serve and gather information from classrooms. DeweyWeb builds on this experience and delivers information that comes from scientists and explorers, and gives students an opportunity to contribute their own observations and discussions.

Indiana University

URL address: **http://www.indiana.edu**

Fig. 9.3
Astronomy, law, music, and philosophy are a few of the departments you can connect to from the Indiana University home page.

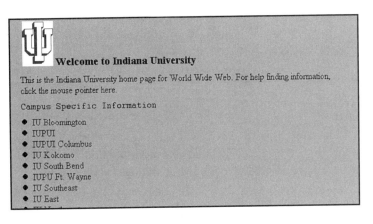

Indiana University is a public university comprised of a residential campus in Bloomington, Indiana, a major urban campus in Indianapolis, and six other campuses located in Gary, South Bend, Fort Wayne, Kokomo, Richmond, and New Albany. The University currently serves 94,000 students, employs nearly 17,000 faculty and staff, and has a budget in excess of $1 billion. It is one of the largest institutions of higher education in the United States.

Indiana University's WWW home page presents a variety of information about the degree programs and has links to each of the eight campuses. A good start, which gives you some idea of how large this institution really is, is the link to a list of Internet servers on all IU campuses. You'll find more than links here to the astronomy, computer science, law, music, philosophy, and numerous other departments and schools—even the Indiana University Press. But be warned, even though it's user friendly, you can get lost just like on a real university campus. Other resources include news, weather, address books, library and research services, and access to Telnet resources.

Geography—What Do Maps Show?

URL address:

http://info.er.usgs.gov/education/teacher/what-do-maps-show/index.html

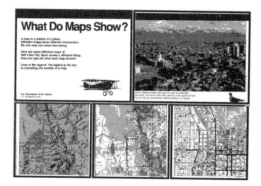

Fig. 9.4
Good map reading skills last a lifetime. This WWW home page provides lessons and material that teach those skills.

If you've ever gotten lost, you know how important a good map can be. How do you read a map? What do map symbols represent? These are just a few of the topics and lesson plans that you can find on this Web site. The focus is information and resources for educators who teach upper elementary and junior high school classes; the goal is to teach students how to use and understand maps. In addition to links for step-by-step lesson plans, there are on-line posters and reproducible activity sheets.

The on-line color poster is a wonderful resource. The poster shows several different views of Salt Lake City. There is an aerial photograph, a relief map, a road map, a topographical map, and a three-dimensional terrain map. You begin with small "thumbnail" images of these maps and click your way through to get ever larger images—final images can print as 8 1/2" x 11". Students will be able to learn the differences between these maps and understand how to read the legends and keys. From the home page you can jump to a list of USGS materials that is available for educational purposes. It's a great WWW application.

IX

Education

Patch American High School

URL address: **http://192.253.114.31/Home.html**

This WWW site really illustrates what a teacher with motivation, students with talent, and a diverse educational program can accomplish. The school is located at Patch Barracks, headquarters for the United States European Command (US EUCOM) in Vaihingen, a small section of Stuttgart, Germany, and serves dependent youth of American military and civilians stationed throughout 19 countries.

Students and faculty at Patch share some of their European experiences on the Web. Home page links include a picture of the school's mascot and a multimedia exhibition about the D-Day Normandy Invasion. Definitely check out the "What's New" section. One link brings up a multimedia presentation about the Maulbronn Abbey.

Other home page links include:

- Student Art Galleries—examine artwork by students.

- The Arab-Israeli Conflict—an interactive communications course.

- Biology Department Zoo—jump to a breakdown of the living world that includes insects, reptiles, and birds. Be sure to check out the picture of Louise, a ten-year-old boa constrictor at the zoo.

- Music—the world band and recent concerts.

If you are a K–12 educator, this might be a good site to begin an interactive classroom project. The school's e-mail address is WWW@patch-ahs.dsi.net.

Educational Libraries

Cornell University's Engineering Library
URL address: **http://www.englib.cornell.edu**

This home page has links to information about the Cornell Engineering Library and its services. It provides information on several electronic library projects and points to ICE (Internet Connections for Engineering); The Engineering Library Gopher; a guide to science and engineering journals, general science, and technology and geology Internet resources.

National Agricultural Library
URL address: **http://probe.nalusda.gov:8000/index.html**

This is the server from the National Agricultural Library—U.S. Department of Agriculture. Some of the links it provides are to plant genome information, animal genome information, agricultural genome Gopher, other biology servers, other WWW information, national agricultural library phone list, and search for projects and researchers.

National Library of Medicine
URL address: **http://www.nlm.nih.gov**

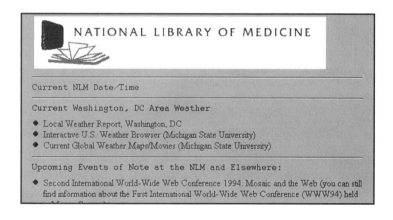

Fig. 9.6
This server offers links to documents and images that deal with the subject of health and medicine.

The National Library of Medicine (NLM), located on the campus of the U.S. National Institutes of Health (NIH) in Bethesda, Maryland, is the world's largest library focusing on a single scientific/professional topic. It maintains more than 4.5 million holdings (including books, journals, reports, manuscripts, and audio-visual items). The NLM offers numerous on-line information services (dealing with clinical care, toxicology and environmental health, and basic biomedical research), has research and development components (including an extramural grants program), houses a History of Medicine collection, and provides several programs designed to improve the nation's medical library system.

North Carolina State's Webbed Library Without Walls
URL address: **http://dewey.lib.ncsu.edu**

The NCSU Libraries handle (catalog or recatalog, or withdraw) about 500 titles a week. The purpose of this service is to organize and disseminate information that relates to the research and educational needs of the students, faculty, and staff of the North Carolina State University. The System offers the following selections: Information systems of the Triangle Research Libraries Network (TRLN); Duke University; North Carolina State University; University of North Carolina at Chapel-Hill; capability to do a search of the NCSU Libraries catalog, as well as other databases and indexes and several electronic texts.

St. Joseph County Public Library
URL address: **http://sjcpl.lib.in.us**

From this home page you can access the library's databases and the SJCPL on-line catalog that contains more than 500,000 records and includes the holdings of three area public libraries—SJCPL, Mishawaka-Penn Public Library, and the Plymouth Public Library (Plymouth, Indiana). The Community Connection contains information on over 1,200 community organizations and services.

University of Georgia Libraries
URL address:
http://scarlett.libs.uga.edu/1h/www/darchive/hargrett/wpa.html

Take a trip on this server and examine a collection of photographs that chronicle the various Work Progress Administration (WPA) projects that were built in Georgia, including streets, airports, schools and recreation facilities, flood control, and fine arts projects.

Virginia Tech
URL address: **http://borg.lib.vt.edu**

The Scholarly Communications Project of University Libraries, Virginia Polytechnic Institute, and State University. Electronic journal titles available include The Community Services CATALYST, Journal of Counseling and Development, Journal of Technology Education, Journal of the International Academy of Hospitality Research, and Journal of Veterinary Medical Education.

Educational Resources

AskERIC Virtual Library

URL address: **http://eryx.syr.edu/Main.html**

Fig. 9.7
Even teachers
sometimes have
questions. The
AskERIC Virtual
Library is a
repository of
information for
teachers and offers
an on-line virtual
librarian who can
answer specific
questions.

What could be better than a virtual librarian who never says, "Be quiet!"?
The AskERIC Virtual Library is an ongoing project building a digital library
for educational information. You navigate through it as you would any real
library. It offers a multimedia slide show that explains what AskERIC is and
how to use it (includes audio narration). You can ask the virtual librarian
questions with an on-line mail interface. Go to the reference section to search
for subject-specific Infoguides, lesson plans, and AskERIC Frequently Asked
Questions. This is an extremely valuable resource for educators.

Astronomy—Mars Surveyor MENU

URL address:
http://esther.la.asu.edu/asu_tes/TES_Editor/MsurveyorMENU.html

NASA's Mars Surveyor Program is the "next big thing" in the exploration of
Mars. It will begin with the launch of Mars Global Surveyor in November 1996.
The program proposes to send additional orbiters and landers to Mars every 26
months from 1996 to 2006. For now you can access information provided by
the Arizona Mars K–12 Education Program through the NASA Planetary Data
System Infrared Subnode, located at Arizona State University, Tempe.

Biology—LBL Imaging and Distributed Computing Group

URL address: **http://george.lbl.gov/ITG.html**

The Imaging and Distributed Computing Group of Lawrence Berkeley Laboratory contains information about the "Whole Frog" project, an experiment in
applying scientific imaging to education. The Whole Frog document includes
images, movies, and pointers to 3D frog anatomy data.

IX

Education

Britannica Online
URL address: **http://www.eb.com/**

Fig. 9.8
The Encyclopedia
Britannica now
offers on-line
information about
a world of subjects
via the WWW.

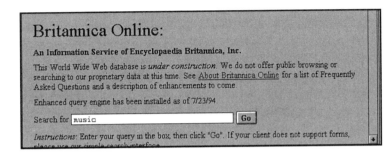

The database is experimental on the WWW and contains the full text of The
New Encyclopedia Britannica, 15th Edition. The automatic conversion has
not been checked by the editors, so equations may be rendered incorrectly or
not displayed at all. This is a fun site to visit.

CEA Education Outreach Page
URL address: **http://cea-ftp.cea.berkeley.edu/Education/**

This Web site offers a great collection of links for educators who are just getting
their feet wet with educational capabilities of the Internet and the WWW. Collected by the Center for EUV Astrophysics at Berkeley, California, you will find
home page links to the broad categories of K–12 outreach, distance learning,
public outreach, undergraduate outreach, and links to other educational sites.
There is also an on-line questionnaire that you can fill out to help make this
site more receptive to your needs. From the distance learning link you can find
information about how your classroom/students can connect to the Internet.

Cisco Educational Archive
URL address: **http://www.cisco.com/cisco/edu-arch.html**

An educational resource center sponsored by Cisco Systems Incorporated that
provides information to assist educators and schools in connecting with educational resources available on the WWW.

Computers—Mosaic Tutorial
URL address:
http://curry.edschool.virginia.edu/murray/tutorial/Tutorial.html

This tutorial is designed to guide teachers in using Mosaic for the Macintosh
as an instructional resource. It is divided into two main parts: "Mosaic: The
Basics" and "Creating a Mosaic Document." An on-line reference is also available to perform limited searches of these two main sections.

Computers—One Giant Leap; Networks: Where Have You Been All My Life

URL address: **http://www.tc.cornell.edu/Edu/SQ/Gibson/**

This essay won a 1994 "Networks: Where Have You Been All My Life?" essay contest sponsored by the U.S. Department of Education's National Center for Education Statistics, the National Science Foundation, and the National Aeronautics and Space Administration.

Computers—PCLT Exit Ramp

URL address: **http://pclt.cis.yale.edu/pclt/default.htm**

PC Lube and Tune supplies introductions, tutorials, and education on technical subjects to ordinary computer users through hypertext articles. Major articles include "Introduction to PC Hardware," "Introduction to SNA," "Introduction to TCP/IP," and "PC Serial Communications." A project is under development to create an easy-to-install package of shareware tools.

DeweyWeb: Journey North

URL address: **http://ics.soe.umich.edu**

An experiment in building a Web environment that students expand upon. Based on the World School's Journey North activity, the primary feature of the experiment is a series of maps that students can change as they enter observations of wildlife migration.

Dictionaries—Liz Brigman's WWW Page

URL address: **http://is.rice.edu:80/~liz**

This Web site offers a variety of links to reference materials. You can keyword search the *Oxford Dictionary* to find a definition of a word; *Roget's Thesaurus* to get a synonym or antonym; and the *Dictionary of Computer Terms* to find out the difference between a "byte" and a "bit."

Dictionary—English/German

URL address: **http://www.fmi.uni-passau.de/htbin/lt/lte/ltd**

Wohin wollen wir fahren? This WWW site will be a big help if you want to translate this ("Where shall we go?"), or learn how to say it—in German, of course. When you connect, a little entry box appears at the bottom of your screen. Simply type in a word and it will be translated. In addition to a simple translation of the word, you get a few German phrases that incorporate the word. For example, type in "World" and the search brings back "Welt" as well as "ein Mann von Welt" (a man of the world), "auf die Welt bringen" (bring into the world), and a few other useful expressions.

IX

Education

Dictionary—Genes
URL address: **http://mickey.utmem.edu/front.htm**

This WWW server offers an electronic dictionary (a database really) about genes. The dictionary contains data on about 13,700 loci, which are genes and anonymous DNA segments.

Geography—Project GeoSim (Geography Education Software)
URL address: **http://geosim.cs.vt.edu/index.html**

This Web server includes detailed information about Human Population (HumPop), a multimedia tutorial program; International Population (IntlPop), a population simulation program; Migration Modeling (MigModel), a migration modeling and simulation program; and Mental Maps (MMap), a geography quiz program.

Geography—USGS Education
URL address: **http://info.er.usgs.gov/education/index.html**

Some of the links this server provides are to the U.S. Geological Survey National Center Tour Information, the USGS Library System, the GeoMedia, What's Under Your Feet, Fact Sheets, and Dinosaurs at the Museum of Paleontology, U.C. Berkeley.

HungerWeb Home Page
URL address: **http://www.hunger.brown.edu/hungerweb/**

The server introduces two new facilities: an interactive Hunger Quiz, and a gateway to send e-mail to the President. It is designed to be both a general education platform and a research resource. The site includes an extensive integrated database on politics, the environment, economics, and ethics relevant to hunger and a broad collection of compelling introductory material. The service encourages submissions, including research, advocacy, projects, and case and clinical studies.

InfoVid Outlet: The Educational & How-To Video Warehouse
URL address: **http://branch.com:1080/infovid/c100.html**

This server is a guide to educational, instructional, and informative videos from around the world, with more than 3,500 titles on a wide variety of subjects.

Intercultural-Email-Classroom-Connections
URL address: **http://www.stolaf.edu/network/iecc.html**

This Web resource is designed to help teachers seeking partner classrooms for international and cross-cultural electronic mail exchanges.

Janice's K–12 Cyberspace OUTPOST
URL address: **http://k12.cnidr.org/janice_k12/k12menu.html**

The site offers a collection of resources within the K–12 Web-space as well as other things related to educational use of the net. References are made to K–12 virtual libraries, NSF projects and project maps, and other "cool stuff" for kids.

JASON Project Voyage
URL address: **http://seawifs.gsfc.nasa.gov/JASON/JASON.html**

Fig. 9.9
Students and teachers can use the WWW interface to the JASON Project to look into volcanoes, tour Mayan ruins, and explore coral reefs.

This Web site puts a new spin on the class field trip. Instead of going to the pond behind the school, your students can look into the mouth of a volcano. This is a great home page for educators and students who want to explore and learn about the environment on Earth. Some links include individual "letters" from the rain forest. Definitely worth the trip.

Language Bank of Swedish
URL address: **http://logos.svenska.gu.se/lbeng.html**

Links to information about the Language Bank of Swedish, the Catalogue of Machine-Readable Texts and Lexical Data, the Language Bank Gopher Server, and the Language Bank Concordance System are provided here. There are also links to Scandinavian text archives and other text archives. Text is in Swedish and English.

Language—Esperanto Home Page
URL address:
http://utis179.cs.utwente.nl:8001/esperanto/hypercourse/

Esperanto is a "universal" language that has been in existence for more than 100 years. Not belonging to any specific country, Esperanto helps people from many different countries communicate. The Esperanto server provides links to both background information as well as a hypermedia tutorial on the language—so "klik hier voor de korse."

IX

Education

Literature—Electronic Text Center
URL address: **http://www.lib.virginia.edu/etext/ETC.html**

Fig. 9.10
This WWW home page is a gateway to thousands of electronic hypertext versions of great literature.

From the University of Virginia, this WWW site is a gateway to thousands of electronic hypertext documents and works of literature. Most of the home page links are self explanatory, such as British Poetry 1780–1910. When you select "Electronic Text Searchable Through the Web" you receive a new menu that offers access to Middle English Texts, the King James and Revised standard version of the Bible, and a 16MB collection of Early Modern English material, including an early English dictionary.

Math and Science—The Hub
URL address: **http://hub.terc.edu/**

An Internet resource for mathematics and science education, the Hub provides services that can help you create and publish reports, curricula, projects in progress, and requests for proposals.

National Center on Adult Literacy (NCAL)
URL address: **gopher://litserver.literacy.upenn.edu**

The ability to read and write are essential tools for living and working in the modern world. The National Center on Adult Literacy provides leadership in research and development in the field of adult literacy. This Gopher server includes information on literacy programs throughout the U.S. and in foreign countries. You can jump to any of four organizational units that focus on different aspects of literacy: The National Center on Adult Literacy, which engages in research and development on adult literacy in the United States; the International Literacy and Education Program (ILEP), which provides a worldwide network for literacy training and development; the Penn Group on Literacy Studies (PGLS), which engages in a broad range of university-based research projects; and the Literacy Technology Laboratory (LTL) which promotes the use of new technologies for learning and instruction.

Pacific Forestry Center
URL address: **http://www.pfc.forestry.ca/**

This center is located at the Canadian Forest Service in Victoria, British Columbia. The server provides an introduction, staff profiles, recent publications, a contact list, research programs, and an advanced forest technologies program.

Science Bytes—University of Tennessee
URL address: **http://loki.ur.utk.edu/default.html**

Science Bytes includes a series of illustrated articles designed for school children and their teachers.

The Explorer
URL address: **http://unite.tisl.ukans.edu/xmintro.html**

Part of an effort to establish a simple means of delivering a full range of information resources to educators and students, this site has significant resources in mathematics and the natural sciences. *Explorer News* is an educational newsletter that comes out several times a month and offers ideas for lesson plans and teaching events. One issue, for example, focuses on Global Change and Ozone Depletion, a unit lesson plan that includes background information on the Earth's ozone layer and hands-on activities. You can download these programs and resources to your PC for future reference or use.

U.S. Department of Education
URL address: **http://www.ed.gov/**

A few of the goals of the USDOE include: To assure access to equal educational opportunity for every individual and to improve the quality of education. If you have an interest in education in the United States, this is a good Web site. Begin with a jump to the Goals 2000 on-line library, which provides the full text of Goals 2000, and fact sheets and other information about the Act, which is designed to help America reach the National Education Goals and to move every child toward achieving high academic standards (**ftplink/webs/Goals_2000.web**).

Xerox PARC PubWeb Server
URL address: **http://pubweb.parc.xerox.com/**

This is an initiatory World Wide Web server running at the Xerox Palo Alto Research Center in Palo Alto, California. It includes links to the Xerox Corporation WWW server, a map viewer, PARC Research related Digital Libraries, color photos, bitmap photos, and the epicenter of the Southern California Earthquake.

IX

Education

K–12

Armadillo's WWW Server
URL address: **http://chico.rice.edu/armadillo/**

This Web server is a collaborative effort between the Houston Independent School District and Rice University. It presents resources and instructional material to support an interdisciplinary course of study with a Texas theme. Pertains mostly to education on the K–12 level.

Glenview District 34 Schools
URL address: **http://www.ncook.k12.il.us/dist34_home_page.html**

A K–8 district in Glenview, Illinois, with a server for several schools of this suburb north of Chicago. You can access the on-line catalogs of the district's primary libraries. There are also numerous other links for educators and students, including one called "goodies," which brings up a large list of hyperlinks to education-related topics.

Hillside Elementary School
URL address: **http://hillside.coled.umn.edu/**

Fig. 9.11
Learn how sixth graders are making an impact on the Information Superhighway when you visit this home page.

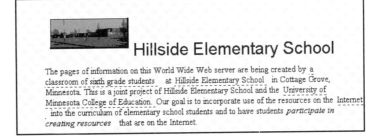

Hillside Elementary School

The pages of information on this World Wide Web server are being created by a classroom of sixth grade students at Hillside Elementary School in Cottage Grove, Minnesota. This is a joint project of Hillside Elementary School and the University of Minnesota College of Education. Our goal is to incorporate use of the resources on the Internet into the curriculum of elementary school students and to have students *participate in creating resources* that are on the Internet.

Sixth graders at this school develop the server, which is part of a joint project between the school and the University of Minnesota. It focuses on integration of the Internet into the curriculum of elementary level education. The goal is to have students not only look at the Internet and take information from it, but to actively participate in building and shaping their own part of the Information Superhighway.

Illinois Mathematics and Science Academy
URL address: **http://www.imsa.edu/**

The Illinois Mathematics and Science Academy is the nation's only three-year residential, public high school for students with talent in the fields of science and mathematics. It is also the state of Illinois' research and development laboratory for K–12 mathematics and science education.

Ithaca, New York Kids on Campus
URL address: **http://www.tc.cornell.edu/Kids.on.Campus/KOC94/**

This program is designed to increase computer awareness and scientific interest among Ithaca-area third-, fourth-, and fifth-grade students through hands-on activities, innovative videos, and demos. It provides a graphical interface to a wide variety of information resources on the Internet.

Monta Vista High School—News
URL address: **http://www.mvhs.edu/newsmenu.html**

The school is located in Cupertino, California. It focuses on integrating the Internet in a high school setting.

Murray Elementary School
URL address: **http://curry.edschool.virginia.edu/murray**

In collaboration with the Curry School of Education at the University of Virginia, Murray Elementary School has established a home page that has a variety of educational resources, including a Macintosh Mosaic Tutorial for K–12 educators.

NASA Langley HPCC
URL address: **http://k12mac.larc.nasa.gov/hpcck12home.html**

The home page for the High Performance Computing and Communications K–12 Program is an educational outreach program involving five high schools in the Tidewater area of Virginia. The focus of this pilot program is to investigate and develop curriculum integration computational sciences in K–12 education.

Princeton High Schools
URL address: **http://www.prs.k12.nj.us**

Located in Princeton, New Jersey, this is a student-run server with reference material and a school newspaper.

IX

Education

Ralph Bunche Elementary School
URL address: **http://mac94.ralphbunche.rbs.edu/**

This home page is run by a graduate student of the school, and includes the school newspaper, student work, and a pointer to the school's Gopher.

Smoky Mountain Field School
URL address: **http://www.ce.utk.edu/smoky.html**

The University of Tennessee Division of Continuing Education maintains this WWW home page for the Smoky Mountain Field School. The school offers supervised wilderness adventures for people of all ages and levels of experience. There are links to a current program schedule, which has topics like "Family Hiking in the Smokies" and "Insections of the Smokies." There is also registration information on-line.

Virginia L. Murray Elementary School
URL address: **http://curry.edschool.Virginia.EDU:80/murray/**

The school is located in Ivy, Virginia, and serves approximately 250 students in grades K–5. With funding from a local grant, Albemarle County, the PTO, and the school's budget, Murray established a direct Internet connection. This home page was developed by graduate students at the Curry School of Education as a part of a Technology Infusion Project with Albemarle County Schools.

Colleges and Universities—U.S.

Arizona State University—Infrared Subnode
URL address: **http://esther.la.asu.edu/asu_tes/**

Arizona State University provides the Infrared Imaging subnode, a subsidiary of the Geosciences Node of NASA's Planetary Data System. It is located at the Thermal Emission Spectroscopy Laboratory at Arizona State University, Tempe, Arizona.

Baylor College of Medicine
URL address: **http://www.bcm.tmc.edu/**

The server provides information about The Molecular Biology Computational Resource (MBCR). Here you can find the MBCR Guide, a hypertext manual on how to do just about anything for which a molecular biologist uses a computer. There are also links to a number of biological databank services on the Internet. There is information about The Department of Human and Molecular Genetics, for links of general interest to molecular biologists.

Carnegie Mellon University: The English Server
URL address: **http://english-server.hss.cmu.edu/**

The server is a student-run cooperative that publishes humanities texts electronically at Carnegie Mellon University.

Clemson University Computational Science and Engineering Resources
URL address: **http://diogenes.cs.clemson.edu/CSE/homepage.html**

Clemson University's server represents a collection of educational resources for the areas of computational science and engineering. It contains links to servers such as Netlib, mailing lists on CSE, relevant newsgroups, and contacts for academic materials.

ECSEL Coalition
URL address: **http://echo.umd.edu/**

The Engineering Coalition of Schools for excellence in Education and Leadership is funded by the National Science Foundation coalition of engineering schools and is engaged in a five-year effort to renew undergraduate engineering education and its infrastructure. This server provides general information, dissemination, and links to ECSEL research projects and other Engineering Education Coalitions.

Harvard University Graduate School of Education
URL address: **http://golgi.harvard.edu/hugse**

Fig. 9.12
If you've always wanted to "go to Harvard," just enter this URL address.

The home page of this Web server provides information about the school and links to other education-related resources.

Northwestern University—Learning Through Collaborative Visualization
URL address: **http://www.covis.nwu.edu/**

The CoVis server at Northwestern University has information about research and development of approaches to high school science education through collaborative project work with advanced networking technologies, collaborative software, and visualization tools. It is funded by the National Science Foundation and various industry partners and sponsors.

North Carolina State University College of Engineering
URL address: **http://www.eos.ncsu.edu/coe/coe.html**

This server contains information about all aspects of the operations, including undergraduate and graduate programs, the research program, staffing, student activities and organizations, computer operations, and extension services. It has links to several other departments.

NMSU Astronomy
URL address: **http://charon.nmsu.edu/**

It serves information about the Department of Astronomy's people, facilities, research, and educational activities. It also provides links to access images that show the collision of the comet Shoemaker-Levy 9 with Jupiter.

Oklahoma State University
URL address: **http://a.cs.okstate.edu/welcome.html**

Information about the Department of Computer Science at Oklahoma State University, Stillwater, Oklahoma. The server provides links to information about department resources, campus resources, Internet resources, and more.

University of California—College of Engineering
URL address: **http://ucrengr.ucr.edu/**

From the University of California, Riverside, the site provides information on courses, faculty, degree programs, and research centers. The research centers include VIS Lab, a research center for computer visualization and image processing; Systems Clinic, an opportunity for students to participate in solving industry-related problems; CE-CERT, an industry-University-government partnership for research in air pollution control; and UCM.E.P., the University of California Manufacturing Extension Program.

University of Chicago—Ancient Near East
URL address: **http://spirit.lib.uconn.edu/archnet/near_east.html**

The server is of the Oriental Institute of the University of Chicago. It provides mainly Egyptological material including announcements and the newsletter of the Archaeological Institute of America, the archives of the Ancient Near East, announcements and the newsletter of the American Schools of Oriental Research, information about the Oriental Institute, and other research on the Ancient Near East.

University of Massachusetts
URL address: **http://webserver.cogsci.umassd.edu/welcome.html**

The Computer and Information Science Department at the University of Massachusetts, Dartmouth, currently provides links to its research activities and writings, as well as its educational programs for graduates and undergraduates.

University of North Carolina at Chapel Hill
URL address: **http://sunsite.unc.edu/unchome.html**

The UNC-CH Office of Information Technology's SunSITE Project Sun Microsystems Information Page provides information on the Sun Archives, newsgroups, and all the SunSITEs in the world! It also provides Cisco Inc. archive information, including back issues of The Packet, and the Cisco Educational Archive and Resources Catalog Home page—CEARCH.

University of Pennsylvania
URL address: **http://www.upenn.edu/**

This server contains several topics of interest, links with other web servers on the Penn campus, provides gateways to PennInfo, the University's campus-wide information system, and to Gopher servers at Penn and worldwide. Currently featured is information in the fields of engineering, educational technology services, physics, medicine, computer and information sciences, statistics, math, virtual language, cognitive science, and economics.

University of Tennessee
URL address: **http://loki.ur.utk.edu/default.html**

The Office of University Relations has developed a Web server containing general information about the university, bicentennial information, on-line photographs of the pieces included in the sculpture tour of the Knoxville campus, profiles of twelve University of Tennessee faculty or alumni who have gained national recognition for their contributions, and an official listing of the WUOT-FM radio program guide complete with articles, images, and daily programming schedules.

University of Texas—ARLUT
URL address: **http://www.arlut.utexas.edu/home.html**

The Applied Research Laboratory, University of Texas server provides links to a variety of Web information resources. Especially worthwhile is the Internet Resources Meta-Index, which you can keyword search to locate information.

University of Washington Computer Science & Engineering
URL address: **http://www.cs.washington.edu/**

Information accessible on this server includes an overview of the department and its research, descriptions of the graduate educational programs and research summaries, as well as on-line technical reports. Also, home of the WebCrawler, a WWW searcher.

Colleges and Universities—International

Australia—Australian National University
URL address: **http://coombs.anu.edu.au/CoombsHome.html**

Located at the Australian National University, Canberra, the Coombsweb keeps track of information resources of value to researchers in the field of social sciences, humanities, and Asian studies.

Austria—University of Salzburg
URL address: **http://www.cosy.sbg.ac.at/welcome.html**

The server is from the University of Salzburg, Austria. It provides information on documents in German and English. It also provides a hyperlink map of Austria and Europe.

Belgium—Brussels University
URL address: **http://www.iihe.ac.be/**

This server provides information about Brussels University—Belgium, the Library Information inquiry and Referral Network (LIRN) project, the Belgian Multimedia Integrated Conferencing for European Researchers (MICE) NSC, and gateways and search tools.

Canada—Mount Allison University
URL address: **http://ollc.mta.ca/tenb.html**

This server is located at Mount Allison University in Sackville, New Brunswick, Canada. The TeleEducation New Brunswick Network is used to deliver university, community college, and other educational courses to all areas of the province of New Brunswick.

Canada—University of Saskatchewan
URL address: **http://www.usask.ca/**

Local information is about the university, its departments and organizations, as well as views of the students. Canadian-based information is about the systems, the Web, and its government.

Chile—University of Chile—
Departamento de Ciencias de la Computación
URL address: **http://www.dcc.uchile.cl/**

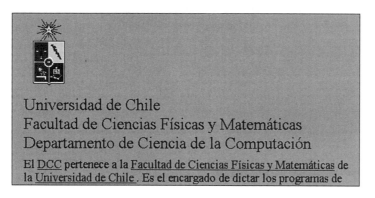

Universidad de Chile
Facultad de Ciencias Físicas y Matemáticas
Departamento de Ciencia de la Computación

El DCC pertenece a la Facultad de Ciencias Físicas y Matemáticas de
la Universidad de Chile . Es el encargado de dictar los programas de

Fig. 9.13
This Web server
will give you a
sense of the type of
programs that are
offered in universi-
ties in foreign
countries.

The server provides information about the University of Chile. It
includes links to several departments and general information about the
University.

Finland—University of Turku
URL address: **http://www.funet.fi/resources/map.html**

This server includes a map and information from the University of Turku—
the second largest educational entity in South Western Finland.

Germany—University of Kaiserslautern
URL address: **http://www.uni-kl.de/**

This site is from the University of Kaiserlautern, Germany. Most of the text is
presented in German. There are information links to the departments, the
institute itself, and the servers.

Italy—Center for Advanced Studies
URL address: **http://www.crs4.it/HTML/homecrs4.html**

From the Center for Advanced Studies, Research and Development in
Sardinia, Italy, the server provides links to CRS4 groups and projects, local
resources, CRS4 contributions to the Web, local area information, selections
of Italian literature in HTML form, and annotated maps, political maps,
physical maps, and satellite maps.

IX

Education

Singapore—Ministry of Education
URL address: **http://www.moe.ac.sg/**

The Ministry of Education (Singapore) server provides information on the education system in Singapore. It promotes education via the Internet by collating relevant educational resources and grouping them by subjects.

Slovenia—University of Ljubljana
URL address: **http://www.fer.uni-lj.si/**

Information from the University of Ljubljana, Slovenia, including links to the history of the faculty, research activities, educational programs, research labs, an e-mail address search, and an English-Slovene electronic dictionary.

Computer Science Programs—U.S.

Brigham Young University Computer Science
URL address: **http://www.cs.byu.edu/homepage.html**

Information about the Computer Science Department at Brigham Young University, including a virtual tour of the department building, information about the department mission, faculty classes, resources, and laboratories in the department.

Caltech Concurrent Supercomputing Facilities
URL address: **http://www.ccsf.caltech.edu/ccsf.html**

Information about the facilities at Caltech, USA. It is located on the campus of the California Institute of Technology, which supports and maintains a variety of massively parallel supercomputers for the Concurrent Supercomputing Consortium.

Cornell
URL address:
http://helpdesk-www.cit.cornell.edu/CITSHDHome.html

Got a question—go to an electronic help desk. This server has information about Cornell University and a variety of links to other WWW servers that contain information about computers and computer applications. There is a link to the "Free On-Line Dictionary of Computing," the Internet computer index, and the Global Prepress center, a site that helps with desktop publishing.

Georgia State University—Mathematics and Computer Science
URL address: **http://www.cs.gsu.edu/**

Located at Georgia State University, Atlanta, Georgia. It provides information about graduate and undergraduate courses and degrees, faculty, research, department and university resources, other math and computer science resources, Internet resources, and information about Atlanta.

Indiana University Computer Science Department
URL address: **http://cs.indiana.edu/home-page.html**

If you want to be a computer programmer, check out the course descriptions for classes offered by this department, including "Assemblers and Compilers." In addition to the classes, you can jump to documents that offer technical reports, overviews of the labs, and research projects. Advanced computer science applications include a robotics lab and high performance computing. There are also broad links to WWW resources and search tools.

MIT—Artificial Intelligence Laboratory
URL address: **http://www.ai.mit.edu/**

The Massachusetts Institute of Technology (MIT). The AI lab's research ranges from computer-based learning, vision, and robotics to development of new computers. There are links to these various research areas. A visit to this site will give you some insight into where computer applications will be in the next decade as artificial intelligence moves from the pages of science fiction to the real world.

Old Dominion University Department of Computer Science
URL address: **http://www.cs.odu.edu/index.html**

This server provides an introduction to the department, a brochure of the work in progress, a catalog of courses, lab information, and general education requirements.

Stanford University
URL address: **http://kanpai.stanford.edu/epgy/pamph/pamph.html**

The Education Program for Gifted Youth is located at Stanford University. The program is a continuing project offering computer-based courses in mathematics and the mathematical sciences for bright young students through the Stanford Continuing Studies Program. When you visit this site you can learn about the courses and students involved in this program.

IX

Education

University of Florida
URL address: **http://www.cis.ufl.edu/**

Fig. 9.14
Learn about the
computer science
curriculum at the
University of
Florida when you
visit the Web
server.

Information about the Computer and Information Sciences at the University of Florida. It provides links to departmental resources and a collection of other Web sites.

University of Maryland Advanced Computer Studies
URL address: **http://www.umiacs.umd.edu/**

From the University of Maryland Institute for Advanced Computer Studies. The institute was established to broaden support for computing research throughout the University system, focusing on interdisciplinary topics of computing. The server provides links to faculty, systems staff, departments, and research.

University of Washington Computer Science & Engineering
URL address: **http://www.cs.washington.edu/**

The server provides links to the Puget Sound region and Seattle and the university and its departments. There is also a summary of various research fields including mobile computing.

University of Iowa
URL address: **http://caesar.cs.uiowa.edu/**

Information from the Department of Computer Science at the University of Iowa, Iowa City. This server provides information about the computer science department colloquia, the Iowa Virtual Tourist, and Doctor Fun, a daily cartoon for the Internet.

University of Rochester
URL address: **http://www.cs.rochester.edu/**

The server provides information on the Department of Computer Science at the University of Rochester, Rochester, New York. It provides links to the department brochure, technical report collection, anonymous FTP archive, a department subway map, and other information about the university.

University of Wisconsin Computer Sciences
URL address: **http://www.cs.wisc.edu/**

Computer Sciences Department at the University of Wisconsin—Madison, Wisconsin. This site includes information about the Computer Systems Lab, research projects, courses, technical reports, and admissions.

Wesleyan University Department of Mathematics and Computer Science
URL address: **http://www.cs.wesleyan.edu/**

Information about Wesleyan University. Links to what's new, the students and staff, local news and information, topics in computing, islands in the Net, Clipper encryption, and more.

Yale University Computer Science Department Overview
URL address: **http://www.yale.edu/HTML/YaleCS-Info.html**

Information from Yale University. The server provides links to general information about the University, the Linda Group, and the Vision and Robotics interdisciplinary research group at Yale.

Computer Science Programs— International

Australia—James Cook University
URL address: **http://coral.cs.jcu.edu.au/**

Information from the James Cook University Department of Computer Science, Australia. It includes links to a department handbook, technical reports, subject information, a technical seminar series, an Australian Computer Science Academics Database, TP/TP library, a list of electronic libraries, and functional programming.

British Columbia—University of British Columbia—Computer Science
URL address: **http://www.cs.ubc.ca/home**

This server provides information about the University of British Columbia Computer Science Department in Vancouver, British Columbia, Canada. You can access an on-line Webster dictionary and thesaurus.

Denmark—The University of Aarhus
URL address: **http://www.daimi.aau.dk/**

Home page for the University of Aarhus, Denmark, Department of Computer Science. Provides information on research activities and groups, personnel, and general information about the archives.

Germany—TU Chemnitz-Zwickau, FakInf.html
URL address: **http://www.tu-chemnitz.de/~uer/FakInf.html**

The server provides links to all types of information about the Department of Computer Science at Technical University of Chemnitz—Zwickau, Germany. The information is in German.

Germany—University of Erlangen
URL address:
http://www.informatik.uni-erlangen.de/tree/Departments

Information about the University of Erlangen-Nurnberg, Germany. Listed are links to some of the Departments of the IMMD including Research and Operating and Distributed Systems.

Germany—University of Hannover
URL address:
http://www.tnt.uni-hannover.de/data/info/www/tnt/welcome.html

The Institut fuer Theoretische Nachrichtentechnik und Informaationsverarbeitung (TNT) at the University of Hannover provides information about the institute's people, research, and education on scientific topics like AI, signal processing, audio and video coding, and other subjects of interest.

Greece—National Technical University
URL address: **http://www.ntua.gr/**

Information for the National Technical University of Athens, Greece. Some links include What's New, the Mandelbrot Explorer—exploring the Mandelbrot fractal through X Mosaic, as well as frequently asked questions.

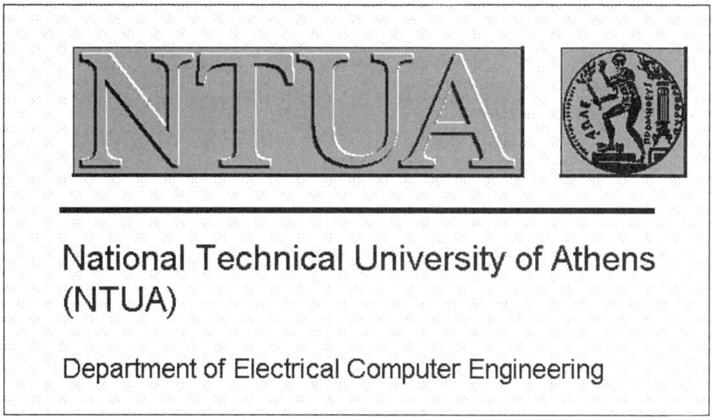

National Technical University of Athens
(NTUA)

Department of Electrical Computer Engineering

Fig. 9.15
In addition to
computer sciences,
you can view some
interesting visuals
created by
Mandelbrot
fractals at this
Web site.

Ireland—Dublin City University—Centre for Software Engineering
URL address: **http://www.compapp.dcu.ie/CSE/CSE_home.html**

Information about Dublin City University in Ireland. The University and
the WWW site help Irish software developers enhance their quality and
productivity.

Ireland—Trinity College
URL address: **http://www.cs.tcd.ie:/welcome.html**

From Trinity College, Dublin, Ireland. The server provides information and
links to the O'Reilly Institute and the University of Limerick, as well as all
types of information about the department itself.

Italy—Department of Computer Science at University of Pisa
URL address: **http://www.di.unipi.it/welcome.html**

Home page for the Department of Computer Science at the University of Pisa,
Italy. You can find information about the department and programs of study
in computer science, its documentation, and a large icon collection.

Japan—University of Aizu
URL address: **http://www.u-aizu.ac.jp/**

The university is dedicated to research and education in computer science.
It provides a hypermedia research profile brochure, People Advancing
Knowledge for Humanity, and an introduction to information on the
University and its faculty.

IX

Education

Netherlands—TU Delft
URL address: **http://www.twi.tudelft.nl/TWI/Overview.html**

Information about TU Delft, Netherlands. It provides links to information about the faculty, departments in pure mathematics, statistics, probability theory and operations research, applied analysis, information systems, and technical informatics.

Norway—University of Trondeim—Activities in Artificial Intelligence
URL address: **http://www.ifi.unit.no/ai.html**

Information from the University of Trondeim, Department of Informatics, Norway. Links are available to knowledge-intensive problem solving and machine learning, case-based reasoning, knowledge acquisition and modeling, integrated architectures, and connectionism.

Singapore—National University of Singapore—ISS Resource Guide
URL address: **http://www.iss.nus.sg/**

The Institute of Systems Science at the National University of Singapore has a home page that provides information about its location, facilities, and research and educational programs.

South Africa—Rhodes University Computing Services
URL address: **http://www.ru.ac.za/**

The main campus server is from the Computing Centre, Rhodes University, Grahamstown, South Africa. It provides Rhodes-specific information, as well as information relating to networking in South Africa.

Sweden—Uppsala University
URL address: **http://www.csd.uu.se/**

Home page from the Computer Science Department at Uppsala University, Sweden. The server provides links to local information, general information, faculty and staff, courses, projects, and technical reports.

United Kingdom—Computational Phonology
URL address: **http://ftp.cogsci.ed.ac.uk/phonology/CompPhon.html**

This service is from the Centre for Cognitive Science at the University of Edinburgh. It offers documents and directories about this field as well as the Association for Computational Phonology. It includes a directory of computational phonologists around the world and past newsletters of the ACP.

United Kingdom—Department of Computer Science, University of Exeter

URL address: **http://www.dcs.exeter.ac.uk/**

Information about the University of Exeter, UK. It includes links to research papers, postgraduate study details, and personnel information.

United Kingdom—Department of Computing, Imperial College, London

URL address: **http://www.doc.ic.ac.uk/**

Information about Imperial College of Science, Technology and Medicine, University of London, UK. It provides links to the department's staff, advanced languages and architectures, distributed software engineering, logic programming, theory, and formal methods.

United Kingdom—University of Birmingham School of Computer Science

URL address: **http://www.cs.bham.ac.uk/**

This site provides information about the Computer Science Web Server at this University in the UK. It provides links to campus and regional information, the main library catalogue, what's new, and hypertext regarding the Object Oriented C++ Programming course.

United Kingdom—Oxford University Computing Laboratory

URL address: **http://www.comlab.ox.ac.uk/**

From the Oxford University Computing Laboratory, UK. The Laboratory is one of the world's leading centers for the study, development, and exploitation of computing technology. It has responsibilities for all academic aspects of computing—teaching, basic research, and collaboration with industry on applied research. The server provides links to information about all aspects of the University.

United Kingdom—The University of Manchester Computer Graphics Unit

URL address: **http://info.mcc.ac.uk/CGU/CGU-intro.html**

Located in the UK, the server provides high-performance interactive computer graphics facilities on a range of workstations. The CGU is part of Manchester Computing Centre, one of the regional super-computing centers that provide facilities to the UK academic community. Services are available to all departments of the UM, UMIST, and users of the national super computers.

IX

Education

United Kingdom—University of Wales College of Cardiff
The COMMA Information Server
URL address: **http://www.cm.cf.ac.uk/**

From the University of Wales College of Cardiff, UK. The server provides information about the Department and its research interests, lecture notes for computer science courses, support pages for users, and recreational pages.

Regional and Community Education

Austin Texas User Group
URL address:
**http://www.quadralay.com/www/Austin/AustinOrgs/AWWWUG/
AWWWUG.html**

The server of the Austin WWW User Group in Austin, Texas, provides a technical and organizational infrastructure to support the local community. Its mission is to promote the academic, commercial, and educational use of the Web.

Michigan Department of Education—MDEnet
URL address: **http://web.mde.state.mi.us:1024/**

This system is designed to help arrange communication and information sharing between the Department of Education and the educational community in Michigan. The Department is developing an internal collection strategy to locate, format, and archive popular documents and files for placement on its Gopher server.

The College and University List

This list can be an immensely valuable resource for high school students who want to learn more about their potential choices for a college degree. Rather than send letters to 30 colleges asking for their course information and details about the school, jump on the Web and get it all in less than a day! Of course, anyone with an interest in academic subjects can find valuable information in these Web servers. Here are some tips on using this section.

First, this list simply includes the URL addresses (there isn't enough space to describe all these home pages). Second, many schools have more than one WWW home page, possibly more than one Web server (the MIT list includes 68 addresses)—each providing access to different information or departments within the school.

Here is an example that will give you some clues as to what the addresses point to. The listing for Georgia State University has three WWW addresses.

1. http://chara.gsu.edu

2. http://www.cs.gsu.edu

3. http://www.gsu.edu

The Internet DNS address structure (described in chapter 1) breaks the address down into domains. All of the addresses in this section end with *.edu,* for education. In this example the name to the left of .edu is .gsu, which stands for Georgia State University. The first address links to the Georgia State University Astronomy Department. You really couldn't guess this, but the acronom "chara" comes from one of the first menu items on the home page you receive, which offers:

CHARA—The Center for High Angular Resolution Astronomy

CHARA Array—Proposed optical imaging array

HLCO—The Hard Labor Creek Observatory

PEGA—The Program for Extragalactic Astronomy

The Be Star Newsletter—The electronic journal of Be star observation.

Astronomy Graduate Study at GSU. Fill out a quick form for information by postal mail.

GSU Astronomy FTP information

Publications of interest to amateur and professional astronomers

Observing forecast, current conditions, and current U.S. weather map

The second address points to the Georgia State University Mathematics and Computer Science Department's home page—lots of information about mathematics and computer science. Here the short address "cs" refers to computer science. Other common address codes include math for mathematics, psych for psychology, and eng for engineering.

In this example, address number three is the Georgia State University home page. The home page has links to all the other departments and resources at the university. It is here that a prospective college student can learn that GSU is the second-largest university in Georgia; more than 22,000 students attend the school and there are approximately 50 graduate and undergraduate degrees in 250 areas of study through six colleges. The clue to the fact that this URL is University's home page is that the address (www.gsu.edu) doesn't have any other subdomain pointers in it, only:

.www	.gsu	.edu
World Wide Web	Georgia State University	EDUcation

IX

Education

United States College and University Web Servers List (.edu Domain)

University of Alaska

http://saturn.uaamath.alaska.edu

University of Arizona

http://info.ccit.arizona.edu

http://info-center.ccit.arizona.edu

http://lanka.ccit.arizona.edu

http://lion.ccit.arizona.edu

http://www.cs.arizona.edu

http://miles.library.arizona.edu

http://bozo.lpl.arizona.edu

http://seds.lpl.arizona.edu

http://obsidian.math.arizona.edu

http://papago.rc.arizona.edu

http://www.arizona.edu

Arizona State University

http://enuxsa.eas.asu.edu

http://enuxsa.eas.asu.edu

http://enws324.eas.asu.edu

http://mosaic.eas.asu.edu

http://info.asu.edu

http://esther.la.asu.edu

University of California at Berkeley

http://neon.cchem.berkeley.edu

http://www.cchem.berkeley.edu

http://cea-ftp.cea.berkeley.edu

http://cs-tr.cs.berkeley.edu

http://cs-tr.cs.berkeley.edu

http://ftp.cs.berkeley.edu

http://docs34.berkeley.edu

http://http.icsi.berkeley.edu

http://netinfo.berkeley.edu

http://neutrino.nuc.berkeley.edu

http://ocf.berkeley.edu

http://remarque.berkeley.edu

http://ucmp1.berkeley.edu

http://www.berkeley.edu

http://xcf.berkeley.edu

http://ucmp1.berkely.edu

Boise State University

http://gozer.idbsu.edu

Bowling Green State University

http://hydra.bgsu.edu

Bradley University

http://bradley.bradley.edu

http://www.bradley.edu

Brandeis University

http://www.cs.brandeis.edu

Bridgewater College

http://www.bridgewater.edu

Brown University

http://www.chem.brown.edu

http://www.cog.brown.edu

http://elbow.cs.brown.edu

http://www.cs.brown.edu

http://home.eos.brown.edu

http://ftp.brown.edu

http://garnet.geo.brown.edu

http://home.geo.brown.edu

http://lager.geo.brown.edu

http://gopher.brown.edu

http://pion.het.brown.edu

http://www.het.brown.edu

http://www-geo.het.brown.edu

http://www.hunger.brown.edu

http://www.iris.brown.edu

http://ns.brown.edu

http://www.physics.brown.edu

http://www.planetary.brown.edu

http://www.brown.edu

Boston University

http://buphy.bu.edu

http://conx.bu.edu

http://med-amsa.bu.edu

http://robotics.bu.edu

http://spiderman.bu.edu

http://web.bu.edu

http://www-busph.bu.edu

SUNY at Buffalo

http://www.acsu.buffalo.edu

http://www.cedar.buffalo.edu

http://mirach.cs.buffalo.edu

http://www.cs.buffalo.edu

http://wheat.eng.buffalo.edu

http://zia.geog.buffalo.edu

http://mcbio.med.buffalo.edu

http://wings.buffalo.edu

http://www.wings.buffalo.edu

Brigham Young University

http://acm.cs.byu.edu

http://lal.cs.byu.edu

http://www.cs.byu.edu

http://www.math.byu.edu

Cal Poly State University

http://www.calpoly.edu

California Institute of Technology

http://alumni.caltech.edu

http://www.ama.caltech.edu

http://avalon.caltech.edu

http://ccfs.caltech.edu

http://www.cco.caltech.edu

http://ccsf.caltech.edu

http://www.ccsf.caltech.edu

http://cithe501.cithep.caltech.edu

http://cs.caltech.edu

http://www.galcit.caltech.edu

http://www.gg.caltech.edu

http://gopher.caltech.edu

http://expet.gps.caltech.edu

http://www.gps.caltech.edu

http://brando.ipac.caltech.edu

http://www.ipac.caltech.edu

http://kaa.caltech.edu

http://electra.micro.caltech.edu

http://www.pcmp.caltech.edu

http://robby.caltech.edu

http://www.theory.caltech.edu

http://www.ugcs.caltech.edu

http://www.caltech.edu

California State University

http://www.hal.csuhayward.edu

http://www.mcs.csuhayward.edu

California State University, Chico

http://www2.ecst.csuchico.edu

California State University, Long Beach

http://gothic.acs.csulb.edu

Calvin College and Seminary

http://calvin.edu

http://mcmellx.calvin.edu

http://unicks.calvin.edu

http://www.calvin.edu

Carleton College

http://www.carleton.edu

Carnegie-Mellon University

http://alycia.andrew.cmu.edu

http://www.contrib.andrew.cmu.edu

IX

Education

http://orac.andrew.cmu.edu

http://heretic.pc.cc.cmu.edu

http://clockwork.ws.cc.cmu.edu

http://ce.cmu.edu

http://strauss.ce.cmu.edu

http://porsche.boltz.cs.cmu.edu

http://c.gp.cs.cmu.edu

http://p.gp.cs.cmu.edu

http://legend.gwydion.cs.cmu.edu

http://anther.learning.cs.cmu.edu

http://hopeless.mess.cs.cmu.edu

http://robocop.modmath.cs.cmu.edu

http://fuzine.mt.cs.cmu.edu

http://musashi.mt.cs.cmu.edu

http://sodom.mt.cs.cmu.edu

http://thule.mt.cs.cmu.edu

http://www.mt.cs.cmu.edu

http://byron.sp.cs.cmu.edu

http://gs13.sp.cs.cmu.edu

http://gs71.sp.cs.cmu.edu

http://mixing.sp.cs.cmu.edu

http://www.cs.cmu.edu

http://www.ece.cmu.edu

http://gaisberg.edrc.cmu.edu

http://logan.edrc.cmu.edu

http://paneer.ndim.edrc.cmu.edu

http://engsh-server.hss.cmu.edu

http://hp8.ini.cmu.edu

http://janus.brary.cmu.edu

http://www.brary.cmu.edu

http://basisk.cimds.ri.cmu.edu

http://frc.ri.cmu.edu

http://www.frc.ri.cmu.edu

http://b.stat.cmu.edu

http://www.cmu.edu

Carroll College

http://carroll1.cc.edu

Case Western Reserve University

http://biochemistry.bioc.cwru.edu

http://caisr2.caisr.cwru.edu

http://ftp.cwru.edu

The Claremont Colleges

http://chs.cusd.claremont.edu

http://www.cusd.claremont.edu

Clarkson University

http://fire.clarkson.edu

http://omnigate.clarkson.edu

Clemson University

http://clancy.clemson.edu

http://cmcserver.clemson.edu

http://diogenes.cs.clemson.edu

http://www.cts.clemson.edu

http://beast.eng.clemson.edu

http://www.math.clemson.edu

http://www.clemson.edu

Cleveland State University

http://gopher.law.csuohio.edu

University of Colorado

http://adswww.colorado.edu

http://bruno.cs.colorado.edu

http://mcbryan.cs.colorado.edu

http://piper.cs.colorado.edu

http://www.cs.colorado.edu

http://cuboulder.colorado.edu

http://noaacdc.colorado.edu

http://puppis.colorado.edu

http://refuge.colorado.edu

http://saturn.colorado.edu

http://sslab.colorado.edu

http://www.colorado.edu

http://www-sgc.colorado.edu

Colorado State University

http://www.colostate.edu

Columbia University

http://gutentag.cc.columbia.edu

http://www.cc.columbia.edu

http://www.ctr.columbia.edu

http://www.ilt.columbia.edu

http://lawnet.law.columbia.edu

http://rainbow.ldeo.columbia.edu

http://lamont.ldgo.columbia.edu

http://www.ilt.tc.columbia.edu

Cornell University

http://helpdesk-www.cit.cornell.edu

http://stos-www.cit.cornell.edu

http://cs-tr.cs.cornell.edu

http://simlab.cs.cornell.edu

http://www.cs.cornell.edu

http://dri.cornell.edu

http://www.gated.cornell.edu

http://fatty.law.cornell.edu

http://www.law.cornell.edu

http://w4.lns.cornell.edu

http://chare.mannb.cornell.edu

http://aruba.nysaes.cornell.edu

http://lylahfive.resfe.cornell.edu

http://gopher.tc.cornell.edu

http://ibm.tc.cornell.edu

http://www.tc.cornell.edu

http://astrosun.tn.cornell.edu

Creighton University

http://phoenix.creighton.edu

Dartmouth College

http://ausg.dartmouth.edu

http://cagari.dartmouth.edu

http://coos.dartmouth.edu

http://cs.dartmouth.edu

http://www.cs.dartmouth.edu

http://geminga.dartmouth.edu

http://picard.dartmouth.edu

http://www.dartmouth.edu

University of Denver

http://nyx.cs.du

http://nyx10.cs.du

http://mobetter.ac.du

http://www.chem.du

http://www.cs.du

http://www.ctl.du

http://www.mis.du

http://porter.netcom.du

Dixie College

http://sci.dixie.edu

http://www.sci.dixie.edu

Embry-Riddle Aeronautical University

http://blackbird.db.erau.edu

The Exploratorium

http://isaac.exploratorium.edu

http://www.exploratorium.edu

Florida Institute of Technology

http://sci-ed.fit.edu

Florida State University ACNS

http://garnet.acns.fsu.edu

http://gopher.fsu.edu

http://eucd.math.fsu.edu

http://ftp.met.fsu.edu

http://www.scri.fsu.edu

http://sis.fsu.edu

http://www.fsu.edu

IX

Education

Franklin and Marshall College

http://www.fandm.edu

Georgia Institute of Technology

http://moralforce.cc.gatech.edu

http://howe.ce.gatech.edu

http://isye.gatech.edu

http://ejc.math.gatech.edu

http://mern.gatech.edu

http://penguin.gatech.edu

http://www.gatech.edu

SUNY Geneseo

http://mosaic.cc.geneseo.edu

Georgetown University

http://gusun.georgetown.edu

http://www.georgetown.edu

George Mason University

http://absolut.gmu.edu

http://www.science.gmu.edu

Georgia State Board of Regents

http://k-9.oit.peachnet.edu

http://catfish.valdosta.peachnet.edu

Georgia State University

http://chara.gsu.edu

http://www.cs.gsu.edu

http://www.gsu.edu

Gustavus Adolphus College

http://www.gac.edu

Hahnemann University

http://ubu.hahnemann.edu

Hanover College

http://www.hanover.edu

Harvard University

http://adswww.harvard.edu

http://cfa-www.harvard.edu

http://courses.harvard.edu

http://www.das.harvard.edu

http://gopher.dfci.harvard.edu

http://fas-gopher.harvard.edu

http://golgi.harvard.edu

http://gopher.harvard.edu

http://hea-www.harvard.edu

http://hols.harvard.edu

http://hrl.harvard.edu

http://hsph.harvard.edu

http://huh.harvard.edu

http://huhepl.harvard.edu

http://count51.med.harvard.edu

http://twod.med.harvard.edu

http://weeds.mgh.harvard.edu

http://oir-www.harvard.edu

http://phys2.harvard.edu

http://sao-www.harvard.edu

http://string.harvard.edu

http://chan4.student.harvard.edu

http://cmiyagis.student.harvard.edu

http://egstein.student.harvard.edu

http://ibhan.student.harvard.edu

http://mgelman.student.harvard.edu

Harvey Mudd College

http://www.hmc.edu

University of Hawaii

http://ftp.cfht.hawaii.edu

http://www.cfht.hawaii.edu

http://pegasus.ed.hawaii.edu

http://spectra.eng.hawaii.edu

http://www.eng.hawaii.edu

http://gopher.hawaii.edu

http://hccadb.hcc.hawaii.edu

http://kawika.hcc.hawaii.edu

http://pulua.hcc.hawaii.edu

http://www.hcc.hawaii.edu

http://irtf.ifa.hawaii.edu

http://jach.hawaii.edu

http://uhcarl.b.hawaii.edu

http://www.soest.hawaii.edu

Hope College

http://smaug.cs.hope.edu

Idaho State University

http://pharmacy.isu.edu

Illinois Mathematics and Science Academy

http://gluon.imsa.edu

http://imsasun.imsa.edu

http://www.imsa.edu

Indiana University

http://astrowww.astro.indiana.edu

http://ftp.bio.indiana.edu

http://cica.indiana.edu

http://ftp.cica.indiana.edu

http://www.cica.indiana.edu

http://loris.cisab.indiana.edu

http://www.cisab.indiana.edu

http://cogsci.indiana.edu

http://www.cs.indiana.edu

http://gopher.indiana.edu

http://infotech.indiana.edu

http://ist.indiana.edu

http://polecat.law.indiana.edu

http://www.law.indiana.edu

http://www.music.indiana.edu

http://tarski.phil.indiana.edu

http://iuis.ucs.indiana.edu

http://scwww.ucs.indiana.edu

http://www-iub.ucs.indiana.edu

http://www.indiana.edu

http://www-iub.indiana.edu

Indiana University-Purdue

http://chem.iupui.edu

http://www-b.iupui.edu

Iowa State University

http://www.cc.iastate.edu

http://www.cs.iastate.edu

http://info.iastate.edu

http://www.b.iastate.edu

http://www.pubc.iastate.edu

Jackson State University

http://tiger.jsums.edu

Johns Hopkins University

http://gopher.hs.jhu.edu

http://muse.mse.jhu.edu

http://merlot.welch.jhu.edu

Kansas State University

http://depot.cis.ksu.edu

http://www.cis.ksu.edu

http://www.ecc.ksu.edu

http://www.eece.ksu.edu

http://www.engg.ksu.edu

http://www.ksu.ksu.edu

http://godiva.ne.ksu.edu

http://www.ksu.edu

Kent State University

http://www.mcs.kent.edu

Kestrel Research Institute

http://kestrel.edu

Lake Forest College

http://br2.lfc.edu

IX

Education

Louisiana Tech University

http://aurora.latech.edu

http://info.latech.edu

Louisiana State University

http://unix1.sncc.lsu.edu

Loyola College

http://www.loyola.edu

University of Maine

http://gopher.ume.maine.edu

Maricopa Community College District

http://hakatai.mc.dist.maricopa.edu

http://www.emc.maricopa.edu

Marine Biological Laboratory

http://alopias.mbl.edu

Massachusetts Institute of Technology

http://ai.mit.edu

http://martigny.ai.mit.edu

http://prep.ai.mit.edu

http://www.ai.mit.edu

http://www-swiss.ai.mit.edu

http://alecto.mit.edu

http://alexander-hamilton.mit.edu

http://anxiety-closet.mit.edu

http://arsenio.mit.edu

http://bresn.mit.edu

http://consult-www.mit.edu

http://cremer.mit.edu

http://delcano.mit.edu

http://earthcube.mit.edu

http://eddie.mit.edu

http://eecs-test.mit.edu

http://far.mit.edu

http://farnsworth.mit.edu

http://foundation.mit.edu

http://gopher.mit.edu

http://jack-vance.mit.edu

http://japaninfo.mit.edu

http://jazz.mit.edu

http://joet.mit.edu

http://lancet.mit.edu

http://lcs.mit.edu

http://amsterdam.lcs.mit.edu

http://bronze.lcs.mit.edu

http://cag-www.lcs.mit.edu

http://clef.lcs.mit.edu

http://export.lcs.mit.edu

http://im.lcs.mit.edu

http://info.lcs.mit.edu

http://jukebox.lcs.mit.edu

http://ltt-www.lcs.mit.edu

http://medg.lcs.mit.edu

http://paris.lcs.mit.edu

http://reading-room-www.lcs.mit.edu

http://sls-www.lcs.mit.edu

http://sparta.lcs.mit.edu

http://theory.lcs.mit.edu

http://tns-www.lcs.mit.edu

http://tower.lcs.mit.edu

http://www.lcs.mit.edu

http://www-im.lcs.mit.edu

http://www-ni-gateway.lcs.mit.edu

http://www-psrg.lcs.mit.edu

http://macpythia.mit.edu

http://marie.mit.edu

http://debussy.media.mit.edu

http://microworld.media.mit.edu

http://rg.media.mit.edu

http://nmis03.mit.edu

http://rtfm.mit.edu

http://sipb.mit.edu

http://sobolev.mit.edu

http://sturgeon.mit.edu

http://synergy.mit.edu

http://the-tech.mit.edu

http://timesink.mit.edu

http://tk-www.mit.edu

http://uu-gna.mit.edu

http://uu-nna.mit.edu

http://vance.mit.edu

http://web.mit.edu

http://www-genome.wi.mit.edu

http://www-erl.mit.edu

http://www-techinfo.mit.edu

University of Memphis
http://www.memphis.edu

Memphis State University
http://www.memst.edu

Merit Computer Network
http://merit.edu

http://nic.merit.edu

MHPCC (Maui High Performance Computing Center)
http://pipene.mhpcc.edu

University of Miami
http://www.ir.miami.edu

http://iitcsun10.med.miami.edu

http://iitcsun3.med.miami.edu

http://www.rsmas.miami.edu

Miami University
http://m-media.muohio.edu

Michigan State University
http://ah3.cal.msu.edu

http://web.cal.msu.edu

http://burrow.cl.msu.edu

http://web.cl.msu.edu

http://indian.cps.msu.edu

http://web.cps.msu.edu

http://puck.egr.msu.edu

http://esalsun10.ent.msu.edu

http://gopher.msu.edu

http://pads1.pa.msu.edu

http://rs560.msu.edu

http://web.msu.edu

http://www.msu.edu

Mississippi State University
http://www.cs.msstate.edu

http://www.erc.msstate.edu

http://msuinfo.ur.msstate.edu

http://www.msstate.edu

University of Missouri at Columbia
http://teosinte.agron.missouri.edu

http://www.phlab.missouri.edu

Mt. Wilson Observatory
http://www.mtwilson.edu

National Air and Space Museum
http://ceps.nasm.edu

National Astronomy and Ionosphere Center
http://naic.edu

http://www.naic.edu

National Radio Astronomy Observatory
http://info.aoc.nrao.edu

http://zia.aoc.nrao.edu

http://fits.cv.nrao.edu

http://info.cv.nrao.edu

http://fits.nrao.edu

http://info.gb.nrao.edu

IX

Education

National Supercomputing Center for Energy and the Environment

http://www.nscee.edu

New Jersey Institute of Technology

http://eies.njit.edu

http://eies2.njit.edu

http://it.njit.edu

New Mexico State University

http://www.apo.nmsu.edu

http://charon.nmsu.edu

http://crl.nmsu.edu

http://vitoria.nmsu.edu

New Mexico Institute of Mining and Technology

http://nmt.edu

http://www.nmt.edu

New York University

http://edgar.stern.nyu.edu

http://www.nyu.edu

North Carolina State University

http://www.acs.ncsu.edu

http://www.catt.ncsu.edu

http://www.eos.ncsu.edu

http://dewey.b.ncsu.edu

http://ericmorgan.b.ncsu.edu

http://www.mmrc.ncsu.edu

http://meawx1.nrrc.ncsu.edu

http://www.tx.ncsu.edu

http://www.ncsu.edu

University of Notre Dame

http://orange-room.cc.nd.edu

http://undhe6.hep.nd.edu

http://www.nd.edu

Northeastern University

http://ftp.ccs.neu.edu

http://jh.ccs.neu.edu

http://www.ccs.neu.edu

http://www.cs.neu.edu

http://www.dac.neu.edu

Northwestern State University

http://lsmsa.nsula.edu

Northwestern University

http://antioch.acns.nwu.edu

http://daneel.acns.nwu.edu

http://pubweb.acns.nwu.edu

http://words.acns.nwu.edu

http://www.acns.nwu.edu

http://holmes.astro.nwu.edu

http://rossi.astro.nwu.edu

http://www.astro.nwu.edu

http://www.covis.nwu.edu

http://asgard.eecs.nwu.edu

http://tup.eecs.nwu.edu

http://www.eecs.nwu.edu

http://asp.esam.nwu.edu

http://www.ils.nwu.edu

http://www.brary.nwu.edu

http://math.nwu.edu

http://gopher.math.nwu.edu

http://hopf.math.nwu.edu

http://www.math.nwu.edu

http://voltaire.mech.nwu.edu

http://www.mmss.nwu.edu

http://www.psych.nwu.edu

http://www.speech.nwu.edu

http://www.nwu.edu

NOAO

http://ctios2.ctio.noao.edu

http://ctiot6.ctio.noao.edu

http://iraf.noao.edu

http://claret.kpno.noao.edu

http://coral.kpno.noao.edu

http://mocha.kpno.noao.edu

http://sunspot.noao.edu

http://blazing.sunspot.noao.edu

http://esf.sunspot.noao.edu

http://ftp.sunspot.noao.edu

http://vtt.sunspot.noao.edu

http://www.sunspot.noao.edu

http://argo.tuc.noao.edu

http://argo.tuc.noao.edu

http://daikon.tuc.noao.edu

http://icarus.tuc.noao.edu

http://tucana.tuc.noao.edu

http://www.tuc.noao.edu

http://www.noao.edu

Nova University

http://alpha.acast.nova.edu

Oakland University

http://gopher.acs.oakland.edu

http://mars.acs.oakland.edu

http://www.acs.oakland.edu

http://unix.secs.oakland.edu

Obern College

http://cs.obern.edu

Occidental College

http://apa.oxy.edu

http://gate.oxy.edu

Ohio State University

http://www.acs.ohio-state.edu

http://kirk.cgrg.ohio-state.edu

http://archive.cis.ohio-state.edu

http://www.cis.ohio-state.edu

http://hertz.eng.ohio-state.edu

http://hartke.b.ohio-state.edu

http://beetle.marion.ohio-state.edu

Ohio Supercomputer Center

http://osc.edu

http://www.osc.edu

Oklahoma State University

http://a.cs.okstate.edu

http://math.okstate.edu

http://ftp.math.okstate.edu

http://www.okstate.edu

Old Dominion University

http://www.cs.odu

http://xanth.cs.odu

Oregon State University

http://gopher.cs.orst.edu

http://www.csos.orst.edu

http://engr.orst.edu

Pennsylvania State University

http://euler.bd.psu.edu

http://opus.chem.psu.edu

http://random.chem.psu.edu

http://www.xray.hmc.psu.edu

http://www.math.psu.edu

http://info.pop.psu.edu

http://www.pop.psu.edu

http://bjt105.rh.psu.edu

http://www.psu.edu

Pittsburgh Supercomputer Center

http://pscinfo.psc.edu

University of Pittsburgh

http://artemis.phyast.pitt.edu

http://www.pitt.edu

SUNY College at Plattsburgh

http://bio420.hawk.plattsburgh.edu

Plymouth State College

http://www.plymouth.edu

IX

Education

Portland State University

http://gopher.cs.pdx.edu

http://ursula.ee.pdx.edu

http://www.ee.pdx.edu

SUNY College at Potsdam

http://gopher.dc.potsdam.edu

Princeton University

http://princeton.edu

http://astro.princeton.edu

http://www.cs.princeton.edu

http://bpd.student.princeton.edu

http://wombat.princeton.edu

http://www.princeton.edu

Purdue University

http://thunder.atms.purdu

http://mentor.cc.purdu

http://gopher.cs.purdu

http://www.cs.purdu

http://purgatory.ecn.purdu

Reed College

http://reed.edu

http://www.reed.edu

Rensselaer Polytechnic Institute

http://cs.rpi.edu

http://www.cs.rpi.edu

http://ftp.rpi.edu

http://wolf3.vlsc.rpi.edu

http://www.rpi.edu

Rice University

http://chico.rice.edu

http://softb.cs.rice.edu

http://es.rice.edu

http://harpo.rice.edu

http://hex.rice.edu

http://is.rice.edu

http://riceinfo.rice.edu

http://softb.rice.edu

http://vm.rice.edu

Rochester Institute of Technology

http://www.csh.rit.edu

University of Rochester

http://lancelot.cif.rochester.edu

http://lancelot.cif.rochester.edu

http://vein.cs.rochester.edu

http://www.cs.rochester.edu

http://sherman.pas.rochester.edu

Rockefeller University

http://pisa.rockefeller.edu

Rutgers

http://aristarchus.rutgers.edu

http://gandalf.rutgers.edu

http://info.rutgers.edu

http://ndb.rutgers.edu

http://www.usacs.rutgers.edu

http://www.rutgers.edu

http://www-ns.rutgers.edu

Saint John's University—College of St Benedict

http://bingen.cs.csbsju.edu

University of San Diego

http://teetot.acusd.edu

University of Southern California

http://info.broker.isi.edu

http://info.internet.isi.edu

http://venera.isi.edu

http://www.isi.edu

Chapter 10

Government Resources

Every year on April 15th millions of Americans make a last minute rush to send in federal taxes. The money, of course, goes to fund the largest economic engine in the world—the U.S. Government. The many different operations of the government account for approximately 11 percent of the nation's more than $5 trillion gross national product.

In theory, all of this money funds services that are of value to U.S. citizens—education, transportation, agriculture, defense. It is difficult to get a handle on the many services that are available, not to mention all the legislative issues, government documents, and research programs. In an effort to get information out to the public, the government and its various departments, agencies, divisions, and branches now use the World Wide Web system to distribute multimedia resources.

This effort begins to demystify government programs and makes it easier for ordinary citizens to "get involved" in the government decision-making process. The Department of Energy (DOE), for example, is enormous and oversees thousands of research efforts that range from the development of solar energy to testing nuclear weapons. Some of this research moves into private industry, which creates commercial applications (more efficient gasoline) and new job opportunities. There are more than 20 DOE laboratories and sites across the U.S. that maintain WWW servers.

On a practical level you can jump to a Web site that has information about efforts by the U.S. Fish and Wildlife Service to protect endangered species in your state, or learn how legislation impacts social security benefits, or search the Library of Congress for a specific book. State and local governments also maintain WWW servers. These provide useful resources for business people, tourists, and local residents.

FreeNets offer another mechanism for electronic access to federal, state, and local government resources and information. FreeNets began as electronic bulletin board systems (BBSs) where members of a community could use their computer to dial in and connect with a variety of local information. The first community FreeNet began in Cleveland in the mid-1980s. The name FreeNet comes from the fact that they are free of charge (except for long distance connect fees if you connect through a telephone number instead of the Web) and they use electronic networks for information delivery. FreeNets are non-profit, public service organizations. As such, these electronic towns strive to serve the members of a community with access to useful information. With their emphasis on the local community, you will find that FreeNet databases include calendars of events for museums and town meetings, public service directories, tips on local education, health care, gardening, and other subjects.

To reach a broad audience, many FreeNets now offer access via the Internet (usually a Telnet session) and the World Wide Web in addition to a dial-in BBS phone number. FreeNets now exist in communities across the U.S. and Canada. Like a real town, FreeNets maintain an electronic post office, public town hall, recreation center, library, museums, and schools. When you connect with a FreeNet you begin with a menu that resembles a city plan. Each menu selection represents a "building" that contains topical information. If you select school house, for example, you will receive a series of links and documents that relate to education.

If you want to find out where your tax dollars are going, or simply need to know about your town's emergency response procedures, check out the resources in this chapter. There are three categories: FreeNets, State and Local Government, and U.S. Government.

FedWorld

URL address: **http://www.fedworld.gov**

Have you ever read a newspaper article or listened to a radio report that cites a government study or report? This WWW site is the place to go if you want to see that report for yourself. The National Technical Information Service maintains this home page to help people deal with the challenge of accessing the vast amount of U.S. Government information. How vast? NITS provides users access to over two million documents, studies, and databases, and adds about 1,300 titles each week. This WWW server is extremely popular and has been accessed more than a half million times.

From the home page you have three main choices. First, you can go to the FedWorld FTP Site, which includes information on business, health, the environment, and the White House and National Performance Review. Second, you can link to the FedWorld Telnet site, which has information about 50 different agencies—you can order publications and learn about federal job opportunities. Third, you can click on an alphabetical index, which will help you locate and then access specific federal WWW sites. Rather than displaying a long list of servers, the alphabetical section has subject categories, such as Environmental Resources, which then opens a menu of servers that focus on that topic. This is a good starting point to jump into the U.S. Government.

Fig. 10.1
FedWorld represents a collection of hyperlinks to millions of government publications.

Library of Congress

URL address: **http://lcweb.loc.gov/homepage/lchp.html**

Fig. 10.2
The Library of Congress WWW home page is your gateway to the world's largest collection of information about published works.

If your local library doesn't have the book or resource you need, take an electronic trip to the digital card catalogs and shelves at the Library of Congress WWW home page. Each week approximately 5,000 people log into this server. If you are looking for a specific book (by author, subject, or title) click on the icon that begins a Telnet session to LOCIS (**telnet://locis.loc.gov**), the Library of Congress Information System. The menu selections at LOCIS include:

1. Library of Congress Catalog

2. Federal Legislation

3. Copyright Information

4. Braille and Audio

5. Organizations

6. Foreign Law

To search use first word	Examples
subject	browse solar energy
author	b faulkner, william
title or series	browse megatrends
partial LC call #	b call QA76.9
LC record #	loci 80-14332

The home page also sports links to some great exhibits and collections. The American Memory Project focuses on American culture and history with catalog items and digital reproductions including prints and photographs. You weave your way through a few links into the collections page where you find photographs from the Civil War (1861-1865) by Matthew Brady; portraits of literary figures and artists by Carl Van Vechten (1932-1964); and color photographs from the Farm Security Administration (1938-1944).

Another home page link is the Country Studies. This represents a series of documents that examine the political, social, and economic conditions in countries around the world such as Ethiopia, Egypt, the Philippines, and South Korea. If you are researching a project or paper, check out the Global Electronic Library that offers links to several WWW indexes and search tools.

State of North Carolina

URL address: **http://www.sips.state.nc.us/nchome.html**

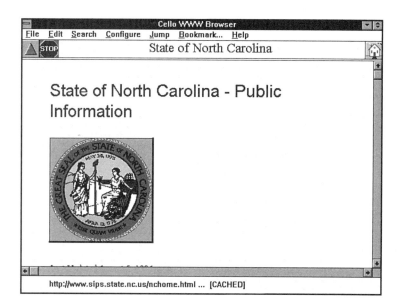

Fig. 10.3
The North Carolina WWW home page lets you access a wonderful multimedia encyclopedia that offers information about the 400-year history of the state.

What do Sir Walter Raleigh and the Wright Brothers have in common? They both played an important role in the history of North Carolina. This state takes the bull by the horns when it comes to the Information Age. From the home page, go to the FAQ document that does a good job of explaining how the state and state agencies are taking advantage of electronic communications. There is also a link to North Carolina and the Information Superhighway.

Several public agencies have contributed to the resources you can access from this home page. If you want to find out what elected representatives are doing, jump to the status of bills from the North Carolina General Assembly. Other home page links include:

Center for Geographic Information and Analysis

Division of Environmental Management

Office of State Personnel Job Vacancies

State Library

Cooperative Extension Service

Institute for Transportation Research and Education (ITRE)

Research Triangle Institute (RTI)

Weather In North Carolina

The State Library maintains an electronic multimedia guide to the Old North State—the North Carolina Encyclopedia. This fun and easy-to-use resource for adults and children combines text and visuals to give the reader a good understanding of the state's economy, educational and cultural assets, and the state's system of government. There are also overviews of the geography, the 100 counties, and 400-year history of the state. It's a great tool for education, tourist promotion, and business information.

National Capital FreeNet (NCF)

URL address: **http://www.ncf.carleton.ca/**

Fig. 10.4
Located on a Web server in Canada, the home page for the National Capital FreeNet has links to thousands of documents and resources for both the region and the country.

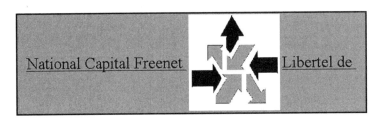

This URL address provides WWW access to the Ottawa, Canada FreeNet. The home page has a menu that offers five selections. The first and second choices are "Survival Guides" for new users (#1 is in English and #2 is in French). These selections bring up menus that provide advice on topics such as "Navigating Menus" and "Using the File System." Selection #3, NCF Information, jumps to the NCF FreeNet main menu, where you will find approximately 18 different service areas. There aren't a lot of fancy graphics here, but you could spend days going through all the links from this menu. A few examples include:

- *The Government Center.* Where you can weave your way to reports on Canadian national politics or to an organizational chart of the Ottawa police.

- *Professional Associations.* Find out about the Canadian Association of Journalists or other associations.

- *Schools, Colleges, and Universities.* Links range from Global Education to the Ottawa Board of Education.

- *Science, Engineering, and Technology Center.* Topics range from museums to women in engineering.

From the home page, menu item #4 brings you to the NCF message of the day, which is a list of new services and information resources. Finally, menu item #5 brings up a hypertext "GO" list. This is an alphabetical listing of all the special interest groups (SIGS) that offer information or newsgroup messages via the NCF.

FreeNets

Cambridge Civic Network
URL address:
**http://www.civic.net:2401/cambridge_civic_network/
cambridge_civic_network.html**

This Web server opens the door to information about civic organizations and resources in the Cambridge, Massachusetts, area. Through exploration of the links, local residents can get involved in programs and organizations that will shape the future of the community.

Denver, Colorado
URL address: **telnet://freenet.hsc.colorado.edu**

When you begin the Telnet session, login as guest. Some of the main menu selections include the World Futures Assembly Hall; Colorado health-care building; arts building; business and industrial park; community center and recreation area; and the courthouse and government center.

Detroit FreeNet
URL address: **http://http2.sils.umich.edu/~pegjones/HomePage.html**

The top of this home page displays a small color image of the city of Detroit. Useful links include a map of the counties in the area and a "Meta-Index," which offers links to educational resources (including a list of schools that maintain Gopher sites), area entertainment, transportation, and weather information.

Eugene, Oregon
URL address: **http://www.efn.org/**

This Web site is home base for the Eugene FreeNet, also known as the Oregon Public Networking (OPN) Web Page. One link is to a broad-based Gopher menu (URL address **gopher://efn.efn.org/**) where you can check a calendar that identifies dates for many local events ranging from free blood pressure checks for seniors to a Neville Brothers concert. There is also a link to *Oregon Online*—the state government Gopher that offers a broad range of documents, including information about current elections, candidate profiles, and ballot measures. One unique link from the home page brings up a list of other WWW home pages developed by OPN members.

Grand Rapids, Michigan
URL address: **http://www.grfn.org/**

This is a good WWW site to visit prior to your next trip to Grand Rapids. The information and links range from local weather forecasts to details about local attractions and modes of transportation.

Twin Cities FreeNet
URL address:
http://free-net.mpls stpaul.mn.us:8000/proto_top.html

In addition to the standard FreeNet links for government, education, and recreation, the Twin Cities home page has links to a medical arts building and information about the individual neighborhoods near St. Paul and Minneapolis.

Vancouver, British Columbia
URL address: **http://freenet.vancouver.bc.ca**

If you like one-stop shopping, this home page should be one of your first stops to an exploration of Canada and the Web. The mission statement will give you some idea of the broad scope of information that you can access here:

> "The Vancouver Regional FreeNet Association is dedicated to the development, operation and ownership of a free, publicly accessible community computer utility in the Lower Mainland of British Columbia providing the broadest possible range of information and possibilities for the exchange of experience, ideas and wisdom."

The people who maintain the server live up to this goal by beginning with links that take you to other WWW servers and information about Vancouver (this link begins a Telnet session), British Columbia, Canada, other FreeNets in the U.S., and global WWW home pages.

Victoria, British Columbia
URL address: **http://freenet.victoria.bc.ca/vifa.html**

This home page provides a useful link to a hyperlink list of all the WWW servers in British Columbia, commercial and non-commercial. There are also links to game resources, WWW hypertext magazine collections, and gateways to other FreeNets.

Other FreeNet Addresses

FreeNets Home Page
URL address: **http://herald.usask.ca/~scottp/free.html**

This WWW resource has lists (and links) to FreeNets around the world. Peter Scott at the University of Saskatchewan Libraries in Canada maintains the information as a "public service." Your choices include FreeNet access via WWW, Gopher, and Telnet. There are also FreeNet mailing lists, newsgroups, reference documents, and conference schedules.

Buffalo, New York
URL address: **telnet://freenet.buffalo.edu**

Cleveland, Ohio
URL address: **telnet://freenet-in-acwru.edu**

Halifax, Nova Scotia
URL address: **http://www.cfn.cs.dal.ca**

Montreal, Quebec
URL address: **http//thym.remm.uqam.ca**

Saskatoon, Saskatchewan
URL address: **http://www.usask.ca~fogel/freenet.html**

State and Local Government

Arizona—Phoenix
URL address: **http://www.rtd.com/arizona/phoenix/index.html**

In addition to being the state capital, Phoenix is the largest city in Arizona. This home page has numerous links to the history, cultural activities, social services, and city governments that are in the area.

California—Bay Area Governments
URL address: **http://www.abag.ca.gov/index.html**

The San Francisco Bay area encompasses a wide geographic area and several different government entities. This home page directs you to regional agencies, local governments, and a calendar of events. There is also a link to a list of state agencies such as the California Environmental Protection Agency and the Department of Forestry and Fire Protection

California—Palo Alto
URL address: **http://www.city.palo-alto.ca.us/home.html**

This is the heart of Silicon Valley, where computers and chips are a way of life and a means for making a living for thousands of residents. Find out about housing, visit the city library, retrieve demographic studies, learn about the schools and parks, and even visit the city council.

California—San Carlos
URL address:
http://www.abag.ca.gov/abag/local_gov/city/san_carlos/schome.html

This town uses its WWW site to open local government to the residents (and anyone else who has an interest). The home page has a letter from the mayor that discusses local education and efforts and procedures by the town and citizens to ensure emergency preparedness. There is an on-line guide to city business, license rules, and rates and news and tips from the fire, police, and parks and recreation departments.

California—San Diego
URL address: **http://white.nosc.mil/sandiego.html**

Tourists and local residents will appreciate this home page. There are guides to restaurants and entertainment as well as specifics about disaster and emergency response procedures, and tax and local school information.

Colorado—Boulder
URL address:
http://bcn.boulder.co.us/government/boulder_city/center.html

Boulder has a reputation for being a city where local residents get involved in government. This home page has links to the city council members including their phone numbers and addresses. There is detailed information about the city council agendas, city emergency preparedness, and weekly city calendars, boards, and commissions.

Illinois—Champaign County

URL address: **http://www.prairienet.org/SiliconPrairie/ccnet.html**

If you are doing business in Champaign county, or plan to relocate to the area, this WWW site has information about communities, living conditions, travel, and government resources.

Massachusetts—Cambridge

URL address:

http://www.ai.mit.edu/projects/iiip/Cambridge/homepage.html

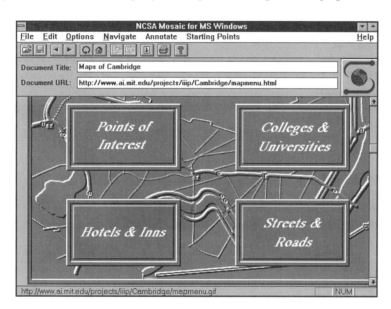

Fig. 10.5
The city of Cambridge's main map menu.

There are several digital maps of Cambridge here (including a subway map), a profile of the city, and links to the Civic Network and state educational resources.

Minnesota

URL address: **gopher://gopher.state.mn.us/**

This site, a Gopher server, offers directories that have information on the Department of Health, Legislature, Department of Transportation, Higher Education Coordinating Board, and the Center for Arts Education.

Rhode Island
URL address: **http://www.ids.net/ri.html**

This is the Rhode Island state information home page with press releases and copies of the Governor's speeches. You can jump to links that include artifacts at the Department of State Archives and the Department of Education. There is also a pointer to information on Providence, which even includes local bus and movie schedules.

Texas
URL address: **http://www.texas.gov**

URL address: **file://sun.stac.dir.texas.gov/TEXAS_homepage.html**

This WWW server provides access to resources of state agencies. You can begin your tour by reading a letter from the Governor—from there jump to sites and documents from several state agencies.

Texas—Austin
URL address: **http://www.quadralay.com/www/Austin/Austin.html**

Austin is the state capitol of Texas. This WWW site has more than 40 links to information about the local area and government.

Virginia
URL address: **http://www.elpress.com:80/staunton/**

Fig. 10.6

The Woodrow Wilson birthplace and museum is one of several fascinating historical sites you can visit from a link on this Virginia home page.

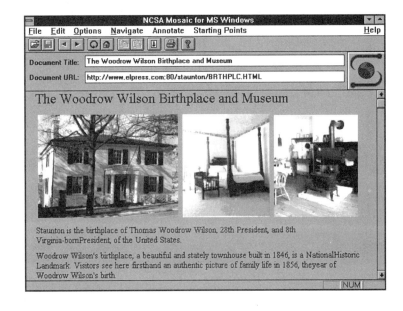

This is the home page for the "Queen City of the Shenandoah Valley." In addition to taking a virtual tour of the historic district and visiting local museums, you can jump into pages that offer details on the city government and county chamber of commerce.

U.S. Government

This section divides government WWW resources into three areas: general information, Legislative, and Executive branch resources. Note that this list represents only a portion of the U.S. Government departments, agencies and bureaus—many are still developing WWW servers.

General Information

FEDIX

URL address: **http://web.fie.com/**

Federal Information Exchange, Inc. (FEDIX) is a commercial company that provides documentation from many different government agencies. One of its goals is to connect institutions of higher education with the federal government in an effort to assist research and educational programs. FEDIX contains data from both the *Commerce Business Daily*, *The Federal Register*, and other government agencies. Try **http://www.fie.com/www/ district.htm** to get a current list of government, commercial, and educational WWW servers located in the District of Columbia.

National Information Infrastructure

URL address: **http://sunsite.unc.edu/nii/NII-Table-of-Contents.html**

Maintained at the University of North Carolina, this home page lets you review the U.S. government's proposal on the goals and development of this national communications system, which will directly tie into the Internet and the World Wide Web.

National Performance Review

URL address: **http://sunsite.unc.edu/npr/nptoc.html**

This home page begins with the phrase "Creating a Government That Works Better and Costs Less." It is a hypertext version of Vice President Al Gore's proposal to improve and reinvent government and includes a short audio message from Mr. Gore and President Clinton.

National Technology Transfer Center
URL address: **http://iridium.nttc.edu/nttc.html**

Technology transfer involves moving the technology and research that oc-curs in our government's facilities and government sponsored activities into the private sector where companies can apply the technology to viable com-mercial applications. This home page offers links to regional, state, and fed-eral activities as well as information on conferences, workshops, and funding that relates to tech transfer.

National Trade Data Bank
URL address:
http://www.stat-usa.gov/BEN/Topics/TradePromo.html

Fig. 10.7
The National Trade Data Bank Web site opens the door to more than 100 databases of information on trade.

This Web site contains trade information gathered by more than 20 federal agencies. The focus is to improve international trade and export opportuni-ties. Topics include export opportunities by industry and product, trade sta-tistics, how-to guides, and socio-economic conditions. From the home page you can search 125 trade and business databases.

North American Free Trade Agreement
URL address: **http://the-tech.mit.edu/Bulletins/nafta.html**

Here you will find more than 50 individual documents that discuss all aspects of this trade agreement between the U.S., Mexico, and Canada.

SunSITE Government Documents
URL address: **http://sunsite.unc.edu/govdocs.html**

This WWW server offers several hypertext versions of federal documents that have a broad interest such as Technology for Economic Growth, the President's Progress Report, National Health Security Plan, and President Clinton's Saturday Radio Addresses (as audio files).

White House Electronic Publications
URL address: **http://www.acns.nwu.edu/us.gov.online.html**

This Web site has numerous links to documents created by the White House, such as press releases, links to searchable databases of White House publications such as the FTP link **ftp://cco.caltech.edu:/pub/bjmccall**, or information that addresses the White House such as the files from the newsgroup **alt.politics.usa.misc**.

Legislative Branch

Currently neither the U.S. Senate nor House of Representatives operate WWW servers. They do, however, maintain Gopher servers that provide electronic documents that are categorized by member and committee, and offer keyword searching. The address for the U.S. Senate Gopher site is **gopher://gopher.senate.gov:70/1** and the address for the U.S. House of Representatives is **gopher://gopher.house.gov:70/1**.

Senator Edward Kennedy does have a Web address: URL address **http://www.ai.mit.edu/projects/iiip/Kenedy/homepage.html**.

Executive Branch

The President has direct control over the Executive Branch of the U.S. Government and all the following departments (Agriculture, Commerce, Defense, and so on) are cabinet level agencies.

Department of Agriculture

Agricultural Genome
URL address: **http://probe.nalusda.gov:8000/index.html**

USDA—Soil Conservation Service
URL address: **http://www.ncg.scs.ag.gov**

The Soil Conservation Service administers programs that help people conserve and improve the country's natural resources. From this home page you can link to comprehensive information about programs and legislative issues that relate to soil, water, air, plants, animals, and human conditions. There are also links to state, regional, and national offices.

Fig. 10.8
Conservation is one of the keynotes to the resources on the U.S. Department of Agriculture home page.

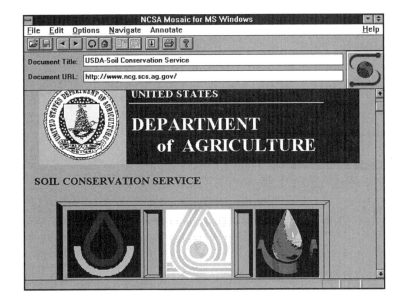

Department of Commerce

Commerce Department
URL address: **http://www.doc.gov**

The Commerce Department's home page has links to documents about the department and dozens of other government-based WWW, Gopher, FTP, Telnet, and WAIS sites. You can jump to the *Commerce Business Daily,* which has a directory of federal government requests for bids on proposals; Federal Tax Forms, which has an index of more than 700 forms that are free to download; and Senate and Congressional sites and directories.

Information Infrastructure Task Force (IITF)
URL address: **http://iitf.doc.gov:70**

If you have an interest in the future of the Internet, the WWW, and the Information Superhighway, take a look. You will find many interesting reports, like one on an Advanced Digital Video in the NII workshop, a calendar of events, and speeches.

National Institute of Standards and Technology (NIST)
URL address: **http://www.nist.gov/welcome.html**

NIST sponsors and conducts a variety of scientific research programs ranging from biotechnology to computer technology. Many efforts, such as the Manufacturing Extension Centers, directly help industry and small business.

National Telecommunications and Information Administration
URL address: **http://www.ntia.doc.gov/**

Organized like a book with a table of contents, the National Telecommunications and Information Administration home page has links to international activities, legislation, spectrum management, and legislative testimony.

National Oceanic and Atmospheric Administration (NOAA)
URL address: **http://www.noaa.gov**

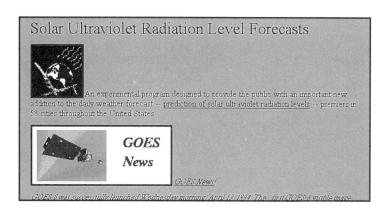

Fig. 10.9
NOAA's home page has links to their current research on solar ultraviolet radiation and other hot topics.

Find out whether you need to put on sunblock 45 today. NOAA is involved with all aspects of scientific research related to the oceans and the atmosphere. For example, this agency monitors and studies the impact of the annual fires that occur in the Western United States. The home page also has a link to an overview of an experimental program that provides 58 cities across the U.S. with daily information about solar ultraviolet radiation levels.

National Oceanographics Data Center
URL address: **http://www.nodc.noaa.gov/index.html**

This is the home page for one of the data centers that NOAA operates. You can find out more about the center and its operations such as how to obtain products (such as data) or submit data.

U.S. Bureau of the Census
URL address: **http://www.census.gov**

The role of the U.S. Bureau of the Census is to constantly collect data about the people and economy of the U.S. It then takes this data and produces volumes of reports. This home page is easy-to-use and incorporates a lot of small icons for areas like Center for Economic Studies, Financial Data, International Programs, and Statistical Briefs—lots of data here. Also try the

Census Phone List (URL address **http://gopher.census.gov:70/1m/Bureau/Who/who)**, a Who's Who list that contains phone numbers for many different services that relate to census information, including census customer service; regional offices; and agriculture, construction, government, housing, and state and local data centers.

Fig. 10.10
The Bureau of the Census home page connects you with volumes of reports, statistics, and data about the population of the United States.

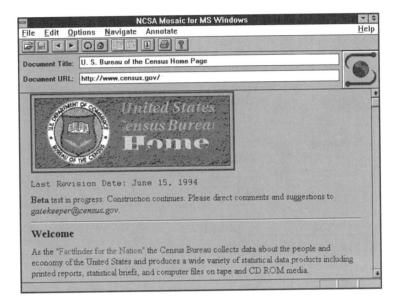

U.S. Patent and Trademark Office
URL address: **http://www.uspto.gov**

Here you will find a variety of information about patents and intellectual property, which brings to light interesting issues about patents as they relate to information and data on computer networks. You can also take a look at info on public hearings of software patent protection.

Department of Defense

The following Department of Defense (DOD) sites are open to the public. However, there are many DOD WWW sites that contain information of a more secure nature and to which access is limited to military personnel only.

ARPA
URL address: **http://ftp.arpa.mil**

This information server is an FTP site that provides some information about the activities and programs of the Advanced Research Projects Agency

(ARPA)—the group that got the Internet started back in the 1960s. It contains information provided by the Computing Systems Technology Office (CSTO). There are details about the High Performance Computing and Communications Program, and links to research and solicitation for government projects. In its goal to become a completely electronic based program, this WWW server will become a central entry point for all ARPA electronic information services.

The Air Force

Air Force
URL address: **http://iitcsun10.med.miami.edu/persons/nick/usaf/**

Fig. 10.11
A wealth of hot links on the Air Force home page should provide you with more information on this service branch than you imagined possible.

Fly high when you start with this home page for the U.S. Air Force. You can jump to the Headquarters for the Air Force or learn about Air Force ROTC or pilot training efforts.

The Army

U.S. Army
URL address: **http://white.nosc.mil/army.html**

This WWW home page for the Army has a variety of links to education and research efforts, even one to the U.S. Military Academy at West Point.

Army Corps of Engineers
URL address: **http://www.usace.mil/cespd.html**

This is the WWW site for the South Pacific Division of the Army Corps of Engineers. You can access bid documents for current projects, public archives, and geographic maps.

X

Government Resources

Army Research Laboratory
URL address: **http://info.arl.army.mil**

The purpose of this WWW site is to enable scientists from government, academia, and industry to discover information about ARL including facilities and research projects.

Defense Information Systems Agency's Center for Engineering
URL address: **http://disa11.disa.atd.net**

A very specialized server with information on "technology insertion activities for information systems in the Department of Defense." The focus is on IS technologies like wireless and ATM—Asynchronous Transfer Mode is a high-speed switching/transmission technology for delivery of broadband voice, video, and data. For the general public there is a test video of the Clementine Moon Shot (455K) and a sound clip from Neil Armstrong—don't forget to sign the visitors book.

The Navy

Navy Online
URL address: **http://www.ncts.navy.mil**

This is your electronic gateway to the Department of Navy on-line resources. You will find fact sheets and public affairs information.

David Taylor Model Basin, Communications & Information Systems Department
URL address: **http://navysgml.dt.navy.mil**

This is another home page for computer enthusiasts. The Communications & Information Systems Department provides the Navy with expertise in the CALS and SGML initiatives, both of which deal with the implementation of electronic documentation and electronic purchase orders.

Naval Research Laboratory
URL address: **http://www.nrl.navy.mil**

This is the Navy's Research & Development lab, which was created in 1923 by Congress. The research focuses on the Naval environments—the sea, sky, and space. You'll find an organizational directory and information about specific research efforts.

Department of Education

U.S. Department of Education
URL address: **http://www.ed.gov**

Established in 1980, the Department of Education focuses on providing access to equal educational opportunities for all individuals. The Department sponsors programs that are designed to improve the quality of the U.S. educational system. From the home page you can jump to information about the National Education Goals, teacher's and researcher's guides to the USDOE, staff, offices, newsletters, and other educational resources.

Department of Energy

Energy Sciences Network—ESnet
URL address: **http://www.es.net**

The Energy Sciences Network is a nationwide computer data communications network managed and funded by the U.S. Department of Energy (DOE) Office of Energy Research (ER). ESnet connects the U.S. energy research community, which consists of the DOE national laboratories and DOE-funded, U.S. universities, to enhance energy research. ESnet facilitates access to scientific facilities, provides information dissemination among scientific collaborators throughout all ER programs, and provides access to ER supercomputer facilities. You can download an electronic brochure, contact information, the ESnet Steering Committee, a map of the network backbone, and individual sites and statistics on network usage. There is also an electronic White Pages that has approximately 130,000 entries.

Fermi National Accelerator Laboratory
URL address: **http://fnnews.fnal.gov**

This server includes information for the general public on Fermilab, which studies high-energy physics—the fundamental particles and forces of nature. It includes information for physicists and other technical professionals in related subjects. Descriptions of education programs are also on-line.

Fig. 10.12

The Fermilab home page offers the public information on one of the most advanced research centers in the world.

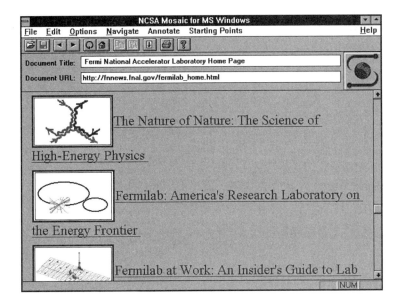

Office of Environment, Safety, and Health
URL address: **http://apollo.osti.gov/eh/eh_home.html**

There's not a lot here. The Office focuses on issues of safety and health for DOE facilities.

Office of Science Education and Technical Information
URL address: **http://apollo.osti.gov/home.html**

This WWW site offers a broad overview of the Department of Energy's efforts with news information, directory of DOE servers, and people, places, and organizations links. There is an unfinished (in construction) link to a national DOE telephone directory.

Office of Energy Research
URL address: **http://www.acl.lanl.gov/DOE/OER.html**

A good overview page for the different types of energy research such as fusion, nuclear, and basic energy.

Office of Fusion Energy
URL address: **http://wwwofe.er.doe.gov**

The home page makes the Office of Fusion Energy's mission clear, which is to, "develop fusion as an environmentally attractive, commercially viable, and sustainable energy source for the Nation and the world." There are lots of links about that subject.

Superconducting Super Collider

URL address: **http://www.ssc.gov**

The Superconducting Super Collider is not being built; however, this home page does offer links to information about the project with a rather sad link entitled "A chronicle of events up to the fatal vote."

Laboratories of the Department of Energy

Argonne National Laboratory

URL address: **http://www.anl.gov**

Located near Chicago, Argonne employs almost 5,000 people who research various aspects of energy. The home page has both audio links as well as links to documents about the Lab's research.

Brookhaven National Laboratory

URL address: **http://suntid.bnl.gov:8080/bnl.html**

Overviews of scientific research programs that examine energy such as the "Relativistic Heavy Ion Collider."

Lawrence Berkeley Laboratory

URL address: **http://www.lbl.gov/LBL.html**

Nine Nobel prize winners have worked at LBL. Start with an introduction to the Lab and then work your way into research news, scientific programs, technology transfer (science that moves into private industry), and educational programs.

Lawrence Livermore National Laboratory

URL address: **http://www.llnl.gov**

This government Research & Development lab has many different projects. From the WWW home page learn about high-performance computing, advanced sensors, and energy technologies.

Los Alamos National Laboratory

URL address: **http://www.lanl.gov/welcome.html**

This home page gives you links to a variety of documents on energy and nuclear weapons research.

National Energy Research Supercomputer Center

URL address: **http://www.nersc.gov**

Located at the Lawrence Livermore National Laboratory, this center is home base for supplying high-performance computer and networking services to the nationwide energy research community. From the home page you can jump to newsletters and newsgroups to find out more specifics, retrieve an introductory brochure, or (if you are a qualified user) request computer and storage allocations.

National Renewable Energy Laboratory
URL address: **http://www.nrel.gov**

NREL's server provides information on renewable energy research, development, and applications including technology transfer of renewable energy research to the private sector, accumulated energy data and resource maps, publications, and business and job opportunities.

Oak Ridge National Laboratory
URL address: **http://www.ornl.gov**

This server provides information on subjects about the laboratory including basic and applied research, media releases, ORNL publications, and educational opportunities.

Pacific Northwest Laboratory
URL address: **http://www.pnl.gov:2080**

Not a lot of links here. The home page describes activities of the lab: "A major part of PNL's activities is specifically focused on resolving environmental issues, such as waste cleanup at Hanford and global climate change."

Princeton Plasma Physics Laboratory
URL address: **http://www.pppl.gov**

Energy research, technology transfer, and lab resources are some of the documents you can read on-line at this site.

Sandia National Laboratory
URL address: **http://www.sandia.gov**

The home page is a long list of links to information about Sandia, such as capabilities, facilities, news and events, and a phone book. There's also a link to New Mexico weather.

Department of Health and Human Services

U.S. Department of Health and Human Services
URL address: **http://www.os.dhhs.gov**

The U.S. Department of Health and Human Services (HHS) is a cabinet agency that focuses on a variety of tasks to maintain and improve the health and well-being of the nation's population. With an emphasis on children, the elderly, persons with disabilities, the poor, and others who are most vulnerable, HHS is the principal government agency responsible for protecting health and for providing human services to Americans. This WWW home page has a multitude of links for information on the mission, programs, organization, initiatives, activities, and impact of this agency.

FDA Center for Food Safety & Applied Nutrition
URL address: **http://vm.cfsan.fda.gov/index.html**

A very valuable source of information about food safety and nutrition, here you can learn about food labeling, find out about the seafood hotline, food borne illness education, cosmetics labeling, and other useful data.

National Institute of Health
URL address: **http://www.nih.gov**

The National Institute of Health Web server will link you with a variety of information about U.S. health programs, resources, and research activities. The home page offers NIH grants and contracts, research opportunities, and topics of molecular biology and molecular modeling.

Social Security Administration
URL address: **http://www.ssa.gov/SSA_Home.html**

Information here is available in English and Spanish. You will find social security news, benefit information (includes disability, survivors, etc.), a social security handbook (a summary of all benefits and policies), speeches, and legislative data.

Department of the Interior

United States Fish and Wildlife Service
URL address: **http://bluegoose.arw.r9.fws.gov/FWSHomePage.html**

If you enjoy the great outdoors you will enjoy this WWW site as it links to information about the National Wildlife Refugee System, saving endangered species, conserving migratory birds, restoring fisheries, and enforcing wildlife laws.

United States Geological Survey
URL address: **http://info.er.usgs.gov**

Start your visit to this home page with an audio or video message. The USGS is a "fact-finding and research organization" that deals specifically with the earth sciences. Many people know about the USGS from the topographical maps they create. There are many links available here.

Assistant Secretary for Territorial and International Affairs
URL address:
http://info.er.usgs.gov/doi/territorial-International-Affairs.html

This department helps with issues related to federal policy in Guam, the U.S. Virgin Islands, American Samoa, and other territories.

Bureau of Indian Affairs
URL address: **http://info.er.usgs.gov/doi/bureau-indian-affairs.html**

This agency works with Indian tribal governments and Alaska Native village communities. Not a lot of links here, just basic information.

Bureau of Land Management
URL address:
http://info.er.usgs.gov/doi/bureau-land-management.html

The BLM manages almost 272 million acres or one-eighth of the nation's land resources. You'll find detailed information about programs and state-by-state contact addresses. You can also jump to the BLM FTP site **(ftp://dsc.blm.gov)**.

Bureau of Mines
URL address: **http://www.usbm.gov**

This home page has links to history, organizational structure, lists of new publications (such as annual state reports), and Internet accessible services.

Bureau of Reclamation
URL address: **http://info.er.usgs.gov/doi/bureau-of-reclamation.html**

The Bureau of Reclamation is known for its large dams and power plant projects. This page will tell you a bit more.

Minerals Management Service
URL address:
http://info.er.usgs.gov/doi/minerals-management-service.html

This service manages most of the mineral resources on the Nation's outer continental shelf. You'll find news releases, state contacts, and an FTP link to more information.

National Park Service
URL address: **http://info.er.usgs.gov/doi/national-park-service.html**

Our national parks began with Yellowstone, which was created in 1872. This WWW document gives you information about the Service and its regional offices.

Department of Justice

Federal Bureau of Investigation
URL address: **http://naic.nasa.gov/fbi/FBI_homepage.html**

This home page begins with a $1 million reward for information about 14 unsolved bombings—jump in to learn more.

Department of Transportation

U.S. Department of Transportation
URL address: **http://www.dot.gov**

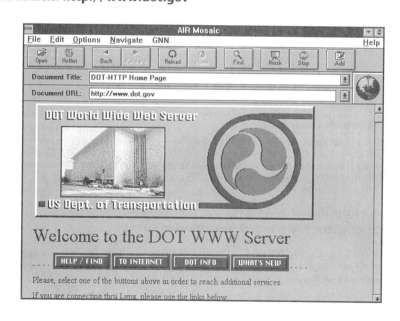

Fig. 10.13
If you own a bicycle, car, or semi, the information in the Department of Transportation home page may be of interest.

When you're driving down the highway you probably aren't thinking about this Web site. But if you need to learn about USDOT programs, find someone who works at USDOT (try a search for "Smith," you'll get quite a few), or find out about procurement and grant management, then check this out.

Independent Agencies and Institutions

Center for Earth and Planetary Studies
URL address: **http://ceps.nasm.edu:2020/homepage.html**

This Regional Planetary Images Facility (RPIF) is a reference library for people who want to review the collection of images from various space missions. There are approximately 300,000 digital images of planets available.

National Aeronautics and Space Administration (NASA)

NASA Home Page
URL address: **http://www.gsfc.nasa.gov/NASA_homepage.html**

This WWW site will connect you to every resource that deals with NASA, national space labs and facilities, research information, and space missions. (Also see the description of this site in the resource listings for chapter 16, "Science Resources.")

NASA Affiliated Institutions

Ames Research Center
URL address: **http://www.arc.nasa.gov**

Located in California, Ames performs a variety of research programs and has the world's most sophisticated wind tunnel.

Dryden Flight Research Center
URL address: **http://www.dfrf.nasa.gov/dryden.html**

This center focuses on high-performance flight research and testing.

Goddard Space Flight Center
URL address: **http://www.gsfc.nasa.gov/GSFC_homepage.html**

The mission of the Goddard Space Flight Center is "to expand knowledge of the Earth and its environment, the solar system, and the universe through observations from space." The home page also has a link to an X.500 address directory.

GSFC SeaWiFS Project

URL address: **http://seawifs.gsfc.nasa.gov/SEAWIFS.html**

This is the home page for NASA's global ocean color monitoring mission, which uses information gathered by satellites to examine the conditions of Earth's oceans.

Jet Propulsion Laboratory

URL address: **http://www.jpl.nasa.gov/ftps.html**

This is a fun WWW site. You can jump to an extensive list of space images, such as the Magellan mission topographic map of the surface of Venus, and then view the GIF images.

Johnson Space Center

URL address: **http://www.jsc.nasa.gov/JSC_homepage.html**

Johnson Space Center plays a major role in space missions. The home page has links to very technical subjects like the Robotics Systems Technology Branch, and Mechanical Design and Analysis Branch.

Kennedy Space Center Home Page

URL address: **http://www.ksc.nasa.gov/ksc.html**

Fig. 10.14
The Kennedy Space Center logo on their home page proudly displays an artistic look at the center and a space shuttle launch.

Built in the 1960s, this is where the majority of the Space Shuttle launches occur today. The home page will let you jump to historical archives, space shuttle mission overviews, and a list of upcoming events.

Langley

URL address: **http://www.larc.nasa.gov/larc.html**

Langley's mission is broad and ambitious: "To be the world leader in pioneering science and innovative technology to ensure U.S. aeronautical and space preeminence." Find out more from this WWW site.

Scientific & Technical Information Program
URL address: **http://nova.sti.nasa.gov**

This Web site provides documents that explain NASA programs, as well as a comprehensive NASA thesaurus that will let you know, for example, that Argon-Oxygen atmosphere is a narrower term for cabin atmosphere.

Government Consortia

Army High Performance Computing Research Center
URL address: **http://www.arc.umn.edu/html/ahpcrc.html**

This is a university-based Research & Development consortium that focuses on computing.

National Center for Atmospheric Research
URL address: **http://http.ucar.edu/metapage.html**

NCAR uses supercomputers to learn about the atmosphere and weather. For skiers, the home page has a link to a Colorado Ski Report.

National Consortium for High Performance Computing
URL address: **http://info.lcs.mit.edu**

Learn all about the meetings, conferences, courses, workshops, and member institutions in this consortia for computing.

More Federal Information— Government Gophers

The following are U.S. Government Gopher sites that offer documents (many of them are compressed), which you can either view on-line or download.

Congressional Information from Library of Congress
URL address: **gopher://gopher.loc.gov:70/11/congress**

Environmental Protection Agency
URL address: **gopher://futures.wic.epa.gov:70/1**

Extension Service USDA Information
URL address: **gopher://zeus.esusda.gov:70/1**

Federal Communications Commission (FCC)
URL address: **gopher://gopher.fcc.gov:70/1**

Federal Government Information from Library of Congress
URL address: **gopher://gopher.loc.gov:70/11/federal**

Federal Networking Council Advisory Committee
URL address: **gopher://fncac.fnc.gov:70/1**

National Center for Education Statistics
URL address: **gopher://gopher.ed.gov:10000/1**

United States Budget 1995
URL address: **gopher://gopher.esa.doc.gov:70/11/BUDGETFY95**

White House Information Service
URL address: **gopher://gopher.tamu.edu:70/11/.dir/president.dir**

X

Government Resources

Chapter 11

Health and Medicine

Health and medicine are subjects that impact every man, woman, and child. The topic is important and controversial. With a national health bill that exceeds $900 billion and approximately 37 million uninsured Americans, the U.S. health-care system faces tremendous challenges as government, health-care providers, employers, and employees look for positive changes in the quality, cost structure, and coverage of medical care. Conference proceedings, proposals, statistics, and opinions on the issue of health care exist on many WWW servers.

Millions of people live with medical conditions ranging from allergies to diabetes to migraine headaches. Medical institutions and commercial firms conduct a never-ending quest for cures, medication, and fitness programs that will help people live longer, happier, healthier lives. The WWW offers a tremendous amount of specific information as well as "pointers" to resources for several areas of health and medicine. These include:

- Specific diseases (such as AIDS)

- Conditions (such as pregnancy)

- Emergencies (such as poisons)

- Good health practices (exercise programs and nutrition)

The resources in this section are in categories that help you find the information that fits your specific medical interest or requirement. The section "General Health Resources by Topic" categorizes Web home pages that relate to general health themes, such as allergies and family medicine. "Health Centers" lists those institutions that focus on a very specific area of medical research or information, such as the Center of Food Safety and Applied Nutrition. "Medical Education" lists institutions that have programs that train individuals to provide medical care, and the "Research" section lists organizations that focus on the research aspects of medical science. You should note that there is some overlap in these broad categories, and an institution in the "Health Centers" section may also perform education and research activities.

Abdominal Training FAQ

URL address:
http://clix.aarnet.edu.au/misc.fitness/abdominal-training.html

If you want to keep your abdominal area in tip-top shape, or simply want to eliminate a "spare tire," this is the WWW address for you! Located at the University of Queensland, Australia, this series of Frequently Asked Questions is an introduction to the basic principles of training the abdominal area. The creation of this set of WWW documents was motivated by frequent questions on the topic in the newsgroup **misc.fitness**. You can also get this information via anonymous FTP from **rtfm.mit.edu** in (**ftp://rtfm.mit.edu/ pub/usenet/misc.fitness/Abdominal_Training_FAQ**). The table of contents has links to individual documents that provide advice on common questions about mid-section exercise. These include:

Question 4: How do I exercise the abs?

Question 5: What's wrong with situps?

Question 6: What are good ab exercises?

Question 7: Is there a specific order I should do exercises in?

HealthNet

URL address: **http://debra.dgbt.doc.ca:80/~mike/healthnet**

HealthNet should be one of your first destinations in your exploration of health and medicine on the Web. Developed by the Communications Development Directorate of Industry Canada, the main goal of the project is to raise awareness about health-care applications for the Information Superhighway. HealthNet uses the WWW to educate health-care providers, governments, private groups, and any individuals who have an interest in health care and about what types of electronic health services are currently available and the future developments that may be feasible.

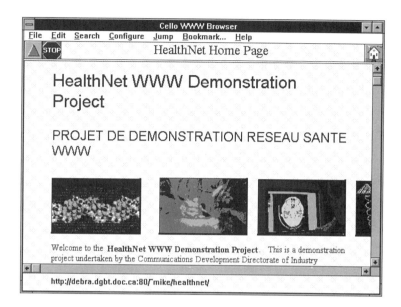

Fig. 11.1
The hyperlinks on
the HealthNet
home page bring
you to government
agencies and
educational
institutions
around the world.

The HealthNet WWW Demonstration Project accomplishes this education in
two ways. First, it provides a comprehensive set of hypertext links to medical
and health-care resources currently available on the Internet/World Wide
Web. Second, it provides an interactive "hands-on resource" for demonstrat-
ing future medical and health-care applications for the Information Superhighway. HealthNet hyperlinks take you to the following categories of
health-related information:

- Biotechnology initiatives and health-care human resource planning

- Clinical and administrative applications

- Government health-care sites

- Health-care applications for the electronic highway

- Hypertext list of Internet health-care resources and contact information

- Medical and health research applications

- Medical education and community health applications

The HealthNet WWW Demonstration Project is an international and collaborative effort. Available publicly via the Internet, it welcomes participation
from anyone who wants to contribute ideas, materials, or comments. For
updates on the HealthNet WWW Demo or to keep up on other topics related
to health-care networking in Canada, subscribe to the HealthNet listserv.

Send a message to **listserv@calvin.dgbt.doc.ca** with the message sub-scribe healthnet and place your name in the body of the text. You may want to review the procedures for sending electronic mail covered in chapter 1, "The Internet."

U. S. Department of Health and Human Services

URL address: **http://www.os.dhhs.gov**

Fig. 11.2
This Web server provides access to a vast amount of information that U.S. government agencies maintain on documents and programs related to health.

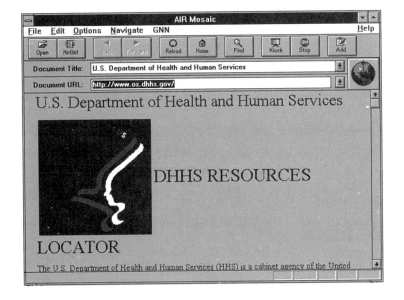

A cabinet agency of the United States Federal Government, the U.S. Department of Health and Human Services (HHS) focuses on programs that both maintain and improve the health and well-being of the nation's population. The agency emphasizes programs that help children, the elderly, persons with disabilities, and the poor. The Department administers social security benefits, prevents and controls disease, alcohol and drug abuse, conducts and supports medical and biomedical research, promotes child development, and assures the safety and efficacy of drugs. HHS administers nearly 300 grant programs that directly serve or assist one out of every five Americans.

The purpose of this WWW server is to provide information on the mission, programs, organization, initiatives, and activities of the U.S. Department of Health and Human Services. From the top of the home page you can jump to an alphabetized listing of specific programs that begin with "AIDS Related

Information" and finish with "Social Security Statistics." There is also a link to the Catalog of Federal Domestic Assistance Programs (**http:// www.sura.net/gsa.html**), which the General Services Administration maintains. From this server you can perform searches to locate information about financial and nonfinancial assistance programs. The HHS home page also provides links to information and resources made available by the various organizations that comprise HHS and other health-related agencies. Here are a few places you can jump to:

Health Organization	Internet/WWW address
Centers for Disease Control (CDC) FTP	**file://ftp.cdc.gov**
Food and Drug Administration (FDA) Telnet— "bbs"	**telnet://fdabbs.fda.gov**
National Center for Food Safety and Applied Nutrition (CFSAN)	**http://vm.cfsan.fda.gov/index.html**
National Center for Toxicological Research (NCTR) Gopher	**gopher://gopher.nctr.fda.gov**
National Institutes of Health (NIH)	**http://www.nih.gov**
National Institute of Allergy and Infectious Diseases (NIAID) Gopher	**gopher://gopher.niaid.nih.gov**
National Institute of Mental Health (NIMH) Gopher	**gopher://gopher.nimh.nih.gov**
National Institute of Environmental Health Sciences (NIEHS) Gopher	**gopher://gopher.niehs.nih.gov**
National Library of Medicine (NLM)	**http://www.nlm.nih.gov**

XI

Health and Medicine

Palo Alto Medical Foundation

URL address: **http://www.service.com/PAMF/home.html**

A nonprofit organization, the Palo Alto Medical Foundation encompasses a research institute and health-care and education divisions. At the facility approximately 160 physicians provide medical care for more than 110,000 people. Scientists conduct research in the areas of human health concerns, including immunology and infectious diseases, cholesterol metabolism, heart and cardiovascular dynamics, and cancer cell biology. Instructors in the health-care division teach classes in a wide variety of areas related to health promotion including early diagnosis and prevention.

From the home page you can access the monthly publication *HealthNews* (**http://www.service.com/PAMF/healthnews/home.html**), which is published by the Palo Alto Medical Clinic/Health Care Division of the Palo Alto Medical Foundation for Health Care, Research and Education. There are also links to a community health calendar and health education and support groups.

Rapid changes are occurring in the U.S. health-care system. The quality of care, rising costs, and benefits are some of the important issues that face individuals, companies, and medical providers. The hypertext link "The Symposium—Can Managed Care Heal America?" (**http://www.service.com/PAMF/symposium.html**) brings you to documentation on this conference, a follow-up of five separate conferences that address the costs and administration of health care.

Stanford University Medical Center

URL address:
http://med-www.Stanford.EDU/MedCenter/welcome.html

Fig. 11.3
When you jump to this home page you access the information resources of the oldest medical center in the Western United States.

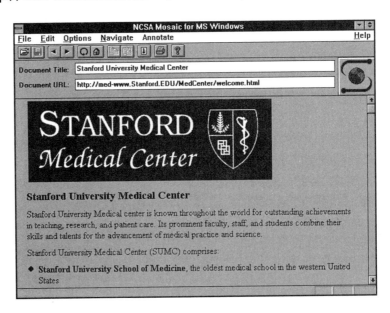

The Stanford University Medical Center (SUMC) is internationally recognized for its outstanding achievements in teaching, research, and patient care. From the home page you can jump to a page of phone numbers for the departments in the Medical Center, and there are numerous links to other biomedical resources. You can also follow links to detailed information about the facilities and services of the following entities, which are part of SUMC.

- Stanford University School of Medicine (SUSM)

  Through its educational programs, SUSM conducts extensive research in many areas of medicine.

- Stanford University Clinic

  The Stanford University Clinic is made up of more than 100 outpatient clinics where members of the medical school faculty focus their activities in medical practice and medical education.

- Stanford University Hospital

  The Stanford University Hospital is a university-owned, nonprofit organization that provides acute and tertiary care to local, national, and international patients.

- Lucile Salter Packard Children's Hospital at Stanford

  Lucile Salter Packard Children's Hospital is an independent, nonprofit pediatric teaching hospital that provides acute and tertiary care exclusively for children.

General Health Resources By Topic

All you have to do is walk into a pharmacy and look across rows and rows of over-the-counter medicines and ointments to realize that health, like the human body, is a very diverse subject area. The following WWW sites are broken down into broad categories that relate to specific health resources and subjects. These include:

AIDS

Exercise

Mental Health

Allergies

Family Medicine

Nutrition

Cancer

XI

Health and Medicine

Genetic Disorders

Poisons

Clinical Alerts

Handicap Information

Substance Abuse

AIDS

AIDS Information
URL address: **http://nearnet.gnn.com/wic/health.03.html**

The National Institute of Allergy and Infectious Disease maintains a special section of its Gopher for AIDS information. It also provides an on-line newsletter on the treatment of AIDS.

AIDS
URL address: **gopher://odie.niaid.nih.gov/11/aids**

There are links to a lot of information about AIDS, including study recruitment information, nursing HIV/AIDS, general information, the National Commission on AIDS, U.S. community AIDS resources, and international AIDS resources.

Allergies

Clark County (Nevada) Pollen/Spore Reports
URL address: **http://www.unlv.edu/CCHD/pollen/**

You can find out about pollen/spore reports in two ways. Available are the Roto-rod, which provides weekly pollen counts at various places around the Las Vegas valley, and the Burkhard Spore Trap, which gives daily pollen counts sampled at Sunset Park. The reports are maintained by the Clark County Health District POCD.

National Institute of Allergy and Infectious Diseases (NIAID) Gopher
URL address: **gopher://gopher.niaid.nih.gov**

These documents contain a variety of information about different allergies.

Cancer

Breast Cancer Information Clearinghouse
URL address: **http://nysernet.org/breast/Default.html**

Fig. 11.4
The Breast Cancer
Information
Clearinghouse has
useful information
and contacts that
focus on the
research, issues,
and treatment of
breast cancer.

An Internet-accessible resource providing information on breast cancer obtained through many organizations. Current sources represent government health agencies, hospitals, libraries, hospices, and nonprofit agencies.

Breast Cancer Information Clearinghouse
URL address: **http://nearnet.gnn.com/wic/health.09.html**

A server containing practical information about breast cancer, questions and answers, graphics for a breast self-exam, and support group listings. It also provides links to other cancer-related Internet resources.

CancerNet (NCI International Cancer Information Center)
URL address: **http://nearnet.gnn.com/wic/med.11.html**

The National Cancer Institute's Gopher and WWW server with information for both physicians and patients.

Japan Access to National Cancer Center
URL address: **http://www.ncc.go.jp/**

This home page for the Japanese National Cancer Center provides a link to the list of all the PDQ statements available on CancerNet. For most of the diseases, two statements are provided for each diagnosis: one for physicians and another for patients.

University of Pennsylvania—OncoLink
URL address: **http://cancer.med.upenn.edu/**

This server is oriented to cancer and is directed to physicians, health-care personnel, social workers, patients, and their supporters. It is subdivided into medical oncology, radiation oncology, pediatric oncology, surgical oncology, medical physics, psychosocial support for oncology patients' families, and other links to other resources. Frequent updates are made.

XI

Health and Medicine

Clinical Alerts

Clinical Alerts
URL address: **http://nearnet.gnn.com/wic/nutrit.02.html**

These alerts are distributed by the National Institutes of Health and the National Library of Medicine for the purpose of getting important findings out to health professionals as quickly as possible.

Cosmetics

Cosmetics in CFSAN
URL address: **http://vm.cfsan.fda.gov/cosmetic.html**

At this site you find a tremendous amount of information on decoding the cosmetic label. Even though cosmetics labels are chemistry-oriented, you can learn to read them and make purchases wisely.

Exercise

Barry's Periodized Workout Plans
URL address:
http://bigdipper.umd.edu/health-fitness/periodization.html

Barry Merriman, a weight lifter, shares his routine on weight and training that was used to gain substantial size and strength. He delves into issues about nutrition, supplements, steroids, and training—he even mentions a college sports medicine textbook.

Family Medicine

Family Medicine Sites
URL address: **http://mir.med.ucalgary.ca:70/1/family**

There are various links to information about family medicine. Because there is such an abundant amount of information here, it is a good place to start looking in your quest for medical answers.

Medicine and Health
URL address: **http://nearnet.gnn.com/wic/med.toc.html**

This site provides a list of many of the links to organizations and newsgroups. A good place to start looking for any specialized area you choose.

Medicine Servers
URL address: **http://white.nosc.mil/med.html**

The medicine servers listed are Health and Medical, The Virtual Hospital, EINet Galaxy, North Carolina State University—Study Carrel Server, Stanford University—Yahoo Server, and Rice University—Information Server.

Virtual Hospital

Fig. 11.5
The Virtual Hospital™ encompasses a variety of hypermedia books that focus on medical issues—browse, look and listen.

URL address: **http://vh.radiology.uiowa.edu**

From the University of Iowa in Iowa City, Iowa, and presented by the Electric Differential Multimedia Laboratory, Department of Radiology at the University of Iowa College of Medicine, this Web server provides a digital medical and health sciences library. This library encompasses a series of hypermedia text books. For example, click on the "Iowa Health Book" and jump to a page where you can learn about heart attacks and strokes. The "UIHC Medical Museum" is another interesting link. It delivers a couple of choices such as a History of Microscopes and a Virtual Hospital demonstration where you move through a series of hypertext documents that tell you how people can take advantage of computer-based health information. This server is both fun and educational.

Genetic Disorders

On-Line "Mendelian Inheritance in Man"
URL address: **http://gdbwww.gdb.org/omimdoc/omimtop.html**

This is the server for the On-Line "Mendelian Inheritance in Man," a comprehensive source on genetic disorders maintained by Johns Hopkins University.

Handicap Information

Handicap News
URL address: **ftp://handicap.shel.isc-br.com** (login anonymous)

A variety of information for disabled individuals including legal, medical, and social service resources.

Mental Health

Florida Mental Health Institute
URL address: **http://hal.fmhi.usf.edu/**

Fig. 11.6
Although the Florida Mental Health Institute Web site focuses on issues about mental health in Florida, any user will find useful information about the broad topic of mental health.

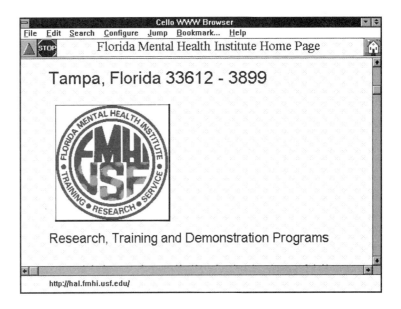

Mental health encompasses a wide range of ailments and conditions that range from depression to Alzheimer's; the role of mental health in our lives is as important as our blood pressure or cholesterol level. The Florida Mental Health Institute focuses on helping individuals in the state maintain and improve their mental health through research, education, and demonstration programs. From the home page you can jump to information about the four departments that comprise FMHI: Aging and Mental Health; Child and Family Studies; Community Mental Health; and the Department of Mental Health Law and Policy. Each of these contains information about their specific topic. You can also jump to a list of scholarly publications that are available.

Nutrition

Cholesterol
URL address: **http://nearnet.gnn.com/wic/nutrit.02.html**

You can find a good explanation of what cholesterol is and how it affects the human body. A good overview of the difference between "good" cholesterol and "bad" cholesterol.

Department of Food Science & Nutrition
URL address: **http://fscn1.fsci.umn.edu/fscn.htm**

This server is located at the University of Minnesota. The Department of Food Science and Nutrition offers undergraduate and graduate programs in nutrition and in food science that prepare students for careers related to food and health. This server provides information on the school and the studies of nutrition and food science from the producer to the consumer.

Poisons

Poisons Information Database (Singapore)
URL address: **http://biomed.nus.sg/PID/PID.html**

This database provides links to information on plant, snake, and animal toxins. There are links to directories of antivenoms, toxinologists, and poison control centers around the world. Information is available in English and Chinese.

Substance Abuse

Alcoholism Research Data Base
URL address: **http://nearnet.gnn.com/wic/med.02.html**

Telnet: **lib.dartmouth.edu**

A database of articles and information about alcoholism and other forms of substance abuse.

Travel and Health
URL address:
http://www.who.ch/TravelAndHealth/TravelAndHealth_Home.html

The World Health Organization, Geneva, provides information regarding diseases, immunizations, and prevention. Be sure to check this resource well in advance of your travel dates.

U.S. National Health Care

History of Medicine
URL address: **http://www.nlm.nih.gov:82/**

The on-line images from the History of Medicine service provide access to nearly 60,000 color and black-and-white images (photographs, artwork, and printed texts) drawn from the collection of the History of Medicine Division at the U.S. National Library of Medicine. The collection is eclectic and includes a photograph of a Greek vase from the 4th century B.C. that shows a bandaging scene, a picture of Abraham Lincoln visiting soldiers' graves at Bull Run, and a scene of American nurses escorting a group of refugee orphans on the beach at Etretat, France, during World War II.

National Health Security Plan
URL address: **http://sunsite.unc.edu/nhs/NHS-T-o-C**

This server contains a summary of the need for reform and support documents that have been released to the public to date. They include the full text of the Health Security Act, the President's address to the Joint Session of Congress as written and as delivered, the President's announcement of the formation of the Task Force on National Health Care Reform, and health care reform today.

National Institute of Health
URL address: **http://www.nih.gov/**

The National Institute of Health, maintained by the Division of Computer Research and Technology, provides biomedical information relating to health issues and clinical protocols, NIH grants and contracts, research opportunities at NIH from the NIH Office of Education, and topics relating to molecular biology and molecular modeling.

National Library of Medicine (NLM)
URL address: **http://www.nlm.nih.gov/**

Fig. 11.7
What's Up, HyperDOC? is a hypertext document that gives you information about new services on the National Library of Medicine Web computer.

A multimedia/hypertext resource of the U.S. National Library of Medicine (NLM), the NLM maintains more than 4.5 million records, including books, reports, and audio-visual materials. The home page provides information about this service, such as What's Up, HyperDOC?, about the NLM, NLM/NIH visitor information, current events at the NLM, contacting people at the NLM, on-line information services, and research and development activities.

Health Centers

Arizona Health Sciences Center
URL address: **http://128.196.106.42/nutrition.html**

This site will remind you that you are what you eat. The WWW server provides a terrific hypertext guide to selected nutrition resources on the Internet/WWW and supports the educational, research, and health-care needs of the Arizona Health Sciences Center community. There are several options for sorting and viewing the resources, which range from medical-based clip art to a food and nutrition newsletter. You can sort by subject, format, or an overall index.

Center for Biomedical and Biophysical Technologies
URL address: **http://citbb.unige.it**

Information resources for the Center for Biomedical and Biophysical Technologies and the Biophysical Institute Labs, School of Medicine, University of Genoa. There are references to information sources on biology, chemistry, cognitive science, mathematics, medicine, physics, and nanotechnology.

Center for Food Safety and Applied Nutrition (CFSAN)
URL address: **http://vm.cfsan.fda.gov/list.html**

Did you know that you spend 25 cents of every dollar on products that are regulated by the FDA? Of this, 75 percent is spent on food. The Center for Food Safety and Applied Nutrition promotes and protects the public health by ensuring that the food supply is safe, nutritious, wholesome, and honest, and that cosmetics are safe and properly labeled. From this WWW home page you can assess a variety of useful consumer information. There are links to help you understand both food and cosmetics labels, a seafood hotline, a list of brochures that you can order from the FDA, and an on-line FDA phone book that has more than 10,000 entries.

Center for Health Law Studies
URL address: **http://lawlib.slu.edu/centers/hlthlaw.htm**

St. Louis University School of Law recognizes public concern with health-care issues, health-care reform, and the impact of law on health-care delivery. The Center represents the School's commitment to increase contributions to education, research, policy analysis, publication and service for law students, practicing health lawyers, and health-care professionals. This WWW home page has links to information about the educational programs, alumni, publications, and research activities.

Center for Neuroscience
URL address: **http://www.uchc.edu/**

This is the home page from the University of Connecticut, located in Farmington, Connecticut, whose server provides information on the Center for Neuroscience.

Historical Center for the Health Sciences
URL address: **http://http2.sils.umich.edu/HCHS/**

The University of Michigan Historical Center for the Health Sciences announces an electronic clearinghouse for information on primary resources in the history of health care and the health sciences as they relate to Michigan. It is designed for use by historians, educators, policy makers, archivists, librarians, and manuscript and museum curators in their work.

Lawson Research Institute
URL address: **http://earthcube.mit.edu/uwo/lri_home.html**

Connected to St. Joseph's Hospital, Lawson Research Institute's research programs attract visiting scientists from around the world. A few of its divisions are maternal and newborn health, adult respiratory distress syndrome, behavioral neurology and neuropsychology research group, Centre for Activity and Aging/Gerontology Group, and Gastroenterology/GI Surgery Group.

Lister Hill National Center for Biomedical Communications
URL address: **http://www.nlm.nih.gov/lhc.dir/lhncbc.html**

Computers are almost as common as stethoscopes in the world of medicine. This is the home page for a research and development portion of the National Library of Medicine in Bethesda, Maryland. Among the principal activities (and hyperlinks on the home page) of the LHNCBC are development of the Unified Medical Language System Project, work on scientific visualization and virtual reality, medical expert systems, natural language processing, computer-aided instruction, machine learning, and the biomedical applications of high speed communication techniques.

Massachusetts General Hospital—Dept. of Neurology
URL address: **http://132.183.145.103/**

You can explore information specific to the hospital, such as a list of current events, the residency program, the brain tumor research fund, or the monthly newsletter *The Neurotransmitter*. There are also links to other medical and neuroscience resources.

National Center for Biotechnology Information (NCBI)
URL address: **http://www.ncbi.nlm.nih.gov**

Information from the National Institute of Health's GenBank Genetic Sequence Database providing a collection of all known DNA sequences. DNA and protein sequence comparison searching against the databases using the BLAST algorithm is also available.

St. Joseph's Health Centre
URL address: **http://earthcube.mit.edu/uwo/homepage.html**

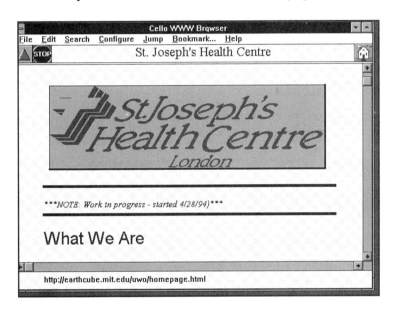

Fig. 11.8
The St. Joseph's Health Centre Web server offers details about educational programs for nurses, medical students, and interns.

Founded by the Sisters of St. Joseph in 1888, St. Joseph's has grown into a major care, teaching, and research center. The Centre provides the most advanced technology with a human touch that stems from the healing mission of the Centre. The home page has links that describe programs for nurses, medical students, and interns.

University of Bonn Medical Center
URL address: **http://imsdd.meb.uni-bonn.de/**

This home page from the University of Bonn Medical Center leads you to links about AIDS, cancer, dentistry, nursing, nutrition, occupational medicine, pharmacy, physics, psychobiology, and telemedicine.

Health-Care Employment

MedSearch America
URL address: **http://www.medsearch.com:9001/**

They may not be the most underemployed sector of the workforce but doctors, nurses, pharmacists, and internists do need jobs. MedSearch America provides access to health-care recruiting. Whether you are a health-care professional looking for a job or a health-care employer looking to fill a position, MedSearch America can be a valuable resource. Job listings, resume postings, and resource services can be searched at any time via this WWW site. One day, for example, there were job listings for a physical therapist in Troy, New York, a clinical dietitian in Aberdeen, Washington, and a director of surgical services in Plantation, Florida.

Medical Education

Advanced Laboratory Workstation Project
URL address: **http://www.alw.nih.gov**

Fig. 11.9
An extremely specialized home page, users can learn about molecular modeling and DNA sequencing.

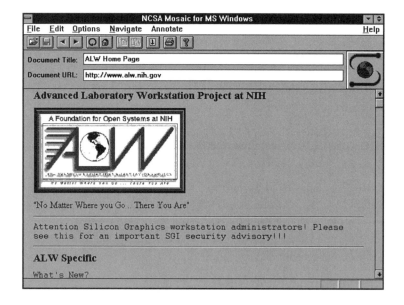

The Advanced Laboratory Workstation Project at the National Institute of Health provides an Andrew File System (AFS)-based and distributed administration and computing project at the NIH. Some of the applications for it include molecular graphics and modeling, medical image processing, gel analysis, DNA and protein sequencing and searching, statistical analysis, and laboratory data acquisition.

Association for Experiential Education
URL address: **http://www.princeton.edu/~rcurtis/aee.html**

Fig. 11.10
If you are involved in medical education you will enjoy learning about the Association for Experiential Education.

With more than 2,000 members, AEE is a broad-based, nonprofit organization that includes people who work in education, mental health, and outdoor education. The focus of the group (and the home page) is experiental educational programs that emphasize health and well-being—experience is a great teacher! You can find out more about the organization when you jump to a description of their annual convention.

Baylor College of Medicine
URL address: **http://www.bcm.tmc.edu/**

The college is located in Houston, Texas, and the home page has links for information on the college and Houston area, the Molecular Biology Computational Resource Guide, the Department of Human and Molecular Genetics, and the Systems Support Center.

Boston University School of Public Health
URL address: **http://www-busph.bu.edu/**

This site is sponsored by the library and maintained by resident students. The server provides information about library services, staff, student announcements, job opportunities, and medical specialties, as well as links to other groups at BUSM.

Edinburgh Chemical Engineering Department
URL address: **http://www.chemeng.ed.ac.uk/**

There are links to information about the university and the department (mostly regarding bioreactors and medical devices) at this site.

Educational Technology Branch
URL address: **http://wwwetb.nlm.nih.gov/**

This server provides information relevant to educational technology in the health profession, the Branch research, and personnel. Also provided are details about the ETB's Learning Center for Interactive Technology.

XI

Health and Medicine

Emory University

URL address: **http://www.cc.emory.edu/welcome.html**

Located in Atlanta, Georgia, it provides information on the School of Medicine and Division of Geriatrics, as well as other subjects.

Indiana University Department of Radiology

URL address: **http://foyt.indyrad.iupui.edu/HomePage.html**

The server from the Indiana University Department of Radiology provides links to radiology events, the division information, medical resources on the Internet, and funding sources for radiologists.

Stanford Health Services Research Training Program

URL address: **http://camis.stanford.edu/HSR.html**

Based in the Division of General Internal Medicine's Section on Medical Informatics, this WWW server has information about the post-doctoral fellowship program in Health Services Research (HSR).

Topics In Primary Care

URL address:

http://uhs.bsd.uchicago.edu/uhs/topics/uhs-teaching.html

Home page for the University Health Services that provides a master list of primary care teaching topics.

University of Geneva—Faculty of Medicine—School of Dentistry—Orthodontics

URL address: **http://www.unige.ch/smd/orthotr.html**

This university server is dedicated to the dissemination of basic and therapeutic knowledge on dentofacial trauma and intends to become a forum on experimental and clinical data.

University of Oklahoma

URL address: **http://157.142.72.77/ouhsc/ouhscokc.html**

The University of Oklahoma is located in Oklahoma City. Its Health Sciences Center houses the schools of allied health, dentistry, medicine, nursing, pharmacy, public health, and graduate college. Included are the phone numbers.

University of Texas Houston

URL address: **http://www.uth.tmc.edu/**

This server contains information about the Health Science Center of the university. It includes campus-wide information on the students, employees, policies, and procedures.

University of Virginia Health Sciences
URL address: **http://www.med.virginia.edu/**

The top of this home page displays a picture of doctors in surgery and a wide shot of the University, which is located in Charlottesville in the foothills of the Blue Ridge Mountains. The home page has links to information about the Health Sciences Center library as well as the schools of medicine and nursing. There is also a link to the topic of education, which brings up further links to subjects that include "Cell Injury and Death" and "Circulatory Disturbances."

U. S. College of Pharmacy
URL address: **http://157.142.72.77/pharmacy/uscop.html**

A partial list organized by state and city. It includes the name of the school, address, and phone and fax numbers. It should be very helpful for a person who is undecided about where he/she wants to attend.

WelchWeb—William H. Welch Medical Library
URL address: **http://www.welch.jhu.edu/**

Designed by the Welch Medical Library at Johns Hopkins University to help the institution's affiliates effectively identify and use Welch resources and services. It includes information about access to Welch databases, library services, instructional opportunities, and publishing assistance.

Yale School of Medicine—Image Processing and Analysis Group
URL address: **http://noodle.med.yale.edu/**

The server from the School of Medicine at Yale. There are links to an assortment of information sources about the Group, the university, and the surrounding area.

Research

Anesthesiology
URL address: **http://www.med.nyu.edu/ruskin/ruskin-intro.html**

The Department of Anesthesiology at NYU is involved in research and clinical anesthesiology. Clinical research interests comprise pharmacology, neurosurgical anesthesiology, electrophysiologic monitoring, and trauma. Basic science interests embody local anesthetics and placental hemodynamics.

XI

Health and Medicine

Biological Imaging and Visualization Lab
URL address: **http://bioviz.biol.trinity.edu/**

Trinity University Biological Imaging and Visualization Lab maintains this Web server. It provides information about Trinity University and the BioViz lab for dynamic visualization and three-dimensional reconstruction of biological images.

Brigham and Women's Hospital, Department of Radiology
URL address: **http://count51.med.harvard.edu/BWH/BWHRad.html**

Fig. 11.11
This is an interesting Web site because there are several on-line educational programs under development, such as the "Nuclear Medicine Electronic Teaching File."

This is a teaching hospital affiliated with Harvard Medical School, located in Boston, Massachusetts. The Department of Radiology is committed to clinical and laboratory research. You can jump to links that describe programs in patient care, training, research, and faculty. There are other links that tell you about the educational programs and medical conferences. In an effort to use computer-based media for education, there is a link to a "nuclear medicine electronic teaching file."

Brookhaven Protein Data Bank
URL address: **http://www.nih.gov/htbin/pdb**

Molecules R Us is an interactive interface to facilitate access for browsing, searching, and viewing the molecular structure data contained within the Brookhaven Protein Data Bank (PDB).

Fujita Health University
URL address: **http://pathy.fujita-hu.ac.jp/pathy.html**

Medical information from the Fujita Health University. Pathy WWW contains some of its text in Japanese. It provides The Textbook of Leukemia (in Japanese), chemotherapy database (in Japanese), on-line case reports (in Japanese), and medical archives (in Japanese). The Pathology Gallery of Hematology is now available.

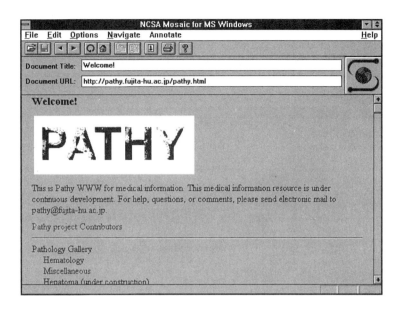

Fig. 11.12
Much of the information available via this home page is in Japanese. Topics include leukemia, chemotherapy, and hematology.

Genome Database
URL address: **http://gdbwww.gdb.org/**

The GDB Human Genome Database supports biomedical research, clinical medicine, and professional and scientific education by providing for the storage and dissemination of data about genes and other DNA markers, map location, genetic disease and locus information, as well as bibliographic information (official, supported).

Institute for Health Informatics
URL address: **http://www.ihi.aber.ac.uk/index.html**

From the University of Wales at Aberystwyth, this server provides information on projects relating to technology in health care.

Lawrence Livermore National Laboratory
URL address: **http://www.llnl.gov**

If you have the right equipment (audio board and speakers) you can begin your tour of this site by listening to a short message from the Director of Public Affairs. Located in Livermore, California, Lawrence Livermore National Laboratory conducts a variety of research programs including a few that focus on health and biomedicine. The home page has links to information on each of the research programs. It is best to begin by selecting Headline News, which brings you to a "visitors center." Then you can perform a keyword

XI

Health and Medicine

search on LLNL press releases to find out what they are doing that may impact your area of interest. For example, a search on the word "medical" brings up several releases, including one that describes efforts by LLNL and a manufacturing firm that reduce the cost of artificial hip replacements.

Fig. 11.13
A U.S. government facility, the Lawrence Livermore National Laboratory provides a variety of information about general health and biomedicine.

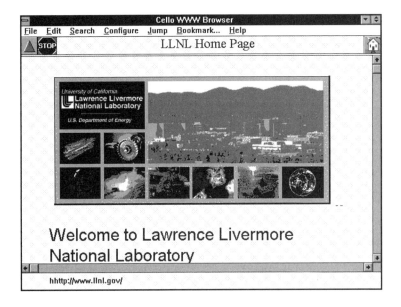

Molecular Virology at the University of Wisconsin
URL address: **http://www.bocklabs.wisc.edu**

The server provides computer-generated and animated images of viruses, topographical maps, digitized electron micrographs of viruses, and tutorial information on selected virology topics.

NIH Molecular Modeling
URL address: **http://www.nih.gov/molecular_modeling/mmhome.html**

This is the National Institute of Health's illustrated hypertext-based primer on molecular modeling methods, software, and applications in the biological sciences. It was created to provide a centralized source of information to the NIT research community and others concerning the major facets of molecular modeling methods and biological applications.

Population Health Summary System
URL address: **http://www.ihi.aber.ac.uk/IHI/phss.html**

This is an example of a very specific Web resource. The Population Health Summary System is developing a summary of the health careers of the entire population of Wales and will be made available to all health-care practitioners in the Principality. The home page has links that describe these efforts.

Chapter 12

History and Geography

Whether it be Julius Caesar's expansion of the Roman Empire, the signing of the American Declaration of Independence, or the enactment of the Chinese Cultural Revolution, bold actions and events in history have a profound effect on our lives today and influence the decisions we make about the future. The World Wide Web is about as close as you can get to a time machine. Jump to a Web server in England to read about and view artifacts from an archaeological exploration of a Roman fort in Scotland, or take an interactive tour of Texas history and see what the Alamo looked like before the famous battle.

From the thick, wet rain forests of Latin America to the dry, sandy dunes of Northern Africa, geography and geology play an equally important role in determining how millions of people live, work, and play. There are maps that show man-made borders as well as the contour of the landscape. You can find and explore both types of maps on the WWW. Try, for example, an interactive global map sponsored by Xerox (URL address **http://pubweb.parc.xerox.com/map**) where you can zoom into different parts of the world, or travel to a Canadian Web site (URL address **http://www.emr.ca**) where you can look at maps and photographs that display the country's tremendous natural resources. The Web transforms history and geography from dull, academic subjects into exciting, important areas of research and exploration. The resources in this chapter are divided into the following categories:

> History
>
> > By continent and country
> >
> > Archaeology
> >
> > Greek and Roman history
>
> Geography

Scrolls from the Dead Sea

URL address:
http://sunsite.unc.edu/expo/deadsea.scrolls.exhibit/intro.html

Fig. 12.1
Scientists and archaeologists unravel the mysteries of the Dead Sea Scrolls— find out how when you visit this interactive exhibit.

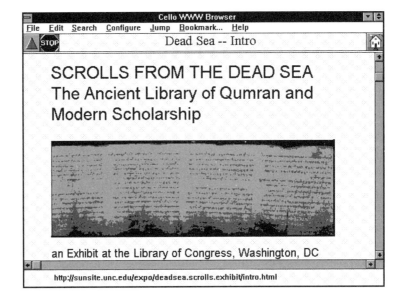

The Ancient Library of Qumran and Modern Scholarship sponsors this exhibit. The physical exhibit is located at the Library of Congress in Washington, D.C., the WWW server is at the University of North Carolina. There are many questions about these mysterious scrolls. Are they indeed authentic? Who were the people who wrote and then carefully hid them? What was the world like when they were written?

This interactive, multimedia exhibit describes the historical context of the scrolls and the Qumran community where they may have been produced. You can read about and relive the story of their discovery—2,000 years after they were hidden. The exhibit encourages viewers to learn about the challenges and activities of archaeology and scroll research.

United States Geological Survey (USGS)

URL address: **http://info.er.usgs.gov**

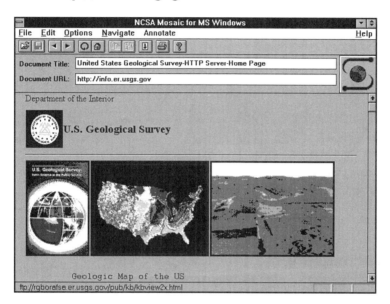

Fig. 12.2
This WWW home site will give you a new perspective on land and natural resources in the United States.

This site uses the multimedia aspects of the Web as a powerful tool for education and exploration. Everywhere you turn there is another clickable image, icon, map, or link. The home page opens with a short introduction that tells you the USGS was established by an act of Congress in 1879 as an agency of the Department of the Interior.

Three large inline images are on the screen—a color picture of a USGS brochure, a color map of the United States that indicates geological contours, and a picture of a mountainscape. Each of these images is a clickable link to other resources. The brochure links to:

National Earth Science Issues

Overview of USGS Services and Activities

Fact Sheets

XII

History and Geography

The color map brings you to Online Files for USA Geology where you can either view a large image of USA Geology or connect to and download ARC information files. The final image, the mountainscape, loads a digital MPEG movie. Some of the other areas you can visit include:

- Education—the USGS library system, the largest earth-science library in the world. Find out what individual collections offer (including maps).

- A list of publications and fact sheets, such as Geology and Human Activity in the Florida Keys or the International Strategic Minerals Inventory report series. Many of these publications are free or have a small fee—you'll learn how to get them.

- The Digital Data Series, which provides information about USGS electronic data such as a geologic map of the sea floor of the Western Massachusetts Bay constructed from digital sonar images, photographs, and sediment samples. These data sources are available as CD-ROMs.

- Employment opportunities with the USGS.

World Map—Xerox PARC Map Viewer

URL address: **http://pubweb.parc.xerox.com/map**

Fig. 12.3
Zoom and pan around the world with this interactive global map.

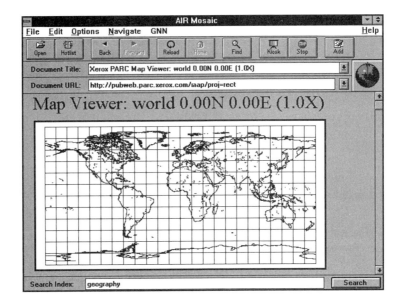

Sponsored by Xerox PARC, this hypermedia world map viewer is custom-made for the WWW. The home page presents a global map. Position your mouse on a section of the map and click. You will zoom in by a factor of two; but don't stop, total zoom-in/zoom-out parameters let you go up to a factor of 25. Utility features allow you to show country borders and rivers. The project was initially created in June of 1993 and improvements are constantly made. Links embedded in the HTML (hypertext markup language) map are controls that change the map rendering. As a result, you can pan or zoom into an area of the map.

History

Africa

African Art
URL address: **http://www.lib.virginia.edu/dic/African.html**

This is an exhibition of African art. From the home page jump to an intro-duction, elements of the African aesthetic, or the exhibition where you can see and read about the Sowei Mask worn over the head of female dancers, a wooden sculpture of a family, or other artifacts.

Europe and Russia

Germany—Database of German Nobility
URL address:
http://faui80.informatik.uni-erlangen.de/html/WW-Person-Engl.html

This WWW database contains biographies, portraits, and the armory of the reigning chairman of a house. The database only contains people of German ancestry—these people don't necessarily live in Germany but do have a Ger-man nobility title. There are several ways to search the database.

Ireland—Thesaurus Linguarum Hiberniae
URL address: **http://curia.ucc.ie/curia/menu.html**

A fancy name for a project that makes computer-based copies of medieval Irish texts. You can browse through a selection of these texts including the *Dream of Oengus*.

XII

History and Geography

Italy—Ariadne

URL address:

http://www.crs4.it/HTML/RUGGIERO/MUSEO/mus_ind.html

Fig. 12.4

Even if you can't read the Italian description of these pieces, there is some exquisite art here to admire.

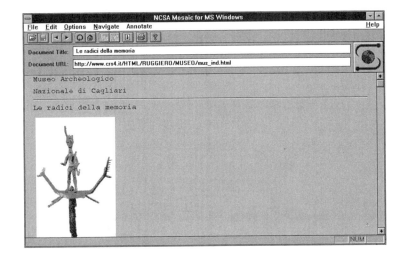

This is the home page for the Archaeological Museum in Cagliari, Italy. There are numerous links to individual exhibits—text is in Italian but an English version is in the works.

Italy—Museum of Physics Department

URL address: **http://hpl33.na.infn.it/Museum/Museum.html**

Fig. 12.5

The home page of the Museum of Physics in Italy features an ancient sundial made in Naples that dates back to 1769.

This Web site offers information about the early instruments at the Institute of Physics located in Naples, Italy. The collection includes 400 physics-based scientific items dating back to 1645, including an antique lens made in Florence. The home page has links to an introduction about the museum, as well as links to the history and description of items in the categories of optics, heat, and electromagnetism. There is also a self-guided tour of this electronic museum.

Russia—Virtual Exhibits
URL address: **http://www.kiae.su/www/wtr/exhibits.html**

Virtual exhibitions from Russia. You can jump between the Kremlin, the Contemporary Fine Arts Center, the Paleontology Institute, and the Soviet Archives. The Russian WWW servers are all under development but are worth a visit.

Middle East

Egypt—Archaeological Survey in the Eastern Desert of Egypt
URL address:
http://rome.classics.lsa.umich.edu/projects/coptos/desert.html

This is a report on a research project that focuses on questions about trade routes, particularly the trans-desert routes, between the Nile Valley and the Red Sea. These routes linked the civilizations of the Mediterranean with those of the Indian Ocean between 300 B.C. and A.D. 400.

Levant cultural multimedia servers
URL address:
http://www.ludvigsen.dhhalden.no/webdoc/levant_servers.html

From Norway (although not including information about Norway), this WWW site is a true potpourri. There are links to historical information and images for the countries of Egypt, Lebanon, and Syria.

Shikhin
URL address: **http://www.colby.edu/rel/Shikhin.html**

A WWW exploration of the location and identification of Ancient Shikhin in Israel. This is a hypermedia overview of the history and archaeology of this ancient site complete with images.

Turkey
URL address: **http://www.ege.edu.tr/Turkiye**

From the Black Sea to the city of Istanbul...browse through the classical architecture and sculpture, the Greek and Roman cities of western Turkey, or get an illustrated tour with Michael Greenhalh of the Department of Art History at the Australian National University.

XII

History and Geography

Asia

Oriental Institute
URL address: **http://csmaclab-www.uchicago.edu/OI/default.html**

Fig. 12.6
View ancient artifacts when you visit this home page. This mummy mask dates back to about 30 B.C.— when you click on the small icon a large GIF image downloads for further examination.

You will find more links than text on this home page. The Oriental Institute is both a museum and research organization that focuses on the study of the ancient Near East. You can explore the museum, archaeology, and philology projects. Start with the first link, the museum, then go to the highlights of the collection where you can select regions of the world such as Cyprus, Egypt, Iran, Mesopotamia, and Syria. You can then move into descriptions and digital images of individual items. For example, the Egyptian collection has the Book of the Dead, a Model of a Butcher Shop, and a Mud Brick Stamped with a Cartouch of Ramses II.

United States

ArchNet—University of Connecticut Anthropology Department
URL address: **http://spirit.lib.uconn.edu/archnet/archnet-ascii.html**

This WWW server is a resource for northeastern archaeology, history, and preservation. Access the University of Connecticut Archaeology Archives or take a virtual tour of the Connecticut State Natural History Museum.

California—Palo Alto Historical Association
URL address:
http://www.commerce.digital.com:80/palo-alto/historical-assoc/home.html

Did you know that Palo Alto, Spanish for "tall tree," was the name given to the California town because of a large twin redwood tree found on the banks of the San Franciaquito Creek? You will learn other interesting details about the history of Palo Alto at this Web site.

D-Day
URL address: **http://192.253.114.31/D-Day/Table_of_contents.html**

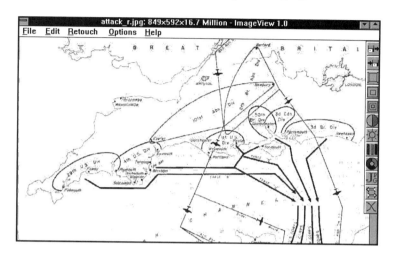

Fig. 12.7
Relive the important campaigns of World War II at the D-Day home page. This image shows the Allied assault plan.

High school students have created this interesting page of links to the history of D-Day with an emphasis on U.S. involvement. There is an archive of Army and Navy News Reels, the *Stars & Stripes* newspaper, famous speeches from the National Archives, and a collection of maps and battle plans from the Center for Military History.

Oregon—World War II Farming
URL address: **http://arcweb.sos.state.or.us/osuhomepage.html**

Not all Americans fought on the front lines during World War II. This is a Web interactive exhibit maintained at the Oregon State University Archives on the subject "Fighters on the Farm Front: Oregon's Emergency Farm Labor Service, 1943–1947." The exhibit commemorates the state's Emergency Farm Labor Service, a program sponsored by the Oregon State College Extension Service to ensure an adequate farm labor supply during and immediately after World War II. This site provides two links, one to information about the exhibit and the other to the exhibit itself. There are 67 images that include photos, posters, and printed documents.

Texas—The Alamo
URL address:
http://www.lib.utexas.edu/LibrariesList/CAH/texas/cah_texas1.html

The Center for American History has a collection that contains books, maps, and other documents that detail the history of Texas from Spanish colonization to the present day. Wind your way through pages in this interactive exhibit of Texas history. View Santa Anna's battle map for the assault on the Alamo or view the oldest photograph taken in Texas—an 1849 daguerreotype that shows the front of the Alamo chapel.

World

History Archives
URL address: **http://www.urz.uni-heidelberg.de/subject/hd/fak7/hist**

This home page for the Heidelberg history archives categorizes its history resources into two areas. First, epochs that include: Antiquity, Middle Ages, Early Modern, and 19th and 20th Century; or, you can search for historical resources by country, which includes: Europe, North and South America, Asia, Africa, and Australia.

Historical Documents
URL address:
gopher://gopher.tntech.edu:70/11gopher_root%3a%5bcampus.as.hist%5d

From the University of Tennessee, this site will connect you to a vast warehouse of historical documents that are significant to countries around the world—from Lincoln's first inaugural address to Clinton's state of the Union address to the manifesto of the Communist party.

History of Science
URL address: **http://nearnet.gnn.com:80/wic/histsci.toc.html**

From the Global Network Navigator, this page has two useful links. One is to the History of Science Server, which opens a gateway to a Gopher that, as the GNN page states, is "an attempt to collect and catalog the writings and papers of respected scientists in a single place." The other link takes you to HOST, which stands for the History and Philosophy of Science and Technology, an academic journal that focuses on scientific history.

International History

URL address: **http://heiwww.unige.ch/iuhei/int-history-politics/**

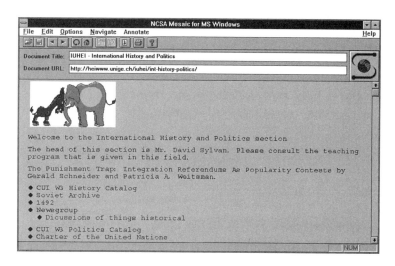

Fig. 12.8
You'll find a variety of historical documents, exhibits, and newsgroups at the International History and Politics Web site.

This WWW site contains links to an assortment of historical resources including the Charter of the United Nations, history newsgroups, the multimedia Soviet Archive, and the 1492 exhibits.

Timelines

URL address: **http://cast0.ast.cam.ac.uk/Xray_www/niel/scales.html**

This is a fun resource that can put your life in perspective. There are links to four of "Neil's Timelines" (Neil maintains this site), which include science and technology, evolutional/geological, cosmological, and scales and measures. You will discover, for example, on the evolutionary scale that millipedes evolved as the first land animals 430 million years ago and primitive sharks came along some 375 million years ago.

United States Holocaust Memorial Museum

URL address: **http://www.ushmm.org**

Located in Washington D.C., this museum (and the Web site) focus on the history and memory of the Holocaust. There are links to general information about the museum itself; educational programs, including a brief history and Frequently Asked Questions and some guidelines for teaching about the subject; the Research Institute, which offers archival information for researchers; and the association of Holocaust organizations, which is a network of organizations.

XII

History and Geography

Greek and Roman

Catalogi Codicum Montis Athonis
URL address: **http://abacus.bates.edu/~rallison/**

Learn about Greek manuscripts of the Philotheou Monastery. Search through an electronic catalog of materials that is maintained at Bates College.

Classics and Mediterranean Archaeology Home Page
URL address: **http://rome.classics.lsa.umich.edu/welcome.html**

Links here to field projects, courses, exhibits, atlases, and bibliographies. A good starting point for a journey into past civilizations.

Leptiminus Archaeological Project
URL address:
http://rome.classics.lsa.umich.edu/projects/lepti/lepti.html

Fig. 12.9
At nearly 200KB, this GIF of an unearthed aqueduct takes a while to download at 14.4K bps but it is worth the wait to see so far back into western history.

This is a multimedia report on the site of Leptiminus and fieldwork from 1990-1993 by Dr. Nejib Ben Lazreg, Institut National du Patrimoine; and Dr. John H. Humphre, Sebastian Heath, and David Stone of the University of Michigan. GIF images support the text report.

Newstead Project
URL address:
http://www.brad.ac.uk/acad/archsci/field_proj/newstead/newstead.html

This project investigates the region around the Roman fort of Trimontium, which is near Newstead in the Borders region of southern Scotland. It describes a number of Roman artifacts ranging from wooden tent pegs to military parade helmets.

Pompeii Forum
URL address: **http://jefferson.village.virginia.edu/pompeii/page-1.html**

Pompeii, A.D. 79, a great volcanic eruption of Mt. Vesuvius devastated this great city. This project focuses on the urban center of Pompeii where the main religious, civic, and commercial activities occurred. From the home page, go to the Forum map that opens a list of specific buildings in the city, such as the Imperial Cult Building. Click on a building name and jump to a variety of pictures.

Archaeology

Archaeological Fieldwork Server
URL address: **http://durendal.cit.cornell.edu/TestPit.html**

Do you enjoy "a dig"? This server provides links to fieldwork opportunities including positions for volunteers, contract work, and field schools. Links on the home page are broken down into Europe, Middle East, and North America.

Archaeology
URL address: **http://spirit.lib.uconn.edu/archaeology.html**

This home page has links to other documents and servers of interest to archaeologists. Selections include the Museum of Cagliari, a survey in the eastern desert of Egypt, Northeastern archaeology, Mediterranean archaeology, the Leptiminus Archaeological Project in Tunisia, the Dead Sea Scrolls Exhibit at the University of North Carolina, and the national archaeological database from the U.S. National Park Service.

Classics and Mediterranean Archaeology
URL address: **http://rome.classics.lsa.umich.edu/welcome.html**

This WWW server collects links to Internet resources that will be of interest to Mediterranean archaeologists. Included are links to field projects, texts and journals, museums, atlases, newsgroups, and mailing lists.

XII

History and Geography

Geography

Antarctica—Maps of Antarctica

URL address:

http://www.hmc.edu/www/people/teverett/antarctica/Maps.html

Fig. 12.10
The Maps of
Antarctica Web
server shows how
specific locations
on this continent
relate to other
areas of the world.

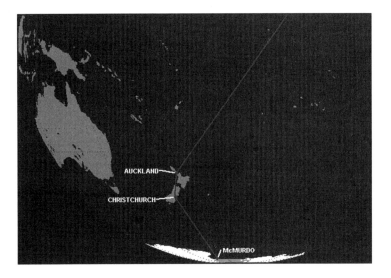

A nice selection of color graphic maps of Antarctica that show the relationship between locations on this continent to the rest of the world with highlighted lines. Specific areas include McMurdo Station and its vicinity, Taylor
Valley, and McMurdo Dome. All the maps are GIF images and load fairly
quickly.

Digital Relief Map of the U.S.

URL address: **http://ageninfo.tamu.edu/apl-us/**

This is a great resource for exploration of the geography of the United States.
You begin with a home page image of the U.S. that is divided into a grid.
When you click on a specific grid area you get two-color shaded relief maps
of the area. One shows coastlines, boundaries, and rivers and the other has a
topographical view. You can then select one of these maps to continue to
"zoom" into the specific area you want to view. The overall map coverage
area ranges from 65 to 125 degrees West longitude and 25 to 50 degrees
North latitude. The server also has high-resolution images of the state of
Wyoming.

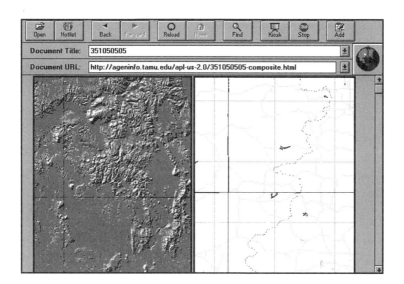

Fig. 12.11
The Digital Relief Map of the U.S. Web server offers both a topographical and an boundary map view of all sections of the country.

Geographic Name Information System
URL address:
gopher://mudhoney.micro.umn.edu:4324/7geo%20search

Use this WWW interface to a Gopher server that looks up the names of towns and cities across the U.S. Enter New York, for example, and you will find that there is more than one "Big Apple"; New Mexico, Florida, Texas, Iowa, and Kentucky all have towns with the name New York. Click on one of these towns to get detailed information about telephone area codes, population, latitude, longitude, elevation, zip codes, and counties in the area.

Geography—Indexes and WWW Resources
URL address: **http://honor.uc.wlu.edu:1020/-ge**

An extensive list of WWW servers by geographic location. First all 50 states, then country by country. When you select a state or country you get a new list of servers in that area, many of which provide information on the geography and history of the area.

Map Collection
URL address:
http://www.lib.utexas.edu/LibrariesList/PCL/Map_collection/Map_collection.html

This address connects you with information about the Perry-Castaneda Library Map Collection (some 200,000+ maps) at the University of Texas at Austin. You can weave your way through links to different parts of the world,

XII

History and Geography

for example, start with Maps of Africa, and then select Botswana to retrieve the map. Many of the maps were created by the Central Intelligence Agency.

Fig. 12.12
All of the maps here may not be the most aesthetically pleasing, but with over 200,000 maps including this census map of Indiana (blown up to show central Indiana—home of Macmillan Computer Publishing and Que) you are bound to find a map that suits your needs.

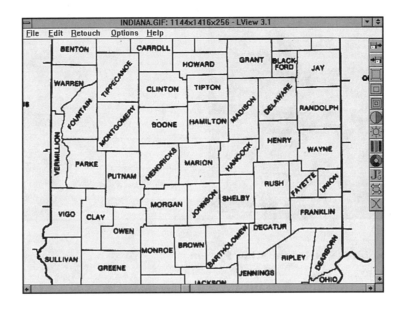

Mars Atlas
URL address:
http://fi-www.arc.nasa.gov/fia/projects/bayes group/Atlas/Mars/

If you enjoy out-of-this world geography, travel to this Web server, which offers a browsable, zoomable, scrollable atlas of Mars. The project is a spin-off of an "image super-resolution project" at NASA Ames Artificial Intelligence Research Branch. It shows the locations (footprints) of thousands of high-resolution Viking Orbiter images. You begin with a high (1440 x 740 pixel) or low res (600 x 300 pixel) image of Mars and you then select specific areas for further exploration. There are also links to images of Jupiter, Saturn, Uranus, and Neptune.

Peru—Red Cientifica Peruana
URL address: **http://www.rcp.net.pe/rcp_ingles.html**

This WWW server represents the central point for the Internet network in this country. It provides a neat overview of this Latin American country with maps, descriptions of the land, the economy, and government.

Project GeoSim
URL address: **http://geosim.cs.vt.edu/index.html**

Project GeoSim has a WWW server that distributes Geography Education software developed by the Departments of Geography and Computer Science at Virginia Tech. The software runs on MS-DOS, Macintosh, and DECstations running X-Windows. The GOPHER address, **gopher://geosim.cs.vt.edu/1**, is also available.

Railroad Maps
URL address:
http://www-cse.ucsd.edu/users/bowdidge/railroad/rail-maps.html

Some of the featured maps you can access via this server include the London Underground, San Francisco Bay Area Rapid Transit (BART), Long Island Railroad, Paris Metro, and Tokyo and Cambridge, Massachusetts train systems.

Space Remote Sensing
URL address: **http://ma.itd.com:8000/welcome.html**

According to their home page description, "The Institute for Technology Development/Space Remote Sensing Center (ITD/SRSC) is a not-for-profit organization dedicated to the development and commercialization of remote sensing (satellite imagery) and Geographic Information System technologies into the private and public sectors." The research from this organization helps create new maps and improve farm management techniques.

The Jason Project
URL address: **http://seawifs.gsfc.nasa.gov/scripts/JASON.html**

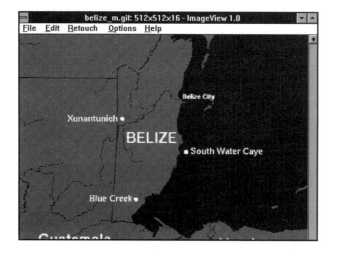

Fig. 12.13
This map of Belize is just one of the many geographic resources that are available via The Jason Project Web site.

This is an educational program that helps school students learn more about our planet's geography and environmental issues. Dr. Robert D. Ballard started the project in 1989 after he received thousands of letters from children who were interested in how he found the RMS Titanic. The program uses computer and video technology to tell about explorations. Teachers can access ideas for educational curricula that accompany the project. From the home page you can jump into a voyage to the volcanoes of Hawaii or a journey to the rain forests of Belize.

Chapter 13

International Web Resources

From a user's point-of-view, the most exciting aspect of the World Wide Web is that you can read, view, and listen to the thoughts of people around the globe from the comfort of your study or living room. With a few clicks of the mouse, you can jump between ten or 20 countries in less than an hour. Learn about cultures and traditions; plan a vacation or business trip; understand the legal and economic systems; discover the latest scientific activities in international research centers; or find out about organizations or associations that relate to your own interests or professional pursuits. These are a few of the thrilling, educational, and useful activities that you can perform via the global WWW.

As you leap from continent to continent, you will notice that most Web sites have either made English their official language, or offer both a native language and English. However, there are still many WWW servers that only have information in a native tongue. This, too, is part of the special international flavor of the medium, and if you either know a foreign language, are learning a foreign language, or simply have an interest in looking at information that is written in a foreign language, you will enjoy visiting these servers. Some countries, like Japan and Russia, provide advice on how to obtain a WWW browser that displays information in their unique character set (Japanese and Russian).

The first portion of this chapter lists international resources by specific category, such as art, cuisine, education, travel, and scientific research. The last section has an alphabetical listing of WWW servers in countries in all regions of the world. These servers have been selected as good starting places to quickly access a variety of different information, ranging from tips for tourists to business opportunities.

Gateway to Antarctica

URL address: **http://icair.iac.org.nz/**

Fig. 13.1

Did you know
that less than
five percent of
Antarctica's land is
without perma-
nent ice or snow?
This is one of the
many interesting
facts you'll learn
when you visit
Gateway to
Antarctica.

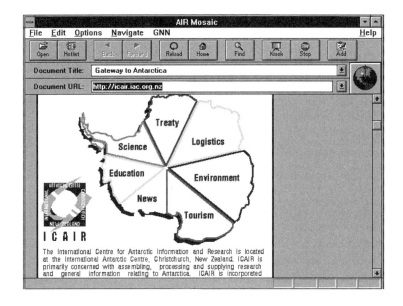

Covered by 90 percent of the world's ice, which has an average thickness of
about 2,000 meters, most people consider the continent of Antarctica to be
a cold and mysterious place. Now, thanks to sponsorship by the National
Science Foundation, you can visit the South Pole without getting frostbite.
This WWW server links you with interesting information about the geological history of the continent, the impact that Antarctica has on the world's
environment, opportunities to travel to the continent (physically), and
Antarctica gifts.

You will learn that the climate for most of Antarctica is that of a cold desert.
In the region of the South Pole, about seven centimeters of snow accumulates
annually and it has an annual mean temperature of -49°C. As the ice sheet
reflects most of the sun's heat back into the atmosphere, it collects almost no
heat and significantly influences world weather patterns. Antarctica received
tremendous media attention when it was discovered that ozone depletion,
known as the Ozone Hole, was getting larger over the South Pole. This WWW
server contains annual program reports for several nations that are involved
in experiments on the continent.

If you're even more adventurous, there are links to help you take the next step—a trip to Antarctica. Learn about Southern Heritage Expeditions, a company specializing in expedition cruises to Antarctica and Subantarctic Islands, and Arctic Adventures, a Norwegian Company that specializes in Arctic tours. Or order a free copy of the Antarctic Gift Shop Catalog.

New Zealand

URL address:

http://www.cs.cmu.edu:8001/Web/People/mjw/NZ/MainPage.html

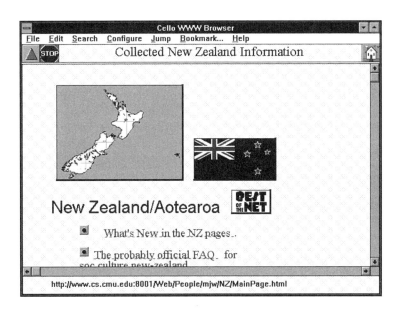

Fig. 13.2
Special tips on hitchhiking and sightseeing are a few of the many useful tidbits you get when you visit the New Zealand WWW home page.

When you visit this home page, you increase your knowledge of this country as you learn that New Zealand is situated the same distance eastward from Australia as London is to Moscow, and that it is bigger than Connecticut, but smaller than Canada. This just scratches the surface of the many interesting and useful things you will learn about New Zealand. Sports enthusiasts can find out about windsurfing and water-skiing in the beautiful waters surrounding the country. Hikers can receive detailed information about "tramping," the art of walking in the outdoors. If you are involved in international trade, or simply want to buy a new sweater, you will learn that wool is one of the major exports. And, if you enjoy dabbling in international cooking, you can jump to various recipes, including this one for Pavlovas:

3 egg whites	1 teaspoon vinegar
3 tablespoons cold water	1 teaspoon vanilla essence
1 cup castor sugar	3 teaspoons cornflour

Beat egg whites until stiff, add cold water, and beat again. Add castor sugar gradually while still beating. Slow beater and add vinegar, vanilla, and cornflour. Place on greased paper on greased tray and bake at 150° C (300° F) for 45 minutes, then leave to cool in the oven.

Other home page links bring you to subdocuments, which offer yet more links to information about New Zealand, such as:

New Zealand News Stories

Travel and Tourist Information

Physical Environment: Geography, Natural History, Environment

History, People, Language and Culture

Recreation, Entertainment, and Sports

Government and Public Affairs

Singapore Online Guide

URL address: **http://www.ncb.gov.sg/sog/sog.html**

A travel agent would have a difficult time pulling together this much information about Singapore. This electronic version of the Singapore Official Guide is issued by the Singapore Tourist Promotion Board (STPB) and is free to all tourists and travelers. The first edition is a prototype being developed by the Digital Media Center (DMC) of the National Computer Board.

The hyperlinks on the home page very closely represent the type of information that you would find in a good travel guide: places to visit, hotels, shopping, and more. To make your journey even more interesting, an interactive tour agent gives you a customized mini-tour of Singapore. And if you don't see what you need, you can keyword search articles about Singapore to get more specific information. When you have finished visiting this WWW server, you'll be ready to pack your bags. Here are some of the main selections and topics you can jump to from the home page:

Introduction

What To Expect in Singapore

Multi-Cultural Traditions

Things to See and Do

Shopping in Singapore

Feasting in Singapore

Touring the Region Map of Singapore

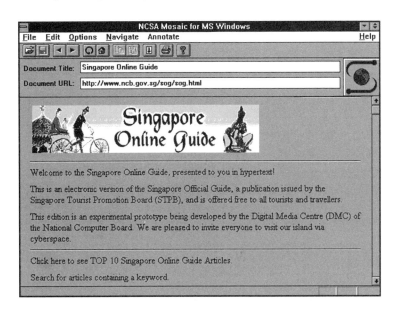

Fig. 13.3
This WWW resource provides an interactive tourist information guide complete with an electronic tour agent.

Nippon Telephone and Telegraph Corporation

URL address: **http://www.ntt.jp**

Nippon Telephone and Telegraph Corporation and its subsidiaries provide a broad range of telecommunication services in Japan, including telephone, telegraph, leased circuit, data communication, and miscellaneous services. NTT also sells terminal equipment.

Fig. 13.4

Learn about the Nippon Telephone and Telegraph Company and jump to a variety of interesting Japanese resources.

In addition to providing general information about its overseas offices and NTT service information, this home page provides linkage to the following 12 laboratories that are part of its R & D department:

Basic Research Laboratories

Software Laboratories

Communication Switching Laboratories

Telecommunications Networks Laboratories

Network Information Systems Laboratories

Human Interface Laboratories

Transmission Systems Laboratories

Radio Communication Systems Laboratories

LSI Laboratories

Opto-Electronics Laboratories

Interdisciplinary Research Laboratories

Communication Science Laboratories

A unique feature of the NTT WWW information is the way it provides Japanese documents. It refers to five browsers that present information in Japanese (all in a UNIX environment).

Window-To-Russia

URL address: **http://www.kiae.su:80/www/wtr**

Window-to-Russia is a Moscow-based project created by Relcom Corporation, initiated to give the worldwide network community a means of WWW access to a variety of information resources from and about Russia. Some resources are in Russian. (To view these Russian texts you need to install KOI-8 Cyrillic fonts.) Main menu links offer the following resources:

Arts, Culture, History, and Human Sciences

Business Opportunities

Science, Technology, Computers, and Software

Other Russian Web-Servers

Russia-Related Sources Outside Russia

Art and Entertainment

Dublin Pub Review
URL address:
http://www.dsg.cs.tcd.ie:/dsg_people/czimmerm/pubs.html

These are the most complete descriptions of Dublin's venues on the Internet. It is divided into two sections: pubs and nightclubs. Each entry comes with a short review and the address.

Electric Gallery
URL address: **http://www.elpress.com/gallery/homepage.html**

The Electric Gallery provides you with the opportunity to view an exhibition and appreciate quality art electronically. It contains an exclusive collection of original native Haitian paintings for view and sale.

Kylie Minogue
URL address: **http://www.eia.brad.ac.uk/kylie/index.html**

The site provides hypertext about the Australian singer Kylie Minogue. The discography has links to samples from each of the songs and pictures from album and single covers, as well as other related areas like fan mail and newsletters.

Nando.Net
URL address: **http://www.nando.net/welcome.html**

It includes samples of many newspapers, journals, cartoons, schedules, games, stories, and statistics. Daily updates.

Ohio State University at Newark, Art Gallery
URL address: **http://www.cgrg.ohio-state.edu/mkruse/osu.html**

Art Gallery exhibits the work of local, national, and international artists. Exhibitions are available to the public.

Associations and Organizations

Association for Experiential Education
URL address: **http://www.princeton.edu/~rcurtis/aee.html**

AEE is a nonprofit, international membership organization with roots in adventure education. It is committed to the development, practice, and evaluation of experiential learning in all settings. With more than 2,000 members in over 20 countries, AEE's membership consists of individuals and organizations with affiliations in education, recreation, outdoor adventure programming, mental health, youth service, physical education, management development training, corrections, programming for people with disabilities, and environmental education.

ATM Forum
URL address: **http://www.atmforum.com/**

An international nonprofit organization formed with the objective of accelerating the use of ATM (Asynchronous Transfer Mode) telecommunications products and services through a rapid convergence of interoperability specifications. In addition, the Forum promotes industry cooperation and awareness. Currently, the ATM Forum consists of over 500 member companies, and it remains open to any organization that is interested in accelerating the availability of ATM-based solutions.

Bay Area Model Mugging

URL address: **http://www.ugcs.caltech.edu/~rachel/bamm.html**

This organization is a worldwide self-defense organization for women. BAMM is a member of IMPACT International.

Graduate Institute of International Studies

URL address: **http://heiwww.unige.ch/**

Explore Internet history and politics, economics, law, art galleries, music, and more.

Global Fund for Women

URL address: **http://www.ai.mit.edu/people/ellens/gfw.html**

This is an international grant-funding organization that supports groups committed to women's well-being and full participation in society.

International Association of Open Systems Professionals

URL address: **http://www.uniforum.org/**

The International Association of Open Systems Professionals has announced their World Wide Web server. It contains information about the association, its programs, and services.

International Commission on Illumination

URL address: **http://www.hike.te.chiba-u.ac.jp/ikeda/CIE/home.html**

The International Commission on Illumination, CIE from its French title Commission Internationale de l'Eclairage, is an organization devoted to international teamwork and the exchange of information among its member countries on matters relating to the science and art of lighting. Its publications and disks are available from the CIE National Committees and the CIE Central Bureau in Vienna.

International Council on Monuments and Sites

URL address: **http://hpb.hwc.ca:7002/ICOMOS_description.html**

Fig. 13.5
Preservation of the world's historical monuments is the focus of this WWW site.

No one would be very happy if the great pyramids of Egypt or the Anasazi cliff dwellings in the U.S. Southwest suddenly disappeared. The International Council on Monuments and Sites is an international, non-governmental organization dedicated to the conservation of the world's historic monuments and sites. The organization has national committees in over 80 countries. The home page has links to documents and treaties between nations that address the preservation of historic sites, and there are links to other "heritage conservation" organizations.

International Organization for Plant Information
URL address: **http://life.anu.edu.au/biodiversity/iopi/iopi.html**

This Web site contains links to hypermedia taxonomic information—a fancy way of saying databases on plant information. IOPI came into being in 1991 at a meeting hosted by the Australian Biological Resources Study. Forty-nine botanists from 11 countries participated, and an idea was born to consider the establishment of a global plant species information system. Learn more information through the many links available from this site.

International Society for Optical Engineering
URL address: **http://www.spie.org/**

This nonprofit professional association—The International Society for Optical Engineering—is dedicated to advancing research and applications in the optical sciences. This site provides many links to information relevant to the topic.

International Space and Science
URL address: **http://krakatoa.jsc.nasa.gov/ss/issaip/issaip.html**

Space enthusiasts can find all kinds of ISSA information with these links to Agenzia Spazione Italiana, Canadian Space Agency, European Space Agency, National Aeronautics & Space Development Agency, Russian Space Agency, the space station home page, JSC Home page, and the NASA Home page.

Rotary
URL address: **http://www.tecc.co.uk/public/PaulHarris/**

With some 26,000 Rotary clubs around the world, the Rotary organization is indeed a global effort. There is much information for the casual browser, as well as for those who are interested in details of joining or creating a local Rotary chapter. One link will provide you with a list of Rotary BBS and Internet connections. The Rotary effort is dedicated to alleviating suffering around the world.

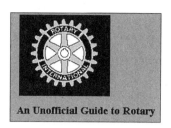

An Unofficial Guide to Rotary

Fig. 13.6
Lots of links to information about the global Rotary organization and its chapters.

Southampton University Astronomy Group
URL address: **http://sousun1.phys.soton.ac.uk/**

The group provides an index of recent International Astronomical Union telegrams. To avoid breaching the copyright on the circulars, the full text of the telegrams is only available locally. If you have your own legitimate source for these documents, this search tool will tell you in which telegrams to look for news on certain astronomical objects and events.

Business and Legal

Cleveland State University
URL address: **http://www.law.csuohio.edu/**

The home page for The Joseph W. Bartunek III Law Library in Ohio serves links to legal Internet resources, OhioLINK, and other library Telnet sites, the technical and computer information center, and experimental CGI gateways.

Electronic Industries Association of Japan
URL address: **http://fuji.stanford.edu/orgs/UCOM.html**

Established by the Electronic Industries Association of Japan (EIAJ), it promotes the import of semiconductors while contributing to the development and maintenance of free international trade. There is information about UCOM California's purpose, activities, and services provided to U.S. semiconductor chip manufacturers.

Employee Ownership
URL address: **http://www.fed.org/fed/**

Get information and strategies on international developments in employee ownership and equity compensation methods. Have access to the latest research and statistics from case studies of successful employee-owned firms.

Social Security Administration
URL address: **http://www.ssa.gov/SSA_Home.html**

Offers public information about retirement, survivors, disability, and other Social Security Administration programs, the status of the SSA Trust Fund, and legislation affecting SSA. Do you have employees in other countries? International Agreement information is available.

Trade Law
URL address: **http://ananse.irv.uit.no/trade_law/nav/trade.html**

This server contains various international trade treaties, conventions, laws and rules, and other trade instruments.

Fig. 13.7
This is the place to visit if you need to learn about sale or carriage of goods, insurance, or other matters of international law.

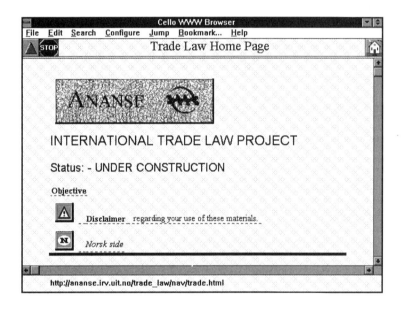

Uruguay Round—Final Act (24-May-1994)
URL address: **http://heiwww.unige.ch/gatt/final_act/**

This server contains the results of the Uruguay Round of multilateral trade negotiations and is available at the Graduate Institute of International Studies.

Washington College of Law
URL address: **http://sray.wcl.american.edu/pub/wcl.html**

This server is for the Washington College of Law at the American University. It focuses mainly on the European Community, United Nations, and other international law documents. You can view a list of links to international materials, U.S. legal documents, and help in other areas.

Computer Technology

Also see the listings in the Computer Resource section.

Institut Dalle Molle d'Intelligence Artificelle Perceptive (IDIAP)
URL address: **http://www.idiap.ch/**

A publicly funded research institute located in the Le Valais region of Switzerland. Researchers at the institute work on computer vision, handwriting recognition and OCR, expert systems, neural networks, optical computing, and speech recognition.

University of Aizu
URL address: **http://www.u-aizu.ac.jp/**

Established in 1993 to provide you with education and research in computer science. The hypermedia research profile brochure is People Advancing Knowledge for Humanity.

Upsilon Pi Epsilon Honor Society
URL address: **http://www.cs.purdue.edu/upe/upe-main.html**

The first and only international honor society for the Computing Sciences. It was founded to recognize scholarly activities and professionalism. Many chapters honor faculty as well as students with membership. The home page has a listing of all chapters.

Stony Brook
URL address: **http://www.sunysb.edu/**

Research informatics focusing on math, chemistry, earth space sciences, electrical engineering, and theoretical and x-ray physics. It also provides links to research-related and economic development opportunities.

Conferences

Association for Computing Machinery
URL address: **http://info.acm.org/**

The information available through ACM's Internet services provides you with details on a range of subjects, including conferences, calls for papers, ACM periodicals and books, ACM special interest groups, members' services, chapters, technical outreach programs, and the ACM International Collegiate Programming Contest.

Departamento de Ciencias de la Computaci_n
URL address: **http://www.dcc.uchile.cl/**

The first WWW server in Chile, it provides information about the Department of Computer Science and includes a map of WWW/Gopher servers in Chile. It also includes information about The 20th International Conference on Very Large Databases.

First WWW Conference
URL address: **http://www1.cern.ch/WWW94/Welcome.html**

The Best of the Web '94 awards were announced in 12 categories and a WWW Hall of Fame was created. The exhibit should serve as an example for the rest of the Web.

Management Briefing Seminars
URL address: **http://ott22.engin.umich.edu/mbs/mbsdoc.html**

An international conference held annually at the Grand Traverse Resort of Michigan's Grand Traverse Bay. Keeps you up to date on issues facing the automotive industry, manufacturing, and quality assurance.

UIAH Entrypoint
URL address: **http://www.uiah.fi/**

The University of Art and Design Helsinki provides information on The International Symposium on Electronic Art (ISEA) and The International Conference on Colour Education.

Cooking, Food, and International Cuisine

Boston Restaurant List
URL address: **http://www.osf.org:8001/boston-food/boston-food.html**

In addition to detailed reviews of recommended restaurants in and around Boston, there's also an on-line forum for submitting new or updated restaurant reviews.

Grapevine
URL address: **http://www.opal.com/grapevine**

This Web-accessible magazine is dedicated to wine lovers. It carries reviews and information about wines and vineyards from all over the world.

Italian Recipes from the University of Minnesota
URL address:
gopher://spinaltap.micro.umn.edu/11/fun/Recipes/Italian

Provides a list of links to several types of dishes and how many of the individual recipes are available. Everything from carbonara (3) to spaghetti sauce (6). The person who submitted the recipe usually tells where he/she got it from, and may include a few other interesting details.

Oriental Recipes from the University of Minnesota
URL address:
gopher://spinaltap.micro.umn.edu/11/fun/Recipes/Oriental

A list of links to recipes for several types of dishes. Some of them include barmi-goregn, Chinese spaghetti, potstickers, sagh, sambal-bajak, sambal-lilang, shu-mei, sukiyaki, and tofu-meat. Included with the recipe is a note from the provider about where it is from.

Tex-Mex Recipes from the University of Minnesota
URL address:
gopher://spinaltap.micro.umn.edu/11/fun/Recipes/TexMex

A list of links to recipes for foods that will make your mouth (and eyes) water. There are chalupas, enchiladas, fajitas, quiches, salads, salsa, tex-mex beans, refried beans, tacos, tortilla-cass, and tucson-tostadas. There is a bit of information about the origin of the recipe included.

Education and Careers

Also see the resources listed in Education/International.

Alternative Careers
URL address:
http://snorri.cpac.washington.edu/ysnarchive/Alt_Careers/Alt_Careers.html

A collection of stories about scientists who have created new careers for themselves other than academic research in their Ph.D. field. Contributions are welcome if your story might be of value to others.

Fig. 13.8
From carpets to drapes, the textile industry plays an important role in our everyday life. Visit this server and find out about the industry and one of the nation's largest textile schools.

College of Textiles
URL address: **http://www.tx.ncsu.edu/**

The North Carolina State University College of Textiles is the largest of its kind in the United States. It offers one of only two accredited Textile Engineering programs in the country, and produces more than half of the textile graduates in the U.S. each year.

Griffith University
URL address: **http://www.gu.edu.au/**

Here you will find information about the university, its structure, work, and people. It is located in the Brisbane-Gold Coast corridor of Australia.

Institut für Theoretische Nachrichtentechnik und Informationsverarbeitung
URL address:
http://www.tnt.unihannover.de/data/info/www/tnt/org/tnt/overview.html

At this site you will find information about the Institut für Theoretische Nachrichtentechnik und Informationsverarbeitung at the University of Hannover (Germany). If you are interested in more details, you can select one of these items: structure of the Institute, research, education, and staff and equipment. Information is in German and English.

Lakemedelsstatistik
URL address: **http://www.ls.se/**

This is a medical information system, located in Stockholm, called MedLink. It distributes medical information via the Web to all the doctors and nurses in Sweden.

Norsk Regnesentral
URL address: **http://www.nr.no/**

The Norwegian Computing Center is a research institute dedicated to studies of information technology and applied statistics. Information is presented in Norwegian and English. The Center is located in Oslo.

University of Montreal
URL address: **http://www.droit.umontreal.ca/english.html**

The server of the Centre de Recherche en Droit Public and the Faculty of Law at the University of Montreal is experimental. It allows links to information on Canadian and Quebec Law as well as to other legal sources in the world.

University of Saarland, Germany
URL address: **http://www.jura.uni-sb.de/indexengl.html**

Most of the information at this law-related server site is in the German language. There are links to codes and sources of law, news bulletins, exemplary cases, and the Internet virtual library.

University of Waikato
URL address: **http://www.droit.umontreal.ca/english.html**

The School of Law is located in Te Piringa in New Zealand. From this home page you can access the law school handbook, courses offered, staff profiles, and other sites.

XFIND index of CERN
URL address: **http://crnvmc.cern.ch:80/FIND/DICTIONARY?**

This server provides a dictionary that combines the Free On-line Dictionary of Computing and a natural English dictionary. Its files were preprocessed at CERN. If you incorrectly spell the word you want to have defined, it gives you correctly spelled words that it thinks you meant to enter. You may choose the correct one from there. It will then go on to give the definition and other related information.

Environmental

Center for Atmospheric Science
URL address: **http://www.atm.ch.cam.ac.uk/**

Located at the University of Cambridge, UK, this server provides information such as degrees offered, seminars, and information about the UK Universities Global Atmospheric Modelling Programme (UGAMP).

EcoWeb
URL address: **http://ecosys.drdr.virginia.edu/EcoWeb.html**

An environmental WWW server that provides and connects users to environmental information on the local, state, regional, and global level. Telnet and dial-up access are also available.

Forensic Science
URL address: **http://ash.lab.r1.fws.gov/**

The USFWS Forensic Laboratory is a part of the U.S. Fish and Wildlife Service Division of Law Enforcement. Its mission is to provide forensic support to federal, state, and international wildlife agencies.

Geological Survey of Finland
URL address: **http://www.gsf.fi/**

This server contains information on research activities and international services. The GSF, which was established in 1885, is a government-funded agency responsible to the Ministry of Trade and Industry.

ICE House—Information Center for the Environment
URL address: **http://ice.ucdavis.edu**

Fig. 13.9
Saving the environment is a task that requires the efforts of many people and organizations. This home page will point you toward some of the key players in this important endeavor.

The Center is a cooperative effort between environmental scientists at the University of California and a number of state, federal, and international organizations that focus on environmental protection. The home page has links to information about a wide variety of environmental organizations, events, and documents, such as "Man and the Biosphere" and the "California Rivers Assessment." Jump to the John Muir (of Sierra Club fame) exhibit and find out everything there is to know about this important historical figure in the environmental movement.

International Electric Grand Prix Association
URL address: **http://www.elpress.com/iegp/iegp.html**

The International Electric Grand Prix Association goes on-line with its Drive Clean '94 slate of events on a WWW server hosted by Electric Press, Inc. Events include the Exide Electric Grand Prix and the 1994 World Clean Air Road Rally to Disneyland. Photographs, sound bites, and video clips shatter myths about electric cars.

Ocean Research Institute
URL address: **http://www.ori.u-tokyo.ac.jp/**

Server for the Ocean Research Institute at the University of Tokyo. It has links to an outline of the university, research units and facilities, other oceanographic institutions and data centers, research vessels, and other services at ORI.

School of Ocean and Earth Science and Technology
URL address: **http://www.soest.hawaii.edu/**

This server comes from the University of Hawaii at Manoa. It consists of a list of organizations, academic programs, facilities, and research programs. There are even old, spectacular images of hurricanes that might be of interest.

Interesting Sites and National Travel Guides

For more WWW resources about travel-related information check out the listings in chapter 18, "Sports, Hobbies, Games, Travel, Cooking, and Recreation."

Australia
URL address: **http://life.anu.edu.au/education/australia.html**

This is a guide to compile available information resources about Australia to distribute via the WWW. It contains links to facts and figures, maps, travel information, government and history, and much more. This guide can be a great help while you are making your vacation plans.

Brazil
URL address: **http://www.rnp.br**

This is a WWW server that is maintained by the National Research Network in Rio de Janeiro. It offers links to other WWW servers in Brazil and Latin

ESTONIA!
URL address: **http://www.eenet.ee/english.html**

This server provides a map of Estonia and links to the following: Where is Estonia?; Estonia; World; About Estonia; EENet WHOIS, and also netfind. You can access this information in Estonian.

Europe
URL address: **http://s700.uminho.pt/europa.html**

Fig. 13.10
Use this Web server's hypermedia map of Europe to quickly jump to one of the European countries.

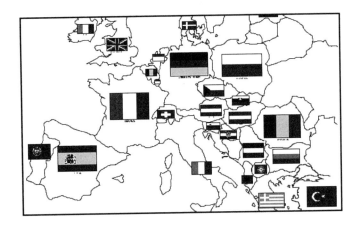

If you haven't taken a European trip yet this year, you must check out this terrific WWW home page—from it you can jump to many countries in Europe. There is a hypermedia map and when you click on a flag for a particular country, you jump to a server in that country.

France
URL address: **http://cuisg13.unige.ch:8100**

An assortment of links to resources and information about France.

Global Network Navigator—Travelers' Center
URL address: **http://gnn.interpath.net/gnn/meta/travel/index.html**

Before you plan your next trip, be sure to visit the GNN Travelers' Center. You can get a quick update on the editor's notes, visit a specific region, country, state, or city guide for help, and receive information on staying healthy in several of the countries you may want to visit. This one is packed with information, so plan to spend some time browsing.

Iran
URL address: **http://tehran.stanford.edu**

Information about the culture, people, language, art, and literature of Iran. There are GIF images and audio files that you can download.

Ireland: The Internet Collection
URL address: **http://itdsrv1.ul.ie/Information/Ireland.html**

This server contains links to various sources that contain information on Ireland. A few of the areas are: maps, the virtual tourist guide to Ireland, photos from the weather satellites, and genealogical research in Ireland.

Fig. 13.11
You can find everything from Irish pubs to Irish music via this home page, which presents an interactive map of Ireland.

Ireland: Virtual Tourist Guide
URL address: **http://www.bess.tcd.ie/ireland.html**

This server contains lots of information about Ireland, including Irish universities, Irish genealogy, the Irish language, Irish literature and theater on the Web, Irish music on the Web, Irish economics, politics, current affairs, and other tourist guides to Ireland.

Jerusalem Mosaic
URL address: **http://shum.cc.huji.ac.il/jeru/jerusalem.html**

With a recorded history of some 4,000 years, Jerusalem is familiar to many people. This server links to a lot of information and maps. You can even sign the Visitors' Book!

Lebanon
URL address: **http://www.ludvigsen.dhhalden.no**

This WWW home page lets you explore information about Lebanon and the Middle East. The resources are broad and range from historical information to lists of restaurants.

Museums of Paris
URL address: **http://mistral.enst.fr/~pioch/louvre/museums.html**

This server contains presentations about the three major art museums in Paris, each dedicated to a certain period. Featured are the Louvre, the Le Mus'ee d'Orsay, and the Centre Georges Pompidou (Beaubourg). You will find the history of the museum and the masterpieces most intriguing.

New Zealand
URL address:
http://www.cs.cmu.edu:8001/Web/People/mjw/NZ/MainPage.html

A home page with links to information about travel and tourist information of New Zealand. Connections include environment, history, language and culture, universities, recreation, and entertainment.

Norway
URL address: **http://www.nta.no/uninett**

Run by the Norwegian Televerkets Forskningsinstitutt, this server has links to documents, images, and movies. The University of Oslo uses this computer and all information is in Norwegian.

Penang
URL address: **http://www.uni-mb.si/**

Universiti Sains Malaysia, Penang Web Server is now operating. The server provides general information of USM, academic programs, research, and more. Also included for potential visitors to Penang Island is tourist information about Penang that includes maps, pictures, interesting places to visit, and local food.

Peru
URL address: **http://www.rcp.net.pe/rcp_ingles.html**

Fig. 13.12
If you want to learn Spanish, or learn about the Spanish culture in Peru, this WWW home page can help.

Are you learning Spanish? One of the hyperlinks on this home page will bring up a Spanish language tutorial. There are also several sources of information links about Peru, its system, and the networks of Latin America and the Caribbean at this site. The RCP, which is the Internet Network of Peru, reaches 23 of the 24 provinces that make up that country. It functions as the center of the 200 affiliated institutions.

Portugal
URL address: **http://s700.uminho.ptPortugal/portugal.html**

This home page brings you to an assortment of useful tourist information about Portugal.

Russia
URL address: **http://www.hyperion.com/koreth/russia/**

This is an illustrated account of a two-week tour of Russia that the author took with Muscovite friends in 1993. Browse through descriptions and enjoy the pictures; it's a good way to "travel" on a budget.

Russian Academy of Science
URL address: **http://ucmp1.berkeley.edu/pin.html**

The Paleontological Institute of the Russian Academy of Science in Moscow, Russia, is the world's largest paleontological institute. The museum, which is run by the Institute, is open to the public and has "loaned" some of its exhibits for use on the WWW Virtual Library because it does not have an Internet line of its own.

Russian and East European Studies
URL address: **http://www.pitt.edu/~cjp/rees.html**

This is a directory of Internet resources listed by discipline. There are links to language, literature, music, art, culture, government and public affairs, education, business, history, geography, etc. There are also links to national home pages and other major sites.

Russia—Moscow Kremlin On-line Excursion
URL address: **http://www.kiae.su/www/wtr/kremlin/begin.html**

This on-line excursion was organized jointly by State Museums of the Moscow Kremlin, COMINFO Ltd., and Relcom Corp. It begins by letting you select links that you wish to visit, such as Red Square or Cathedral Square, and goes on from there. These materials are part of an on-going project to put Moscow Kremlin on CD-ROM.

Singapore
URL address: **http://www.ncb.gov.sg/sif/issues.html**

This newsletter is a publication of the Singapore International Foundation that is dedicated to increasing and improving the interaction of Singapore and Singaporeans with the world. It covers lifestyle, events, and culture.

Slovakia—Cavern Stary Hrad
URL address: **http://hron.ef.tuke.sk/sh/sh-a.html**

This server allows you to go spelunking in the Caverns of Stary Hrad in Kosice, Slovakia. They were discovered in 1967 and are still bringing forth new discoveries. During this tour you can almost feel what it's like to be down there.

Slovenija
URL address: **http://www.ijs.si/slo.html**

The presentation of Slovenia is now spread over the J. Stefan Institute and the University of Maribor servers. Both now jointly offer general geographical, cultural, tourist, and other information about Slovenia and some hints about Slovenian wine and food recipes. Links to other WWW and Gopher servers in Slovenia, as well as links to on-line information and library services, are provided.

Turkey
URL address: **http://www.metu.edu.tr**

Located close to Ankara, the Middle East Technical University sponsors this WWW information and server. You find information about the University, as well as links to other resources in Turkey (most information is in Turkish).

Vatican Exhibit
URL address:
http://sunsite.unc.edu/expo/vatican.exhibit/Vatican.exhibit.html

Millions of pilgrims and tourists come to Rome every year. It holds treasures of architecture, art, and history. The Vatican Exhibit provides a connection to several links, a few of which are the Vatican library, archaeology, humanism, and orientation to Rome.

International Communication

International Marine Signal Flags
URL address: **http://155.187.10.12:80/flags/signal-flags.html**

Try the international marine signal flags character set to send useful mes-sages. Strung end-to-end and hung from bow to stern from the rigging, they are also used to decorate the ship for festivities and ceremonies. The home page has GIF images of each flag.

People and Cultures

Aboriginal Studies Register
URL address:
http://coombs.anu.edu.au/ResFacilities/AboriginalPage.html

This provider keeps track of information facilities of value and significance to researchers in the field of Aboriginal and Indigenous Peoples studies. It is sponsored via the Australian National University's Coombsweb.

Judaism and Jewish Resources
URL address: **http://www.acm.uiuc.edu/signet/JHSI/judaism.html**

This has a rich source of links to information about Jewish resources. A few of them are: Israel sensitive map (this is a visual interface to all the WWW and Gopher servers in Israel), the Shamash Project, Jerusalem One, the Hebrew calendar, Dead Sea Scrolls, and an introduction to Judaism.

Latin American Studies
URL address: **http://lanic.utexas.edu/las.html**

Visit this home page for links to studies of Latin America in general, Latin America-related services, Argentina, Brazil, Bolivia, Chile, Colombia, Costa Rica, Ecuador, Mexico, Peru, Uruguay, and Venezuela. When you click on a country name you get a list of several servers/WWW documents that are either in the country, or have information about the country.

Obituary Page
URL address: **http://catless.ncl.ac.uk/Obituary/README.html**

This is a register of the names, dates, and causes of death of well-known people around the world. You can register a death via this site or mail details for entry. Most of the names are provided by readers.

Vikings Home Page
URL address: **http://control.chalmers.se/vikings/viking.html**

This contains lots of information about the Viking Age (793-1050), its Native Vikings and culture, and a small Swedish-Viking-English Dictionary. There are also links to information about the Vikings of Russia.

Publications

Complexity International
URL address: **http://life.anu.edu.au:80/ci/ci.html**

This is a research journal whose publishers' intent is to make the publication entirely Web-based hypermedia. Contributions are invited.

IKEDA Lab
URL address: **http://www.hike.te.chiba-u.ac.jp/**

Hirokai Ikeda and Yasuhiko Higaki announce a shared electronic publication of the IEC Standard 417 to the Internet as trial bases, with permission of the Central Office of the International Electrotechnical Commission (IEC). The original paper-based publication from the IEC in Geneva, has been reproduced as a hypertext with graphics in the Ikeda Laboratory. The standard is for graphical symbols for use on equipment. It has been maintained and will continue to be maintained and supplemented by the IEC SC3C, in accordance with the needs in the fields of electrotechnology.

International Teletimes
URL address:

http://www.wimsey.com/teletimes.root/teletimes_home_page.html

This is a general interest magazine, published in Vancouver, Canada, and distributed all over the world. It covers a wide variety of subjects.

Mother Jones
URL address: **http://www.mojones.com/**

This has grants available for documentary photographers. Check the classifieds, travel opportunities, surveys, internship opportunities, letters to the editor, views on politics, and more.

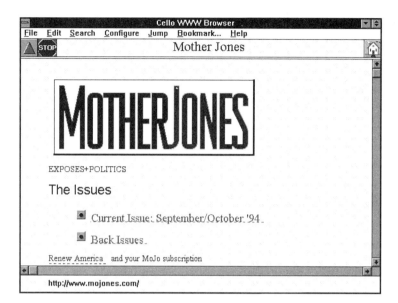

Fig. 13.13
You can explore electronic versions of internationally focused Mother Jones dating back to 1993.

Science and Research

Athens High Performance Computing Laboratory
URL address: **http://www.hpcl.cti.gr/**

AHPCL is in Athens, Greece. It is a nonprofit organization formed by the University of Athens, the National Technical University of Athens, and the Computer Technology Institute of the University of Patras, to do research and development in High Performance Computing and Networking (HPCN). The Laboratory is the owner of a Parsytec GCel 3/512 massively parallel, 512-node computer, and this server focuses mainly on issues involving this machine and work done on it.

Australian National University Bioinformatics
URL address: **http://life.anu.edu.au:80/**

ANU's Bioinformatics Facility provides hypermedia information on the Internet under a number of themes, including biodiversity, bioinformation, biomathematics, and complex systems.

Daresbury Laboratory
URL address: **http://www.dl.ac.uk/**

The Laboratory is based near Warrington in northwest England. Its research facilities include 2 Ge V synchrotron radiation source; advanced computing facilities, including parallel computers; and RUSTI, the Research Unit for Surfaces, transforms and interfaces are made available to users from the UK and other countries.

Gemini 8m Telescopes Project
URL address: **http://www.gemini.edu/**

The goal is to build two telescopes, one on Mauna Kea, Hawaii, the other on Cerro Pachon, Chile. The scientific goal of these telescopes is to produce near-diffraction-limited images at infrared wavelengths. If that doesn't tell you enough, try some of the links to the "Scientific Specifications" or a "Gemini Newsletter." This is a great resource if you have an interest in telescopes.

Marine Research
URL address: **file://ua.nrb.ac.uk/pub/rvshome.html**

The purpose of Research Vessel Services is to provide support for marine research undertaken by the Natural Environment Research Council (NERC)-supported scientists. This service is located in Barry, South Wales, and has links to several other sites, including the RVS mission statement, organization, resources, current research cruises, and other sites and images.

SRI International
URL address: **http://www.sri.com/**

Fig. 13.14
SRI International is one of the largest research firms in the world. This home page can tell you more about the organization and its programs.

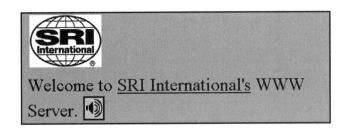

SRI International, formerly the Stanford Research Institute, has links to:

The Artificial Intelligence Center (AIC)

The Collaborative Environment for Concurrent Engineering Design (CECED) project

The Computer Science Laboratory (CSL)

The Virtual Perception Program

With more than 3,000 employees, offices in countries around the world, and revenues that exceed $300 million, SRI is one of the world's largest contract research firms. Its main operating groups are engineering research, science and technology, business and policy, and the David Sarnoff Research Center.

Sports and Recreation

Here are a few representative international sports resources on the WWW. You will find a more comprehensive list of sports resources in chapter 18.

Footbag Club
URL address: **ftp://gregorio.stanford.edu/www/footbag/SUFC.html**

The home page provides information on the international sport of footbag. Pick up on events, festivals, tournaments, demos, and regular meetings.

Taekwon Do and other Martial Arts in Munich
URL address: **http://www.bl.physik.tu-muenchen.de/k2/budo_english/**

Here is some information about traditional Taekwon Do in Munich, Germany, and the neighboring area. This site describes this and other martial arts and gives information about related schools. Information is in English and German.

World Wide Web Server Summary

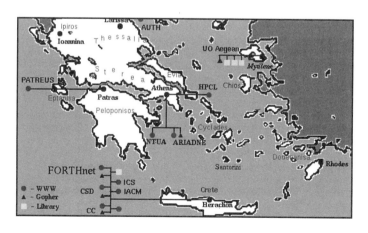

Fig. 13.15
This is the home page for the WWW sensitive map of Greece. When you click on a specific area, such as the island of Crete, or a town, such as Patras, you travel to information about that location.

Fig 13.16
With this sensitive map of Chile you select an area of interest, such as Tourism, to learn about what the country has to offer.

Fig. 13.17
The sensitive map of Israel lets you click on areas that represent WWW or Gopher servers for specific institutions, such as the Tel-Aviv University.

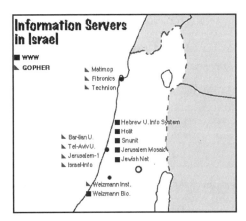

Following is a summary of some of the WWW servers located in countries around the world. The URL addresses represent computers/home pages that are good starting points for each country, although it should be noted that most countries have many more WWW servers and home pages than those listed here. Many of these servers present information in the language of the nation, such as Japanese, Portugese, Norwegian, etc. So prepare yourself for some of the same challenges that would present themselves if you were to travel to these countries in person.

A listing after a URL address that states (sensitive map) is NOT part of the address. This is only a note to let you know that the server provides a graphic, hypermedia map of the country that has links to other WWW resources in the country. There are three types of sensitive maps. One allows you to click on any area of the map, at which point you go to a server or document that has information about that region. The map of Greece is an example of this.

A second type brings up a map along with icons of general areas of interest, such as tourism or the economy, which take you again to a server or document that highlights those areas of interest. The sensitive map of Chile is an example. A third type of map highlights and has links to specific WWW or Gopher servers at specific locations, such as a university or government office. The sensitive map of Israel provides an example.

AFRICA
URL address: **http://osprey.unisa.ac.za/0/docs/africa.html**

South Africa
URL address: **http://www.ru.ac.za**

URL address: **http://www.und.ac.za/prg/prg.html**

ANTARCTICA
URL address: **http://icair.iac.org.nz**

ASIA
China
URL address: **http://www.ihep.ac.cn/china_www.html**

Hong Kong
URL address: **http://www.cuhk.hk/hkwww.htm**

Japan
URL address: **http://www.ntt.jp/SQUARE/www-in-JP.html**

URL address: **http://www.ntt.jp/japan/map** (sensitive map)

Taiwan
URL address: **http://peacock.tnjc.edu.tw/ROC_sites.html**

Thailand
URL address: **http://www.chiangmai.ac.th/Servers-th.html**

AUSTRALIA AND NEW ZEALAND
Australia
URL address: **http://life.anu.edu.au/links/ozmap.html**

New Zealand
URL address:
http://www.cs.cmu.edu:8001/Web/People/mjw/NZ/MainPage.html

CANADA
URL address:
http://www.sal.ists.ca/services/w3_can/www_index.html

EUROPE

Europe Overall
URL address: **http://s700.uminho.pt/europa.html**

Austria
URL address: **http://www.ifs.univie.ac.at/austria.html**

Belgium
URL address: **http://info1.vub.ac.be:8080/Belgium_map/index.html**

Croatia
URL address: **http://tjev.tel.etf.hr/hrvatska/prijava.html**

Czech Republic
URL address: **http://www.cuni.cz:81/cesnet/cesnet-map.html**

Denmark
URL address: **http://info.denet.dk/dk-infoservers.html**

URL address: **http://www.daimi.aau.dk/denmark.html**

URL address: **http://www.dd.dk/Denmark**

Finland
URL address: **http://www.funet.fi/resources/map.html**

URL address: **http://www.cs.hut.fi/suomi.html**

France
URL address: **http://web.urec.fr/docs/www_list_fr.html**

URL address:
http://web.urec.fr/france/france.html (sensitive map)

Germany
URL address:
http://www.chemie.fu-berlin.de/outerspace/www-german.html

Greece
URL address:
http://www.forthnet.gr/hellas/hellas.html (sensitive map)

Hungary
URL address: **http://www.fsz.bme.hu/hu-infoservers.html**

Iceland
URL address: **http://www.rfisk.is/english/sites.html**

URL address: **http://www.isnet.is/WWW/servers.html**

Ireland
URL address:
http://itdsrv1.ul.ie/Information/IrishServerList.html

Italy
URL address: **http://www.mi.cnr.it/NIR-IT/NIR-list.html**

URL address: **http://www.mi.cnr.it/NIR-IT/NIR-map.html** (sensitive map)

Netherlands
URL address:
http://www.eeb.ele.tue.nl/map/netherlands.html (sensitive map)

Norway
URL address: **http://www.ii.uib.no/~magnus/norway.html**

URL address: **http://www.service.uit.no/homepage-no** (sensitive map)

Poland
URL address: **http://info.fuw.edu.pl/pl/servers-list.html**

URL address: **http://info.fuw.edu.pl/poland.html** (sensitive map)

Portugal
URL address: **http://s700.uminho.pt/Portugal/all-pt.html**

Slovakia
URL address: **http://www.tuzvo.sk/list.html**

Slovenia
URL address: **http://www.ijs.si/slo.html** (sensitive map)

URL address: **http://www.tuzvo.sk/uvt.html**

Spain
URL address: **http://www.gae.unican.es/general/es-servers.html**

URL address: **http://www.uji.es/spain_www.html**

Sweden
URL address: **http://www.sunet.se/map/sweden.html** (sensitive map)

Switzerland
URL address: **http://www.math.ethz.ch/~zari/admin/chw3.html**

URL address: **http://heiwww.unige.ch/switzerland/** (sensitive map)

United Kingdom
URL address: **http://src.doc.ic.ac.uk/all-uk.html**

URL address: **http://www.ucs.ed.ac.uk/General/uk.html**

MIDDLE EAST

Israel
URL address:
http://shum.cc.huji.ac.il/israel_sens.html (sensitive map)

Turkey
URL address: **http://www.bilkent.edu.tr/turkiye.html**

URL address: **http://www.metu.edu.tr/Turkey**

MEXICO AND CENTRAL AMERICA

Costa Rica
URL address: **http://ns.cr**

Mexico
URL address: **http://info.pue.udlap.mx/mexico.html**

URL address:
http://info.pue.udlap.mx/www-mex-eng.html (sensitive map)

RUSSIA AND COUNTRIES OF THE FORMER SOVIET UNION

Estonia
URL address: **http://www.eenet.ee/english.html**

Russia
URL address: **http://www.kiae.su/www/wtr/kremlin/begin.html**

SOUTH AMERICA

Argentina
URL address: **http://www.ar:70**

Brazil

URL address: **http://www.rnp.br/cern.html**

URL address: **http://www.rnp.br/cern.html**

Chile

URL address: **http://www.dcc.uchile.cl/servers.html**

URL address:
http://www.dcc.uchile.cl/chile/chile.html (sensitive map)

Equador

URL address: **http://mail.usfq.edu.ec/root.htm**

Peru

URL address: **http://www.rcp.net.pe/rcp.html**

UNITED STATES OF AMERICA

The Virtual Tourist: hypermedia map of the U.S. with links on individual states.

URL address: **http://wings.buffalo.edu/world/na.html**

Alaska

URL address: **http://info.alaska.edu:70/1s/Alaska**

Hawaii

URL address: **http://www.eng.hawaii.edu/hawaiisvc.html**

Chapter 14

Issues, Politics, Religion, and World Events

This chapter lists WWW resources that provide information about organizations, services, and events of a social nature. Perhaps the most noble use of communication technology is as an instrument of social change, whereby electronic data is transformed from bits and bytes into information that touches peoples hearts and moves them to take action to improve the lives of other people—individuals who may live across the street or across the globe.

There is justifiable concern that only the well-to-do, those who can afford powerful computers and Internet connections, will take advantage of the technology and applications of a system like the World Wide Web—that we will see the creation of a society of information haves and have-nots. There is, however, another scenario that envisions a situation where information about organizations that help the have-nots reaches others who pitch in to help, and where technology reaches a broad audience through outlets like libraries, schools, government facilities, and public information kiosks. Several organizations focus their efforts on ensuring the useful development of communications technology. The Electronic Frontier Foundation, for example, lobbies for legislation that will ensure that individual rights mandated by the U.S. Constitution and Bill of Rights are protected with respect to new communications technologies and infrastructures.

The potential for the WWW to have a positive impact on the lives of individuals and society in general is real. You can connect to a database at Columbia University to search for employment opportunities, jump to the Amnesty International home page and find out about human rights conditions and issues in hundreds of countries (and how you can help), search through on-line images of missing children sponsored by the National Center for Missing and Exploited Children, or get practical environmental tips from the electronic version of *The Citizen's Handbook* on a Web site at the University of North Carolina. Religion and religious organizations also have a presence on the Web, and these home pages offer links to a variety of educational resources and social services. Specific resources in this chapter are in the following categories:

Children

Crime

Employment

Environmental issues

Human sexuality and marriage

Non-profit organizations

Law and legal resources

Philosophy

Politics and political issues

Public policy and world events

Publications

Religion

Amnesty International

URL address:
http://www.traveller.com/~hrweb/ai/ai.html

Fig. 14.1
The Amnesty International home page brings you to resources that focus on global human rights.

The famous Amnesty International logo, a candle wrapped in barbed wire, tells you a lot about this organization. Founded in 1961, Amnesty International focuses on issues and events that examine and improve human rights around the world. The home page begins with links that provide information about the organization and its goals. You can get fact sheets, obtain an introductory brochure, or learn how to join.

There are also links to the specific information that the organization is known for, such as the Urgent Action Network (UAN), which issues "calls to action" in cases where a person's life is in danger, someone has disappeared, is being tortured, or is not receiving proper medical care. Click on the link to Amnesty International Printed Reports and Documentation to bring up a searchable list of all documents including country reports, the Annual Report, and reports on regions or issues. You can then order any of these reports. There is also an electronic directory of Amnesty International offices and contact people around the world.

Legal Information Institute

URL address: **http://www.law.cornell.edu/lii.table.html**

Fig. 14.2
This home page is a great resource if you need to find information about the legal profession or specific legal rulings.

You will enjoy this home page if you are in the legal profession, have ever used a lawyer, or simply have an interest in the major legal rulings of our time. The Legal Information Institute connects the resources of the Cornell Law School with the legal profession, other law schools, and the world via the Internet. In fact, all LII "publications" are electronic and the LII created and owns the copyright on the Cello WWW browser.

From the home page, there are links to a variety of hypertext documents including Supreme Court decisions, issues that relate to civil rights, U.S.

Patent and Copyright Acts, legal proceedings from U.S., state, and international cases, an e-mail directory of the faculty of all U.S. law schools, and links to international legal resources. You can perform keyword searches on many of the archives.

Click on the "Search U.S. Supreme Court Syllabi" link to get an index that allows you to search all Supreme Court decisions archived at the Case Western Reserve FTP site (URL address **ftp://ftp.cwru.edu**). The result of a search is a hypertext document that contains links to all the opinions in cases that relate to your search. Thus, if do a search on the word "gun," you get a list of several cases, one being HAROLD E. STAPLES, III, PETITIONER v. UNITED STATES (May 23, 1994). You can learn that Justice Thomas delivered the opinion of the Court, which states that the National Firearms Act makes it unlawful for any person to possess a machine gun that is not properly registered with the Federal Government. You can also jump to other interesting legal resources, such as law schools or "German Legal Materials (in German) from the Juristisches Internetprojekt" and "South African Politics (including Constitution, Interim Flag, and Ballot)."

Jerusalem Mosaic

URL address: **http://shum.cc.huji.ac.il/jeru/jerusalem.html**

Fig. 14.3
When you jump to this home page in Israel, you can take an interactive tour of the sights and sounds of Jerusalem.

Travel to Israel and take this wonderful guided tour of Jewish history and religion, which dates back some 4,000 years. Jerusalem Mosaic is a "guided tour" that gives you the impression you are actually visiting this great city, the capital of the state of Israel, with its many monuments associated with the great biblical figures of past ages. From this home page, you can see the site of the mystic hill-city founded in the third millennium BC, and the "Urusalim," which appears in pottery inscriptions at the beginning of the second millennium. Listen to the Song of Jerusalem or view maps, paintings, and photographs of Jerusalem.

The tour combines these many forms of media in an interactive tour. You travel through an assortment of "gates" to look at and read about different parts of the city. The gates offer categories of images including faces, maps, paintings, and views. There are a number of aerial photographs, which give you a unique perspective. A passage describes the types of images you will view: "We peek into the different neighborhoods and observe the roofs, squares, streets, and gardens, along with the numerous historical buildings which beautify the city." Other home page links connect you with:

Main events in the history of Jerusalem

More information about Jerusalem

Other Hebrew University information servers

Jobnet

URL address: **http://sun.cc.westga.edu:80/~coop/localhome.html**

Getting a job can be just a little easier with the help of this WWW server. The home page represents a collection of employment resources and job leads collected from the WWW, Usenet news, and listservers. You can access information about employment trends, statistics, and career opportunities. Jobnet also provides links to several employment services and organizations that list jobs, such as Academe This Week from the *Chronicle of Higher Education*, the Academic Position Network, the On-line Career Center, and government databases that list federal employment opportunities. Frequently, the links connect with Gopher servers, which you then navigate through submenus until you find specific descriptions for job openings.

Children

Adolescence
URL address:
**http://galaxy.einet.net/galaxy/Community/TheFamily/
Adolescence.html**

Having difficulty communicating with your teenager? Or, are you a teenager? This WWW site offers information on the subject of parenting teenagers as well as links to information for teenagers.

Child Relief You (CRY)
URL address: **http://homechheese.eas.asu.edu/info/sso/cry.html**

Children around the world face very adult issues and problems, but they frequently have little protection or advice. This home page addresses issues of unfair child labor and hunger and looks for relief to these problems with a focus on conditions in India.

Children
URL address:
http://galaxy.einet.net/galaxy/Community/The-Family/Children.html

This Web home page has links that bring you to information about a variety of aspects of the childhood years. For educational purposes there are poems, stories, songs, and activities. There is also information about the problem of child abuse.

Florida Health Baby Hotline
URL address: **http://freenet3.scri.fsu.edu:81/ht-free/fhbaby.html**

Whether you are about to become a parent for the first time or are having a second or third child, this WWW site offers useful information. It provides links to information about prenatal care, breast feeding, and how to keep babies healthy.

GEMS—Missing Kids
URL address: **http://www.gems.com/kids/index.html**

This section allows you to view the images from the Missing Children Database. If you discover information about any of these children, you can contact (1-800-THE-LOST) and inform the National Center for Missing and Exploited Children (NCMEC).

Home-Schooling
URL address: **http://www.armory.com/~jon/HomeSchool.html**

If you've got a living room, you've got a classroom. Home schooling is becoming a popular method for educating children. From the home page you can access home-schooling resource lists by state and special interest, historical documents, and electronic books. There are also links to ERIC, the Educational Resources Information Center, and OERI INet, a Gopher run by the U.S. Department of Education that offers information and free educational software.

Infants
URL address:
http://galaxy.einet.net/galaxy/Community/The-Family/Infants.html

The information on this Web page begins with material on prenatal care. You can access links to resources and documents on issues of infant care, such as the dangers of pesticides and lead poisoning as well as advice on nutrition and day care.

Missing Children Database and Forum
URL address:
http://www.scubed.com:8001/public_service/missing.html

Now on the Internet, this database contains information about and pictures of children who are missing. The database is maintained by the National Center for Missing and Exploited Children (NCMEC).

Phone Friend
URL address:
http://freenet3.scri.fsu.edu:81/ht-free/phfriend.html

Do your children get lonely, scared, or bored when they are home alone after school? This Web site has information about a telephone service that is a companion to children who live in the Tallahassee area. Parents will be happy to learn that PhoneFriend supports and makes children feel confident about taking care of themselves when they must be alone.

Teaching Parenting
URL address: **http://joe.uwex.edu/joe/1993fall/iw5.html**

This WWW home page describes a program that distributes educational materials to parents of young children. It is currently in effect in several Ohio counties through support by McDonald's restaurants. The information at this site may inspire other communities to begin similar programs.

Crime
Center for Innovative Computer Applications

URL address: **http://www.cica.indiana.edu/projects/Police/index.html**

This Web site offers information about how the Indiana State Police Department is being assisted by computers in their efforts to solve crimes. Learn how photographic images that are taken at the crime scene are digitized and enhanced with computer technology.

XIV

Issues

Center to Prevent Handgun Violence

URL address:

**http://www.psych.nwu.edu/biancaTroll/lolla/politics/handguns/
handgun.html**

This non-profit organization is dedicated to the prevention of gun violence.
The organization works with as many resources as possible to prevent further
bloodshed. This page has several links, including one that jumps to a letter
from Sarah Brady.

FAMM

URL address:

**http://www.psych.nwu.edu/biancaTroll/lolla/politics/famm/
famm.htm**

This Web page has information about Families Against Mandatory Mini-
mums, a non-profit organization that opposes the mandatory sentencing
laws passed in 1986 for offenders convicted of drug crimes.

Employment

Employment Opportunities and Resume Postings

URL address: **http://galaxy.einet.net/GJ/employment.html**

This is a comprehensive list of links to educational, government, and private
sector job opportunities. Most of the sites listed are Gopher sites with documents that describe positions.

Employment Resources

URL address: **http://alpha.acast.nova.edu/employment.html**

Jobs, jobs, jobs. This Web page has links to the following resources, which
focus on employment opportunities: Academic Position Network; Chronicle
of Higher Education; Employment Opportunities (EINet Galaxy); ESPAN's
Interactive Employment Network; MedSearch America; Online Career Center;
Job Banks (UT Austin); Job Banks (Latino network); and Jobs in Federal Government.

Engineering Employment Expo

URL address: **http://stimpy.cen.uiuc.edu/comm/expo/**

Sponsored by students of the Engineering Council of the University of Illinois, Urbana-Champaign, this job fair allows students and members of the
community to meet with representatives from over 100 companies in order
to obtain information about summer and permanent employment opportunities. Links on the home page tell you how to get involved. There is also a

list of companies that attend the job fair, and some of the company names are links to the Web servers of those companies.

Fig. 14.4
This Web site provides information about an annual job fair in which more than 100 companies provide information about employment opportunities.

Interest Groups

URL address:

http://alpha.acast.nova.edu/cgi-bin/news-lists.pl?jobs

This site contains the network mailing lists of several Usenet news groups. Get the latest scoop about jobs in Israel, American jobs and grants, openings in specific areas such as libraries, physics, and television, classes and seminars, volunteers, and employment issues.

International Employment Listings

URL address: **gopher://sun.cc.westga.edu:70/1/coop/JobNet/**

You can search for international jobs by subject area, including corporate, education, government, science, and social services.

Resume Server

URL address: **http://ibd.ar.com/Resume/**

This is a long list of hypertext resumes. It is free to list and read these resumes, which are generally a couple of pages long and include a date stamp that tells you when the individual put his or her resume on the system.

Environmental Issues

Citizen's Handbook

URL address:

**http://sunsite.unc.edu/nc/nc_env_handbook/
R_Table_of_Contents.html**

The Citizen's Handbook of North Carolina's Environmental Information Sources addresses a wide range of environmental issues affecting the state. Just a few of the topics covered in this electronic version of the handbook are

XIV

Issues

agriculture, soil, air quality, resources, energy, and hazardous materials. Learn how to dispose of pesticides, where to purchase organic farming supplies, and what the dangers of radon radiation are. The hypertext document gives government and non-government information sources and is also available in hard copy.

Energy Efficient Housing in Canada
URL address: **http://web.cs.ualberta.ca/~art/house/**

If only we could build our homes in such a manner that they take full advantage of the sun's heat during the cold season and the cooling shade of trees when it's hot outdoors. This site provides links to information about energy efficient home construction. It is useful for people who are building new homes and for people who are remodeling existing structures.

Environmental Resource Center
URL address: **http://ftp.clearlake.ibm.com/ERC/main.html**

This Web site has information for consumers who have an interest in environmentalism. The Center is a cooperative effort between private industry and government that focuses on the collection and distribution of information about environmentally positive activities.

Jalan Hijau: 40 Tips
URL address: **http://www.ncb.gov.sg/jkj/env/greentips.html**

Jalan Hijau is a Singapore-based environmental group. This is an electronic version of a flyer, "40 Tips to Go Green," which was initially distributed by the group during Earth Day 1992. It gives tips for use at home, on the road, while you're shopping, and at work. It also provides an address that you can write to for more information.

National Environmental Scorecard
URL address: **http://www.econet.apc.org/lcv/scorecard.html**

This Web site provides information about the environmental voting records of U.S. Senators and Representatives. One link enables you to see the changes brought about in environmental politics during 1993 and describes the work that remains.

The EnviroWeb
URL address: **http://envirolink.org/start_web.html**

This Web site has several links to sources of information on the environment, as well as methods of adding new documentation to the EnviroWeb. You can, for instance, go to the EnviroProducts Directory for a list of "green" products, services, and businesses you may wish to support. Or, you can jump to the

Virtual Environmental Library, which the home page describes as "the most comprehensive clearinghouse of environmental information available in electronic format. The EnviroLink Network's staff not only gathers information from other on-line resources, but also works with organizations, governments, and individuals to put useful information and ideas on the Internet."

Fig. 14.5
Visit the EnviroWeb home page if you want to learn about "green" companies, or get ideas about environmental efforts for your own home or family.

XIV

Issues

Human Sexuality and Marriage

Marriage
URL address:
http://galaxy.einet.net/galaxy/Community/TheFamily/Marriage.html

Just what is marriage and how does it relate to the family? This site has links to information concerning the history of marriage, separation and divorce, child custody, same sex marriage, and other related topics.

Mortality Attributable to HIV Infection
URL address: **http://herbst7.his.ucsf.edu/Issue1/AIDSmort1992.html**

Updated data from the National Vital Statistics System that was obtained from death certificates filed in all 50 states and the District of Columbia.

Preventing HIV and AIDS
URL address:
http://www.psych.nwu.edu/biancaTroll/lolla/politics/aids/aids.html

This is a site of extensive information links relating to issues of HIV and AIDS. Much of the information is from the U.S. Center for Disease Control. It also provides a link to the "AIDS Parlor," where you can add your own comments and read what other readers have written.

Queer Resources Directory
URL address: **http://vector.casti.com/QRD/.html/QRD-home-page.html**

This is a resource page for gays and lesbians that includes newsletters from chapters of the Gay and Lesbian Alliance Against Defamation and the Gay Games, as well as covering such issues as gays in the military, religion, and other topics.

Law and Legal Resources

Corporate Law
URL address: **http://www.law.uc.edu/CCL**

The Center for Corporate Law, at the University of Cincinnati's College of Law, maintains this WWW server, which contains data that assists lawyers in the practice of corporate and securities law. You can, for example, learn about the Public Utilities Holding Company Act of 1935 or the Securities Investor Protection Act of 1970.

Federal Communications Law Journal
URL address: **http://www.law.indiana.edu/fclj/fclj.html**

The Indiana University School of Law maintains this home page, which allows you to do a full text search of all back issues, as well as read the publication on-line.

Westlaw
URL address: **gopher://wld.westlaw.com**

This is a searchable database of more than 675,000 law firms, branch offices, and specific lawyers across the nation. You can get addresses, phone numbers, and contact names. Be as specific as possible in your search; a search for "Denver" retrieves 200 listings.

Nonprofit Organizations

ACLU
URL address: **gopher://pipeline.com:70/11/society/aclu**

The American Civil Liberties Union is a nonprofit organization that fights for individual rights and regularly litigates cases that relate to First Amendment rights and other issues. The Gopher site offers newsletters, speeches, legislative alerts, and Supreme Court rulings. It also tells you how to order ACLU publications or how to join the organization.

Computer Professionals for Social Responsibility
URL address: **http://www.cpsr.org/home**

This is a nonprofit, public interest organization that focuses on the effects of computers on society with topics that tie together computers, freedom, and privacy. You can browse through reports and publications. Hot topics include technologies like Caller ID and the Clipper Chip security system.

Electronic Frontier Foundation
URL address: **http://www.eff.org**

The Electronic Frontier Foundation (EFF) focuses on ensuring that individual rights mandated by the U.S. Constitution and Bill of Rights are protected with respect to new communications technologies and infrastructures. This home page provides information about the organization and its activities.

Florida Mental Health Institute
URL address: **http://hal.fmhi.usf.edu**

This home page overviews the research, training, and demonstration programs that FMHI performs to strengthen mental health services in Florida. There are links to publications, such as *An Overview of Judicial Enforcement of the Fair Housing Amendments Act of 1988,* and other resources.

Foundation for National Progress
URL address: **http://www.mojones.com/masthead.html**

Founded in 1975, this nonprofit organization focuses on educating and empowering people for progressive changes. FNP publishes *Mother Jones* magazine and administers Mother Jones Reporting Internships.

Global Fund for Women
URL address: **http://www.ai.mit.edu/people/ellens/gfw.html**

Global Fund for Women is an international grant-making organization with the mission "to provide funds to seed, strengthen, and link groups that are committed to women's well-being and that work for their full participation in society; to encourage increased support for women's programs globally; and to provide leadership in promoting a greater understanding of the importance of supporting women's full participation internationally."

GURUKUL—The Teacher's Family
URL address: **http://www.acsu.buffalo.edu/~naras-r/gurukul.html**

This is the home page for GURUKUL, a nonprofit organization founded by a group of students. The server and the organization promote rural education in India and the Third World. The focus for education begins with issues of literacy and housing.

INFACT's Tobacco Industry Campaign
URL address: **http://sunsite.unc.edu/boutell/infact/infact.html**

The issue of smoking seems to have only two sides—you're for it or against it. This Web site helps you learn the answers to questions like, "What are the

XIV

Issues

effects of second-hand smoke?" and "Why are certain tobacco companies being boycotted?" The focus is to reduce the marketing of tobacco to children and youth around the world.

Mother Jones: Not for Profit
URL address: **http://www.mojones.com/not.for.profit.htm**

This site provides access to approximately 20 non-profit organizations to familiarize you with some of the hottest issues of the day. A few of the topics are refugees, lesbian rights, housing, midwifery, parenting, Quaker beliefs, environment, and anthroposophy.

National Charities Information Bureau Standards
URL address: **http://www.ai.mit.edu/people/ellens/Non/ncib.html**

The links on this WWW home page can help you evaluate the governance, policy, and program fundamentals of national charities.

National Child Rights Alliance
URL address: **http://www.ai.mit.edu/people/ellens/NCRA/ncra.html**

NCRA is the only national organization directed entirely by youth and adult survivors of abuse and neglect. Child abuse not only refers to physical abuse, rape, and murder, it can also involve deprivation of safety, food, medical care, and shelter by society at large. This home page provides links to documents and resources which bring these topics to light.

NRA
URL address: **http://www.nra.org**

The National Rifle Association provides information about gun ownership, safety, and legislative issues.

Philosophy

American Philosophical Gopher
URL address: **gopher://apa.oxy.edu**

This site provides information on the association, a philosophical calendar, grants, calls for papers, books, and philosophical images.

File Room
URL address:
http://fileroom.aaup.uic.edu/FileRoom/documents/homepage.html

Produced by the Raldolph Street Gallery in Chicago, Illinois, this home page offers an illustrated archive on censorship. You'll find everything from definitions to case studies to anti-censorship resources.

Philosophy
URL address: **http://english-server.hss.cmu.edu/Philosophy.html**

This is a definitive resource for people who have an interest in philosophy. You can find out about the American Philosophical Association, or read articles about and by all of the world's great philosophers—Aristotle, Bacon, Descartes, Kant, Locke, and Nietzsche to name a few. These are all large files, so you'll want to download them to your hard drive to read later.

Politics and Political Issues

Anarchy List
URL address:

http://www.cwi.nl/cwi/people/Jack.Jansen/anarchy/anarchy.html

Fig. 14.6
Anarchy—the word itself almost sounds dangerous. Go to this home page to find out more.

This site has a mailing list and archive of postings regarding the issue of anarchy as a structure for society.

Electronic Democracy Information Network
URL address: **gopher://garnet.berkeley.edu:1250/11**

Information at this Gopher site is designed to increase awareness of events and resources that will have a positive impact on everything from revitalization of inner-city communities to the creation of a global peacetime economy.

Government, Law, and Society
URL address: **http://english-server.hss.cmu.edu/Govt.html**

How does the world of politics impact our everyday lives? Visit this server and find out. There's everything from an overview of Democratic and Republican party platforms to information about Ross Perot's book *United We Stand*.

XIV

Issues

Read speeches, campaign stories, and political documents that tie the efforts of politicians into the impact on education, jobs, the environment, and feminist issues.

Rec.guns
URL address: **http://sal.cs.uiuc.edu/rec.guns/**

Fig. 14.7
The large icon of a gun on this home page tells you immediately that the site has links to information about owning and using guns.

Links on this home page bring you to information about types of guns, gun safety, terminology and acronyms, the National Rifle Association, and the constitutional right to keep and bear arms. Visit this site if you are thinking of buying a gun either for sport or safety. You will learn both your rights and responsibilities as a gun owner. Much of the information is collected from gun news groups.

Public Policy and World Events

Crisis in Rwanda
URL address: **http://www.intac.com/PubService/rwanda/**

A plane crash on April 6, 1994, that killed the Presidents of Rwanda and Burundi began the now tragic, bloody civil war. The Web site contains information and documents about relief organizations, statistics of the war, and human rights issues. There are maps of the vicinity and reports on actions.

Food Gatherers
URL address: **http://garnet.msen.com:70/1/causes/fgs**

Food Gatherers, a food service serving Washtenaw County, Michigan, is putting up hunger-related and food rescue information. Among other items, there's the text of *Keeping It Out of the Dump,* which includes some history of food resources in case you're interested in starting or joining a food rescue group.

Fourth World Documentation Project
URL address: **ftp://ftp.halcyon.com/pub/FWDP/WWW/fwdp.html**

Organized by the Center for World Indigenous Studies, this FTP site maintains archives of more than 300 documents on Fourth World nations. The information includes essays, position papers, UN documents, and speeches.

Graduate Institute of International Studies
URL address: **http://heiwww.unige.ch:80/**

Subjects include international history and politics, economics, and law. There is a variety of interesting publications, such as *Ten Years of Turbulence: The Chinese Cultural Revolution* and *World Financial Markets.*

Human Dimensions Research Programs and Global Environmental Change
URL address: **http://www.ciesin.org/TG/HDP/HDP-home.html**

The name of this server is a mouthful, but the resources are timely and global. The focus here is information and research efforts that will help one understand and make positive changes to the global condition, which includes environmental, social, and political issues.

Human Rights
URL address: **http://www.idt.unit.no/~isfit/human.rights.html**

The site links contain an enormous amount of information about human rights and related issues. At the site the U.S. State Department maintains on human rights, there is a report from 1993 for almost every country in the world.

HumPop and IntlPop
URL address: **http://geosim.cs.vt.edu/huip.html**

This Web site offers two multimedia tutorial programs: HumPop, which lets you interact with a population change simulation program, and IntlPop, which allows you to simulate population growth.

HungerWeb
URL address: **http://www.hunger.brown.edu/hungerweb/**

The home page begins, "In the 5 minutes you spend surfing through the HungerWeb more than 120 children will die because of hunger...What are we going to do about it?" This site offers several links to address the seemingly insurmountable issue of hunger, which plagues about one-fifth of the people on this planet. We have the resources to overcome hunger, we need to educate ourselves and take action.

Institute for Social Studies
URL address: **http://andante.iss.uw.edu.pl/issgen.html**

Located at the University of Warsaw in Poland, this WWW server focuses on social topics and provides both English and Polish documents. One such example is an article in the *Warsaw Voice*, called "Foxes and Hedgehogs." The article addresses the impact of age, sex, marital status, and residence on the psychological condition of Poles. You'll be amazed to learn that in most Western countries, age accounts for four percent of depression, whereas in Poland it is as high as 43 percent.

International Institute for Sustainable Development (IISD)
URL address: **http://www.iisd.ca/linkages/index.html**

The IISD publishes the Earth Negotiations Bulletin. This home page is a clearing-house for information on international meetings that relate to the global environment and development. For example, you can jump to resources about the International Conference on Population Development in Cairo, a gallery of photos, or the Earth Negotiations Bulletin.

PeaceNet Home Page
URL address: **http://www.igc.apc.org/igc/pn.html**

This nonprofit organization, and the Web site, deal with human rights. It collects current information about related issues and assists in the effective communication and cooperation of human rights communities throughout the world.

Planet Earth
URL address: **http://white.nosc.mil/info.html**

This is a monster! There are lots of WWW resource links on this home page (if you don't have a lot of RAM, load the text version or disable inline graphics). The Community Resource links are quite good. You can, for example, get a listing of the environmental voting records for legislators by state (the National Environmental Scorecard).

Population Research Institute
URL address: **http://info.pop.psu.edu**

The Population Research Institute supports population research at Penn State. There are working papers from the Association of Population Centers, including rural center bibliographies, such as North Carolina's rural aging program and Penn State's center on aging and health in rural America.

Population Studies Center
URL address: **http://www.psc.lsa.umich.edu/**

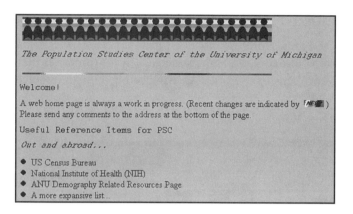

The Population Studies Center of the University of Michigan

Welcome!

A web home page is always a work in progress. (Recent changes are indicated by [NEW]) Please send any comments to the address at the bottom of the page.

Useful Reference Items for PSC

Out and abroad...

- US Census Bureau
- National Institute of Health (NIH)
- ANU Demography Related Resources Page
- A more expansive list...

Fig. 14.8
How does global population impact society? Visit the Population Studies Center home page to find out.

The PSC sponsors research and training programs. From the University of Michigan, this home page points you to a variety of global demographic information such as health, fertility, labor force characteristics, and migration. You can browse through abstracts of their publications on these and other subjects.

Public Policy Education
URL address: **http://joe.uwex.edu/joe/1993winter/tp1.html**

This document provides a short article about public policy, the title is "The Need of an Informed Populace to Make Wise Public Policy."

Social Science Information Gateway
URL address: **http://sosig.esrc.bris.ac.uk/**

Located at the University of Bristol in the U.K., this server lets you search for specific social science resources on the WWW. The topics are broad, ranging from feminism to politics to social welfare. Each topic then takes you to more documents. If you select feminism, for example, you can open up a file that contains biographies of 500 famous women.

World Summit for Social Development
URL address: **http://www.iisd.ca/linkages/topics/10topice.html**

This home page provides details about the preparation and events of the annual World Summit for Social Development and preparations for the Summit, which was created after approval of U.N. resolution 47/92. The goal is to alleviate and reduce poverty, expand employment, and enhance social integration on a global scale.

XIV

Issues

Publications

American Employment Weekly
URL address: **http://branch.com:1080**

This web site features information about the publication *American Employment Weekly,* which contains help wanted ads in job categories that include accounting, banking, data processing, engineering, human resources, manufacturing, and sales.

ANSWERS
URL address: **http://www.service.com/answers/cover.html**

Fig. 14.9
This is the home page for ANSWERS, a magazine for people who have aging parents.

Subtitled *The Magazine for Adult Children of Aging Parents,* this publication is written for anyone that faces questions, issues, and concerns that relate to having an aging parent. The magazine covers aspects of taking care of an elderly parent, including how to deal with the emotional impact and where to get help if you need it. The Web site offers sample articles and a subscription form.

National Health Security Plan Table of Contents
URL address: **http://sunsite.unc.edu/nhs/NHS-T-o-C**

The complete executive summary and all supporting documents on the National Health Security Plan.

Prison Legal News
URL address: **http://www.ai.mit.edu/people/ellens/PLN/pln.html**

This is an electronic version of a monthly newsletter published and edited by prisoners in Washington state. Their motto: "Working to Extend Democracy to All," speaks of the desire to uphold their rights in the judicial system. A sample copy is available as well as a yearly subscription.

Tax
URL address: **http://www.scubed.com:8001/tax/tax.html**

Fig. 14.10
Doing your taxes
is never easy, but
this Web site
offers on-line
information and
tax forms that
may make it a
little less painful.

A Taxing Times information server now has more than 450 of the 750 IRS tax
forms, instructions, and publications on-line. State forms for California and
New Jersey are also available. Many of the forms are available as PostScript
and TIFF files and all of the forms are free.

Religion

Baha'i Faith
URL address: **http://herald.usask.ca/~maton/bahai.html**

Fig. 14.11
The Baha'i faith is
one of the world's
major religions
and this Web page
has links that
provide informa-
tion for learning
and worship.

Although a large percentage of Americans don't know about the Baha'i faith,
it is one of the world's major religions. This home page provides background
information and resources for study and worship.

Bethany Christian Services
URL address: **http://www.bethany.org/bethany/what_we_do.html**

This home page provides a variety of social services with a focus on
Christianity.

Catholic Resources
URL address:
http://www.cs.cmu.edu:8001/Web/People/spok/catholic.html

This home page has a list of hyperlinks to other Catholic resources on the Web.

Christian Musicians
URL address: **http://csclub.uwaterloo.ca/u/gjhurlbu/ccm.html**

This is a large Web page that offers GIF images of many Christian musicians and some information about their work.

Christian Resource List
URL address: **http://saturn.colorado.edu:8080/Christian/list.html**

This home page has numerous pointers to Christian resources and organizations, as well as four on-line Bibles, devotionals, history and culture, documents, and news groups.

Global Jewish Networking
URL address: **http://www.huji.ac.il/www_jewishn/www/t01.html**

This home page offers a tremendous number of Jewish resources, including libraries, catalogs, WWW servers, reading lists, information about the Holocaust, conferences, software resources for Hebrew support, and much more!

Judaism and Jewish Resources
URL address:
http://sleepless.acm.uiuc.edu/signet/JHSI/judaism.html

You'll find a variety of interesting Jewish resources here, including a link to the Israel touch screen map—a visual interface to all WWW and Gopher servers in Israel, Jewish mailing lists, and news groups. It also has links to commercial companies that provide Jewish goods and services.

Kabbalah Software
URL address: **http://nysernet.org/~kabbalah/kabbalah.html**

This home page describes the software that offers clip art, educational software, Hebrew utilities, Torah study tools, and Jewish calendar programs.

Orthodox Page in Europe
URL address: **http://www.york.ac.uk/~em101/Orthodox.html**

Housed at the University of York in the U.K., this page offers numerous resources for orthodox Christians ranging from the Mount Athos Greek Manuscripts Catalog to icons, prayers, and the Divine Liturgy.

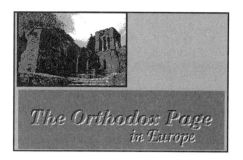

Fig. 14.12
Orthodox
Christians can
find many
different resources
at this home page
located in the
United Kingdom.

Religious Society of Friends
URL address: **http://www.uidaho.edu:80/~norum933/quaker/**

This is the home page for the Society of Friends, more commonly known as the Quakers. This page contains information about the society and its meetings.

Religion Database
URL address: **http://schiller.wustl.edu/DACLOD/daclod?id=00076.dcl**

This is a true smorgasbord of hyperlinks to religious information. You find links to Jewish music and art, the Baha'i Faith, Islam, Mormon, and even a system to provide your horoscope.

Religion Page
URL address:
http://hakatai.mcli.dist.maricopa.edu/smc/ml/religion.html

A great home page for people who are interested in learning about many different religions. There are links to documents, books, bibliographies, and other WWW religion servers that include Buddhism, Christianity, Confucanism, Hinduism, Islam, Judaism, Native American religions, Taoism, shamanism, and religions of India.

Taoism
URL address:
http://www.pcs.cnu.edu/student/patrick/MyHomePage.html

There is a lot of information about Taoism here, including electronic versions of the *Tao Teh Ching* translations, a copy of Sun Tzu's *The Art of War,* and pointers to other WWW resources on Taoism.

XIV

Issues

Chapter 15

Publications: News, Periodicals, and Books

Digital ink. It allows writers, editors, publishers, and readers to distribute articles, stories, and books on the Web and it enables users to enjoy a rich tapestry of multimedia information. Electronic publications are here and they have several advantages over their hard-copy cousins. The impact and power of news relies on rapid distribution. An electronic news story can move from the event through the communications process and onto a WWW server in less than an hour—even television has a hard time competing with this type of "instant" publication.

Besides "speed-to-market," electronic publications have a second unique quality. Anyone with access to a WWW server can be a writer/publisher. This capability has had a profound impact on the scientific/academic community. Several years ago, after a researcher or academic professional wrote an article, a rather lengthy peer-review and publishing process meant that it could take more than six months before the material became available to the public. Now, by self-publishing on the Web, these same individuals can bring their ideas, theories, and research results "to market" much faster. Likewise, young authors who want to publish articles or stories can find a WWW outlet that will get their words out to the world via electronic magazines that cost less than five dollars to create and distribute.

This shouldn't suggest that all scientists and all writers are madly throwing vast quantities of unqualified manuscripts onto the WWW. Indeed, many electronic journals still require peer-review, and commercial electronic magazines have editors who rework copy and reject manuscripts. However, as you weave your way through the resources in this chapter, you will come across works that probably would not have been published in the mainstream system that produces hard-copy reading material—and some of the electronic reading is very good!

Electronic publications come in the same flavors that appear in hard copy—books, magazines, journals, newspapers, and newsletters. There is a phenomenal quantity of electronic books available via the WWW. There are plenty of classics, including the complete works of William Shakespeare, which reside on a server at MIT. And there are many new publications, such as the electronic version of the *Big Island of Hawaii Handbook,* a guide for travelers who want to explore Hawaii. Authors who write with the intention of "publishing" on the Web often include hyptertext and hypermedia links in the manuscript.

Magazines usually have a broad audience and are published either on a weekly or monthly schedule. Journals and newsletters normally focus on a specific subject for a narrow audience. They publish weekly, monthly, or quarterly. Because there is no cost for paper, printing, or distribution, all of these electronic publications can incorporate graphics, photographs, audio, and—like the Global Network Navigator News—even video. These are truly multimedia publications. They unanimously use hypertext to let readers jump from chapter to chapter, from front page to a story, or from an icon to an image, audio, or video clip. You'll find that many of the "commercial" electronic publications, which are digital versions of the hard-copy issues, offer only a few articles. They are really "teasers" designed to get you to subscribe. Nevertheless, they are fun to browse through, and you can't beat the no-charge sticker price.

There are benefits for you, the reader, as well. Using the WWW, you can find an article or story on just about any subject you can think of. You can read materials that you might not normally subscribe to or have access to. And, because the WWW is global, you can jump to newspapers and publications in Russia, Italy, or other foreign countries without worrying about postage or timeliness. So, get a cup of tea or coffee, sit back, and enjoy reading global electronic publications. The categories for these resources include:

Authors

Books and Brochures

Book and Literature Resources

College Publications

International Literature

Newspapers

Magazines and newsletters

Journals

Radio

Gazette Telegraph

URL address: **http://usa.net/gazette/today/Gazette.html**

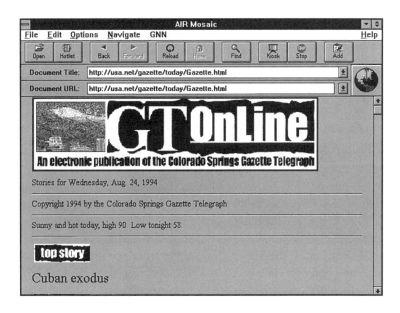

Fig. 15.1
The Colorado
Springs *Gazette
Telegraph* brings all
of the features of a
real daily newspa-
per to the WWW.

From the full-color masthead to the icons for different sections, this WWW
home page is a great example of an electronic version of a newspaper. Under
the banner, you have the current weather conditions and a headline for the
top story of the day, followed by a little one-paragraph teaser to make you
want to jump to that story. Next, a few more headlines, then icons for
weather, local, nation, sports, world, business, and arts and entertainment.

You can leave mail for the *Gazette* staff when you click an icon that opens a
form for your name, e-mail address, and an area for your letter. Or, join a
reader discussion area where you can either read comments from other readers, like a newsgroup, or leave your own message for other readers. Even
though this is a daily publication, you can jump to an archive of the previous
week's issues.

XV

Publications

Project Gutenberg

URL address: **http://med-amsa.bu.edu/Gutenberg/Welcome.html**

Gopher: **gopher.tc.umn.edu/Libraries/Electronic Books**

FTP site: **ftp://mrcnext.cso.uiuc.edu/etext/NEWUSER.GUT**

If you enjoy literature, especially the classics, you will love this WWW server. Project Gutenberg began in 1971 when Michael Hart began to enter the text of famous literature into electronic files stored in the mainframe at the Materials Research Lab at the University of Illinois. Between 1971 and today, more than 100 texts have been added to the collection.

There are two significant features to all the books. First, they are all stored as ASCII text, which means you can easily read and download them to any type of computer system. Second, all the books are in the public domain, which means you don't have to worry about issues of copyright when you download and use the books. Some of the authors represented include Emily Bronte, Edgar Rice Burroughs, Charles Dickens, Nathaniel Hawthorne, Herman Melville, William Shakespeare, Mary Shelley, Henry David Thoreau, Mark Twain, and Jules Verne.

It should be noted that there are three different addresses for this resource. You can use any of these addresses to access Gutenberg publications. The Gutenberg Web server is located at the Medical Library at the Boston University School of Medicine. It began operation in 1993 as a means to facilitate access to the electronic texts available at the main Gutenberg computer—an FTP host. The pages on this server represent links to documents stored on the FTP host. The good news is that, unlike an FTP connection, you don't have to remember file names, directories, or FTP commands—you just point and click to view and download the books. You can also try URL address **http://info.cern.ch/roeber/fgmr.html** to access an unofficial Gutenberg Master Index.

Electronic Newsstand

URL address: **gopher://gopher.enews.com:70/11**

The Electronic Newsstand was founded in July 1993 to provide Internet users a means by which they could access information created by many different magazine (hard copy) publishers. Like a traditional newsstand, you can browse, at no charge, through these publications.

The subjects cover every area of interest—computers, technology, science, business, economics, foreign affairs, arts, sports, and travel. Each publisher provides an on-line table of contents and a few articles that have been pulled from a current issue. You also can keyword search the archives on specific publications for articles. These articles are really teasers, which will hopefully encourage you to order a single copy or a subscription to the publications via The Newsstand e-mail or 800 number. A few of the publications that you will find here include *Animals, Business Week, Inc. Magazine, Computerworld, Canoe & Kayak, Fiber Optics News*, and *Federal Employees News Digest.*

Center for the Study of Southern Culture

URL address: **http://imp.cssc.olemiss.edu**

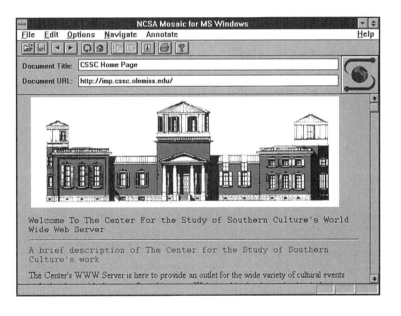

Fig. 15.2
You'll find a variety of electronic publications that focus on activities and culture of the American South at this home page.

For more than 16 years, the Center for the Study of Southern Culture at the University of Mississippi has sponsored educational and research programs about the American South. The Center offers BA and MA degrees in Southern Studies. This WWW home page provides an outlet for information about the cultural activities of the region. From the home page, you can jump to lists of events in each state in the region.

The Center also publishes several periodicals that you can peruse from the home page. These include:

- *Southern Culture Catalog*. Contains videos, sound recordings, and periodicals.

- *The Southern Register*. A Newsletter of the Center for the Study of Southern Culture containing updates on current activities, such as the study of the culture of a 28,000-acre quail-hunting reserve.

- *Living Blues*. A journal of the African-American blues tradition.

- *Living Blues: Blues Directory*. A guide to the blues music industry.

- *Reckon*. The magazine of southern culture.

- *Rejoice!* A gospel music magazine.

- *Old Time Country*. The source for traditional country music.

CBC Radio Trial

URL address: **http://debra.dgbt.doc.ca/cbc/cbc.html**

Fig. 15.3
From this home page, download a variety of audio programs from the Canadian Broadcasting Corporation.

The Canadian Broadcasting Corporation and the New Broadcast Services Laboratory of the Communications Research Centre (CRC), in association with the Communications Development and Planning Branch of Industry Canada, sponsor this WWW radio service.

From the home page you can jump to a list of CBC radio products, an overview of program transcripts that are available, program listings, and samples of digital radio programs. The digital radio program files are in the "au" audio file format. A 10-minute story takes approximately 5MB. Program samples include:

- *Quirks And Quarks*. CBC Radio's science program.

- *The Idea of Canada*. A program in which Canadians talk about what Canada means to them.

- *Sunday Morning*. A current affairs program.

- *Basic Black*. This program features people who have unusual jobs and hobbies.

- *Brand X*. A pop culture entertainment magazine.

Another WWW site, **http://www.cs.cmu.edu:8001/Web/Unofficial/ Canadiana/CBC-News.html**, maintains audio files of the daily Canadian Broadcast News programs.

Authors

Asimov, Isaac
URL address:

http://www.lightside.com/SpecialInterest/asimov/asimov-faq.html

This has got to be the definitive Q&A about Isaac Asimov. It has everything from answers to "Where was he born?" to "What books have been written about him?"

Carroll, Lewis
URL address: **http://cs.indiana.edu/metastuff/dir.html**

This Web server offers electronic versions of *Alice's Adventures in Wonderland* and *Alice Through the Looking Glass*—Mr. Carroll would have loved hypertext.

Clarke, Arthur C.
URL address: **http://wired.com/**

Go through *Wired* magazine home page to access this 1993 interview with Clarke.

Jordan, Robert
URL address: **http://faser.cs.olemiss.edu/jordan/jordan.html**

This home page includes Robert Jordan Frequently Asked Questions, plus fan material related to the author's *Wheel of Time* series. The information was collected from discussions on Usenet.

Pratchett, Terry
URL address: **http://web.cs.nott.ac.uk/~nlc/pratchett.html**

This home page is an index to sites that feature information on Terry Pratchett.

XV

Publications

Shakespeare
URL address: **http://the-tech.mit.edu/Shakespeare.html**

This is a complete archive of Shakespeare's works.

Stoker, Bram—Dracula
URL address:
http://www.cs.cmu.edu:8001/Web/People/rgs/drac-table.html

This is a hypertext version of Bram Stoker's horror novel, *Dracula*. Start with Chapter 1, "Jonathan Harker's Journal," and weave your way through to Chapter 27, "Mina Harker's Journal," with a lot of vampire bites in between.

Stross, Charles
URL address:
http://www.lysator.liu.se/sf_archive/sub/Charles_Stross/index.html

This is a collection of short stories, from *Interzone* and other sources, by U.K. author Charles Stross.

Tolkien, JRR
URL address:
http://csclub.uwaterloo.ca/u/relipper/tolkien/rootpage.html

This is a resource guide and index of Internet resources relating to Tolkien and his fiction—clubs, newsgroups, and dictionaries.

Books and Brochures

ANIMA
URL address: **http://www.wimsey.com/anima/ARTWORLDhome.html**

Find out what's going on in the art world. Here, you have reviews and listings of visual, performing, literary, and video arts. Choose the art form you have an interest in, then weave down to specific documents, such as the Fine Art Forum that students at Griffith University in Australia produce to discuss art and technology.

Citizen's Handbook of North Carolina's Environmental Information Sources
URL address:
http://sunsite.unc.edu/nc/nc_env_handbook/R_Table_of_Contents.html

Learn how to be good to the environment. Compiled by Susan E. Hass, this electronic environmental guide offers 11 topic chapters. Chapters are then arranged into alphabetical listings of governmental and non-governmental sources for information and publications. Many of the documents and "green tips" are simple things that everyone can do to help preserve environmental resources and reduce pollution.

For Sale By Owner

URL address: **http://www.human.com/mkt/fsbo/fsbo.html**

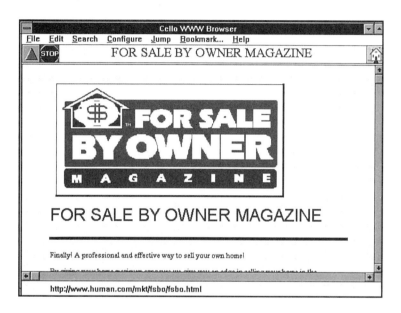

Fig. 15.4
If you are looking to buy or sell a home, here is a unique new resource.

This electronic publication is for home buyers and home sellers who want to check out listings or place an ad. A hard-copy version is distributed in Santa Cruz, Santa Clara, and Monterey counties.

Hacker Crackdown

URL address:
http://www.scrg.cs.tcd.ie/scrg/u/bos/hacker/hacker.html

This is an electronic version of *The Hacker Crackdown* by Bruce Sterling. Sections include: Crashing The System, The Digital Underground, Law and Order, and the Civil Libertarians.

Moon Publications

URL address:
http://bookweb.cwis.uci.edu:8042/Books/Moon/hawaii.html

XV

Publications

Fig. 15.5
The *Big Island of Hawaii Handbook* uses all of the multimedia aspects of the WWW to let you explore Hawaii in an exciting, interactive manner.

This is a hypertext travel guide based on J.D. Bisignani's *Big Island of Hawaii Handbook*. It uses the multimedia of the WWW, presenting text, maps, photos, and audio to tell you about the "Big Island," its land, culture, history, and recreational opportunities.

Samples of Electronic Publishing
URL address: **http://www.elpress.com/samples/samples.html**

Fig. 15.6
If you are planning an on-line publication, this is an excellent place to look for samples and examples.

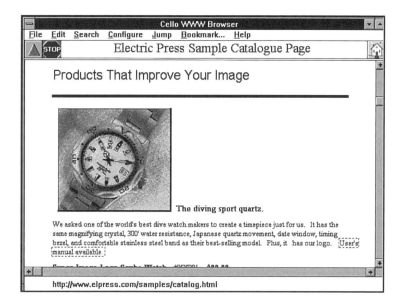

This is a commercial WWW server that demonstrates a variety of electronic publications that use hypermedia. Examples include an electronic catalog for direct mail purposes, an electronic newsletter with photographs, and a product brochure.

The Doomsday Brunette
URL address: **http://zeb.nysaes.cornell.edu/CGI/ddb/demo.cgi**

This is an electronic sci-fi novel that occurs in the year 2056. Unfortunately you don't get the entire book for free, but check it out.

Book and Literature Resources

Association des Bibliophiles Universels
URL address: **http://www.cnam.fr/ABU/EssaisHtml/ABU.html**

URL address: **http://www.cnam.fr/ABU/principal/ABU.v2.html**

Founded in 1993, the Association des Bibliophiles Universels (ABU) offers on-line texts of French public domain literature. It also includes some information about the organization (in French).

Books
URL address:
http://hakatai.mcli.dist.maricopa.edu/smc/ml/Books.html

If reading is one of your passions, you will enjoy visiting this Web site. This is an on-line collection of full text books and documents. Files for the books are large and will take several minutes to download.

Bryn Mawr Classical Review
Gopher: **//gopher.lib.Virginia.EDU:70/11/alpha/bmcr**

BMCR is a review of classical literature distributed over the Internet.

Clearinghouse for Subject-Oriented Internet Resource Guides
URL address: **http://http2.sils.umich.edu/~lou/chhome.html**

From the University of Michigan, University Library School of Information and Library Science, this WWW site offers a searchable resource for publications on the humanities, social sciences, science, and other subjects.

Global Population Publications
URL address: **http://www.pop.psu.edu:70/1m/library/catalog**

This is an extensive hypertext list of library catalog titles that deal with issues of global population growth and world demographics. Sample publications titles include *Adolescent Mothers in Later Life* and *Population Factors in Development Planning in the Middle East.* When you click on the title of a publication, you get information about the author, the publisher, publication date, and library call number.

Indexes of On-line Books
URL address: **http://nearnet.gnn.com/wic/lit.18.html**

Published fiction usually is available on the Internet only if it is out of copyright. This is the home page for the Global Network Navigator Indexes of On-line Books, many of which are either very recent, or have not even been published in hard copy.

Information Arcade
URL address: **http://www.arcade.uiowa.edu**

Located at the University of Iowa (in the library), the Information Arcade is a facility that provides UI students, faculty, and staff access to electronic source materials and to information sources on the Internet.

Internet Book Information Center
URL address: **http://sunsite.unc.edu/ibic/IBIC-homepage.html**

This is a hypertext guide to information about books on the Internet. The WWW Virtual Library literature is maintained by the Internet Book Information Center. The server is provided courtesy of SunSITE, a joint project of Sun Microsystems and the University of North Carolina-Chapel Hill. The IBIC's mission is to provide Internet-based access to useful, interesting information about books.

Lysator Computer Society
URL address: **http://www.lysator.liu.se**

Lysator is an association for computer-interested students at Linköping University in Sweden. Lysator manages its own machines and provides links to three interesting art and literature sections: The Science Fiction/Fantasy Archive, which collects SF and fantasy reviews, bibliographies, newslists, electronic magazines, and artwork; Project Runeberg, which publishes electronic texts in Scandinavian languages; and Anime and Manga, which are Japanese comics and animations that enjoy a growing cult status.

Macmillan Computer Publishing

URL address: **http://www.mcp.com/**

Find information on the best computer book publishers in the world. Books from Que, SAMS, New Riders, Alpha, Brady, and Hayden are featured here. You can review a sample chapter or table of contents from current books. This site also contains a wealth of reference articles pulled from these leading books to answer your questions about computer software and hardware. You can order any Macmillan Computer Publishing book directly from this Web site. Download software associated with best-selling titles. (This site will become available in December, 1994.)

On-Line Books

URL address: **http://cs.indiana.edu/metastuff/bookfaq.html**

This on-line directory of electronic books that you can find on the Internet is a good place to start your search for a particular title.

Science and Magic

URL address:

http://www.lysator.liu.se/sf_archive/sftexts/lists/Science_and_Magic

This server has information about books that bridge the gap between science fiction and fantasy.

The Global Network Navigator

URL address: **http://nearnet.gnn.com**

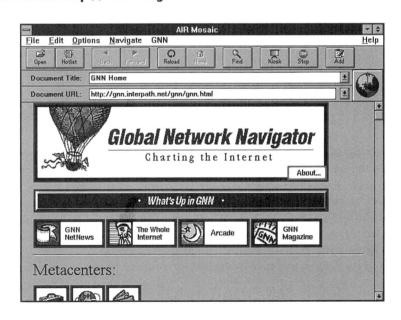

Fig. 15.7
The Global Network Navigator WWW site provides one-stop shopping for many electronic news publications.

XV

Publications

The Global Network Navigator combines a variety of the WWW resources into icons on the home page. There are links to news and periodicals, such as overviews of the Lonely Planet books, and guides that have tips and directions to remote and interesting travel destinations.

College Publications

Georgetown Gonzo
URL address: **http://sunsite.unc.edu/martin/gonzo.html**

This is a publication of satire from Georgetown University, which, as the home page states, is "unofficial, unsponsored, and Underground." It contains article titles like "Enter the Duck: A Kung Fu Play in One Act" and "Hamlet was a College Student."

The Bucknellian
URL address: **http://www.bucknell.edu/bucknellian**

Fig. 15.8
The Bucknellian is an example of a student-run University newspaper on the WWW.

This is the WWW home page for the student-run newspaper of Bucknell University located in Lewisburg, Pennsylvania. There are articles about the arts, social and political issues, and topics that relate to university events.

The Tech
URL address: **http://the-tech.mit.edu/The-Tech**

This is the electronic version of MIT's oldest (since 1881) and largest newspaper. There are articles in each issue that focus on the world and nation. Other sections of the paper include columns, arts, and sports. You also can send a letter to the editor via a special "Comment" button in every issue.

International Literature

China News Digest
URL address: **http://www.cnd.org:80/**

This home page provides links to current news and to Chinese classic novels.

Ireland: CURIA Irish Manuscript Project
URL address: **http://curia.ucc.ie**

URL address: **http://curia.ucc.ie/curia/menu.html**

The Irish Literature archive, known as the Thesaurus Linguarum Hiberniae, collects and puts on-line Irish literature dating from 600 to 1600 AD. It's a bit hard to go through, but many interesting Irish texts are available.

Ireland: Irish Constitution
URL address: **http://www.maths.tcd.ie/Constitution/index.htm.**

This is the English text of Bunreacht Na hE/ireann—the Irish Constitution. For the surfer whose browser is not capable of using the ISO-Latin1 character set, you can choose a plain text format.

Russian and East European Studies
URL address: **http://www.pitt.edu/~cjp/rslang.html**

Here, you will find links to Russian literature and history.

Swedish Language Bank
URL address: **http://logos.svenska.gu.se/**

The Language Bank of Swedish, a text archive at Gloumteborg University's Department of Swedish, is comprised of approximately 30 million words of fiction, legal texts, and newspapers. This Web server provides information about the collection, as well as a Telnet connection to the Language Bank's on-line concordance system.

Magazines and Newsletters

AM/FM
URL address: **http://www.tecc.co.uk/public/tqm/amfm**

This WWW site is a monthly newsletter that features events and personalities in the United Kingdom radio industry. This electronic publication includes back issues that date from July of 1992. There are not a lot of images here, but there are solid reports about the business.

Answers
URL address: **http://www.service.com/answers/cover.html**

The Magazine for Adult Children of Aging Parents is written for anyone who faces questions, issues, and concerns that relate to having an aging parent. The magazine covers aspects of taking care of an elderly parent, including how to deal with emotional impact and where to get help if you need it. Sample articles and a subscription form are available electronically.

Big Dreams
URL address: **http://www.wimsey.com/~duncans/**

This electronic newsletter is devoted to personal development and starting your own business.

Cambridge University Science Fiction Society
URL address: **http://myrddin.chu.cam.ac.uk/cusfs/ttba**

This Web site provides the magazine of the Cambridge University Science Fiction Society. It contains fiction, reviews, poetry, and artwork.

Capacity Index
URL address: **http://www.wimsey.com/Capacity/**

At this Web site, you'll find an art and culture publication with poetry and other artistic endeavors from Canada.

Cyberkind
URL address: **http://sunsite.unc.edu/shannon/ckind/title.html**

Fig. 15.9
The Cyberkind WWW site illustrates the type of new writing that is available on the Web.

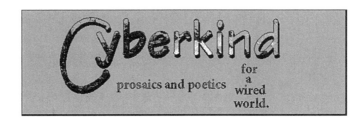

A WWW magazine of Net-related fiction, nonfiction, poetry, and art, Cyberkind features prose and art submitted by the Internet population. All genres and subjects are included with the condition that there is some connection to the Internet, cyberspace, computers, or the networked world. Features range from articles about writers and the Internet to computer-related mysteries to hyperlinked poems. There is also a variety of graphic art.

International Teletimes
URL address:
http://www.wimsey.com/teletimes/teletimes_home_page.html

Fig. 15.10
Teletimes is a monthly WWW publication that has articles on subjects ranging from travel to film.

From a WWW server in Vancouver, Canada, *Teletimes* is a general-interest electronic publication—and there really is something for everyone. Each monthly issue focuses on a topic, such as history or TV and film. One issue that focuses on travel has articles that include "Hawaii Pubcrawl" by Ken Eisner and "Toronto to Vancouver by Train" by Paul Gribble.

Internet World
URL address: **http://www.mecklerweb.com/MecklerWeb/demo.html**

This is the home page for MecklerWeb, a WWW information gathering place sponsored by Mecklermedia. In addition to *Internet World*, an electronic version of the monthly magazine for Internet users, MecklerWeb helps companies put information about their products and services on the Web.

Interserve Magazine
URL address: **http://www.interserv.com**

Start out with graphics ON for this home page—it only has icons. This is really an electronic connecting station with links (and instructions) that will let you access Internet newsgroups via Mosaic and other services.

InterText Magazine
URL address: **http://ftp.etext.org/Zines/InterText/intertext.html**

This is an electronic magazine of fiction stories and articles. There are more than 20 issues on-line which provide for lots of good reading.

MagNet Magazines
URL address: **http://branch.com:1080/magazines/magazines.html**

This WWW page will help you subscribe to "real," non-electronic magazines like *Atlantic Monthly* and *Golf Illustrated*.

Mogul Media
URL address: **http://www.mogul.no/mogul/artikler/artikler.html**

XV

Publications

From Norway, Mogul Media brings you a variety of research articles that focus on new media, such as "The Effect of the Media User Interface on Interactivity and Content" by Terje Norderhaug. Some articles are in English, but it wouldn't hurt to brush up on your Norwegian.

Morpho Review
URL address: **http://morpo.creighton.edu/morpo**

This is a nice, bi-monthly collection of stories and poetry that is color-coded—a white bullet indicates a story and a green bullet indicates poetry. Each page has a forward and a backward icon for easy navigation.

Mother Jones
URL address: **http://www.mojones.com/motherjones.html**

Fig. 15.11
Did you miss Woodstock '94? You can read all about it in *Mother Jones*.

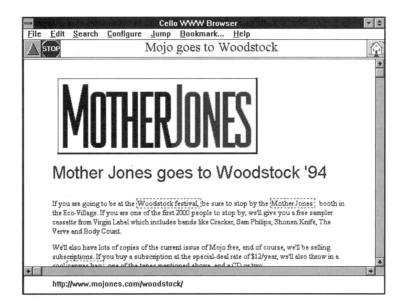

This is an international magazine that contains exposes and progressive political commentary. There are articles about specific legislators, political races, U.S. foreign policy, political activists, and education. There's a lot of hypermedia (images especially) at this WWW site.

NCSA Access
URL address: **http://www.ncsa.uiuc.edu/Pubs/access/accessDir.html**

From NCSA (National Center for Supercomputing Applications), this magazine contains articles about the issues and research that NCSA deals with, such as "Enhancing Reality with VR" and "Supercomputing and the Environment."

PC Magazine

URL address: **http://www.ziff.com/~pcmag**

Published by Ziff-Davis Publishing Company, *PC Magazine* (the hard copy) provides PC product evaluations, such as reviews of CD-ROMs, to a circulation of more than one million readers. This is an electronic version of the publication. Also check out the address (**http://www.ziff.com/~pcweek/best_news.html**), which lists some other electronic publications.

Postmodern Culture

URL address:
http://jefferson.village.virginia.edu/pmc/contents.all.html

This is a joint project published by North Carolina State University, Oxford University Press, and the University of Virginia's Institute for Advanced Technology in the Humanities. There are links to numerous fictional stories, poetry, articles, and reviews—usually esoteric, but interesting subjects such as Ann Larabees' "Remembering the Shuttle, Forgetting the Loom: Interpreting the Challenger Disaster." You can keyword search these archives.

PowerPC News

URL address: **http://power.globalnews.com/**

This WWW electronic magazine is published twice a month. The target audience is users and developers who have an interest in news and information about the IBM/Motorola/Apple microprocessors.

San Francisco Bay Area Parent Magazine

URL address: **http://www.internet-is.com/parent**

This electronic version of the monthly magazine includes reviews and calendars of events of interest to parents and children.

XV

Publications

The Reader
URL address:
http://www.wimsey.com/Duthie/The_Reader/Reader.html

This WWW page is the front-end for a quarterly literary review with stories and articles.

Twenty Nothing
URL address:
http://www.mit.edu:8001/afs/athena.mit.edu/user/t/h/thomasc/Public/twenty/intro.html

Fig. 15.13
The graphic of a kayaker on the home page suggests that you will find a lot of fast action in this magazine.

This is a quarterly hypertext magazine written by people in their 20s. There are only two issues here, but they contain interesting articles like "Plainly, Change Comes to Spain," in which the author examines some of the economic changes that have occurred in this country. Or check out "The Bachelor Gourmet"—the title says it all.

Verbiage Magazine
URL address: **http://sunsite.unc.edu/boutell/verbiage/index.html**

This WWW magazine showcases short fiction. Jump from the home page into an index for each issue, then select a story title that sounds interesting. You can also submit fiction (100 to 3,000 words) to this WWW site.

Webster's Weekly
URL address: **http://www.awa.com/w2**

This WWW-only publication comes out every Wednesday. Topics are broad, ranging from music and movies to politics and sex.

Wired Magazine
URL address: **http://www.wired.com**

Kind of a new wave, hip-hop, cyber magazine, *Wired* has a variety of interesting computer-related articles. Here's one example, "*Wired's* Siberia Barnstormers Sprint for the Pacific-Stolen money. Cracked engine cowlings. Personality clashes. Constant crew drunkenness. The daily burdens afflicting the *Wired* team threatened the successful completion of their trans-Siberian Friendship Flight. So did the interest of the KGB. If you want to know more about invisible military sites, hidden film, and blatant extortion, read the latest dispatches filed from Shane Lundgren's Antonov-2 biplane over Russia." There are links to back issues, a mailing list archive, a Clipper Chip archive, and a promotional video (2 megs in QuickTime).

Fig. 15.14
If you can't get enough of the printed version of *Wired*, this site presents some material that's only available electronically.

Workplace Labor Update
URL address: **http://venable.com/wlu/wlu3.htm**

This is a WWW newsletter published by a law firm. It addresses issues of employment law. Links on the home page bring you up-to-date news about violence in the workplace, retroactivity of the 1991 Civil Rights Act, alcohol/drug use, company downsizing, and COBRA health insurance.

Newspapers

Gazeta Online
URL address: **http://info.fuw.edu.pl/gw/0/gazeta.html**

This is the WWW electronic version of Poland's largest daily newspaper, *Gazeta Wyborcza*. Unfortunately, unless your Polish is pretty good, you won't be able to read much of the news.

XV

Publications

Georgia Newspaper Project

URL address:

http://scarlett.libs.uga.edu:70/1h/www/darchive/aboutgnp.html

This contains information about a microfilm archive of some 1,200 public and private Georgia newspapers. One fun feature is a link from the home page that brings you to a set of icons of the mastheads of Georgia newspapers. Click on a masthead to get a description of the newspaper.

L'Unione Sarda

URL address: **http://www.crs4.it/~ruggiero/unione.html**

This is an on-line version of this Italian newspaper. There are hundreds of articles and back issues here, but you need to be able to read Italian!

News Observer

URL address: **http://www.nando.net/nando.html**

Raleigh, North Carolina's daily newspaper.

Palo Alto Weekly

URL address: **http://www.service.com/PAW/home.html**

This is the electronic version of a newspaper that has a weekly circulation of 50,000. This version comes out twice a week. There is a home page link to "Palo Alto: The First 100 Years," as well as links to articles about child care, education, the community, and housing.

Saint Petersburg Press

URL address: **http://www.spb.su/sppress/index.html**

Fig. 15.15
This WWW site has articles from the Saint Petersburg Press, a weekly Russian newspaper (it's written in English).

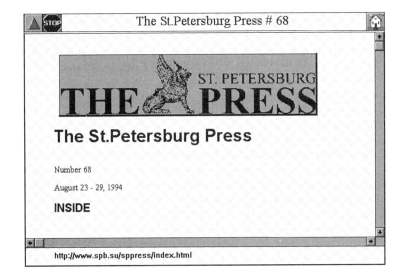

Live from Russia, this is an HTML version of the weekly, English-language newspaper. Major article categories include Business, Culture, and News. Articles like "Local Police Help Smash Million-Dollar Nuclear Crime Gang" have somewhat sensational titles. Be sure to check out the personal listings in the classified section, which include listings such as "20 year-old English, Russian-speaking nice lady from Finland is looking for friend from St. Petersburg...."

Star-Tribune

URL address: **http://www.trib.com/trib_home.html**

This WWW daily newspaper is provided by the Casper, *Wyoming Star-Tribune*. There are also links to other WWW resources.

The Virginian-Pilot

URL address: **http://www.infi.net/pilot/tvp.html**

News (newsgroup information), classified ads, community news, arts and entertainment, and travel are the sections you can jump to from this home page.

Today's News

URL address:
http://www.cfn.cs.dal.ca/Media/TodaysNews/TodaysNews.html

While this Web site does not offer a complete transcript of *The Daily News* from Halifax, Nova Scotia, you will find a story of the day, local and national news summaries, daily listing of metro activities, sports and business, and "Mou's Cartoon," a daily cartoon that is in GIF image format.

USA Today

URL address: **http://alpha.acast.nova.edu/usatoday.html**

URL address: **telnet://spacemet.phast.umass.edu**

These links open Telnet sessions that bring you daily summaries of *USA Today* reports. Logon as guest.

Journals

Chronicle of Higher Education

URL address: **http://chronicle.merit.edu**

URL address: **gopher://chronicle.merit.edu:70/1**

This publication focuses on issues of importance to people who work in higher education. A typical article title is "What They're Reading on College Campuses." There are articles and listings of employment opportunities for teachers and administrators (usually hundreds).

Complexity International
URL address: **http://life.anu.edu.au:80/ci/ci.html**

This is a journal of scientific papers about complex systems including artificial life, chaos theory, and genetic algorithms.

Computer Music Journal
URL address:
file://mitpress.mit.edu:/pub/Computer-Music-Journal/CMJ.html

The "Computer Music Journal" Archive is provided for Computer Music Journal readers and the computer music community. It includes a table of contents, abstracts, and editor's notes for several volumes of CMJ, including the recent bibliography, discography, and taxonomy of the field, and the list of network resources for music. There are also related documents, such as the complete MIDI and AIFF specifications, a reference list, and the text of recent articles.

Conservation Ecology
URL address: **http://journal.biology.carleton.ca**

This is an "in-construction" scientific journal that focuses on research in ecosystems, landscapes, park management, and endangered species.

Cultronix
URL address: **http://english-server.hss.cmu.edu/cultronix.html**

This is a cultural studies journal that uses multimedia to discuss a variety of cultural topics, such as the medical industry or the effects of machine culture.

English Server (Carnegie-Mellon University)
URL address: **http://english-server.hss.cmu.edu**

The CMU English Department sponsors this server—run by its graduate students—for distribution of research, criticism, novels, and hypertexts. It includes SF-related texts on film and television.

Federal Communications Law Journal
URL address: **http://www.law.indiana.edu:80/fclj/fclj.html**

Communications law is a big business as it relates to cable and broadcast television, radio, and now computer communications. This journal comes from the Indiana University School of Law.

Government Information in Canada

URL address: **http://www.usask.ca/library/gic/index.html**

This is a quarterly electronic journal that focuses on articles that relate to the provinces and Canadian government. One example is an article titled "Parliamentary Papers: Change is the Name of the Game" by Brian Land. Some of the information, such as the editorial, is written in French.

Internaut

URL address: **http://www.astro.nwu.edu:80/lentz/**

This journal contains lots of timely articles and FAQs (Frequently Asked Questions) about space. For example, the General Astronomy Information Leaflets, The Nine Planets, a reference to the solar system, and links to other space resources are included.

Journal of Buddhist Ethics

URL address: **http://www.psu.edu/jbe/jbe.html**

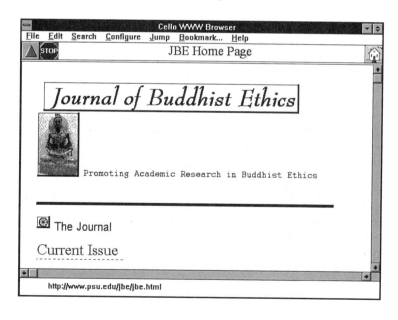

Fig. 15.16
Like many of the Web's electronic journals, the *Journal of Buddhist Ethics* offers timely articles, essays, and a calendar of events.

This is a WWW electronic academic journal that addresses Buddhism with articles like "Kraft's Inner Peace, World Peace: Essays on Buddhism and Non-violence." Bulletins mention different timely topics, such as employment opportunities in religious studies and seminars on Buddhism.

Learned InfoNet
URL address: **http://info.learned.co.uk**

This Web site is sponsored by Learned Information Ltd., a publishers- and conference-organizing company that focuses on information industries. The LI NewsWire link offers abstracts and news about the world of on-line information. Examples of titles include *Europe Acts On Superhighways* and *Electronic Libraries—Visions of the Future*. There is also a link to information about conferences that focus on on-line information.

NASDAQ Financial Executive Journal
URL address: **http://www.law.cornell.edu/nasdaq/nasdtoc.html**

This is a joint project of the Legal Information Institute at Cornell Law School and the NASDAQ (SM) Stock Exchange which contains in-depth articles and interviews such as "Disclosure from the Analyst's Perspective."

Psycoloquy
URL address:
http://info.cern.ch/hypertext/DataSources/bySubject/Psychology/Psycoloquy.html

Sponsored by the American Psychological Association, this electronic publication now has 20,000 readers. It is an interdisciplinary journal that has features on psychology, philosophy, behaviorism, and artificial intelligence.

Secular Web
URL address: **http://freethought.tamu.edu**

This addresses secular issues including atheism, agnosticism, humanism, and skepticism. The site also maintains an archive of free-thought literature called *The Freethought Web*.

Scholarly Communications Project
URL address: **http://borg.lib.vt.edu**

This home page will link you to several different scholarly journals including *The Journal of Fluids Engineering DATABAND*, *The Journal of Technology Education*, and *The Journal of Veterinary Medical Education*.

Telektronikk
URL address: **http://www.nta.no/telektronikk/4.93.html**

This is a huge collection of interesting articles about electronic communications such as "Coordination: Challenge of the Nineties: Multimedia as a Co-ordinating Technology." You can do full text search of the articles. It's truly an international collaboration.

Tree Physiology
URL address: **http://sol.uvic.ca/treephys**

This monthly publication is distributed to more than 60 countries—the electronic version includes reviews, reports, and papers about tree physiology such as the impact of air pollutants on trees, tree growth, reproduction, and environmental adaptation.

Radio

Canadian Broadcast News
URL address:
http://www.cs.cmu.edu:8001/Web/Unofficial/Canadiana/CBC-News.html

This WWW site maintains daily audio files of the CBC radio news broadcasts. There are two daily newscasts—an International broadcast at 8:00 EST and Canadian Domestic News at 17:00 EST. The audio files are 10-15 minutes long. (You can also see the detailed overview of the CBC Radio Trial).

Internet Talk Radio
URL address: **http://juggler.lanl.gov/itr.html**

This is a daily information service that focuses on news and technology about the Internet. Internet Talk Radio is similar in format to National Public Radio and provides in-depth technical information to the Internet community. There are also some general-interest program features like "Taking Care of Planet Earth" and "Technology and Health Care." You download the program to your PC, then play it back with a sound program. Each half-hour program consists of 64,000 bits per second or 15 MBs total. ITR produces between 30 to 90 minutes of programming each day. This digital, cyberspace radio show is produced by the Internet Multicasting Service—a non-profit corporation that resides in the National Press Building. Initial support for the project comes from Sun Microsystems and O'Reilly & Associates.

XV

Publications

Additional Electronic Publications Via Gopher

When you connect with the following Gopher sites, you get an on-screen display of icons that represent individual files, which are documents and articles. Usually the file name provides a good clue as to the type of information that you will find if you click on the icon.

Austin Daily Texan
gopher://ftp.cc.utexas.edu:3003/1/microlib/info/texan/today

Citations for Serial Literature
gopher://dewey.lib.ncsu.edu/11/library/stacks/csl

Electronic Antiquity
gopher://gopher.cic.net/11/e-serials/alphabetic/e/electronic-antiquity

General News Serials
gopher://gopher.cic.net/11/e-serials/general/news

Review of Early English Drama
gopher://vm.utcs.utoronto.ca/11/listserv/reed-l

The Nation
gopher://gopher.igc.apc.org/11/pubs/nation.gopher

Chapter 16

Science Resources

From botany to zoology, the WWW has information about every category of science. Perhaps one reason for this is that computers enhance scientific research. Scientists use computers to record and analyze data from experiments, model images of phenomena not visible to the human eye (such as a 3D image of protein structure or a graphic representation of weather conditions), and store databases that range from catalogs of animal species to dinosaur fossils. The WWW was originally created to assist scientists who work in the area of high energy physics and, as a result, a number of institutions that focus on this complex science have a presence on the Web. But you don't have to have a Ph.D. in nuclear science to enjoy and use the scientific information. There are WWW servers that can help you grow roses, locate the Big Dipper, or develop a lesson plan for a sixth-grade biology class. The broad categories of resources in this chapter include:

Agricultural (botany) and animal sciences

Anthropology

Astronomy

Biology

Chemistry

Complex systems

Engineering

Environmental sciences

Meteorology

Museums

Physics

Resources

Telecommunications

National Aeronautics and Space Administration (NASA)

URL address: **http://hypatia.gsfc.nasa.gov/NASA_homepage.html**

WWW Telnet address: **telnet://spacelink.msfc.nasa.gov/**

Fig. 16.1
The NASA home page is the definitive source of information and links to other resources about space science, technology, and flights.

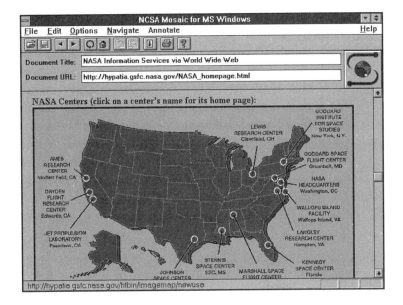

NASA, the U.S. National Aeronautics and Space Administration, is the undisputed world leader in the exploration of space. The NASA mission statement located at the WWW home page declares, "As explorers, pioneers, and innovators, we boldly expand frontiers in air and space to inspire and serve America and to benefit the quality of life on Earth.... We explore the universe to enrich human life by stimulating intellectual curiosity, opening new worlds of opportunity, and uniting nations of the world in this quest."

Because it is federally funded, NASA makes information about its programs available to the public. Many of the NASA materials are designed for use by educators and students who access information about NASA's scientific projects, space missions, educational programs, and newsletters. NASA Spacelink, which is a Telnet site, provides lesson plans, GIF digital images, educational software, and schedules for NASA Select TV, a television channel that NASA makes available to cable companies and others who have access to a satellite downlink system.

Delving into NASA's resources on the Web is similar to exploring outer space—it is enormous, and one destination quickly opens up new avenues for discovery. NASA's WWW home page contains a map of the United States that highlights the primary NASA-connected institutions. Each of the "hot buttons" for the locations on the map links users to these institutions.

Here are a few of the WWW sites available from the NASA home page. You can also go to them directly.

NASA Jet Propulsion Laboratory
URL address: **http://www.jpl.nasa.gov/ftps.html**

NASA Langley Research Center Home Page
URL address: **http://mosaic.larc.nasa.gov/larc.html**

NASA Spacelink (interactive session). This is probably the site most used by public school teachers and students.

TELNET address: **telnet://spacelink.msfc.nasa.gov/**

NASA Headline News
URL address:
http://cs.indiana.edu/finger/gateway?nasanews@space.mit.edu

NASA/Kennedy Space Center Home Page
URL address: **http://www.ksc.nasa.gov/ksc.html**

Dinosaurs—Honolulu Community College

URL address: **http://www.hcc.hawaii.edu/dinos/dinos.1.html**

Dinosaurs are everywhere—movies, television programs, t-shirts—and now on the Web. Did you know that the Triceratops lived 70 million years ago, grew to 30 feet long, and weighed seven tons? Take this wonderful trip to the WWW server at Honolulu Community College where you can learn (or teach) about dinosaurs. There are some terrific images of these prehistoric creatures and the exhibits in this electronic museum contain artifacts from around the world.

Fig. 16.2
When you jump to this home page you travel to the time of the dinosaurs. See images of T. Rex and other prehistoric creatures.

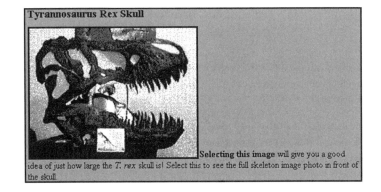

From the home page you begin a guided tour, which you can either read or hear (by clicking on the audio icon). You get the feeling that a real guide stands beside you as a voice says, "We could not afford nor did we have the space for the full Tyrannosaurus Rex skeleton, so we did also purchase here on the right a full Tyrannosaurus Rex hind leg. It stands 12 to 13 feet tall as you can see there, and as you look at this leg, the bones of the feet and the leg, you can see very much the connection with birds...."

Australian National Botanic Gardens

URL address: **http://155.187.10.12:80/index.html**

Fig. 16.3
Go "down under" and learn about the thousands of plants that grow in Australia.

Australia has a lot more to offer than kangaroos and beer. The logo for this WWW home page, a Banksia branch with one flowering and one fruiting inflorescence superimposed over a map of the Australian continent, gives you some idea about the topic—plant life in Australia. This WWW site is a valuable resource for both the serious gardener and the professional botanist.

Located in Canberra, the Australian National Botanic Gardens maintain a collection of some 90,000 native plants from all parts of the continent. Learn about the science and the gardening requirements for flowers, plants, and trees. The "Flower of the Week" link provides information about a specific flower that is in bloom at the Gardens. You can almost smell the aroma as you read the descriptions—"The perfume of golden wattles pervades throughout the gardens, whilst banksias, grevilleas and hakeas continue to flower." Other home page links bring you to:

ANBG Integrated Botanical Information System (IBIS)

Bibliography of plant identification

A selection of botanical glossaries

Australian Nature Conservation Agency Libraries

Centre for Plant Biodiversity Research (CPBR)

Australian Biological Resources Study (ABRS)

Australian Network for Plant Conservation (ANPC)

National Renewable Energy Laboratory

URL address: **http://www.nrel.gov**

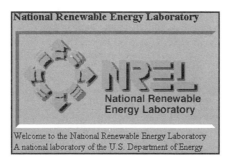

Fig. 16.4
Wind power, photovoltaics, biofuels—these are some of the renewable energy technologies that you find at the NREL home page.

Scientific research plays an important role in the understanding and application of resources and technologies that simultaneously provide energy and improve the environment. NREL, a national laboratory of the U.S. Department of Energy, is renowned for its research activities in renewable energy.

NREL's WWW server provides information about the laboratory and research activities, which encompass photovoltaics, wind energy, biofuels, biomass power, fuels utilization, solar industrial and building technologies, and solar thermal electric and waste management. From the home page you can access information about this research, commercial and experimental applications, energy resource maps, publications, business partnerships—even job opportunities at the lab.

Agricultural (Botany) and Animal Sciences

Agricultural Information Links
URL address: **http://moose.cs.indiana.edu/internet/agri.html**

This home page offers links to a variety of agricultural information including livestock reports and market prices. Main links include agricultural information at Penn State, CSU Fresno, Clemson, Purdue, and Cornell.

Agricultural Genome World Wide Web Server
URL address: **http://probe.nalusda.gov:8000/about.html**

URL address: **http://probe.nalusda.gov:8000/animal/index.html**

Fig. 16.5
There's a wealth of useful plant, animal, and biology information on this page.

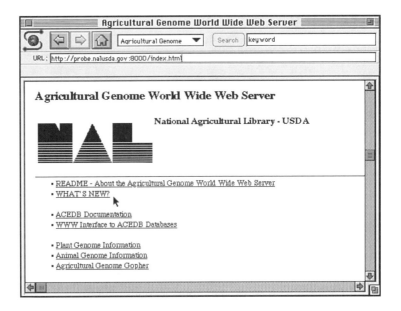

The Agricultural Genome WWW server is a service provided by the USDA and the National Agricultural Library in Beltsville, Maryland. This information is useful to farmers or anyone who may have an interest in plants, animals, or biology. There is even a link to a National Agricultural Library telephone list.

Animal Sounds

URL address: **http://info.fuw.edu.pl/multimedia/sounds.animals**

Do you want to hear a bat? A cow? A donkey? This server maintains an enormous collection of animal noises. Download and play these short sound bites.

FDA Animal Drug Database

URL address: **http://borg.lib.vt.edu/ejournals/vetfda.html**

The Generic Animal Drug and Patent Restoration Act of 1988 requires that a list of all FDA-approved animal drug products be made available to the public. This information is available via the Veterinary Medical Informatics Laboratory server at Virginia Polytechnic Institute and University.

Guess the Animal

URL address: **http://www.cis.upenn.edu/cgi-bin/mjd/animal?intro**

This is a computer game in which you think of an animal and the computer tries to guess what it is. During a recent game, the computer lost—it guessed "Maine coon cat," when the actual answer was a simple house cat.

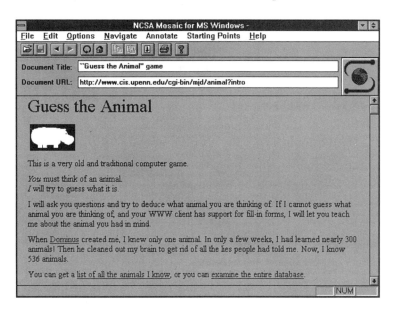

Fig. 16.6
Play a game of
Guess the Animal
at this page.

Insects—CSU Gillette Entomology Club

URL address: **http://www.colostate.edu/Depts/Entomology/ent.html**

Fascinated by the world of insects? Take a peek at slide 281, a close-up of Vanessa cardui (painted lady butterfly), or slide 364, a visually stunning image of Agrosoma placetis (adult leafhopper on chili leaf). The Gillette Entomology Club at Colorado State University offers a large collection of insect slides for sale, including comprehensive lists of insects that are pests.

Fig. 16.7
Neat bug pictures
and more infest
this site.

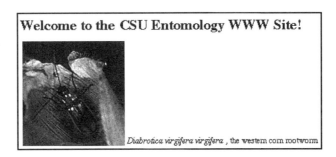

Welcome to the CSU Entomology WWW Site!

Diabrotica virgifera virgifera , the western corn rootworm

Japanese Dairy Cattle Improvement Program
URL address: **http://ws4.niai.affrc.go.jp/dairy/dairy.html**

An overview of several Japanese Dairy Cattle Improvement Programs including genetic evaluation, dairy bull progeny testing, and a dairy herd improvement program.

Fig. 16.8
Moo.

Mammal Species of the World
URL address:
gopher://nmnhgoph.si.edu/00/.docs/mammals_info/about

This checklist contains the names of the 4,629 known species of mammals. They are categorized in a taxonomic hierarchy that includes order, family, subfamily, and genus. Caution—be sure to include the period before the word "docs" in the URL address!

Meat Animal Research Center
URL address: **http://sol.marc.usda.gov**

Home page for the USDA Meat Animal Research Center located in Clay Center, Nebraska.

New York State Agricultural Experiment Station
URL address: **http://aruba.nysaes.cornell.edu:8000/about.htm**

The New York State Agricultural Experiment Station is a part of the New York State College of Agriculture and Life Sciences. There is information on a variety of animal sciences including pest management, plant genetics, and horticultural sciences.

Plant Genome Information
URL address: **http://probe.nalusda.gov:8300**

The data contained in the Plant Genome server comes from collaborators who collect, organize, and evaluate data for individual specimens.

Prescription Farming
URL address: **http://ma.itd.com:8000/p-farming.html**

The Space Remote Sensing Center sponsors this WWW server. By using satellite and computer technology, farmers can detect trouble-spots such as bug infestations and customize fertilizer use in specific sections of a field.

University of Delaware College of Agricultural Sciences
URL address:
gopher://bluehen.ags.udel.edu:71/hh/.recruit/AgriculturalSci.html

Complete information on this school, which has a greenhouse laboratory and a 350-acre teaching and research complex that maintains beef cattle, sheep, swine, horses, poultry, and a dairy herd.

Veterinary Medicine Educational Network
URL address: **http://www.vetnet.ucdavis.edu**

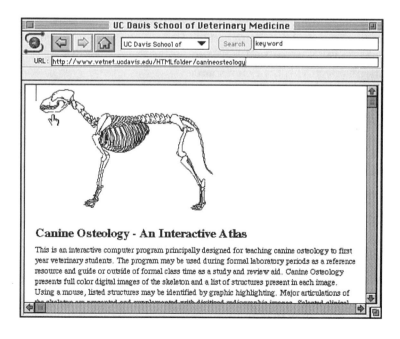

Fig. 16.9
The Veterinary Medicine Educational Network.

This server contains academic program information and links to other veterinary medicine schools and colleges.

W.M. Keck Center for Genome Information
URL address: **http://keck.tamu.edu/cgi/goals/goals.html**

This center provides computer hardware and software to support the study of plant and animal genomes of agricultural and biomedical interest. The site houses information of interest to both the agricultural and the biomedical communities and promotes interaction and exchange of information between these communities.

Anthropology

Anthropology Laboratory
URL address: **http://elab-server.usc.edu/anthropology.html**

This home page is a powerful tool for anthropologists who are involved in fieldwork, research, publication, and education. You can jump to documents that make use of the WWW as a tool for anthropology, including a version of a Mambila transcript with digitized recordings and noun classification in Swahili.

A large number of the World Wide Web's available anthropology resources are also indexed through this site, making it a pointer to such important sources as the Anthropology and Culture Archives at Rice University, Yale University's Peabody Museum of Natural History, the Bishop Museum in Honolulu, and the Center for World Indigenous Studies' Fourth World Documentation Project. This is a rich resource.

Astronomy

Aurora Borealis
FTP address: **ftp://xi.uleth.ca/pub/solar/Aurora/Images**

If you enjoy seeing images of auroral activity, here is an FTP site that houses a great many of them. You can download them into your own computer.

American Astronomical Society
URL address: **http://blackhole.aas.org/AAS-homepage.html**

This WWW address takes you to the American Astronomical Society home page. From here you can learn about the society and meeting schedules or jump into a wide array of options.

Astronomy

URL address:
**http://info.cern.ch/hypertext/DataSources/bySubject/astro/
Overview.html**

When you connect with this home page you are at "T minus 10" about to head to other worlds. Check out indexes at NASA, the XXII General Assembly of the International Astronomical Union, the Sloan Digital Sky Survey, the STELAR project, the Space Telescope Electronic Information System, or the Astrophysics Data System project. The National Solar Observatory home page is also available through CERN's Astronomy home page.

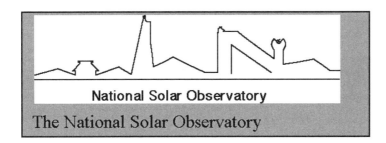

Fig. 16.10
See the stars and more from this page.

Companies

FTP address:
ftp://furmint.nectar.cs.cmu.edu/usr2/anon/space-companies

This FTP site provides a list of companies related to the space industry. Whether you are looking for a job or just interested in seeing who is involved, this is a good point of information.

Planetary Information

URL address: **http://astrosun.tn.cornell.edu/Home.html**

This is the WWW server home page on astronomy information from Cornell University. It includes the archives of *Icarus*, the international journal of solar system exploration, among other resources.

Rensselaer Space Society

URL address: **http://www.rpi.edu/~hassag/space.html**

Find out about the Rensselaer Space Society located at Rensselaer Polytechnic Institute. This server contains many links to other space-related servers.

Space Flights
FTP address: **ftp://archive.afit.af.mil/pub/space**

FTP address: **ftp://kilroy.jpl.nasa.gov/pub/space**

The Orbital Element Sets from NASA, and others, are available at these FTP sites. For individuals trying to track space flights, this is valuable information.

Space Students
URL address: **http://seds.lpl.arizona.edu/**

This WWW server is offered by the Students for the Exploration and Development of Space, based in Arizona. If you are a student and want to find others who are serious about space, check this out.

Fig. 16.11
The Space
Students page.

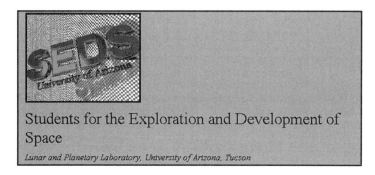

Biology

Biosciences
URL address: **http://golgi.harvard.edu/biopages/all.html**

This home page may take longer than usual to load, not because there are a lot of fancy graphics but because of the vast number of hyperlinks here—perhaps more than 100, and many that relate to biology and the sciences. The hyperlinks to information are categorized first by provider, then by subject, and cover the areas of anthropology, archaeology, evolution, biological journals, biological molecules, Internet resources, biological software and data FTP archives, and molecular evolution. You could spend a day going back and forth from this home page!

Marine Biological Laboratory

URL address: **http://alopias.mbl.edu/Default.html**

Founded in 1888, MBL, located in Woods Hole, Massachusetts, is America's oldest marine lab. This server offers in-depth information about the lab and biological sciences that relate to marine life. You can learn about research and education programs, browse through the Women of Science project files, or reference an on-line catalog of marine flora and fauna specimens.

Proteins and Enzymes—Johns Hopkins Bioinformatics

URL address: **http://www.gdb.org/hopkins.html**

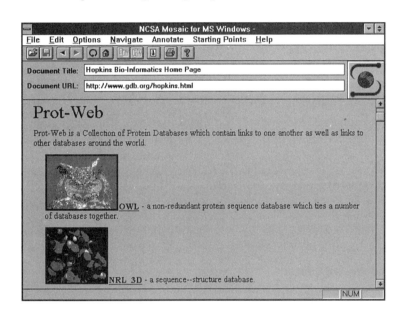

Fig. 16.12
Proteins and enzymes—the building blocks of life—are features at this WWW home site. The protein database, which Johns Hopkins maintains, is a collection of protein sequences and structures.

Shark Images

URL address: **http://ucmp1.berkeley.edu/Doug/shark.html**

The shark is one of the oldest living organisms on the planet, with a history that dates back some 400 million years. If you have a fascination with this creature, or want to take a close-up look at the Great White shark, this Web site will oblige. In all, there are 14 separate images of sharks.

Chemistry

Crystallographic Data Centre
URL address: **http://www.chem.ucla.edu/chempointers.html**

This home page has links to a variety of chemistry sites and documents that focus on the study of crystals. These include the Cambridge Crystallographic Data Centre, the Chemistry Server at the Center for Scientific Computing (Finland), the Chemical Physics Preprint Database, the Computer Center Institute for Molecular Science, the Department of Applied Molecular Science (SOUKAN), Crystallography in Europe, and the chemistry departments at major universities and institutes worldwide.

Chemical Physics Preprint Database
URL address: **http://www.chem.brown.edu/chem-ph.html**

This is a joint chemical/physics database maintained by the Department of Chemistry at Brown University and the Theoretical Chemistry and Molecular Physics Group at the Los Alamos National Laboratory. The target audience is the international theoretical chemistry community.

Crystals
URL address: **http://www.unige.ch/**

Link to the Geneva University server, then choose Crystallography to find information regarding crystallography in Europe on a WWW server maintained by the European Crystallographic Committee.

Pacific Forestry Center
URL address: **http://pine.pfc.forestry.ca**

Fig. 16.13
Visit this home page and the next time you "knock on wood," you'll think about the science behind the material.

A description of the Canadian Advanced Forest Technologies Program, this WWW server takes you into the field of wood and wood product research. This is a great home page if you want to get involved in advanced forestry.

Periodic Table
URL address: **http://www.cchem.berkeley.edu/Table/index.html**

The Periodic Table is available on-line from this server at Berkeley. It is clickable! When you click on an element's symbol, you see a full explanation, as shown in the graphic.

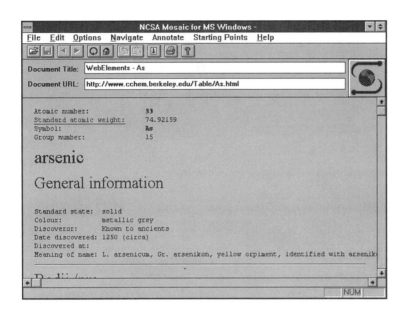

Fig. 16.14
The periodic table was never this much fun in school.

XVI

Science Resources

Complex Systems

Complex systems represents a field of scientific study that has become popular in the past decade. It should come as no surprise that the world we live in is "complex"—events, animals, and plants all constantly interact. Hence, the study of these interrelationships is termed complex systems. The specific areas of scientific study include artificial life, biocomplexity, cellular automata, chaos, criticality, fractals, learning systems, neural networks, nonlinear dynamics, parallel computation, and self-organization. These areas of scientific research represent a new paradigm for scientists as research begins to cut across traditional disciplines such as biology or chemistry.

Artificial Intelligence

Gopher address: **gopher://life.anu.edu.au:70/11/complex_systems/ai**

Of course, if scientists are studying artificial life, certainly they are studying artificial intelligence! This Gopher site at the Australian National University is a good one.

Artificial Life On-Line

URL address: **http://alife.santafe.edu/**

Check out this WWW server on artificial life from the Santa Fe Institute. This is a good place to start looking at the study of complex systems.

Fig. 16.15
You can explore
the science behind
artificial life via
this home page.

Cellular Automata—Tutorial for Beginners
URL address:
http://life.anu.edu.au:80/complex_systems/tutorial1.html

This WWW server in Australia provides a hypermedia tutorial on cellular automata.

Complex Systems Information on the Internet
URL address: **http://www.seas.upenn.edu/~ale/cplxsys.html**

Head towards this WWW server to find a guide to Internet resources on complex systems.

Complexity International
URL address: **http://life.anu.edu.au/ci/ci.html**

The hypermedia journal *Complexity International* publishes papers of original, previously unpublished work in the field of complex systems.

Fractals—Fractal Microscope
URL address:
http://www.ncsa.uiuc.edu/Edu/Fractal/Fractal_Home.html

Fig. 16.16
The Fractal
Microscope page.

The Fractal Microscope is of major interest to scientists working with complex systems. This WWW server is a home page and can take the visitor to many other resources.

Fractals—Images

URL address: **http://www.cnam.fr/fractals.html**

This WWW server in France offers numerous images of fractals.

Fractals—Mandelbrot Set

Gopher address:
gopher://life.anu.edu.au:70/I9/.WWW/complex_systems/mandel1.gif

To download the basic Mandelbrot set shown in GIF format, go to this site.

Fractals—Tutorial

URL address:
http://life.anu.edu.au:80/complex_systems/tutorial3.html

This home page provides a hypermedia tutorial on fractals and scale.

Fuzzy Logic—Tutorial

URL address: **http://life.anu.edu.au:80/complex_systems/fuzzy.html**

This WWW server in Australia provides a hypermedia tutorial on fuzzy logic.

Virtual Reality

URL address: **http://eta.lut.ac.uk/**

This WWW server is from the United Kingdom Virtual Reality Special Interest Group.

Engineering

Chemical Engineering

URL address: **http://www.che.ufl.edu/WWW-CHE/index.html**

Chemical engineering information from a variety of sources is indexed here. This index provides WWW jump points to chemistry departments at the University of Florida, Edinburgh University, Rensselaer Polytechnic Institute, the University of California (Riverside), Virginia Polytechnic Institute and State University, Kansas State University, and the Cornell University School of Chemical Engineering.

Civil Engineering at Georgia Tech

URL address: **http://howe.ce.gatech.edu/WWW-CE/home.html**

Take the WWW route to Georgia Tech's home page to learn more about the institution and its work in the field of civil engineering.

Cornell's Engineering Library
URL address: **http://www.englib.cornell.edu**

If you are on the hunt for information regarding engineering, check out this WWW server at Cornell's Engineering Library.

Electrical Engineering
URL address: **http://epims1.gsfc.nasa.gov/engineering/ee.html**

If you want to know what NASA has to do with electrical engineering, check out this WWW server.

Engineering Case Study Library
URL address:
http://www.civeng.carleton.ca/cgi-bin/ecl-query/ECL/abstract s.db?html-url=1

This catalog lists cases available from the ASEE Engineering Case Program, which are currently distributed by the Rose-Hulman Institute of Technology. The cases are accounts of real engineering work written for use in engineering education, and cover most engineering disciplines. A small number of cases are available electronically.

Industrial Engineering
URL address: **http://isye.gatech.edu/www-ie/**

Georgia Tech offers information on industrial engineering via its WWW server. Naturally, you'll also find out about the university while visiting this site.

Materials Engineering
URL address: **http://m_struct.mie.clarkson.edu/VLmae.html**

Clarkson University hosts this WWW site and maintains information regarding materials, engineering, and its university programs.

Mechanical Engineering
URL address: **http://CDR.stanford.edu/html/WWW-ME/home.html**

A Stanford WWW home page that takes you well into the world of mechanical engineering. This has lots of jump points and information.

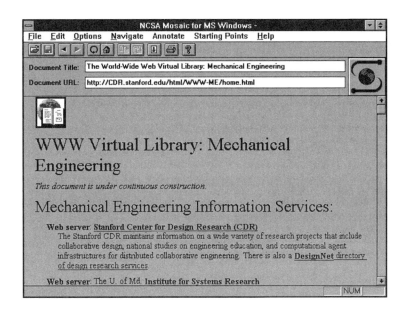

Fig. 16.17
The Mechanical
Engineering
section in the
Virtual Library.

Nuclear Engineering

URL address: **http://neutrino.nuc.berkeley.edu/NEadm.html**

This frequently updated site is in Berkeley, and serves as the WWW Virtual
Library for nuclear engineering. Many WWW sites are accessible from here,
including the Chernobyl database and a nuclear safety site.

UIUC Student Engineering Council

URL address: **http://stimpy.cen.uiuc.edu/**

The University of Illinois Urbana-Champaign is home of one of the most
active Student Engineering Councils in the country. Every year they sponsor
many student-run events for student engineering societies, the College of
Engineering, and the community. Two of the largest events are the Engineering Employment EXPO and the UIUC Engineering Open House.

Environmental Sciences

Climate—Centre for Atmospheric Science

URL Address: **http://www.atm.ch.cam.ac.uk/**

Located at the University of Cambridge, UK, is information on the Center
itself, such as degrees offered and seminars, as well as information about the

UK Universities Global Atmospheric Modelling Programme (UGAMP). This includes a connection to the UGAMP FTP server, which offers software and publications.

Climate—German Climate Computer Center
URL address: **http://www.dkrz.de/index-eng.html**

This is the WWW server of the German Climate Computer Center. The English part of this server is still under construction but is definitely worth checking out. The German Climate Computer Center is a supercomputing center for climate research and is charged with providing the German climate research community with computational, archival, and post processing resources. Here you find information about the German Climate Computer Center, climate research, conferences, and workshops.

Environmental Research Institute of Michigan (ERIM)
URL address: **http://www.erim.org**

Fig. 16.18
Remote sensing and image processing are two of the areas of research that ERIM performs.

ERIM is a nonprofit, high-technology organization that performs research and development and related services for its sponsors. They have expertise in the areas of remote sensing techniques and applications, image and signal processing, and technology transfer.

Landscape and Environments
URL address: **http://life.anu.edu.au/landscape_ecology/landscape.html**

At this site, you'll find abstracts that relate to landscape ecology, biogeography, paleoenvironments, paleoclimates, pollen, fire, and weather.

National Oceanic and Atmospheric Administration (NOAA)
Telnet address: **telnet://NOAADIR@nodc.nodc.noaa.gov**

This is an interactive connection to the National Oceanic and Atmospheric Administration database.

Ocean Research Institute (ORI), University of Tokyo
URL address: **http://www.ori.u-tokyo.ac.jp**

The Ocean Research Institute at the University of Tokyo promotes research about the marine sciences. You'll find out about ORI, including the five-year cruise plans for the Institute's research vessels, reports from past cruises, and pointers to other oceanographic web sites.

U.S. Fish and Wildlife Service
URL address: **http://bluegoose.arw.r9.fws.gov**

This WWW server provides information about the National Wildlife Refuge System and topics of interest for wildlife and natural resources management.

Geology

Canada—Natural Resources
URL address: **http://www.emr.ca**

This Web site is similar to the USGS site in the States. Maintained by the Canadian Forest Service, there are links to government departments and resources in energy, geomatics, and minerals.

Canada—The Model Forest Program
URL address: **http://NCR157.NCR.Forestry.CA/MF.HTM**

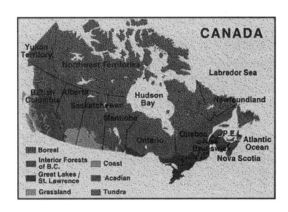

Fig. 16.19
One of the slides in this presentation is a map showing the make-up of the Canadian forest by type of vegetation.

Here is an excellent example of the merging of two technologies. This page contains an interactive photo presentation from Photo-CD on Canada's forests. This is not to be missed!

Finland—Geological Survey
URL address: **http://www.gsf.fi**

This government-run WWW site is responsible for acquiring and making data available (on the Web) about geological information and natural resources in Finland.

MIT Earth Resources Lab
URL address: **http://www-erl.mit.edu/**

A high-end home page that describes the ERL as "primarily concerned with applied geophysics as it relates to tectonophysics, seismology (especially seismic exploration), environmental engineering, and parallel computing."

United Kingdom—Manchester Geology Dept.
URL address: **http://info.mcc.ac.uk/Geology/home-page.html**

Links from this home page go to research, education, and an entertaining HyperGuide to the City of Manchester that includes color maps and directions.

Volcanoes
URL address: **http://www.geo.mtu.edu/eos/**

Get ready to explode. At this home page you will find information about NASA projects that investigate volcanoes, the type of sensing equipment that scientists use, the data that they collect and images of volcanoes.

Meteorology

Current Weather Maps and Movies
URL address: **http://rs560.cl.msu.edu/weather**

This weather database receives weather information from around, and above, the globe, including the Department of Meteorology at the University of Edinburgh, Scotland and NASA readings. Every hour, maps in this database are updated so that you can see weather patterns as they are happening— almost as good as TV weather. In addition to still images, you can view weather movies, if you have viewing software that handles the MPEG format.

Fig. 16.20
The Michigan State University WWW Weather server offers both still images and movies that depict current weather conditions.

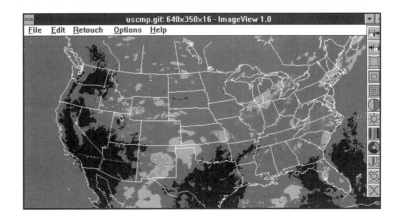

Kochi University—Weather Index

URL address:

http://www.is.kochi-u.ac.jp/weather/index.en.html

Going to the Far East? Located in Japan, this WWW home page offers a collection of images about the Earth's environment and weather information. Specific images of weather conditions in Japan, the Asian area, and the southern hemisphere. Retrieve JPEG, GIF, and MPEG animation (15 frames per second).

MIT Radar Lab

URL address: **http://graupel.mit.edu/Radar_Lab.html**

A unique collection of weather information that includes a weather gallery, a list of frequently asked questions, a hypertext glossary of weather terminology, and a history of radar at MIT. The lab maintains an archive that contains 20 years of observations of storm systems.

NCAR Data Support

URL address: **http://www.ucar.edu/metapage.html**

The National Center for Atmospheric Research (NCAR) supervises research programs and maintains databases of information that relate to meteorology. This WWW home page offers links to some of these resources.

Purdue Weather Processor

URL address: **http://thunder.atms.purdue.edu**

This WWW server uses a software program called WXP to create "weather visualization" for current and past meteorological data. The result is a variety of digital weather maps produced from satellite, surface, air, and radar readings. Weather forecasts range from 48 hours to 7 days—this will help you plan that vacation.

Space Environment Lab

URL address: **http://www.sel.bldrdoc.gov/today.html**

Weather is not limited to events on Earth. When you visit this server, located at the National Oceanic and Atmospheric Administration (NOAA), you can see the "weather" conditions in space and on the sun. A variety of images of the sun show current conditions on the sun's surface and solar radiation patterns.

Museums

Conservation OnLine
URL address: **http://palimpsest.stanford.edu/"**

Conservation OnLine (CoOL) is devoted to information concerning the conservation of museum, library, and archives information. What is science without museums, libraries, and archives?

Dinosaurs—The Berkeley Hall of Dinosaurs
URL address: **http://ucmp1.berkeley.edu/exhibittext/cladecham.html**

The Hall of Dinosaurs has exhibits from around the world. This museum offers a hypermedia tour of the science of paleontology. The graphics are very good and the "hot buttons" provide an effective method of touring the place.

Gems & Minerals—Smithsonian
URL address: **http://galaxy.einet.net/images/gems/gems-icons.html**

The Smithsonian Gem & Mineral Collection. It takes about two minutes (at 14.4 Kbps) to load this home page—but it's worth the wait. A beautiful display of gems and minerals ranging from the brilliant blue azurite to a 68-carat diamond (46 different color images in all) appear on the home page. Click on the name of a gem for further information.

Fig. 16.21
Although you might not be able to buy the 68-carat diamond illustrated on a later screen of this home page, you will enjoy the overview of gems and minerals.

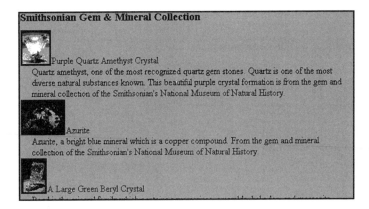

Natural History in London
URL address: **http://www.nhm.ac.uk/**

Natural History Museum, London. The history of the natural sciences is one of the broadest fields of scientific study—learn about our planet and the animals that inhabit Earth.

Physics Instruments Museum
URL address: **http://hpl33.na.infn.it/Museum/Museum.html**

Early instruments of the Institute of Physics of Naples. If you use current physics instruments, you will enjoy touring the exhibits of gadgetry that were once used by scientists and students to learn of our world.

San Francisco Exploratorium
URL address: **http://www.exploratorium.edu/**

An all-time favorite for science buffs in its non-electronic version, this WWW server includes on-line exhibits.

University of California Museum of Paleontology
URL address: **http://ucmp1.berkeley.edu/noinline.html**

Located on the campus of the University of California at Berkeley, the UCMP is responsible for the conservation of paleontological materials, collections development, and research and instructional support. The Museum's collections, rated fourth in size for all collections in America, include protists, plants, invertebrates, and vertebrates.

Physics

Astrophysics—Abstracts
URL address:
http://adswww.harvard.edu/abs_doc/abstract_service.html

This Web server is for researchers, writers, students, and anyone interested in space physics. It connects you to the Astrophysics Data System Abstract Service.

Astrophysics—European Space Information System
URL address: **http://mesis.esrin.esa.it/html/esis.html**

This WWW server comes from the European Space Information System (ESIS), which is the European equivalent to the U.S. NASA program. This site will lead you to explore many other servers around the world.

Astrophysics—Frequently Asked Questions
FTP address: **ftp://rtfm.mit.edu/pub/usenet/sci.space**

Answers to Frequently Asked Questions (FAQ) on the sci.space newsgroup. The purpose of a FAQ site is to reduce the amount of needless question-asking on the newsgroup. It is always a good idea to check out the related FAQ prior to asking general questions on the newsgroup.

Astrophysics—NASA
URL address:
http://sunsite.unc.edu:80/home/fullton/hypertext/nasa.html

NASA hosts this WWW server that contains a variety of astrophysics abstracts. Astrophysics is a very technical but fascinating field of study.

Astrophysics—Space Images
FTP address: **ftp://iris1.ucis.dal.ca/pub/gif**

This FTP site is available on the Web. Here you will find GIF images from Voyager, Hubble, and other sources of space images.

Astrophysics—Space Telescope
Telnet address: **telnet://STARCAT@stesis.hq.eso.org/**

This site offers an interactive session in the Space Telescope—European Coordinating Facility STARCAT archive. Look into this searchable database for more information about how the European telescope community works.

Astrophysics—Space Telescope Science Institute
URL address: **http://stsci.edu/top.html**

This is the WWW server offered by the Space Telescope Science Institute's electronic information service. Space telescopes are more electronic than optical these days, which means that many, many digital images are being created and stored. This is one place to learn more about this field of science.

Astrophysics—Yale Bright Star Catalog
FTP address: **ftp://pomona.claremont.edu/yale_bsc**

This FTP site contains the Yale Bright Star Catalog on Space Physics. This is a place of interest to the very interested!

Atomic and Solid State Physics (LASSP)
URL address: **http://www.lassp.cornell.edu/sethna/sethna.html**

This is the home page for the LASSP World Wide Web server, located at Cornell University. Entertaining science is done here!

High Energy Physics
URL address: **http://heplibw3.slac.stanford.edu/FIND/FHMAIN.HTML**

This Stanford University WWW server provides a free guide to high energy physics software. If you are active in the study of high energy physics, you will find this server very useful.

High Energy Physics
URL address: **http://info.cern.ch./hepix/Overview.html**

This server provides general information about high energy physics. As an overview site, it provides a terrific place from which to jump to more specific information. CERN is also the home of the World Wide Web.

High Energy Physics
URL address: **http://info.desy.de/user/projects/Lattice.html**

Lattice field theory is one area of high energy physics that warrants a server dedicated to describing the various projects going on. This one is located in Germany.

High Energy Physics
URL address: **http://www.cern.ch/Physics/PhysSoc.html**

CERN offers this directory of physics societies on its WWW server. This is a good starting point if you want to locate a physics society for general information, to join, or to subscribe to various print or electronic publications.

High Energy Physics
URL address: **http://slacvm.slac.stanford.edu/find/explist.html**

This Stanford server presents a compilation of experiments' home pages. If you want to keep track of various experiments that are in progress, try this server.

High Energy Physics Newsletters
URL address:
http://www.hep.net/documents/newsletters/newsletters.html

This WWW server presents a compilation of physics newsletters. This is an extremely valuable tool for individuals who seek more information about high energy physics than they can possibly absorb!

Low Temperature Laboratory
URL address:
http://www.hut.fi/English/HUT/Units/Separate/LowTemperature/

This address takes you to Finland, where you can find out what's happening where it is really cold!

Physics
URL address:
http://info.cern.ch/hypertext/DataSources/bySubject/Physics/Overview.html

This server provides a hypertext directory of physics resources. It has links that lead to a mind-boggling array of physics research and information sources.

Physics Experiments Online
URL address:
http://slacvx.slac.stanford.edu/BESWWW/000000/bes.html

This is a point of access through Stanford to the Beijing High Energy Physics experiments.

Resources

Innovator Newsletter
URL address: **http://succeed.che.ufl.edu/SUCCEED/pubs/innovator/**

This newsletter provides information on the education research activities and developments of the Southeastern University and College Coalition for Engineering Education. Also included are publication lists, conference announcements, and relevant information on other initiatives in undergraduate engineering education improvement.

Knowledge Sharing Effort (KSE)
URL address:
http://www-ksl.stanford.edu/knowledge-sharing/README.html

The Knowledge Sharing Effort (KSE) public library is a public directory for information and software related to the ARPA Knowledge Sharing Effort.

The National Institute of Standards and Technology (NIST)
URL address: **http://www.nist.gov/welcome.html**

NIST sponsors and conducts a variety of scientific research programs ranging from biotechnology to computer technology. Many efforts, such as the Manufacturing Extension Centers, directly help industry and small business.

Search for Projects and Researchers
URL address: **http://probe.nalusda.gov:8300/projects.html**

A list of indexes of funded research proposals is provided to allow the user to search for people or topics. The areas covered are the National Institute of Health, the Department of Energy, the National Science Foundation, and the U.S. Department of Agriculture.

Telecommunications

Amateur Radio (a.k.a. Ham Radio)
URL address: **http://buarc.bradley.edu/**

This site provides general information such as: What is Amateur Radio?, Amateur Radio Information, Shortwave/Radio Catalog, University of Hawaii/ Amateur Radio Information, Shuttle Amateur Radio Experiment, the US & Canada Callbook, Amateur Radio Clubs, and Usenet newsgroups.

Chapter 17

Shopping

Would you like to shop in a mall where there are never any parking hassles? Where the stores are never out-of-stock, new merchandise appears on a regular basis, and you are always the first in line? If this appeals to you, explore some of the electronic shopping malls and stores on the World Wide Web. A number of service providers and companies now operate malls where a home page is simultaneously a front door and a directory for many different specialty stores.

Taking full advantage of the multimedia aspects of the WWW, these cyberspace stores offer digital images and sound clips that describe their products and services. If you like the merchandise, you often can fill out an on-line order form and receive the product the next day! Window shopping takes on a new dimension with the global nature of the WWW. Now, it's as easy to visit an exotic or specialty store that's 8,000 miles away as it is to drive downtown. Or, you may want to plan your next visit to a foreign shopping center. Countries like Japan and cities like Singapore have World Wide Web home pages that offer tips on converting sizes for clothing from U.S. to foreign standards or color maps that identify streets and individual shops. From a compact disc of classical music to a bottle of rare Slovenian wine to a high-powered motorboat, there is probably a WWW store that will satisfy your shopping needs.

The resources in this chapter focus on WWW home pages and companies that directly sell products or services, whereas the resources in chapter 7,

"Business on the Web," are primarily large companies, like AT&T or Lockheed Missiles, or services for businesses and business people. The stores in this chapter are in the following categories:

Arts

Books

Computer

Hobbies and recreation

Gifts and products

Services

Internet Shopping Network

URL address: **http://shop.internet.net**

Fig. 17.1
You can search through and purchase 20,000 computer-related products from the Internet Shopping Network's WWW site.

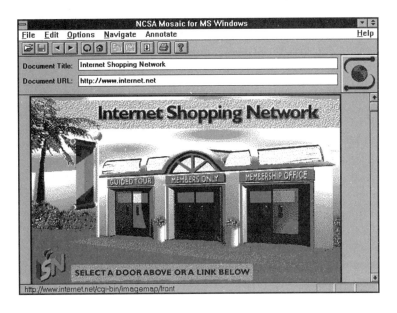

The Internet Shopping Network (ISN) began on-line operation in 1994. The major purpose of this electronic mall is global merchandising. The Internet Shopping Network on-line catalog contains products from more than 800 high technology companies. The home page offers a fantastic image of a shopping center with three doors—door number one is a guided tour of the service, door number two is for members only, and door number three is a membership office. Membership, which is free, means that you have the privilege of ordering, downloading demos, or accessing reviews. Non-members can only window-shop. There is an on-line form for membership, but you must fill it out and fax it back to the company. This is a security measure to protect your credit card information.

Because this service is graphics-intensive, you may want to disable your inline images when you browse. The merchandise in the various stores consists of approximately 20,000 computer hardware and software-related products. When you enter the service, a series of product category icons appear, such as Macintosh products or modems. Jump into a category and begin a search for individual products. It doesn't take long to find the product you're looking for, complete with the ISN price.

Slovenian Wine Shops

URL address: **http://www.ijs.si/vinoteke.html**

Fig. 17.2
When you visit this home page you can learn about rare Slovenian wines and visit vineyards in this European country.

"Vinoteka" is the Slovene word for wine and this home page is a fantastic guide for information about where you can sample and purchase wines in Slovenia. Learn about Vinoteka Bradesko, a store located at the City Fairground in Ljubljana, which offers the largest selection of wines in Slovenia and will let you taste wines. If you get a bit tipsy, try the in-store restaurant.

In addition to reviews of wine stores, there is a database, called the "wine archives," that provides information about the country's best wineries and wines. There is, for example, the Wine Tabernacle in Maribore that sports a collection of almost all post-1945 Slovenia vintages—some bottles that can't be found anywhere else. You may want to remember that the Master Cellarer keeps a secret mini-tabernacle with 50 of the most precious bottles. Click on the name of this or any other highlighted winery and you get a JPEG image of the vineyards, wine cellar, or some other aspect of wine production. The home page also has links to information about wholesale depots and wine specialty shops.

Downtown Anywhere

URL address: **http://awa.com**

Fig. 17.3
The Downtown Anywhere home page has the look and feel of a real town. Do some window shopping!

Downtown Anywhere provides a good example of an electronic town. A bit of amusing self-promotion begins at the home page, which states: "Conveniently located in central cyberspace, Downtown Anywhere is a great place to browse, earn, share, and trade. Everything you can think of is available; just think of making it available. We offer choice real estate and all the amenities to anyone seeking a virtual office, a virtual showroom, or a virtual laboratory in the heart of the new marketplace of ideas."

Like a "real town," Downtown Anywhere has icons that bring you to different locations in the cybertown. For example, you can go to real estate to learn how to sell services and products in this village. There is a library, a financial district, museums, and Main Street with its many shops and services. The jump to Main Street opens the door to a variety of stores, which you can then select to go to their home pages and begin your on-line shopping. For music lovers, there is CDnow!, which claims to have "the largest selection of music CDs on the Internet." If you need to upgrade your computer, try Compusource International—a discount supplier of computer products. If you want to help save the planet, there are at least 140 products in the catalog by Environmentally Sound Products, Inc. And if you just want to make a fashion statement, try t-shirts by Mighty Dog Designs.

Shopping in Singapore

URL address: **http://www.ncb.gov.sg/sog/6.shop.html**

Before you plan your next shopping trip to Singapore, check out this home page. Singapore is a duty-free port and shopping is a major activity. Products range from hand-crafted Asian carpets and jewelry to cameras and electronic goods. There are outdoor bazaars and indoor shopping centers, with most establishments open 12 hours every day. If you are looking for an interesting gift, jump from the home page to the section on Singapore Handicrafts. This describes the Singapore Handicraft Center at Chinatown Point that has more than 60 shops that specialize in oriental treasures like scroll paintings, jade carvings, and embroidered quilts.

Fig. 17.4
Exotic jewelry, hand-made rugs, and spices are a few of the offerings you can sample via the Singapore Shops Web site.

Here is an example of the in-depth descriptions that you can access: "Orchard Road, so-called because of the fruit trees and spice gardens growing here in former days, is the Fifth Avenue, the Champs Elysees, the Via Veneto of Singapore. For sheer volume, quality, and choice, it can rival any one of them. Every shopping center along the stretch from Tanglin Road to Orchard Road to Marina Bay is filled with a myriad of goods from around the world." In addition to inline images of the shops and shopping districts, you can click on little icons to bring up full-screen JPEG maps of the shopping areas. Individual stores are highlighted.

Art

Artists and Works
URL address: **http://lydia.bradley.edu/exhibit/artists.html**

This server provides titles of artwork, descriptions of the piece, medium, size (with and without matting), price, artist name, and address of the gallery where the art is located (physically).

XVII

Shopping

Chez Rampart
URL address: **ftp://ftp.netcom.com/pub/jamesh/chez.rampart.html**

This WWW art gallery features a selection of artwork by Julie Snyder and other artists.

Colorburst Studios
URL address: **http://www.teleport.com/~paulec/catalog.html**

Niobium jewelry is colorful metal-based jewelry. If you're looking for unusual accessories, check out this home page.

Eagle Aerie Gallery
URL address: **http://www.advantage.com/EAG/EAG.html**

Located in Tofino, British Columbia, this gallery features the art of Roy Henry Vickers. The home page provides information about individual pieces, as well as sales information.

ImageMaker—Artistic Gifts for Dog Lovers
URL address: **http://fender.onramp.net:80/imagemaker/**

Artist Monique Akar is on-line with her pen and ink drawings of approximately 156 dog breeds. She creatively captures the essence of each breed and will imprint your selection on quilts, aprons, umbrellas, photo albums, or just about anything you wish for your enjoyment or gift giving. She also has a large selection of porcelain items to choose from.

Pearl St. On-line Gallery
URL address: **http://antics.com/pearl.html**

Fig. 17.5
You will find images of wild-flowers and Southwestern scenes at this WWW gallery.

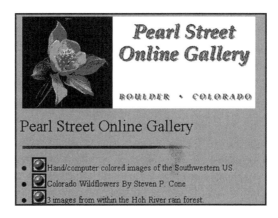

This electronic gallery is located in Boulder, Colorado. The server provides digital images of photographic and computer-enhanced art, such as hand-colored pictures of the Southwest. There is also information about how to send submissions of works to the gallery and how to obtain prints.

Books and Maps

Alternative Textbooks
URL address: **http://www.internex.net/TEXTBOOKS/home.html**

If you're in the market for new and used textbooks, this is the Web site for you. You can link to Stanford texts, which is a book exchange. Some non-book items include world cup soccer memorabilia like t-shirts, polo shirts, souvenirs, and caps.

Computer Softpro Books
URL address: **http://storefront.xor.com/softpro/index.html**

This home page is an extension of Softpro Books—the retail computer bookstore. They are currently in Boston and Denver, but they have the goal to be the best computer bookstore anywhere. They have line-listings and a catalog for on-line use.

Computer Bookstore
URL address: **http://www.nstn.ns.ca/cybermall/roswell/roswell.html**

Located in Halifax, Nova Scotia, Canada, Roswell Electronic Computer Bookstore sponsors this home page. Their WWW database has more than 7,000 titles, which you can search on-line.

Future Fantasy
URL address:
http://www.commerce.digital.com/palo-alto/FutureFantasy/home.html

Fig. 17.6
The world of fantasy is thoroughly explored at this Web site, where you can electronically order books.

This bookstore specializes in science fiction, fantasy, mystery, and horror. You can look through an electronic catalog and place orders via an electronic order form on the WWW. There is also a newsletter.

International—E.J. Brill, Publishers (Netherlands)
URL address: **gopher://infx.infor.com:4900**

The home page enables you to search for publications by using several different methods; the links provide ordering information.

Maps—DeLorme Mapping Order Information
URL address: **http://www.delorme.com/orders/orders.htm**

This electronic store has all kinds of maps. You can link to information about *Street Atlas USA, Global Explorer, MapExpert, GPS MapKit, XMap Professional,* and *The Paper Atlas and Gazetteer* series.

Nautical Bookshelf
URL address: **gopher://gopher.nautical.com:2550/1**

This is the list for everyone interested in anything that would be covered in nautical books. There are references to on-line services, a free book guide, ordering, discounts, and boating tips.

On-Line Bookstores
URL address:
http://thule.mt.cs.cmu.edu:8001/jrrl-space/bookstores.html

This is a list of book publishers, catalogs, and bookstores that you can connect to via the Internet.

Scholastic Inc.
URL address: **http://scholastic.com:2005**

Fig. 17.7
Jump through the links on this home page to find educational books, toys, or games for your children.

Scholastic is a publisher and distributor of children's educational materials, including books, magazines, and now electronic products. Through a link to the "Ultimate Education Store"—an on-line catalog—you can learn about the various products. There is also an electronic Scholastic Newsletter that provides curriculum ideas and a discussion of trends in education.

Tor Books
URL address: **http://sunsite.unc.edu/ibic/Tor-homepage.html**

Tor Books, an imprint of Tom Doherty Associates, Inc., is a New York-based publisher of hard- and soft-cover books. Tor focuses on science fiction and fantasy literature. The home page offers listings of recent and forthcoming books, a newsletter, and pointers to other science fiction resources.

U.S. Judaica Catalog
URL address: **http://tig.com/USJ/index.html**

This Web address links you to an electronic catalog of books on Judaism—it actually starts with a Web site that then opens a second Gopher site. There are also links to other resources on Judaism.

Computer

CD-ROMs—JF Lehmanns Fachbuchhandlung
URL address: **http://www.germany.eu.net:80/shop/jfl/jfl_kat.html**

This WWW home page has links to on-line CD-ROM and book catalogues.

Dell Computer Home Page
URL address: **http://www.us.dell.com/**

On-line shopping for computers, hardware, software, parts, and support. The links on this page make it easy to get information or to order a paper copy of the catalog.

DVAL Visualization Tools
URL address:
http://dval-www.larc.nasa.gov/software/overview.html

Links are available to information about software on the SGI and SUN platforms, and to other visualization tools.

Equipment and Software (by manufacturer)
URL address: **http://gn.update.uu.se:70/1/chp/mf**

This WWW server provides links to several different vendors and manufacturers including Digital Equipment Corporation, Infocom, International Business Machines, and the XKL Systems Corporation.

Fintronic Linux Systems
URL address: **http://www.fintronic.com/linux/catalog.html**

If are looking for a PC that runs a version of UNIX, this company offers PC systems with Linux pre-installed. Linux is a UNIX-like operating system.

Micro Star Software Club
URL address: **http://www.awa.com/bh/microstar/msclub.html**

From this home page you can learn how to become a club member to receive a wide variety of shareware.

Retail Price List
URL address: **ftp://globalvillag.com/pub/www/pricelist.html**

This home page lists suggested retail prices for Global Village products, which are also available from local computer dealers and mail-order resellers.

Software for UNIX Workstations
URL address: **http://www.math.ethz.ch/~www/unix/software.html**

This home page has information about four different categories of software, text processing, calculation, general purpose (graphics, editors, and utilities), and programming (language compilers and development tool kits).

Electronic Malls

The following electronic mall home pages open doors to other vendors and home pages of companies that sell products and services. Depending upon the vendor, there are several ways you can actually make a purchase when you see a product you want to buy. Most purchases are made with credit cards and the methods to place an order include:

- Calling a phone number to place an order.

- Calling the mall or vendor first to establish "membership," whereby you give them your credit card information for future purchases (this helps secure your credit card information) and then shop on-line.

- Shopping on-line and entering credit card information via a WWW form box.

- Sending electronic mail to the company with an order.

Branch Information Services
URL address: **http://branch.com:1080/**

Did you ever think of getting a Bonsai tree or buying clothing from a place that will donate 5 percent of the sale to AIDS related causes? You will find links to unusual and hard-to-find items such as Russian fine art, ergonomic workstation chairs, tuxedos, and gourmet popcorn. Most links just offer product descriptions with some GIF images and phone numbers for ordering.

CommerceNet
URL address: **http://www.commerce.net**

From marketing and selling products to transmitting electronic orders and payments, Silicon Valley-based CommerceNet focuses on the business applications of the WWW.

Commercial Sites on the Web
URL address: **http://tns-www.lcs.mit.edu/commerce.html**

This Web site regularly lists links to commercial sites on the WWW—there are malls, stores, and businesses. You can find the perfect gift or product for that someone special.

CTSNET Marketplace
URL address: **http://www.cts.com/market**

You'll find an interesting collection of merchants at this WWW page, including those that offer rare coins, health and beauty products, and computer equipment.

CyberMall
URL address: **http://www.nstn.ns.ca/cybermall/cybermall.html**

This Web server, which is from Canada, is a storefront for a variety of Canadian vendors. Products and services are broken into four broad categories that include bookstores, disability services, real estate, and telecommunications.

Index of Services
URL address: **http://www.shore.net:/~adfx/1.html**

This Web site offers an extensive list of shopping links you can access from this page. There are more than 125 links to catalogs, services, products, travel ideas, food, spices, and offers for free promotional items.

Internet Business Directory
URL address: **http://ibd.ar.com**

XVII

Shopping

Home page to more than 200 businesses. Start with the link to "Catalogs" where you can get a list of individual companies. For ease of browsing, large catalogs are subdivided with links. For example, Trophies by Edco, Inc. has links to A: Medals; B: Trophies; C: Wooden Plaques; and D: Corporate Overview. The home page also has a link to the Internet Better Business Bureau.

Internet Shopkeeper—a WWW Mall
URL address: **http://www.ip.net:80/shops.html**

Fig. 17.8
The Internet Shopkeeper electronic mall opens doors to businesses from around the world.

People and small businesses from around the world can set up and manage their own shops in this electronic mall. The home page has links to rates and set-up information.

MarketPlace.com
URL address: **http://marketplace.com**

The home page says it all, "Our mission with MarketPlace.com is to offer the Internet community a convenient and useful on-line shopping environment full of information, entertainment, and tools. Many of the items listed are available for purchase here using VISA, MasterCard, or American Express."

NetCenter
URL address **http://netcenter.scruznet.com**

This WWW home page offers "InterActive Yellow Pages." There are stores for compact discs and electronic books as well as computer products.

NetMarket
URL address: **http://www.netmarket.com**

Links from this home page provide access to several good gift stores that sell flowers, music, and discount books.

N_E_T_R_O_P_O_L_I_S
URL address: **http://www.dash.com**

The home page describes this site as "the city of the future." It may be close, as there are links to a variety of resources that are carefully placed in categories that include art, business, education, fun and games, government research tools, and shopping.

Oneworld
URL address: **http://oneworld.wa.com**

From Seattle, Washington, this Web server offers links to companies and organizations in the Northeast. There is Wilson WindowWare, a software company where you can even download some Mosaic shareware during a session, the Asia-Pacific Chamber of Commerce, and a real estate agent who offers properties in the area.

Quadralay MarketPlace
URL address:
http://www.quadralay.com/www/MarketPlaceMarketPlace.html

Home page for shops and vendors that are primarily in the Austin, Texas, area. Other information about the city of Austin and Quadralay's own software products can be found at **http://www.quadralay.com/home.html**.

Retailers
URL address: **http://apollo.co.uk/retailers-usa.html**

From thigh cream to metal roofing and siding, this is the site to look at when you're in the mood for shopping. The server provides names, numbers, addresses, some pricing, descriptions, and everything you will need to get in touch with about 20 retailers.

SPRY World Wide Web Services
URL address: **http://www.freerange.com**

Spry, the folks who offer Internet In a Box, maintain this home page, which points to a number of interesting services, including an electronic mall.

Stanford Shopping Center
URL address: **http://netmedia.com/ims/ssc/ssc.html**

This Web site provides an electronic overview of a *real* mall—the Stanford Shopping Center. There are links to a map of the center, directions, shops by name and type, and links to send a message to the center. The links to individual store names, such as Athlete's Foot and The Gap, bring up a phone number for the store.

Tag Online Mall
URL address: **http://www.tagsys.com**

This Web home page divides company services into useful categories, which are your first links. These include Personal, Business, Retail, Travel, and Miscellaneous Services. An example of a retail store is "Unique Jewelry by Diana Kane"; examples of travel services include tours of New York City and guides to health restaurants in NYC; and an example of a personal service is a directory of accountants.

The Internet Plaza
URL address: **http://plaza.xor.com**

Books, computer network services, software, and cartoons are a few of the offerings on this Internet/WWW mall.UWI Catalogue.

URL address: **http://zapruder.pds.med.umich.edu/uwi/maul.html**

An eclectic collection of "stores" at this home page. There are record labels, like Bulb and Choke, Inc. that sell compact discs, and magazines like *Synergy*.

Village Mall
URL address: **http://crusher.bev.net/mall/index.html**

This site features shopping in the Blacksburg, Virginia, area for local residents and browsers on the Internet. A few of the links you can select are grocery stores, carpentry, bookstores, restaurants, entertainment, and services.

WebScope
URL address: **http://stelcom.com/webscope/customers.html**

You'll find a collection of services and products in this electronic mall. Examples include PC FISHelp, PC software for commercial fishing; Global Leasing Services, equipment leasing; On Target Marketing, direct marketing company; and ARTrageous!, computer clip art. On-line ordering is an option with some vendors.

Hobbies and Recreation

Antique Shops
URL address: **http://www.elpress.com:80/staunton/ANTQS.HTML**

If you are an antique buff, you won't be able to resist the temptation to spend some time at this server—home page for the Staunton Antique Shops. Most of the shops listed are in Staunton, Virginia, but there are several listed for the surrounding area as well. Addresses, phone numbers, and business hours are also given. Happy hunting!

Bikes—Climbing High
URL address: **http://ike.engr.washington.edu/aixcell/climb.html**

This is the home page for the Los Gatos Cyclery, a mountain bike shop that sells Specialized, Trek, and Bridgestone bikes, as well as a wide variety of cycling gear and other sport accessories.

Camping—Guide to the Gear
URL address: **http://io.datasys.swri.edu/Gear.html**

This hypertext guide has links to and evaluations about many kinds of gear. There are directions for making homemade stoves and fire starters, which come in handy at the campsite.

Cards—Non-Sport Cards Page
URL address: **http://empire.umd.edu/**

This WWW server specializes in the art of card collecting. The home page has links that deal with comics, science fiction, and all types of trading cards (including sports related). There's also a list of card companies with addresses and phone numbers.

Crafts, Hobbies & Home Arts—InfoVid Outlet
URL address: **http://branch.com:1080/infovid/c313.html**

This is a comprehensive list of educational and "how-to" videos for learning about crafts, hobbies, and home arts. There is a description of the subject, name of the instructor, and price for the tapes, which are presented by Digitalis Television Productions.

Climbing Hardware
URL address:
http://www.dtek.chalmers.se/Climbing/Hardware/index.html

For all rock climbing enthusiasts, this home page has information about specific hardware and shops that will help you get up those cliffs.

Games—Sundragon Games
URL address: **http://www.sundragon.com/sundragon/home.html**

Do you enjoy games? This home page will help you find and order any of 15,000 strategy, role playing, card, board, or any other type of game you can think of.

Juggling—Infinite Illusions
URL address: **http://io.com/usr/infinite**

Fig. 17.9

The Infinite Illusions home page offers information and products for people who like to juggle.

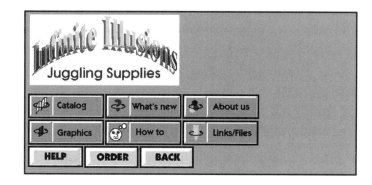

Have you ever been amazed by people who can juggle balls, knives, or flaming torches? The home page for Infinite Illusions Juggling Supplies contains information about products that are in their retail store. You'll also find specific details for ordering.

Marine Supplies—Sailorman
URL address: **gopher://gopher.gate.net/11/marketplace**

Sailorman specializes in new and used marine gear. Inventory constantly changes and there is an area for consignment items. Located in Ft. Lauderdale, Florida, the company also produces special orders—if it is made, they can probably get it.

Running Page
URL address:
http://polar.pica.army.mil/people/drears/running/running.html

This WWW home page contains links to running related products and magazines, as well as volumes of information about the sport itself.

Sports Cards
URL address: **http://www.icw.com/sports/sports.html**

Are you searching for a particular card that is almost impossible to find? This WWW home page will help you locate sports cards and other collectibles with access to items categorized in the areas of football, basketball, baseball, hockey, and singles. Cards are available in multiples or singles by using the on-line order form.

Tennis—The Racquet Workshop

URL address:

http://arganet.tenagra.com/Racquet_Workshop/Workshop.html

If you enjoy the game of tennis, you must get to this site and get there fast! It is brand new and will fill all your tennis needs, whether they are for yourself or a gift item for someone else. There are links to racquets, racquet extras, shoes and socks, tennis apparel, and accessories.

Westminster Supply

URL address: **http://www.icw.com/westminster/medical.html**

For the times you are working on your crafts, you will want to use the type of multipurpose latex gloves that medical personnel have been using for years. There are so many uses for this product! Keep your hands and nails clean while doing mechanical work in your garage or enjoying your favorite hobby. Use these disposable gloves whenever you want to protect your hands.

Whitewater Outfitters

URL address: **http://www.recreation.com/paddling/outfitters/list.html**

If you are looking for guides or equipment, this site is one of the best you'll ever find. The list makes it easy to access information for the area you're looking in. There are links to names, addresses, phone numbers, updates, and comments.

Windsurfing Sports

URL address: **http://www.sccsi.com/Windsurfing/shop.html**

Fill all your windsurfing needs either in the area of Houston, Texas, or on-line. Take lessons at Mud Lake and use the WhySail Mailorder Catalog to buy or rent all the equipment you'll need to enjoy the sport for many years to come.

Music and Video

Compact Disc Connection

URL address: **telnet://cdconnection.com**

This would be a good place to start looking for new music; the on-line catalog has about 80,000 titles.

Compact Disc—Virtual Record Store
URL address: **gopher://owl.nstn.ns.ca:70/11/e-mall**

This is an electronic record store with 3,500 compact disc titles.

Noteworthy Music
URL address:
http://www.netmarket.com/noteworthy/bin/main/ :st=z11pf0v43n|3

or perhaps easier access via the NetMarket Mall at
http://www.netmarket.com

This electronic store features a selection of more than 17,000 compact discs. You can browse or do searches for specific titles, artists, or songs. There are also digital images of CD covers.

Science Television
URL address: **http://www.service.com/stv/home.html**

Do you have a desire or need to learn about the chaos theory? Scientists and students are the target market for the videotapes in this collection.

Products and Gifts

Auction Directory & News
URL address: **http://www.service.com/auction/**

A $50 bidder—will you give me $55? The *Auction Directory & News* is published twice monthly and provides detailed listings of assets from sources like police seizures, S&L failures, military base closures, bankruptcies, and liquidations. You can also get the *Auction Price Guide* to help you decide what your highest bid should be.

Autos—Cars, Cars, Cars
URL address: **http://www.netpart.com:80/jacob/**

Now you can buy any make, model, or year car from Jacob Goldman in Huntington Beach, California. There are links to information about specific cars, so jump to this home page and get that antique or classic you have always wanted.

Autos—Rood Nissan/Volvo
URL address: **http://www.freerange.com:80/rood/index.html**

In the market for a new car? Check out this home page to test drive some autos or learn about the service you can get at Roods'.

Fig. 17.10
Even auto dealers,
like Rood Nissan/
Volvo, have
WWW home
pages.

Cafe MAM—organically grown coffee
URL address: **http://mmink.cts.com/mmink/dossiers/cafemam.html**

Tired of staring at your monitor? Take a coffee break. This is the Web server
for coffee beans and a small selection of advertisement t-shirts and mugs. If
you place your order before noon Pacific Time, they will roast the beans and
ship your selection the same day.

Cyberdeals
URL address: **http://chezhal.slip.netcom.com/index.html**

The subtitle to this home page is "The coolest shop in the entire Internet
universe." You can find out about and purchase high-tech products at or
below manufacturer prices. They even sponsor specials where every hour they
mark-down product prices on-line.

Earrings by Lisa
URL address:
http://mmink.cts.com/mmink/kiosks/earrings/earrings.html

View a selection of earrings from Multimedia Ink Designs in Poway, California. Earrings are made of materials such as turquoise, sterling silver, 14K gold,
real rock materials, glass, clay, plastic, and non-precious metal objects.

Flowers—Absolutely Fresh Flowers
URL address: **http://www.cts.com:80/~flowers**

This home page reminds you that flowers are great for birthdays, anniversa-
ries, thank yous, get wells, congratulations, and, of course, I love yous.

Flowers—Buning the Florist
URL address: **http://www.satelnet.org/flowers/**

Located in Ft. Lauderdale, Florida, this florist has been serving its customers
since 1925. It is now on-line and also can be reached by regular mail, e-mail,
or its 800 number. For whatever the occasion, a gift of flowers is always
appropriate.

Flowers—Grant's FTD
URL address: **gopher://branch.com/11s/florist/**

This may be easier than ordering flowers through the phone book. The server allows you to select and view floral arrangements and fruit baskets. You can order for delivery anywhere in the U.S. and Canada.

Food—Fruit Baskets from Pemberton Orchards
URL address: **gopher://ftp.std.com:70/11/vendors/fruit.baskets**

Now, electronic merchants offer 100 percent satisfaction-guaranteed service. This firm has fruit baskets for personal and corporate occasions and you can order via the telephone, fax, or electronic mail with overnight delivery. Mention "Shop on the World" for a 10 percent discount.

Food—Virginia Diner Catalog
URL address: **http://www.infi.net/vadiner/catalog.html**

Move over Jimmy Carter—no disrespect intended. This gourmet peanut and gift catalog offers peanut-ty selections and other goodies. The Virginia Diner is in Wakefield, Virginia, and offers a peanut recipe of the month on-line (at this writing it was Southern Peanut Pie).

Footware—Rope Sandals
URL address:
http://mmink.cts.com/mmink/kiosks/sandals/ropesandals.html

It doesn't have to be summer to enjoy a nice pair of sandals. This home page offers many selections including six- and two-strap versions in several materials.

Health—Body Wise
URL address: **http://www.cts.com:80/~kylewis**

This home page offers access to information (and ordering) on a myriad of health products, including Beta C and Electro Aloe.

Hello Direct
URL address: **http://www.hello-direct.com/hd/home.html**

Even with the great resources available on the WWW, the telephone remains an important tool for communications. Hello Direct sells every type of telephone and phone accessory you can imagine—cordless, callerID, and digital answering machines. Check it out.

Shirts—Appellation Spring
URL address: **http://www.wilder.com/winery.html**

Q: What do wine and clothing have in common?

A: This home page. Appellation Spring is the WWW source for t-shirts from California wineries. You can click on the names of the various wineries to jump to a short description of the wines and small pictures of the t-shirts (these pictures can be enlarged). You can order shirts via the telephone (old fashioned way) or e-mail (modern way).

Shirts—Mighty Dog Designs
URL address: **http://sashimi.wwa.com/~notime/mdd/Index.html**

The owners of this Web service will design a t-shirt for you. There are even a couple for the Net Surfer and Web Walker. Now you can be the first in your neighborhood or Web circle to wear the styles of the Internet.

Shirts from STUFF
URL address:
**http://www.stuff.com:80/cgi-bin/display_file?filename=/
catalog.html&session_id=cu5bpe.6d5**

A long WWW address gets you to this home page with clickable images of t-shirts. Examples include a Dragon, Wizard, Space Top, and Parachuting Bears.

XVII

Shopping

Shopping in Australia—Glass Wings

URL address:

http://www.aus.xanadu.com/GlassWings/welcome.html

From Australia, this hyper-mall has a variety of products, services, and resources that range from art to games to restaurant reviews.

Shopping in Japan

URL address: **http://www.ntt.jp/japan/TCJ/SHOPPING/00.html**

If you are planning a trip to Japan, stop here first. You can get general information such as shopping hours, tax-free shopping tips, a directory for converting sizes, and a list of weights and measures. Also, jump to resources on where and what to buy.

Shopping in Norway

URL address: **http://www.oslonett.no/html/adv/advertisers.html**

Electronic storefront for several companies in Norway. A real hodge-podge of products and services that includes books, software, consulting, music copyrights, adventure travel, and company profiles.

Solar Panel Power's

URL address: **http://www.wilder.com/solar.html**

Fig. 17.13
Visit this site and you'll learn about a product that captures the energy of the sun and transforms it into electricity you can use for small appliances.

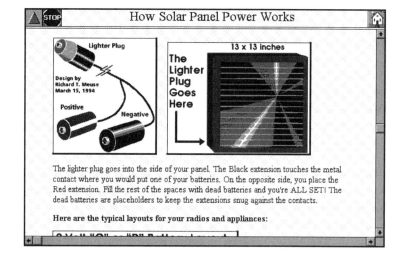

Solar panels capture the energy of the sun and convert it into electricity. This Web site tells you about a portable solar panel product that you can use to play radios and other small items. There is a link to an explanation about how the product works. You can order via e-mail or the telephone.

Vermont Teddy Bear Company
URL address: **http://www.service.digital.com/tdb/vtdbear.html**

Fig. 17.14
Visit the Vermont Teddy Bear Company home page and realize why you don't have to be a child to enjoy a teddy bear.

Need a hug from a bear? This small company located in Shelburne, Vermont, manufactures and sells stuffed teddy bears that are made in the USA.

Wine—Les Vignerons Inc. (The Winemakers)
URL address:
http://www.netmarket.com/wines/bin/main/:st=z11pf0v43n|3

Several interesting links here, you can peruse the selections of wines with pricing for bottles, half, and full cases—items like Dutch Apple, Country Blush, and Pennsylvania Nouveau. You can even see images of the wine labels. Also on-line ordering is available through electronic forms where you enter quantities (certain restrictions on quantities and states for delivery) and credit card information.

Services

Americans with Disabilities—Access Media
URL address: **http://www.human.com/mkt/access/index.html**

The Americans with Disabilities Act requires that employers, schools, and government agencies provide architectural access to their premises and alternative aids and services for people with disabilities. Access Media is a nonprofit organization that provides important documents that relate to the special needs of millions of Americans.

Company Corporation
URL address: **http://incorporate.com/tcc/home.html**

Jump to this home page if you own a small business and you want help with incorporation. Everything can be done on-line.

Document Center
URL address: **http://www.service.com/doccenter/home.html**

This company and its home page specialize in documents. You can order publications about government and industry specifications and standards.

Graphics—Michele-Shine Media
URL address: **http://www.internex.com/MSM/home.html**

Michele-Shine Media creates logos, graphics, and icons for presentations— including on-line presentations.

Hotel Reservations
URL address:
gopher://gopher.gate.net:70/00/marketplace/info-travel-interactive

When you need to travel you can save money through this travel program, which offers 30–40 percent discounts. Independent travelers, either business or leisure, can have access to discounts on hotel rooms booked through Travel InterActive.

Internet Company
URL address: **http://enews.com**

Based in Massachusetts, this company/Web site is a gateway to both the Electronic Newsstand, which offers electronic magazines via the Web, and Counterpoint Publishing, which offers government documents via the Web. Annually the Internet Company helps reply to 10 million inquiries for the Electronic Newsstand and deliver 5 million documents per year via the Internet for Counterpoint Publishing, which specializes in electronic versions of federal information.

Nottingham Arabidopsis Stock Center
URL address: **http://nasc.life.nott.ac.uk/description.html**

Learn about the services and organizational structure of the Nottingham Arabidopsis Stock Center (NASC). Based at the University of Nottingham, U.K., NASC distributes seed free of charge to Europe, Australia, and Africa. The Arabidopsis Biological Resource Centre (ABRC) at Ohio State University (USA) distributes seed to North America and Canada.

Photography and Graphic Arts

URL address:

http://docserver.bnl.gov/com/www/pga/pgahome.html

The home page has links to services that include graphic design, illustration, typesetting and composition, publishing, copy service, printing, computer graphics, photography, and video. The firm, BLN Photography and Graphics Arts, is in the New York area.

Photography—Craig Stewart Studio

URL address: **http://www.sccsi.com/Stewart/craig_stewart.html**

This is the Web page of a commercial photography studio in the Houston, Texas, area. The studio specializes in studio illustration.

Photography—Enrico Ferorelli Enterprises

URL address: **http://branch.com:1080/enrico/enrico.html**

For your corporate photography needs for annual reports, portraits, and advertising, this site directs you to the talents of an international photographer.

Photography—Mary and Michael's Wedding

URL address:

http://www.commerce.digital.com/palo-alto/WeddingPhoto/home.html

Capture those special moments with the help of Mary and Michael Wedding Photography. Located in Palo Alto, California, this home page has lots of links to photos and information about the business.

Resumes—Tips, Pointers, and Buzzwords

URL address:

http://marketplace.com/0/obs/Kennedy/Tips-Buzzwords.html

Here are some ideas for that next electronic resume.

UNIX Security Topics

URL address: **http://ausg.dartmouth.edu/security.html**

This home page has links to 13 sources of information regarding security issues.

Chapter 18

Sports, Games, Hobbies, Travel, Cooking, and Recreation

Sports and computers? You might not immediately think that the world of modems and disk drives would have a connection with the world of athletics, hobbies, or travel—the World Wide Web makes the connection. When it comes to spectator sports like baseball or soccer, WWW sites offer daily reports on the outcome of games. And, to prepare for an event, you can access schedules and statistics of the teams and players. After browsing through a couple of these home pages, you will know more than the television commentators with their fancy computer systems.

Perhaps, rather than watching other people get their exercise, you enjoy making your own muscles work. You may get a rush from competition on the golf course or the ski slopes—there is a WWW server that meets your needs. Do you relish the satisfaction of climbing to the peak of a vertical rise or love feeling the wind as you speed down a tall mountain on your bicycle? Again, there are WWW home pages that focus on these activities. You can learn new tricks and tips that will give you that competitive edge, find out about local and national clubs, and retrieve maps and photographs that point towards unexplored territory.

There are also Web resources that can improve your skills, and interest, in a hobby. There are home pages for chefs, bird watchers, and model enthusiasts. Find a new French recipe or locate advice on training your new puppy. The ultimate in recreation may be adventure travel, where you visit a new country or city and explore the land, culture, and people. There are WWW resources that can help you plan and book that next exciting trip, whether it's to the Louisiana bayou or the Himalayan mountains. The resources in this chapter will lead the way—they're in the following categories:

- Cooking and dining

- Games

- Hobbies

- Recreational sports

- Spectator sports

- Travel

Professional Football Server

URL address: **http://www.mit.edu:8001/services/sis/NFL/NFL.html**

Fig. 18.1
Interested in team-by-team NFL schedules or any other football information? This is the definitive Web site on football.

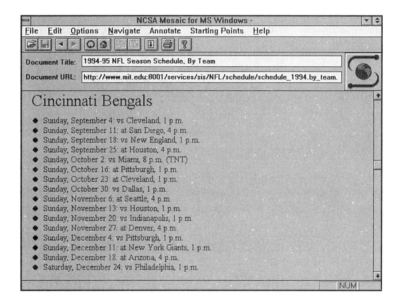

It's third down and four to go. From this home page, by Eric Richard, you can get enough NFL information to become a sports commentator. In fact, the WWW Sports Information system (of which this is part) won the 1994 Best of the Web Contest for "Best Entertainment Site." Divided into conferences, there are team-by-team schedules, round-by-round draft selections, and information on proposed NFL realignments. You can quickly look up statistics from years gone by—choose from the following:

- *Super Bowl History.* Remember Super Bowl XII when Pittsburgh beat Dallas 35 to 31?

- *Super Bowl Standings By Team.* "The Kansas City Chiefs are 1 and 1."

- *Team History and Information.* "The Buffalo Bills' Rich Stadium can handle a screaming crowd of 80,290."

Or, try the Year-By-Year NFL Awards to see a listing of Heisman Trophy Winners dating back to 1935—when Jay Berwanger, a Chicago halfback, took honors. If you like football you'll love this Web site. (Note that the NFL has no connection with this service.)

Games

URL address: **http://wcl-rs.bham.ac.uk/GamesDomain**

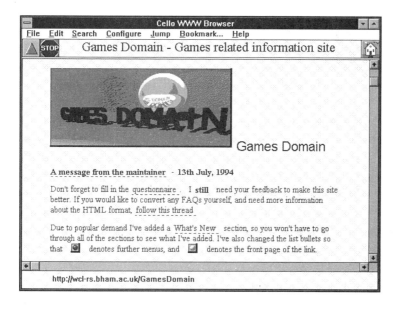

Fig. 18.2
From Checkers to Samurai Showdown, the Games Domain server has information about the rules, clubs and contests for every game imaginable.

You want to know the difference between a Cheat and a Crack in the game *Crusaders of the Dark Savant*? Popular is an understatement for this WWW site. In one month, there were some 55,727 requests for different HTML documents—the equivalent of about 151 requests every hour! After all, this server has more than 140 game-related links.

Not only is Game Domain huge, it's also an easy site to navigate. There are nice features, like a What's New section that instantly tells you about new resources or links that have been added and color-coded bullets in front of menu selections that tell you if there are further submenus. If you start your visit by jumping to Usenet, GamesFAQs will give you basic Q&As for all sorts of games (many of these documents use hypertext).

For the next stop, jump to the Games Related Link: you find at least 50 links to other specific WWW game home pages—from titles like *The World At War: Operation Crusader* to *Othello* (possibly helpful if you play the Microsoft Windows game *Reversi*). There is also a large selection of Games Related FTP links. So if you're into board games, or even bored with games, then get onto this Web site!

Golf Links

URL address: **http://www.gdol.com/golf.links.html**

Fig. 18.3

Visit the Golf Links page to find challenging golf courses around the world or simply get pointers from the pros.

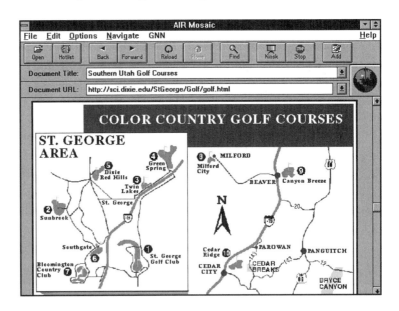

GolfData is the sponsor of this WWW site. They offer great hyperlinks to golf courses and resources on the Web—and around the world. Here is a quick review of some of the links on this page:

■ Southern Utah Golf Courses

URL address: **http://sci.dixie.edu/StGeorge/Golf/golf.html**

If you never thought of Utah as a golf paradise, then this server will change your mind. Many fine courses are located near areas of incredible natural beauty, such as Zion National Park, Bryce Canyon, and Lake Powell. The home page has a fantastic color map of the area with courses indicated. You can click on a course to get more information.

■ Alberta

URL address:
http://bear.ras.ucalgary.ca/brads_home_page/CUUG/golf.html

If you're planning a golf trip to Alberta, Canada, this WWW site has detailed descriptions of many courses such as the Kananaskis course—it has the Rocky Mountains for a backdrop and consists of two 18-hole championship courses.

■ The 19th hole

URL address: **http://dallas.nmhu.edu/golf/golf.htm**

Lots of good golf info here: equipment sources, a golf digest record book, golf associations, and—if you don't already know them—the rules of golf.

■ Princeton golf archives

URL address: **http://dunkin.princeton.edu/.golf/**

A site for the serious golfer, this archive has documents that will tell you how to design a club or calculate slope and handicaps. It also has GIF and BMP images.

Finally, you can learn about the GolfData On-Line service. It is a commercial, electronic bulletin board that contains a database of more than 14,000 golf courses, discount coupons, tips from PGA pro Jeff Maggert, info on golf schools (300 of them), golf resort real estate, and an electronic golf shop—need anything else?

Railroads

URL address:
http://www-cse.ucsd.edu/users/bowdidge/railroad/rail-home.html

From single gauge trains of old to modern passenger trains to information about model railroads, this Web site has it all. The home page offers 17 different areas for exploration. Here is a brief summary of several of the links and some examples of the resources they may open for you:

Fig. 18.4
Whether you enjoy traveling by train, have an interest in old railroad lines, or want to build a model railroad, this Web site will serve your needs.

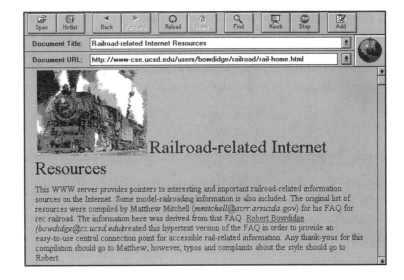

- *Link of the Week.* As it states, a new link each week that, for example, may connect to a JPEG image of a model railroad in Australia.

- *What's New.* Recent additions to the Internet/WWW—possibly a list of hotels that are next to railroad tracks (who needs sleep?).

- *Mailing Lists.* Like the Transit Issues Discussion List.

- *Commercial On-line Services.* Like CompuServe's TrainNet or GEnie's Travel by Rail.

- *Databases.* A database of existing diesels or steam locomotive rosters for Canadian railroads.

- *Railroad Maps.* JPEG, GIF, and Postscript images of the French Metro or the San Francisco BART system.

Rec. Travel Library

URL address:
ftp://ftp.cc.umanitoba.ca/rec-travel/README.html

If you are planning a trip, this is a great resource. The site maintains a library of documents for travelers and tourists. Brian Lucas at the University of Manitoba in Canada operates the site. Links at the home page offer access to more than 15MB of travel information and you can find a file on just about any country in the world. There is also useful information on airfare, cruise reviews, tour operators, and travel agents. There is an electronic newsletter on Caribbean travel. Or, click on the *tourism offices* link and access a database of more than 680 tourist offices worldwide. You keyword search by entering a company name and the database retrieves the address and phone number of the tourist offices in that country.

Cooking and Dining

Coffee Houses In Seattle
URL address: **http://www.seas.upenn.edu/~cpage/mothercity.html**

There are links at this home page that offer reviews of coffee houses as well as coffee brands in Seattle—where more coffee is consumed per capita than in any other U.S. city.

Fig. 18.5
Learn about the best coffees and coffee houses in Seattle, Washington, at this Web site.

Cooking—News Group Recipes
URL address:
http://www.vuw.ac.nz/non-local/recipes-archive/recipe-archive.html

On-line cookbooks are a great resource when you have simply run out of ideas for dinner. This home page represents an archive of recipes that collect in the newsgroup rec.food.recipes.

Cooking—Recipes
URL address: **http://www.cs.colorado.edu/htbin/grepitp**

What's for dinner? This Web site offers recipes for a variety of meals. There are links for cheese and crockpot recipes, pies, grains and cereals, special diets, soufflés, and vegetables.

Gate's Food Page
URL address: **http://sfgate.com/fun/food/**

The next time you're in Washington D.C. try Mark Miller's Red Sage restaurant, or, when in Palo Alto try the Country Fare. From the *San Francisco Chronicle* and *San Francisco Examiner* food pages this site offers links to restaurant pages that represent most large cities. There are also many reviews of eating establishments.

Recipe FAQ Collection
URL address: **http://homecheese.eas.asu.edu/recipes.html**

Connect to this site to access an extensive list of links to other WWW and Internet sites and documents that focus on the art of cooking. There are many Frequently Asked Questions documents as well as links to Gopher, FTP, and WWW sessions. Examples of link titles include the sourdough mailing list and FAQ by FTP, VEGLIFE recipes and Usenet cookbook by Gopher, and cuisine of Karnataka, South India, via WWW.

Recipe Folder
URL address: **http://english-server.hss.cmu.edu/Recipes.html**

An extensive list of home page links to all sorts of recipe documents. There are three main categories: vegetarian, dead animals (which encompasses beef, chicken, pork, and seafood), and a third area that includes desserts, salads, drinks, and regional dishes.

WPI Vegetarian Society
URL address: **http://www.wpi.edu:8080/~veggies/**

If you are a vegetarian and would like some new cooking ideas, say stuffed pumpkin, tomato/avocado salad, lintil casserole, ratatouille, or the rather adventurous exploding sprouts, then try this Web site. From the home page, "The WPI Vegetarian Society is a group of students who enjoy eating Vegetarian food. The group gathers once or twice each term to cook and eat veggie food. Omnivores are more than welcome. E-mail **veggies@wpi.wpi.edu** for more information or with a request to be added to the mailing list." Links include recipes, information about the vegetarian diet, recipes at Carnegie Mellon, and an option to enter a recipe.

Games

Atomic Cafe
URL address: **http://atomic.neosoft.com/Atomic.html**

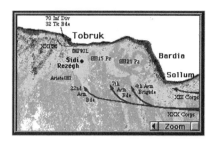

Fig. 18.6
Learn about the
World At War
game series at this
WWW home page.

This home page tells you about the *World At War* computer game series produced by Avalon Hills and Atomic Games. In addition to a detailed description of the individual games, there are some nice graphic images and a few historical facts about WWII.

Game Bytes
URL address: **http://wcl-rs.bham.ac.uk/GameBytes**

Perhaps you'd like to read about a computer or video game before you plunk down your money. *Game Bytes* is an electronic magazine that offers both reviews and images of many different games that are on the market.

Games—Backgammon/Stephen's WWW Backgammon
URL address:
http://www.statslab.cam.ac.uk/~sret1/backgammon/main.html

Double sixes—a good roll. This WWW site will help the uninitiated learn how to play the game; there are rules, books, and newsgroups. Advanced players can jump in and actually play Backgammon on the Internet.

Games—Bridge On The Web
URL address:
http://www.cs.vu.nl/users/staff/sater/bridge/bridge-on-the-web.html

This is the home page for people who love the game of Bridge. You can jump to lists of tournaments, read bridge newsgroups, or connect with either the Stanford University Bridge Club or the University of Warwick Bridge Society. One great link is to OKbridge (**http://www.cts.com/~clegg**), a unique WWW computer site/program that allows four people, anywhere in the world, to play a game of bridge in real time. At any one time, there could be hundreds of people playing OKbridge—professionals and novices.

XVIII

Recreation

Games—Chess
URL address: **http://chess.uoknor.edu/pub/chess/HTML**

URL address: **ftp://chess.uoknor.edu/pub/chess/HTML/homepage**

And Mate! This is a site where you can browse through and download files on World Championship games or utilities that will help you play computer chess games. It is described as "a diverse collection of chess memorabilia for the discriminating chess enthusiast."

Puzzle Archives
URL address: **http://alpha.acast.nova.edu/puzzles.html**

If you like puzzles and brain teasers, visit this site. Both puzzles and their solutions are provided.

The Game Cabinet
URL address: **http://web.kaleida.com/u/tidwell/GameCabinet.html**

An assortment of board game and non-board game rules and information from around the world. The information on this Web site covers not only game rules, but game histories, clubs to join, and reviews of the games.

TrekMUSE!
URL address: **http://grimmy.cnidr.org/trek.html**

"Make It So" might be the motto of this Web site. Find out how to play the interactive Internet game *TrekMUSE!* complete with an MPEG video.

Video Games—Cardiff's Video Game Database Browser
URL address: **http://www.cm.cf.ac.uk/Games**

Video games from Sega, 3DO, and Atari are a few of the products that are reviewed in an extensive list of 1,300 titles that you can access via this Web site. Other links include video game magazine information, newsgroups, and Frequently Asked Questions.

Hobbies

Beer Brewing
URL address: **http://guraldi.itn.med.umich.edu/Beer**

What is the difference between beer and ale? How do you turn hops into a tasty treat? If you'd like the answers to these questions, or some good recipes for your own homebrew, then check out this WWW site.

HAM radio—Bradley University Amateur Radio Club
URL address: **http://buarc.bradley.edu/**

The club is from the Bradley University, in Peoria, Illinois. Many of the links are to local happenings, but there is a link to the Amateur Radio page that will allow you to learn about amateur radio, visit other club home pages, and search for hams on the Internet. Also check out the following sites for more information, including call signs, letters from amateur radio newsgroups, and FCC regulations:

> **http://www.mit.edu:8001/callsign**
> **http://www.acs.ncsu.edu/HamRadio**
> **http://www.mcc.ac.uk/OtherPages/AmateurRadio.html**

Birding
URL address:
http://compstat.wharton.upenn.edu:8001/~siler/birding.html

Birding on the Web

Fig. 18.7
If you like to feed or watch birds, this WWW home page contains a lot of resources.

This WWW site is a great resource for birders with newsletters, exhibits, books, and "bird chat." Be prepared for a slow load time, though, as there are about 20 bird images and logos on the home page.

Beekeeping
URL address: **http://alfred1.u.washington.edu:8080/~jlks/bee.html**

You are invited to learn the ancient art of beekeeping and explore files, photos, and advice on this hobby and business.

Fish—Fish Information Service
URL address: **http://www.actwin.com/fish/index.html**

This is an archive of information about aquariums. It covers both freshwater and marine, tropical and temperate.

Pets
URL address: **ftp://quartz.rutgers.edu (directory pub/pets)**

Although this is not a WWW server, you can find many Frequently Asked Questions about animals, mostly dogs.

Quilting
URL address: **http://ttsw.com/MainQuiltingPage.html**

Fig. 18.8
Quilt history, supply stores, and patterns are a few of the resources available at this Web site.

If you have boxes and boxes of fabric scraps and just can't bear the thought of tossing them away, this may be a good time to develop your quilting skills. At this site you'll learn that the word quilt can be applied not only to a type of bed coverlet or blanket, but also to the ornamental padding and stitching of fabrics for placemats, Christmas stockings, and so on.

Radio Control Sailing
URL address: **http://honeybee.helsinki.fi/surcp/rcsail.htm**

The radio control sailors of Finland share this sailing information with the rest of the Web. They provide descriptions and pictures, along with the Finnish Competition Schedule, which includes results of Finnish and international competitions.

Textiles
URL address: **http://palver.foundation.tricon.com/crafts/index.html**

Do you know what Tvaandstickning is? In English, it's twined knitting! For all you knitters and stitchers, this site, maintained by Diana Lane, provides links to a good selection of patterns, supplies, events, and tips.

Recreational Sports

Bicycle—California Mountain Biking
URL address: **http://xenon.stanford.edu/~rsf/mtn-bike.html**

Bicycle—Colorado Front Range Cycling
URL address:
http://www.lance.colostate.edu/~ja740467/bike/frbike.html

Mountain biking in Colorado with extensive information on clubs and trails.

Fig. 18.9
General information on mountain biking and information on trails in the San Francisco and Northern California areas.

Boating
URL address: **http://www.recreation.com:80/boats/**

Ahoy mate! This WWW server contains a lot of boating information, e-mail lists, links to other boating, the Charter boat directory, and boat classifieds.

Boating—Paddling
URL address: **http://www.recreation.com:80/paddling**

Learn how to prevent the canoe from tipping over! This is the home site for a server that contains information on canoeing, kayaking, and rafting. Find out about clubs and associations, manufacturers, outfitters and guides, and publications.

Climbing Archive
URL address: **http://www.dtek.chalmers.se/Climbing/index.html**

A compilation of climbing material and information for people who enjoy the sport of rock climbing. It includes a daily newsflash, upcoming events, exercise programs, and hardware information.

Fencing
URL address: **http://www.ii.uib.no/~arild/fencing.html**

Touché! For those interested in the art of fencing, you can find books, drawings, clubs, events, and even the Internet fencing encyclopedia at this site. Information is mostly from Europe, Japan, and the U.S.

Fishing
URL address: **http://www.geo.mtu.edu/~jsuchosk/fish/fishpage**

Perhaps you'd like to compare your fish stories to those of other people? The fishing home page offers pictures of fish and a link to the anonymous FTP sites that house the fish GIFS from FLYFISH listserv.

XVIII

Recreation

Frisbee—George Ferguson's Ultimate Frisbee
URL address: **http://www.cs.rochester.edu/u/ferguson/ultimate/**

The WWW server for Ultimate Frisbee fanatics. It is loaded with links to rules, games, and tournament information.

Hang Gliding Mosaic Picture Server
URL address: **http://cougar.stanford.edu:7878/HGMPSHomePage.html**

Fig. 18.10
One of the many great hang gliding photos you can access at this Web site.

The Hang Gliding Picture Server is a WWW server that contains hang gliding- and para gliding-related material, including a collection of hang gliding photos and movies, the hang gliding FAQ, archived issues of a mailing list, and programs related to hang gliding.

Hiking and Camping—Backcountry
URL address: **http://io.datasys.swri.edu**

You don't have to be a boy scout to enjoy getting out into the wilderness. This WWW home page offers links to information about hiking clubs, reviews of outdoor gear, trip reports, and some hypermedia maps.

Kite Flying—Jason's Web Kite Site
URL address: **http://www.latrobe.edu.au/Glenn/KiteSite/Kites.html**

Next time someone tells you to go fly a kite, connect to this WWW home page. Here you'll find JPEG images of single, dual, and quadline kites. There will also be kite plans, newsletters, and other assorted kite flying activities.

Martial Arts
URL address: **http://archie.ac.il:8001/papers/rma/rma.html**

Located in Israel, this page has information about several different forms of martial arts.

Motorcycles
URL address: **http://www.halcyon.com/moto/rec_moto.html**

Fig. 18.11
Tune into this Motorcycle home page before you tune up your bike.

How's your Hog? If you think this refers to a farm animal, check out the agricultural listings—this site has reviews of motorcycles, safety and training, motorcycle images, and racing information.

Fig. 18.12
Find pictures like this classic Harley and more at this page.

XVIII

Recreation

Outdoor Action Program
URL address: **http://www.princeton.edu/~rcurtis/oa.html**

This site is maintained by members of the Outdoor Action Program at Princeton University and much of the information is related to outdoor activities in that area. There are other links to outdoor equipment, rock climbing, paddling, clubs, skiing, and caving.

Running
URL address: **http://www.recreation.com/running/home.html**

This is a network source for running information, including running clubs, event calendars, running WWW Servers, and other Internet information on running.

Scuba—Aquanaut
URL address: **http://www.opal.com/aquanaut**

Aquanaut is a WWW magazine dedicated to recreational and technical scuba diving. There are links to reviews of dive gear and equipment, dive destinations, a database of divable shipwrecks, underwater pictures, and weather maps. Check out the fish pictures!

Fig. 18.13

The world of scuba diving awaits you at this Web server—learn about dive gear and discover terrific underwater locations.

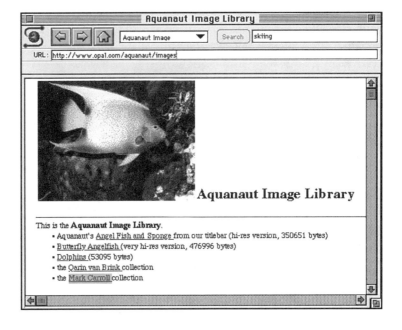

Skiing—Alaska Alpine Club

URL address: **http://info.alaska.edu:70/0/Alaska/rec/aac/class1**

The Alaska Alpine Club offers instruction in ski-mountaineering and climbing every spring at the University of Alaska, Fairbanks campus.

Skiing—Powder Hound Ski Report

URL address: **http://www.icw.com/skireport.html**

If you are in the mood to get out on the slopes and would like to learn about snow and weather conditions, check out this server.

Skiing—World

URL address:
http://www.cs.colorado.edu/homes/mcbryan/public_html/bb/ski/ski.html

Provides bulletin boards to report world skiing conditions for both alpine and Nordic (backcountry).

Skydiving

URL address: **http://www.cis.ufl.edu/skydive**

If you have a fear of heights and don't think you would ever jump out of an airplane, then start with a trip to this home page. You can see pictures and read descriptions about this high-flying sport.

Spelunking

URL address: **http://speleology.cs.yale.edu/**

Spelunking, in plain English, means cave exploration. Spend some time at this site and find out about societies and associations devoted to this sport, equipment, events, and programs. There are also links to photos and cartoons.

SurfNet

URL address: **http://sailfish.peregrine.com/surf/surf.html**

This Web page is your "window to the world's beaches." Find out the expected swell heights for your surfing adventures. Follow links on this home page to learn how to surf, and, before you get wet, view body boarding and surfing photos.

XVIII

Recreation

Fig. 18.14
Surf's up at this
Web site and
you'll find
information about
water temperature,
wave heights, and
tide reports at
beaches around
the world.

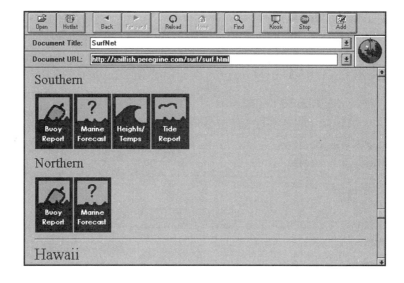

Tennis
URL address:

http://arganet.tenagra.com/Racquet_Workshop/Tennis.html

"Encouraging tennis players everywhere to GO TO THE 'NET for tennis
information and sporting goods." This page offers you links to player news,
equipment tips, tennis news, other WWW tennis resources, and the Racquet
Workshop—an on-line tennis shop.

Unicycling
URL address: **http://nimitz.mcs.kent.edu/~bkonarsk**

You know that funny, yet difficult, sport where people ride a bicycle with
only one wheel? This home page offers frequently asked questions (how
many can there be?), information about unicycle games, and "Red's Night-
mare," a 3.6MB MPEG animation of a red unicycle.

Windsurfing
URL address:

**http://www.dsg.cs.tcd.ie/dsg_people/afcondon/windsurf/
windsurf_home.html**

Spectator Sports

Autoracing Archive

URL address:

http://www.eng.hawaii.edu/Contribs/carina/ra.home.page.html

This service is provided to the racing enthusiasts of the Internet. You will find information on Formula One, IndyCar, and NASCAR racing. It links to race results, schedules, point standings, and other information.

XVIII

Recreation

Baseball Information Center

URL address: **http://www.gems.com/ibic/**

Fig. 18.17
The Baseball
Information
Center page.

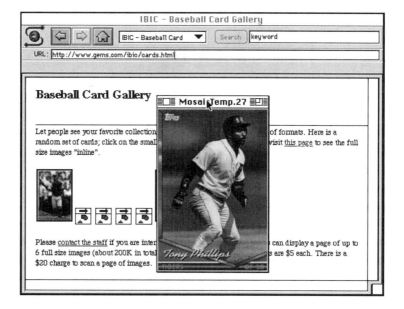

The Internet Baseball Information Center provides access to statistics, fantasy leagues, and discussion groups. There is an annual membership fee, of $25, to help cover the costs of using a commercial stats service—some of the features are only available to members. Links include:

General Information and Frequently Asked Questions

Player Statistics

League Reports

Fantasy Leagues

Baseball Card Gallery

Professional Baseball

Hall Of Fame

Baseball—Fantasy Baseball

URL address:

http://www.cm.cf.ac.uk/User/Gwyn.Price/fantasy_baseball.html

This WWW home page attempts to gather all the information for fantasy baseball available on the Internet into one location.

Baseball Server—Nando X

URL address: **http://www.nando.net/baseball/bbserv.html**

There is more to baseball than beer and boxscores. The Baseball Server's columnists, Bill Arnold and Mark Camps, give you the inside scoop with "Beyond the Boxscore."

Basketball—NBA

URL address:
http://tns-www.lcs.mit.edu/cgi-bin/sports/nba/schedule

URL address: **http://www.mit.edu:8001/services/sis/NBA/NBA.html**

Highlights of games played during the NBA season, NBA schedules, and an NBA sports server.

British Society of Sports History

URL address: **http://info.mcc.ac.uk/UMIST_Sport/bssh.html**

As the home page states, the aims of the Society are: "to promote, stimulate and encourage discussion, study, research, and publication on the history of sport and physical education." Jump to the Sports Historian and you'll quickly realize that American Football has not been the only game in town with articles like "Crowd and Player Violence in Edwardian Cricket" or "English Editors of German Sporting Journals at the Turn of the Century."

European Championships in Athletics

URL address: **http://helsinki94.eunet.fi/**

In addition to voting for your favorite athletes, you can jump to documents that show results of competitions, pictures, and other information about the championships and the town of Helsinki.

Goodwill Games

URL address: **http://www.com/goodwill/index.html**

Lots of features about the 1994 Goodwill Games. There is information about the organization and history, as well as the games' sponsors. St. Petersburg is well represented with a bulletin and gallery.

Figure Skating

URL address:
http://www.cs.yale.edu/HTML/YALE/CS/HyPlans/loosemore-sandra/skate/faq.html

This home page offers the Frequently Asked Question list for amateur and competitive figure skating. You will find information about figure skating as a spectator sport (the file is available in both plain-text (ASCII) and HTML versions). The list posts approximately once a month during the competitive season.

Football—Frequently Asked Questions
URL address: **http://www.ai.mit.edu/~curt/rsfp_faq.html**

This FAQ posts the first and third week of each month.

Hockey—College Hockey Computer Rating
URL address: **http://hydra.bgsu.edu/TCHCR/**

The College Hockey Computer Rating (TCHCR) is the longest-running rating of NCAA Division I college hockey teams. In addition to the ratings you can also link to a schedule of games for each team.

Hockey—Jamaican Bobsledders
URL address:
http://www.mit.edu:8001/afs/athena.mit.edu/user/j/b/jbreiden/hockey/internet/top.html

Home page for the "Jamaican Bobsledders," a team of spirited ice hockey players at the Massachusetts Institute of Technology. The links will lead to information about the bobsledders, game announcements, the roster, team archives, and inspirational material.

Hockey—NHL Schedule
URL address: **http://www.cs.ubc.ca/nhl**

Schedules and other information about the 26 teams that make up the National Hockey League. You can get to the action quickly by linking to a site called playing today, and make your plans with a link to games for a particular date. Other links provide information about your favorite team and ways of following games between divisions.

Hockey—Professional Hockey Server
URL address:
http://maxwell.uhh.hawaii.edu/hockey/nhl94/playoff94.html

This site provides links to so much information it will boggle even the sharpest sports mind. It includes National Hockey League results of the 1993-94 Stanley Cup Playoffs.

Rowing
URL address: **http://www.comlab.ox.ac.uk/archive/other/rowing.html**

Home page for information about the sport of rowing. You can jump to information about individuals located in various parts of the world, Regatta results such as the UK National Championships, and straightforward definitions and rules. There are even photographs and a link to the River and Rowing Museum.

Rugby
URL address: **http://rugby.phys.uidaho.edu/rugby.html**

This WWW server provides access to information about the rules and competitive events in the world of Rugby.

Soccer
URL address:
http://haegar.unibe.ch/~ftiwww/Sonstiges/Tabellen/Eindex.html

Standings, statistics, and scores throughout the world including a large archive file.

Soccer—World Cup USA '94
URL address: **http://sunsite.sut.ac.jp/wc94/index.html**

The level of excitement was high as the United States geared up to host the event, and the rest of the world was in tune while they prepared to participate. You will find links to game sites and schedules, host city information, participating teams, World Cup information, and a good selection of game highlight photos.

World Wide Web of Sports
URL address: **http://tns-www.lcs.mit.edu/cgi-bin/sports/nba**

Need a workout? This Web home page connects you with information on professional, amateur, and hobby sports that include football, basketball, baseball, hockey, soccer, frisbee, cycling, rugby, golf, running, rowing, skating, and tennis. When you are done traveling to all the links, your fingers will certainly have had quite a workout.

Travel

Austria—Salzburg
URL address: **http://www.tcs.co.at/fvp.html**

MPEG videos and documents of Salzburg and the surrounding areas (most of the text is in German).

Canada—Calgary, Alberta

URL address:

http://bear.ras.ucalgary.ca/brads_home_page/CUUG/calgary.html

Find out about the Stampede, learn about the sports teams, parks, accommodations, and hobby clubs that this northern city offers.

Center for the Study of Southern Culture

URL address: **http://imp.cssc.olemiss.edu/**

The Center for the Study of Southern Culture provides links to sources of information on country, gospel, and blues music, a magazine of southern culture, and cultural events for the Southern states region. Get ready for good Southern hospitality.

England—Sunderland Mini-Tourist

URL address:

http://isis.sund.ac.uk/home/gopher/www/hycis/HTML/Sunderland/ MTG.html

The City of Sunderland is located on the coast of northeast England, about 280 miles from London. It is a new city, granted "city" status by the Queen in March 1992. The history of the town goes back much farther, and from this home page you can learn about the city and visit (and view) historical sites such as Hylton castle, Saint Petersburg church, and Queen Alexandria bridge.

Germany—Railroading in Germany

URL address: **http://rzstud1.rz.uni-karlsruhe.de/~ule3/info-trn.html**

This WWW site will let you in on all of the secrets to enjoying travel in Germany by railroad. There are tips, rail fares, descriptions of different types of trains (with pictures), and an overview of overnight travel on the rail.

GNN Travelers' Center

URL address: **http://nearnet.gnn.com/mkt/travel/center.html**

This is a comprehensive travel center: you can get tips on planning and going on your next excursion. There are also links to other WWW travel resources.

Himalayan Expeditions

URL address: **http://www.netpart.com/che/brochure.html**

How about a trip up some of the tallest mountains in the world? Check out this home page before you buy your climbing gear. There are also adventure trips to other places—like Africa.

India
URL address: **http://www.cs.clemson.edu/~nandu/india.html**

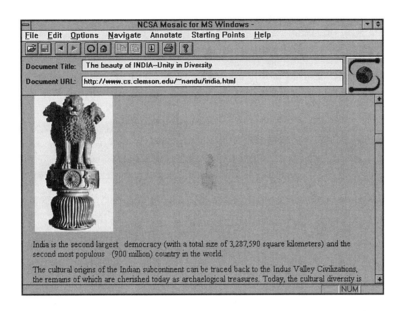

Fig. 18.18
In addition to travel information, this is a valuable site for researching the history and culture of India.

With 25 states, that cover more than 9 million square miles of land, India offers a lot of exploration. This home page offers links that tell you about the languages, religions, and music. There is also information about travel agents that book trips to India and an "adventure summary" of a traveler's trip.

Louisiana—The Barrow House Inn
URL address: **http://sparky.cyberzine.org/html/Inn/innpage.html**

Touted as "The most recommended inn of Audubon's beloved English Louisiana Plantation Country." The inn is located in the heart of St. Francisville, Louisiana.

Missouri Botanical Garden
URL address: **http://straylight.tamu.edu/MoBot/welcome.html**

A 79-acre garden of flora and fauna is here for your sightseeing pleasure. Links take you to information on plants in bloom, educational programs, flora of China, Mesoamericana, and North America. Don't miss the tour—it begins whenever you're ready.

XVIII

Recreation

New England Travel
URL address: **http://www.std.com/NE/netrav.html**

See the beautiful New England states like never before when you visit this Web site. Find out what individual states in New England have to offer for touring, and get tips on lodging and dining.

North Atlantic Cruises
URL address: **http://www.centrum.is/com/vinland.html**

Fig. 18.19

From the relaxation of a pleasure cruise to the excitement of deep water sea angling—this Web site can get you there.

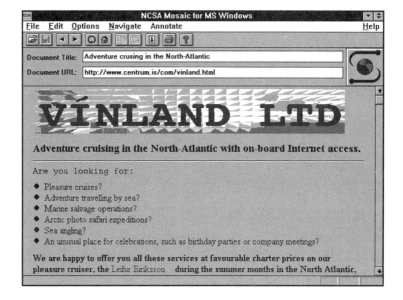

Vinland Limited offers adventure cruises in the North Atlantic. Try a marine salvage operation, sea angling, or a more relaxing pleasure cruise. Links to descriptions of the cruises.

The Avid Explorer
URL address: **http://www.explore.com/**

Take the guesswork out of planning your cruise or land expedition with the vast amount of travel information at your fingertips. There are links to special packages for exceptional values, maps, and weather reports.

Travel Advisories
URL address: **http://www.stolaf.edu/network/travel-advisories.html**

From the U.S. State Department, these advisories provide reports about the safety hazards that may be involved in traveling to foreign countries. You can also subscribe to an Internet mailing list to receive advisories.

Virginia—Arlington County

URL address: **http://www.co.arlington.va.us/**

Fig. 18.20
Across the river from Washington D.C., Arlington has a lot to offer residents and visitors.

Whether you live in Arlington County or simply plan to visit, this server helps you to access information about the area. Home page icons and links bring you to information about the famous statue Iwo Jima, Arlington Cemetery, the Pentagon, the D.C. area, and a regional map. Other resources include tourism, shopping, and restaurants.

Virginia, Staunton

URL address: **http://www.elpress.com/staunton**

Staunton, Virginia is just a few hours from Washington D.C. It is a vacation spot for travelers who have an interest in historic sites, museums, or the great outdoors, that can be found in national parks and forests.

Virtual Tourist

URL address: **http://wings.buffalo.edu/world**

Want to be a world traveler? This home page links you with tourist guides for many foreign locations including Japan and New Zealand.

World Travel—Lonely Planet

URL address:
http://nearnet.gnn.com/gnn/meta/travel/mkt/lp/index.html

Lonely Planet Publications is a publisher of guidebooks for independent travelers. This WWW page connects you to descriptions of all of the guidebooks for different countries—quite a few on Mexico and Latin America. You can also send e-mail for a free subscription to the Lonely Planet Newsletter.

World Travel—International Universities

URL address: **http://venus.mcs.com/^fun/html/uni/main.html**

Going abroad can be a learning experience when you take courses on foreign language and intercultural studies.

XVIII

Recreation

Appendix A

Other Versions of Mosaic for Windows

The first part of this book describes the features available in the Mosaic program developed by NCSA. While this is an impressive program, NCSA saw the need for Mosaic to be further developed and commercialized. To make this possible, NCSA licensed the program to several commercial software companies. These companies developed their own versions of Mosaic based on the NCSA version.

So why would anyone be interested in purchasing one of these commercial versions when the NCSA version is available for free use? In the NCSA version, many features that you expect to work do not. The commercial manufacturers—in some cases—polished most of the rough edges and added some features that weren't finished in the NCSA version.

When it comes to Web cruising, Mosaic is probably the most recognized software for the job. But that doesn't mean it's the only option you have. Shareware programs are available for cruising the Web that are not based on Mosaic.

Another category of software takes the all-in-one approach a step further. In addition to giving you software that performs every task you need on the Internet, this type of software gives you a common interface to access all parts of the Internet. In most cases, this software comes from a service provider that has built a special interface to make using its service even easier. If you are looking for a no-hassle way to use the Web and don't mind sacrificing a few features for ease of use, this software may be for you.

In this chapter, you learn to use the following:

■ AIR Mosaic from SPRY

■ InterAp WebBrowser, a commercial Web browser based on Cello from California Software

■ EINet's WinWeb shareware browser for Windows

■ NetCruiser, an all-in-one special Internet interface from NETCOM

■ The Pipeline, an all-in-one system licensed to service providers all over the country

AIR Mosaic from SPRY

AIR Mosaic is designed as the optimal tool for browsing the World Wide Web. Developed from NCSA's original Mosaic tool, AIR Mosaic incorporates more Windows functionality, and is easier to configure and customize. It's a 16-bit program (the most recent Mosaic is a 32-bit system).

AIR Mosaic features hotlists and advanced menu support; you can incorporate your own Internet finds and quickly access information. You can easily configure fonts, colors, and performance using only one configuration screen.

What Is AIR Mosaic and How Do You Get It?

The AIR series is distributed in two ways—in conjunction with publisher O'Reilly & Associates as part of Internet In A Box, and as part of SPRY's AIR Series of TCP/IP programs. Contact O'Reilly & Associates at 800-998-4269 or **ibox@ora.com**, or SPRY at 800-777-9638 or **info@spry.com**.

The following are the applications included in this suite:

■ **AIR Mosaic.** This is the WWW browser. The features included in AIR Mosaic are described in the next section.

■ **AIR Mail.** This is the e-mail handler for sending and receiving mail on the Internet. AIR Mail contains the printing, mail addressing, binary file attachments, and news folders.

■ **AIR News.** This is the news reader for Usenet news. AIR News has several features, including personalized groups to read from, threading, and custom header support.

- **AIR Gopher.** This is the Gopher interface for searching and retrieving files in a menu driven environment.

- **Network File Manager.** This is the system's FTP utility, which lets you drag and drop files from an FTP site to File Manager. You can copy, create, delete, and move directories and files.

- **AIR Telnet.** This tool lets you connect to Telnet sites as if you were at the site itself, and you can have as many as 15 concurrent Telnet sessions. You can save custom sessions and automatic logins to your favorite sites.

The AIR series also has a GIF and JPEG viewer called ImageView and a uuencode/decode utility.

Features of AIR Mosaic

AIR Mosaic, then, is simply one of a number of applications that you get when you buy Internet In A Box or the AIR Series. You open AIR Mosaic by double-clicking the GNN-AIR Mosaic icon in Program Manager.

> **Note**
>
> GNN stands for *Global Network Navigator*, a World Wide Web publication published by O'Reilly & Associates—the same people who publish Internet In A Box. GNN is available to anyone traveling in Web-space, not just Internet In A Box users.

AIR Mosaic's features include the following:

- Hotlists let you add WWW documents to hotlists with folders and subfolders. You can add multiple hotlists to your AIR Mosaic menu for quick access and you can import NCSA menus from the MOSAIC.INI file—useful if you've been working with Mosaic and created menus.

- A straightforward Configuration dialog box lets you configure Mosaic preferences (colors, fonts, and default home page), viewers, and options. The External Viewers Configuration dialog box enables you to configure viewers or add new ones.

- A *Kiosk* mode enables you to hide the toolbar and other information. Ideal for presentations, it also allows you to set up AIR Mosaic for unattended use. While Mosaic has Kiosk mode, it's "hidden"—you have to start the program using the -k parameter. But in AIR Mosaic you can simply click the Kiosk icon or select the Kiosk menu option.

- A custom caching feature, so that you can access documents you've already browsed in a session. While Mosaic also has caching, it's hidden away in the MOSAIC.INI file, while AIR Mosaic lets you set it from a dialog box.

- Support for "proxy" servers for HTTP, WAIS, FTP, and Gopher. These let a user at a secure site "bypass" the security and get out onto the Web.

- Print WWW document text and graphics as well as save or copy the document text.

Installing AIR Mosaic and Tools

The product's installation procedure is very straightforward. Run the Windows setup program from the first installation disk. The program asks you about each change it makes and tells you when to swap disks.

When you install this product you are installing all the software you need to make a TCP/IP connection. Unlike many products that make installing such a connection difficult, SPRY has done an excellent job of simplifying the procedure. In particular, it has found a simple way to create a login script—and login scripts are the weak point in many Internet products.

> **Note**
>
> Installation is especially easy if you use SprintLink as a service provider. If you plan to use a different service provider's PPP or SLIP, check with SPRY or your provider before purchasing AIR Mosaic to see if configuration files are available for that system. If not, see if you can get some help configuring the software to work with your provider. You will have to enter all the configuration data by hand, and create a login script by using the system's Login Setup dialog box.

> **Note**
>
> You don't have to use SPRY's dialing and connections software. If you already have a service provider and TCP/IP software (such as the Trumpet shareware), you can install AIR Mosaic, skip the service provider section of the installation, and use AIR Mosaic with your current account. This may be the easiest way to use AIR Mosaic with your current account; however, you lose many of the advantages of SPRY's all-in-one package.

Starting AIR Mosaic

To start AIR Mosaic, find the application—in the Internet In A Box program group if you are using that product (see fig. A.1)—and double-click the GNN-AIR Mosaic icon. If you've already started your TCP/IP connection, AIR Mosaic starts right away, otherwise it starts the dialer and makes the connection.

Fig. A.1
AIR Mosaic Icons Program Manager for Internet In A Box.

AIR Mosaic connects you to the SPRY Inc. World Wide Web home page. This is a good place to look for other WWW resources and other Internet resources. From here, you can browse the Internet and connect to other home pages. When you become more experienced, you can build a library of home pages you like—using AIR Mosaic's hotlist feature.

Tip
The Radar Retrieval icon, in the upper right corner of the AIR Mosaic console, spins while the home page is retrieved.

The AIR Mosaic Console

The AIR Mosaic console consists of several components (see fig. A.2). Note the following components:

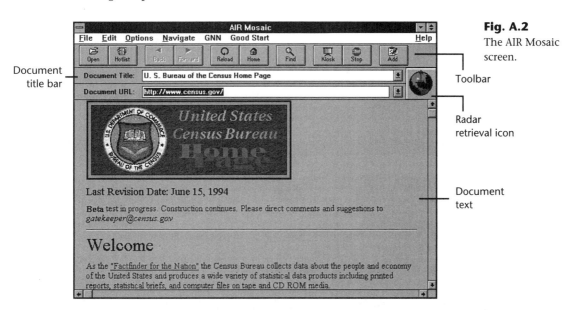

Fig. A.2
The AIR Mosaic screen.

- **The Toolbar.** The toolbar contains shortcut buttons for AIR Mosaic menu items. You can change the style of the toolbar (Picture & Text, Picture only, and Text only). Open the **O**ptions menu and choose Toolbar Style.

- **The Document Title Bar.** The Document Title bar contains the Document Title and Document URL drop-down lists.

  You can go back to any of the previously accessed documents, simply select its title or URL from the lists. You can also change the number of documents displayed in these lists by opening the **O**ptions menu and choosing Configuration.

- The text of the document itself.

- **The Radar Retrieval Icon.** This serves the same function as the spinning globe in NCSA Mosaic.

The Kiosk Mode

AIR Mosaic offers a special mode, *Kiosk mode*, for displaying a data page. Kiosk mode hides all the console information except the actual document (in other words, the Toolbar, Status Bar, Document Title Bar, and the menu items and commands are hidden). This is useful if you give presentations—because it shows a lot of the screen—or if you set up Mosaic on an unattended work-station.

Kiosk mode is actually the same as the Kiosk mode in Mosaic, except that it's not hidden in AIR Mosaic. While Mosaic makes you start the program using the -k parameter, AIR Mosaic lets you start normally, and then go to Kiosk mode at any time using the **O**ptions, **K**iosk Mode command, or by clicking the Toolbar button.

> **Note**
>
> The shortcut movement keys of F (Forward) and B (Back) are very helpful when you move in this mode because the Forward and Back commands are not available.

To exit the Kiosk mode, press the Escape key or Ctrl+K.

Browsing with AIR Mosaic

Hyperlinks in AIR Mosaic are indicated in the same way as the NCSA version: blue underlined text and boxes, or graphics surrounded by a blue border (you

A

can change the color). As with the NCSA version, the mouse turns into a pointing hand when over a hyperlink.

Opening Previous Documents

The Document Title and Document URL drop-down lists contain a listing of the last several documents you accessed in this session. (This is similar to the History feature but provides an easier way to access it.) The lists are identical, except one shows the title of the document (such as SPRY Home Page) and the other shows that document's URL (**http://www.spry.com**). You can go back to any of the displayed documents by choosing the title or URL from the lists. (The latest version of Mosaic no longer has the Title drop-down list box.)

Using Hotlists

Hotlists in AIR Mosaic work quite differently from Mosaic. AIR Mosaic has a hierarchical system of hotlist folders that lets you categorize the hotlist items.

You can access your created hotlist in two ways:

- You can click the Hotlists toolbar button and then double-click the item you want to go to in the Hotlists dialog box.

- You can make hotlists into drop-down menus and choose them directly from the AIR Mosaic menu bar. Select the hotlist in the Hotlists dialog box, and then click the Put this hotlist in the menu bar check box and choose OK.

The Hotlists Dialog Box

To get to the Hotlists dialog box, open the **F**ile menu and choose **H**otlists (see fig. A.3). The Hotlists screen shows all the different hotlists you have. AIR Mosaic comes with two default hotlists pre-loaded—the GNN and Good Start hotlists—but you can add your own.

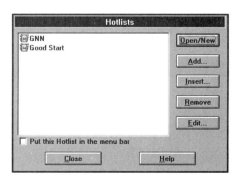

Tip
You can convert any menu you create in NCSA Mosaic into a hotlist. See the end of this section for information.

Fig. A.3
The Hotlists dialog box contains two default hotlists.

A main hotlist, such as the GNN Hotlist, has a flaming icon. Hotlists initially are shown closed: you can open the hotlist by double-clicking the Hotlist icon (see figs. A.4 and A.5). Each Hotlist can contain individual WWW documents, or it can contain folders that house additional documents. You use folders and subfolders to organize your documents any way you want. The documents and folders are listed in a hierarchy similar to the Windows File Manager.

Fig. A.4
Double-click the GNN hotlist to show its individual items.

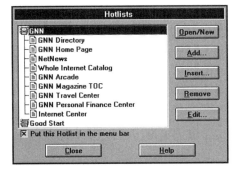

Fig. A.5
The Good Start hotlist comes preconfigured with many interesting and useful sites arranged in folders.

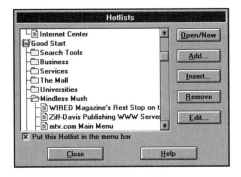

In the Hotlists dialog box, you can create new hotlists, add new hotlist items, edit your existing items, or delete existing items.

To add a hotlist to the menu bar, select Put This Hotlist in the menu bar. You can add as many hotlists to the menu that fit. When you choose this option, the selected Hotlist icon in the Hotlist dialog box changes to an icon containing the letter *M*. When you open one of these hotlist menus, you see a series of cascading menus, one for each folder in the hotlist.

Creating a New Hotlist

To create a new hotlist, follow these steps:

1. Open the **F**ile menu and choose **H**otlists, or click the Hotlist button on the toolbar. The Hotlist dialog box appears (refer to fig. A.5).

2. Click **O**pen/New. You see a Windows Open dialog box.

3. Enter a DOS name for the hotlist. Each hotlist is saved in a file with the HOT file extension.

> **Note**
>
> At this point, you can specify the name of an existing hotlist to load the existing hotlist into the Hotlist dialog box.

4. Click OK.

   Another dialog box appears asking you for the name you want to use for the hotlist (the name that will appear in the Hotlist dialog box). Use any name you want (keep in mind, though, that you may want to use this hotlist as an AIR Mosaic menu item, so you might want to keep the name short). Type a name and click OK. The hotlist is now created and appears in the Hotlist screen with a flaming icon.

Using Folders

You can create folders and subfolders to organize your information.

1. Highlight the hotlist or folder to which you want to add a new folder.

2. Click **A**dd and select Folder in the Add New dialog box that appears.

3. You are asked to name the Folder. Name it and click OK. You have created a new folder.

Adding Documents to a Hotlist

Now that you have a new hotlist and a new folder, you can begin adding documents. To add a document to a hotlist, open the **N**avigate menu and choose Add Document. This adds the document to the hotlist you are currently using—the last hotlist you selected. If you want to place the document into a folder within the hotlist, though, you'll have to use the following method.

Note

If a hotlist isn't selected, this command may not work properly. Using the Hotlist screen, as described below, allows you to specify where you want to add the document.

If you do not have a hotlist selected, use the following steps:

1. Open the **F**ile menu and choose **H**otlist.

2. Select the hotlist to which you want to add the current document.

3. Click **A**dd. You are asked if you want to add a document or a folder; select Document. The Add Document dialog box appears (see fig. A.6). This contains the title and URL of the document you are currently viewing. You can change the name of the document, but do not change the URL!

Fig. A.6
The Add Document dialog box.

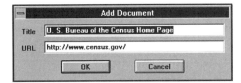

Note

You can also add a document you are not viewing to a hotlist. From the Hotlist dialog box, choose the **A**dd button, select the document, and then enter the URL address and title in the Add Document dialog box.

4. Click OK. The document you specified is added to the hotlist you selected.

Special Feature: Importing NCSA Menus as Hotlists

If you previously used NCSA Mosaic, you may have built an extensive menu of favorite home pages and resources. You can use AIR Mosaic to convert these menus to AIR Mosaic hotlists—you use them as you use those that you have created in AIR Mosaic. To import an NCSA menu as a hotlist, use the following steps:

1. Open the **O**ptions menu and click Import NCSA Menu as Hotlist. You
   see the Import NCSA Menu as Hotlist dialog box (see fig. A.7).

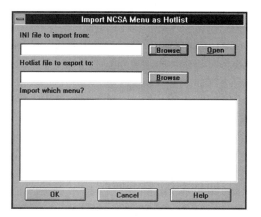

Fig. A.7
The Import NCSA
Menu as Hotlist
dialog box lets you
convert Mosaic
menus to AIR
Mosaic hotlists.

2. In the INI File To Import From text box, type the location and name of
   the MOSAIC.INI file where your NCSA menu information is stored.
   Click the **B**rowse button next to the text box to look through the directories on your PC and select the correct file. After you select the file,
   confirm that it is the correct file you want by clicking the **O**pen button.

3. Specify a hotlist file for this menu. Do not choose an existing hotlist
   unless you want to overwrite the information in that file. You can use
   Browse to find a hotlist file and a directory for the file.

4. Select the menu from the NCSA MOSAIC.INI file you want to import
   (all of the menus in that file appear in a list) as shown in figure A.8.

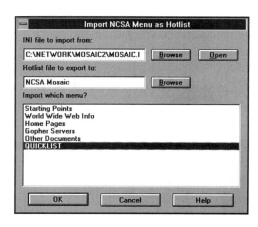

Fig. A.8
The filled in dialog
box with an NCSA
menu selected.

5. Click OK when you're ready to import the file.

Now you can return to the Hotlists dialog box to open the new hotlist you just created.

After you import a menu to a hotlist, you can then place the hotlist on the menu bar if you wish by using the Put this Hotlist in the Menu Bar command.

Saving Documents

You can save WWW documents so that you can open them later (using the Open Local File command) or so that you can use the information in other documents (such as word processing documents). When you save documents, you are saving the HTML source document.

There are two ways to save documents: You can use Load to Disk Mode to save the document to disk as soon as you access it (as described below), or you can save the document source code to disk using the Document Source command.

1. Open the **O**ptions menu and choose **L**oad to Disk Mode.

2. Click a link pointing to a document you want to save. The Save As dialog box appears.

3. Type a name and select a directory to place the file into. (HTML files are saved as an HTM file in DOS.)

4. Click OK.

Here's the other method for saving a document you are already viewing:

1. Open the **F**ile menu and choose **D**ocument Source.

2. In the Document Source dialog box, select **F**ile, and then **S**ave As.

3. Type a name and select a directory in which to place the file.

4. Click OK.

If you see a message saying that the source is not available, it may be because you are using a cached document. Use the Reload command to reload from the original HTML file.

Configuring AIR Mosaic Options

You can easily configure AIR Mosaic using the Configuration dialog box. This dialog box allows you to specify options for displaying elements in the AIR Mosaic Console, such as the Toolbar, Status Bar, images, text files, hyperlinks, and sounds. You can also set the proxy servers for AIR Mosaic, AIR Mosaic's fonts and colors, and which external viewers are used to view graphics and play sounds and movies.

To access the Configuration dialog box, open the **O**ptions menu and choose **C**onfiguration (see fig. A.9). The Configuration options are described in the sections that follow.

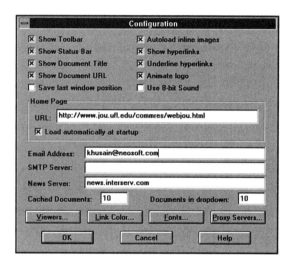

Fig. A.9
The default Configuration dialog box (with the e-mail address and newserver filled in).

General Options

The General Configuration options, shown at the top of the Configuration dialog box, mostly are the same as those in NCSA Mosaic. Some of the options in this dialog are present in NCSA Mosaic, except they can only be changed by editing MOSAIC.INI. Some of the options are the same as in Mosaic, others are not:

- **Save last window position.** You can resize the AIR Mosaic Console window in order to see more (or less) of a WWW document. If you want these size changes to be saved and used during your next AIR Mosaic session, check this option. (In Mosaic you open the File menu and choose Save Preferences to do this.)

■ **Show hyperlinks.** This allows you to hide the hyperlink jumps in a Mosaic document.

■ **Animate logo.** This refers to the radar indicator on the Document Title Bar. It takes additional time to animate this indicator logo. By default, the logo is turned on, because it tells you if a document or image is being retrieved. The time you save by turning off the logo animation, however, is not substantial. You probably only want to turn off the radar indicator if your connection is very slow.

■ **Cached Documents.** This represents how many documents are cached, or kept active, in your PC's memory. If this number is 10, for instance, then 10 documents remain available to you. They don't have to be loaded to go back to them—they immediately appear. If you have a lot of available system memory, you can increase this number. Keep in mind, though, that a high number for cache can affect another application's performance, although AIR Mosaic's performance improves quite a bit. (To change the cache in Mosaic you must edit the MOSAIC.INI file.)

■ **Documents in Dropdown.** This indicates how many of your last-accessed documents appear in the Document Title and Document URL drop-down lists (displayed beneath the Toolbar). A value of 5 means that the last five documents you accessed are displayed in these lists.

Viewer Options

The **V**iewers button in the Configuration dialog box lets you specify the external viewers you want to use. This option is available in NCSA Mosaic only by editing the INI file. AIR Mosaic offers a friendlier way to change the viewer settings. From the Configuration dialog box, press the **V**iewers button. The External Viewer Configuration dialog box appears, as shown in figure A.10.

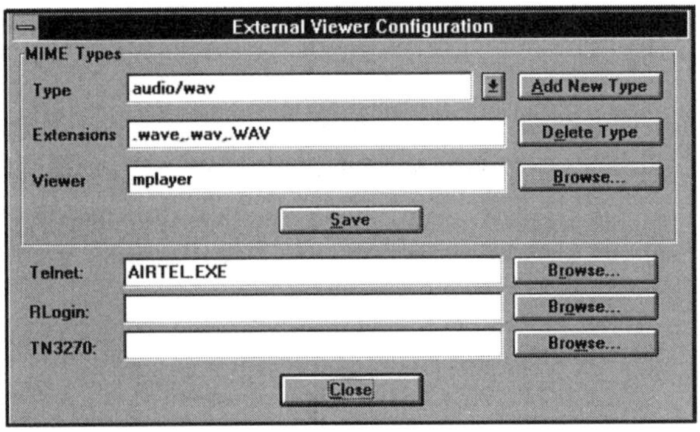

Fig. A.10
The External Viewers Configuration dialog box presents an easy way to configure AIR Mosaic to use external viewers.

To see a list of resources (derived from the MIME multimedia specification) you are likely to find using AIR Mosaic, pull down the Type drop-down list (see fig. A.11). AIR Mosaic has default viewers set up for all resource types; however, it's unlikely that you actually have all of those viewers (or, if you have them, that they are in the right location). Therefore, you can reconfigure to make sure that all the resources you find work properly in AIR Mosaic.

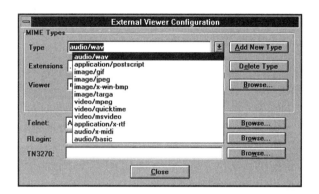

Fig. A.11
The list of viewer types.

To redefine which viewer AIR Mosaic uses for a type of file, follow these steps:

1. Choose the data type from the Type drop-down list.

2. Type the full path and file name of the viewer you want to use in the Viewer field, or choose **B**rowse to find the viewer on your PC (when you locate the viewer and click OK, the Viewer field is filled in automatically).

3. Choose **S**ave. Note that you must choose Save for every type of viewer you want to configure.

4. Choose **C**lose when you are done configuring viewers. The changes take place immediately.

Note

You can also define the applications used by Mosaic for Telnet, rlogin, and tn3270. To do this, type the application you want to use in the appropriate field (choose **B**rowse to search your disk for the correct file and directory name). When you close the dialog box, the changes you made are saved.

AIR Mosaic uses file extensions, found in the hyperlink that is created for the resource, to figure out what resource type the item is, and, consequently, what viewer to use. Therefore, you can create your own resource types and link viewers to them, so that you can use items that don't have resource types set up yet.

For instance, you can access a Gopher site with Mosaic and find some ZIP files. If you have an application that reads ZIP files (such as WinZip), you can define ZIP files in AIR Mosaic as a resource type associated with a viewer. To do this, follow these steps:

1. Click **A**dd New Type in the External Viewer Configuration dialog box (refer to fig. A.10). Specify any name for the new type (such as zipped).

2. Type in the extensions to be considered as zipped files (.zip and .ZIP are used here).

3. Specify a Viewer name and path.

4. Choose **S**ave to store the new Viewer type.

Proxy Servers

AIR Mosaic allows you to specify any Proxy Servers to be used for getting WWW, FTP, WAIS, and Gopher information past Internet firewalls. Click the Proxy Servers button and specify the addresses of your Proxy Servers to have AIR Mosaic use those servers.

> **Note**
>
> A *firewall* is a system used to block outside access to a site, which is connected to the Internet, for security reasons. The firewall can be bypassed by the system's users so they can access resources on the Internet, but to do so the system administrator must specifically allow connections to particular servers.

AIR Mosaic is a very nice system, one that has the added advantage of being bundled with TCP/IP software that is *very* easy to install.

InterAp from California Software

This section is about Web Navigator, an active, powerful tool for business and personal computer users to hunt and gather valuable information from the Web. The Web Navigator browser is an integrated part of a

Windows-compatible suite of telecommunications services called InterAp, which stands for Internet Applications, from California Software (CSI).

The Web Navigator is a smoothly integrated part of the InterAp suite that includes e-mail, a Usenet newsreader interface, modem dialing, FTP, Telnet, and WAIS search services. Because this new Web browser is part of such a useful suite, it will interest customers seeking a single software solution to all their Internet access needs.

Web Navigator stands apart from Mosaic and some other browsers in that it holds a primary home page in the local client machine. On startup, the user immediately has a menu to view, rather than the message Waiting for remote connection. You can replace your primary, local home page, which contains links that are subject to change, with a fresh, up-to-date home page that has new, unbroken links. Just download the new page from California Software. The section, "What Does It Look Like," later in this chapter, covers this process.

> **Note**
>
> California Software says they continue to have a friendly relationship with Thomas R. Bruce, who originally wrote and developed the Web browser called Cello. Tom Bruce provides California Software with advanced technical advice.

Web Navigator and Cello (v. 1.01a) are very much alike, because the Web Navigator was built upon and derived from Cello. This section shows you the important differences between Mosaic and Web Navigator, and shows you the major differences between Web Navigator and Cello, Web Navigator's parent.

Web Navigator is especially interesting because it uses the Windows tools of OLE 2.0 (Object Linking and Embedding 2.0) to integrate itself into a unified suite that deals with all your Internet needs. Also, because it approaches the idea of an initial home page in a new way, the Web Navigator is especially interesting.

Where Do You Get Web Navigator?

Web Navigator is the WWW part of the California Software InterAp suite. But remember, you should ask for InterAp by California Software rather than just the Web Navigator. InterAp will be sold both in retail software stores and directly from California Software.

Tip
Web Navigator (and the whole InterAp suite, for that matter) is compatible with TCP/IP LANs and SLIP and PPP connections that are WinSocket compliant.

Here is the contact information for California Software:

Surface Mail:
California Software Incorporated
4th Floor
4000 Civic Center Drive
San Rafael, California 94903

Voice: (415)491-4371

Fax: (415)491-0402

E-mail: Sales@calsoft.com
                Support@calsoft.com
FTP: ftp.calsoft.com or 199.4.105.10
WWW: http://www.calsoft.com

As usual in the software pricing business, the more copies you buy the more you save. Single users pay the highest prices, and large companies and organizations (who are a primary target audience for this sort of communications suite) can buy site licenses at lower costs per user.

The entire InterAp suite is priced at $295 (December 1994) for single users. Therefore, this browser can only be seen as a bargain if you want what California Software calls the *interoperability* of a single unified suite of Windows OLE 2.0 compliant telecommunications and Internet applications, rather than just the Web Navigator module.

InterAp can be quite a worthwhile investment if you already use other OLE 2.0 compliant programs, such as spreadsheets (for example, Excel 5.0), word processors (Word 6.0), or graphics programs (CorelDRAW! 5.0) and want the drag-and-drop and object linking and embedding features OLE 2.0 offers. This and other feature pros and cons are discussed in more detail in the section "Advantages and Disadvantages," later in this chapter.

The InterAp suite is designed to be customizable, so that large companies and organizations can turn off individual modules if they are undesirable or unneeded. For example, if you already have a great e-mail reader that all your workers use and understand, you don't have to activate the e-mail program in the InterAp suite—you can just leave it turned off.

> **Note**
>
> Another Web Navigator feature you should know about is almost invisible. Web Navigator comes with it's own WinSocket driver; it can supply WinSocket service if you need it.
>
> Web Navigator politely checks to see if you already have WinSocket installed before it does any installing of its own. If it detects an installed WinSocket, Web Navigator announces that fact and moves on without installing another.

What Does It Look Like?

This section gives you a first look at the Web Navigator interface (see fig. A.12). It also describes the interface and the home page.

The InterAp interface is called the LaunchPad. If you double-click the InterAp Manager icon, the LaunchPad toolbar shown in figure A.13 opens. Start the Web Navigator by clicking the globe icon.

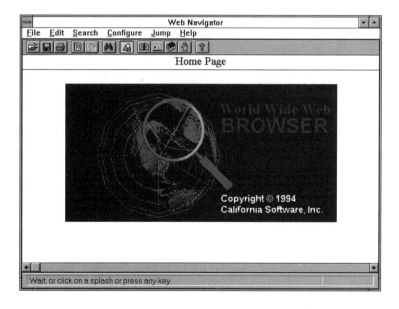

Fig. A.12
Web Navigator opens the World Wide Web to any Windows user.

Fig. A.13
The LaunchPad toolbar.

As mentioned above, Web Navigator loads a local home page from your hard drive as soon as you turn on the Web Navigator. You have no initial lag-time and you don't have to wait for a remote connection or for text and graphics to be returned from a remote site. Figure A.14 shows the top of the home page.

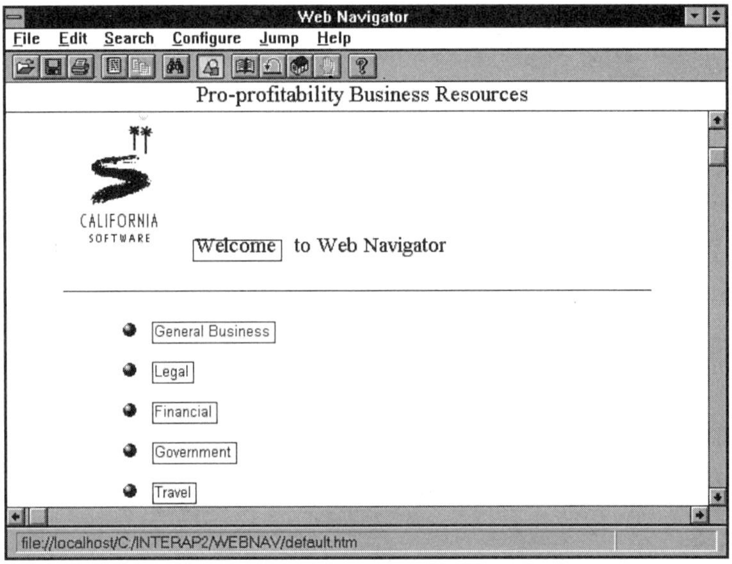

Fig. A.14
Web Navigator comes with its own local home page.

This initial home page is only a sample. California Software gives you a fresh one any time you need it. Or you may want to have them custom design one just for your company or organization. Of course, you can always create your own.

This unique initial feature sets the whole tone for the Web Navigator—California Software wants to insulate you from the UNIX command line and all forms of TCP/IP gibberish by making each transaction simple, visually intuitive, and transparent.

Tip
The Internet is much like a living thing—*always* changing. To accommodate change, California Software encourages users to download a new starting home page, with fresh new connections and up-to-date information.

Tip
If you forget where you are, so to speak, you can always click the right mouse button at the top, near the toolbar, and your current URL will appear in a pop-up box.

Loading a Document by URL

Opening a URL in Web Navigator uses the same command as in Cello. Open the **J**ump menu and choose Launch via **U**RL. Enter the URL in the dialog box and press Enter.

Bookmarks and History

Like Mosaic and Cello, it's easy to mark your place if you find something interesting that you may want to visit again. To place a bookmark in the open document, open the **J**ump menu and choose **B**ookmark. Then choose **M**ark Current document. The Bookmarks dialog box appears (see fig. A.15).

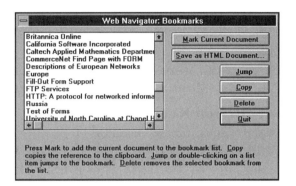

Fig. A.15
Cello's Bookmark dialog is given a facelift in Web Navigator.

Just as in Cello, double-click a bookmark entry to immediately open that document. The remainder of the commands in this dialog box are used in the same way as they are in Cello.

> **Note**
>
> The **S**ave as HTML Document button in Web Navigator's Bookmark dialog box saves the bookmark list as an HTML file that you can open locally. This is the same as the Dump list to **f**ile button in Cello's bookmark dialog box.

Web Navigator's History feature is almost identical to Cello. But Web Navigator has a "spruced up" dialog box (as shown in fig. A.16) to show both the URLs and document titles (Cello shows only the titles).

> **Moving a Bookmark**
>
> To move a bookmark from one group to another, copy it to the Windows clipboard using the Copy button in the Bookmarks dialog box. Open the new group (called a bookmark category) into which you want to move the bookmark. Next, ask to enter a new bookmark in the new group, and then use the clipboard hot keys (Shift+Insert) to paste the bookmark from the clipboard to the new location. Return to the bookmark's previous location and delete it. The final version of Web Navigator may have a simpler way to move bookmarks, but this five-step method works.

Fig. A.16
The Web
Navigator's
History box is
similar to the
dialog box in
Cello.

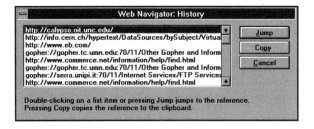

Convenient Function Keys

As you become more familiar with any Windows program, you find that
some menus and keystrokes are part of your normal routine. In many cases,
the most common mouse selections can be duplicated using function keys.
Because macros with mouse movements often fail to work properly, you need
hot keys if you are writing macros for your frequent tasks.

California Software has far exceeded both Cello and Mosaic on this issue by
supplying 12 function keys for the most common operations. Mosaic just
ignores function keys, and Cello uses only a couple.

California Software has provided a full complement of function keys—from
F1 to F12—so that you can use a single keystroke to accomplish a lot.

The Web Navigator hot keys are listed in table A.1. This table lists the function or "f-keys," what the function key does, and on which drop-down menu
the function is found. The letters in boldface are the actual keys you press to
use the hot keys if the function keys are not available. (For more information
on using hot keys in Windows, please see your Windows manual.)

Table A.1 Web Navigator Hot Keys		
Function Key	**Operation**	**Drop-down Menu**
F1	Help **C**ontents	(**H**elp)
F2	**S**ave as...	(**F**ile)
F3	**S**earch again	(**S**earch)
F4	View **S**ource	(**E**dit)
F5	Reload **D**ocument	(**F**ile)
F6	**P**rint	(**F**ile)
F7	Jump **U**p	(**J**ump)

Function Key	Operation	Drop-down Menu
F8	**B**ookmark	(**J**ump)
F9	**H**istory	(**J**ump)
F10	Invokes Hot Key menus, such as Alt	
F11	Return to Home **p**age	(**J**ump)
F12	**A**bort Transaction	(**J**ump)
Alt+F4	**C**lose	(Control Menu*)
Ctrl+Esc	S**w**itch	(Control Menu*)
Ctrl+C	C**o**py	(**E**dit)

* As in all Windows applications, the hot key for accessing the Control Menu is Alt+Space bar. Web Navigator offers another way, also. You can just press F10+Space bar.

The next section, on California Software's NetScripts, is not strictly about Web Navigator, but is about how you can use an OLE 2.0 compliant Internet Web browser, such as Web Navigator, to create powerful interacting macros.

Viewing Source in Windows Write

A good decision on the part of California Software was to use Windows Write as Web Navigator's default word-processing program.

Cello uses Notepad for viewing text files (such as HTML source). It's possible that if you have Windows on your computer, you have (or had) Write on there also. Write came with Windows. Windows Write is a more capable program than Notepad and InterAp takes advantage of it. In particular Write can open very large documents, while Notepad cannot. (This is a limitation in Windows and Windows for Workgroups—Windows NT's Notepad can open large files.)

> **Note**
>
> You can easily change Cello's setup to use Windows Write rather than Notepad.

Other than that difference, the functionality of viewing source in Web Navigator is the same as in Cello. Write lets you either convert the incoming document to Write format, view the document as it is without conversion, or cancel the operation.

A

Appendix A

Starting Points

Web Navigator includes a convenient list of starting points that you may want to check out when Web cruising. The idea is the same as the starting points feature in Mosaic; you choose a starting point—a Web document that the InterAp developers think may be of use. To open a Web document, open the **J**ump menu and choose one of the documents listed at the bottom of the menu. You can get an updated list of starting points from California Software.

NetScripts Macros, Scheduler, and Web Fetch Objects

Because Web Navigator is OLE 2.0 compliant, and part of a full suite of Internet communications services, you can use Web Navigator as part of cross-application macro programs. The InterAp suite allows you to link programs on your computer to remote computers, using a process California Software calls *distributed object communications*.

InterAp does this with NetScripts, a visual basic scripting language that is fully compatible with Microsoft's Visual Basic. You can use NetScript macros to link Internet services such as WWW to your other OLE 2.0 compliant applications, such as Word 6.0, Excel 5.0, and CorelDRAW! 5.0.

Also included in the InterAp suite is a Scheduler; your NetScripts can use the Web at night (or whenever you want, such as daily or weekly at a certain time) for the fastest response times.

This ability to send and receive information from other OLE 2.0 compliant applications opens vast new automation opportunities, including Web Fetch objects, which are only briefly mentioned below.

> **Note**
>
> Although Web Navigator comes packaged with several pre-written NetScripts that may serve your initial, basic needs, California Software also offers to custom produce macros for your exact business needs.

Here are three examples of how you can get Web Navigator and OLE 2.0 to do complex work for you:

- You can prepare a Web macro to automatically retrieve a stock price at certain times each day from a remote Internet site. The retrieved price can then be placed in an OLE 2.0 compliant spreadsheet, and a spreadsheet macro can then be told to compare the price to preset values (or to percent change figures) you determine. If a target, preset level of price or change in price occurs, the spreadsheet macro is ordered to send an e-mail message to you, your stock broker, your clients, or anyone you want.

■ If you find a Web site that you think would be especially interesting to a friend or customer, you can send them an e-mail message with a Web "Fetch" object attached to it. This gives another Web Navigator user more than a plain URL, because they won't have to type or cut-and-paste anything. All they do is click the Web Fetch object; they're connected to the remote site automatically.

■ To keep up to date on new developments, you can search the Web for new advances by topic area. Keyword searches are already available through WebCrawler and Veronica, but with Web Navigator, you can have the search done automatically daily, once a week, or once a month. Or in the middle of the night, with the result stored neatly in your word processor's format waiting for your return in the morning.

Help and Documentation

Context-sensitive help is available in Web Navigator, and the Windows hypertext help documentation looks very nice. Figure A.17 shows the help contents page.

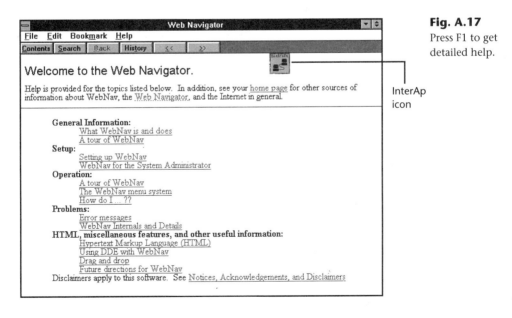

Fig. A.17
Press F1 to get detailed help.

InterAp icon

As the mouse cursor moves over the button bar, yellow help "balloons" pop up to tell you what each button does. This is especially helpful when you are learning the program.

Also, on the help contents page you'll find an integrated help service for the InterAp suite called INTERAP™ on-line help, including tutorials and visual demonstrations. To open this service, click the InterAp icon in the upper right part of the screen. Figure A.18 shows you the opening page.

Fig. A.18
An extra level of InterAp help is always available.

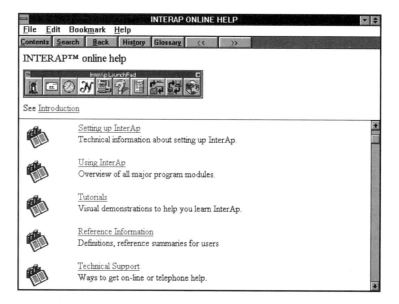

This INTERAP™ service is designed to stay on top of all other windows until you close it.

The bottom of the Web Navigator screen also contains a status line. If you open a drop-down menu up above, the status line always tells you in just a few words the most important tasks for which that menu is used.

Advantages and Disadvantages

While the unique function keys mentioned are not enough to sway a customer to purchase a $295 software program, they do once again demonstrate the customer convenience orientation of the Web Navigator. This section reviews the reasons you should consider buying this suite-with-a-Web-browser, and provides a few notes to check to be sure that it meets your needs.

Disk Cache of Entire Sessions

Web Navigator gives the appearance of more rapid responsiveness than old versions of Mosaic. In Web Navigator, as in Cello before it, the previous screens are stored on the hard disk and appear immediately. You can always tell if you are viewing a cached document by looking in the status bar—the [CACHED] indicator is shown if it is (see fig. A.19).

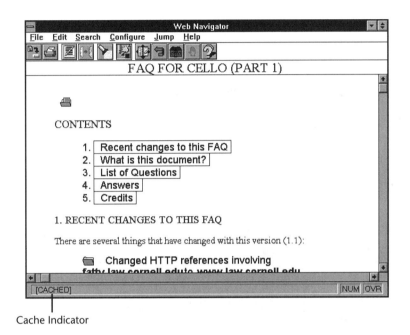

Fig. A.19
Cached pages are clearly marked in the lower left corner when they are loaded.

Cache Indicator

Unfortunately, too many WWW sites still don't provide clear warnings about the sizes of the attached hypertext document. You can "accidentally" download a very large page or a series of graphics that takes several minutes to complete. With Web Navigator, you don't have to dread going back through that page later during your session because it was stored on your hard drive automatically. If you click a link to any previous page in the current session, it appears instantly.

California Software is adding another useful feature to Web Navigator (though it wasn't available at the time this chapter was written). You'll be able to save history lists for future use. Travel around the Web today, save the history, and then come back and reuse the list next week or next month.

Drag and Drop (OLE 2.0)

One of the more important things that California Software means by "InterAp has interoperability" is that text can be moved to and from the Windows clipboard, the InterAp e-mail program, and to and from other OLE 2.0 compatible applications on the user's computer.

The addition of a Select All option on the Edit menu is one of the nicest new features in Web Navigator. This feature allows you to avoid clicking and dragging through an entire document, if you're sure you want to select it all. Once selected, the text can be moved to any OLE 2.0 compliant application, the InterAp e-mail program, or the Windows clipboard. This is an especially welcome feature because NCSA Mosaic does not yet have a copy feature.

On-Line Forms

Web Navigator has added support for on-line forms. These forms work in the latest versions of NCSA Mosaic, but not in Cello. Figure A.20 is a form from Encyclopedia Britannica Online's search service, and figure A.21 is a similar form from CommerceNet's keyword search service.

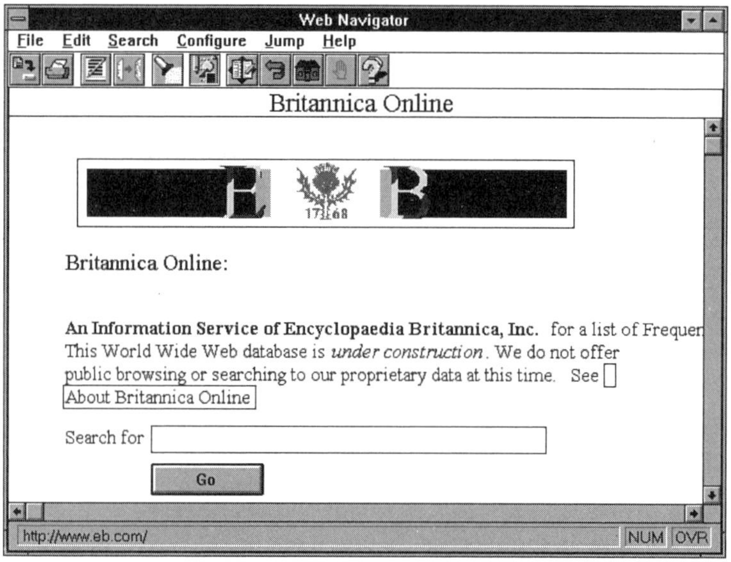

Fig. A.20
You can fill in forms when you read Web pages to supply information or to search for information.

To fill in a form, all you do is click the blank and start typing. Click each blank in turn to fill in a multi-question form.

When you are ready, you indicate you are done by clicking Done, Go, Send, Search, or Submit. Some forms pages even let you reset the form if you want to start over again.

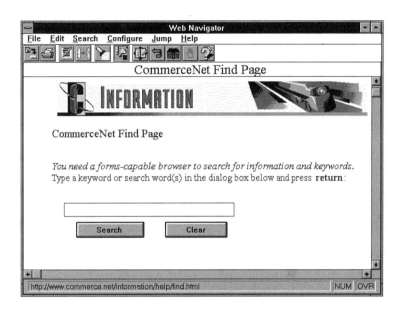

Fig. A.21
CommerceNet
allows you to clear
the form if you
want to start over.

A

Appendix A

Abort Transaction

The excellent Abort Transaction feature started in Cello as a familiar red oc-tagonal Stop sign. (Clicking this Stop sign performs the same function as clicking the spinning globe in Mosaic.) Abort Transaction can be used when you discover a remote site is sending you too much material, when you want a short text, or when another priority presents itself during your busy work-day.

Windows 32-bit Mode Is Not Required

Web Navigator makes full use of one of the most advanced Windows fea-tures, OLE 2.0. On the other hand, it doesn't require that Windows 3.1 users upgrade to 32-bit mode, as does Mosaic. Web Navigator runs quickly, and has advanced features such as session caching, without the trouble, hard disk space requirements and fear of major change that upgrading your Windows version from 16-bit to 32-bit processing may cause.

The Bottom Line

The bottom line is that with full OLE 2.0 compatibility and well-developed second generation Web browser services (session caching, bookmark manage-ment, and so on), Web Navigator is an exciting new entry in the Internet software arena that first-time users and long-time users can both enjoy.

WinWeb from EINet

WinWeb is a neat little World Wide Web viewer from EINet (Enterprise Integration Network), a service provider owned by Microelectronics and Computer Technology Corporation (MCC). EINet has created a Web site they call EINet Galaxy, and the main Galaxy document appears as WinWeb's home page—though you can select whatever page you want as the home page, of course. And, like Mosaic, WinWeb is free for noncommercial use. There's also a Macintosh version, MacWeb.

Installing WinWeb

At the time of writing, EINet had released Version 1.0 A2 of WinWeb; that's an alpha version, a prerelease version. Version 1.0 A2 is out there, and you can use it, but don't be surprised if you run into bugs. When I used WinWeb, though, I found it to be pretty stable.

You can find WinWeb at the **ftp.einet.net** FTP site, in the /einet/pc/winweb directory. Or, if you are already working with a WWW viewer, you can get WinWeb off the World Wide Web at **http://galaxy.einet.net/EINet/ WinWeb/WinWebHome.html.** (In this document you'll find a link currently called /einet/pc/winweb/winweb.zip. Set up your browser to download, because clicking on the link causes the EINet site to send the WINWEB.ZIP file to your system.)

When you download the ZIP archive file, extract the WinWeb files into a directory you've created for WinWeb. Create a Program Manager icon for the program. And that's it. You've installed WinWeb. Start your Internet connection, double-click the icon, and WinWeb starts. You can see the Galaxy home page in figure A.22; you see this page when you first start WinWeb.

You don't have to use this page as your home page. If you prefer to use another—the one provided by your service provider, for instance, or even one on your computer's hard disk—open the **O**ptions menu and choose Set **H**ome Page. The Set Home Page dialog box appears (see fig. A.23).

The EINet Galaxy Home Page option is the default option, but you have two other choices. If you have already navigated the viewer to the page you want to use as the home page, simply select the Current Page option and then choose OK. Or type the URL of the page you want to use into the URL text box and then choose the OK button.

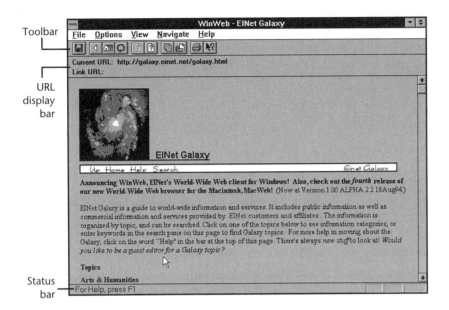

Toolbar

URL display bar

Status bar

Fig. A.22
The WinWeb window, showing the default home page.

A

Appendix A

Fig. A.23
The Set Home Page dialog box lets you choose the home page you see each time you start WinWeb.

The WinWeb Toolbar

Let's take a quick look at the WinWeb toolbar (which you can turn off using the **V**iew, **T**oolbar menu option if you prefer). The toolbar buttons are shown in figure A.24.

- **Save to File.** Turns on loading documents to file (the same as Options, Load to file).

- **Back.** Returns to the previous document (the same as Navigate, Back).

- **Home.** Displays the home page (the same as Navigate, Home).

- **Reload.** Reloads the current document (the same as Navigate, Reload).

- **Search.** Lets you search the current document (the same as Navigate, Search).

- **Search Einet Galaxy.** Lets you search the ElNet Galaxy WWW system (the same as Navigate, Search ElNet Galaxy).

- **History.** Displays the History List (the same as Navigate, History List).

- **Hot List.** Shows or removes the hotlist (the same as Navigate, Hotlist).

- **Print.** Prints the current document (the same as File, Print).

- **Help.** Turns the mouse pointer into a help pointer—clicking a screen component then displays a help file for that component.

Fig. A.24
The WinWeb toolbar has some very useful tools.

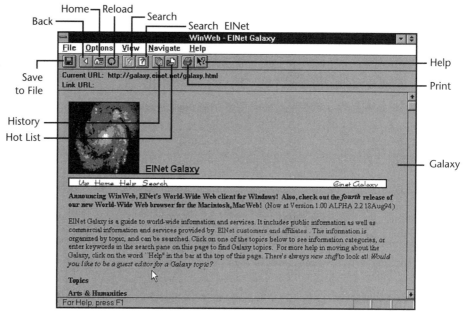

Note

Version 1.0 A2 does not have an on-line help system for the program; all the help tools, including buttons and menu options, do not work at present.

Using WinWeb

WinWeb is not as sophisticated as Mosaic or some of its derivatives, but for many users its simplicity more than makes up for that. It doesn't have as many options as Mosaic, but what it does have is pretty well designed. It's also smaller than Mosaic—the executable file takes up about a third as much disk space as Mosaic—and uses less memory. But perhaps most important is that it's a 16-bit application, so Windows 3.1 and Windows for Workgroups users don't need to add the Win32's 32-bit upgrade. The Win32 versions of Mosaic will outperform it, but WinWeb is faster and more stable than the early 16-bit NCSA Mosaic 1.0.

The basics are the same as with any WWW viewer, of course: click links to go places. When WinWeb is transferring a document it displays a small dialog box with a Cancel button inside it. You can just click the button to stop the transfer.

Let's look at the other navigational tools (see the menu commands in table A.2).

Table A.2 The Navigation Menu Commands	
Command	**Action**
Navigate, **B**ack	Displays the previous document.
Navigate, **H**ome	Displays your home page (which is set using the Options, Set Home Page command).
Navigate, Load **U**RL	Displays a dialog box that you can type a URL into. When you choose the OK button, the document is displayed.
Navigate, Reload	Reloads the current document.
Navigate, **C**ancel	Cancels the current document-loading operation. Use this if you clicked a link and the document is taking too long to load.
Navigate, **S**earch	Searches the current document. You can enter a search keyword.
Navigate, Search ElNet **G**alaxy	Even if you are not currently at the ElNet Galaxy home page, you can still search the Galaxy system for information.
Navigate, His**t**ory List	Displays the History List, so that you can go back to a previous document.
Navigate, Hot**l**ist	Displays or closes the hotlist. Use the hotlist to take a shortcut to documents you saved in the hotlist earlier.

Using the Hotlist

Mosaic uses a hotlist, a sort of bookmark system, to help you find your way back to documents you know you will return to. WinWeb has a similar system, though the current version doesn't let you add the hotlist to the menu bar. Instead, there's a Hotlist dialog box that you can keep open, or open when you need it.

If you are viewing a World Wide Web document that you think you'll want to return to, choose **N**avigate, Hot**l**ist. The dialog box shown in figure A.25 appears.

Fig. A.25
Use the Hotlist dialog box to keep a record of your favorite WWW documents.

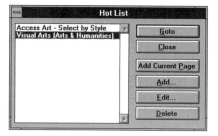

Choose the Add Current **P**age button to see another small dialog box, into which you can type an item name, or accept the document title. Choose the OK button in that dialog box and the entry is added to the Hotlist box.

You can also add items to the Hotlist box without going to the document first. Choose **A**dd to see another small dialog box, this time with space for an item name and its URL. Type both in and choose the OK button to add the entry to the list.

When you've finished adding items to the Hotlist dialog box, close the box by clicking the **C**lose button. You don't have to close the box, though. This dialog box is always on top—it remains above all your other Windows applications, WinWeb included. You can push the dialog box off screen just a little, but have it ready when you want it.

When you need to go to one of the documents you've added to your hotlist, and if you didn't leave the box open, use the **N**avigate, Hot**l**ist option again to open it. Then simply double-click the document you want to go to. Or select the document and click the Goto button.

Using the History List

The History List can also stay open all the time, if you want. Choose the **N**avigate, His**t**ory List menu option. The History dialog box appears (see fig. A.26). It is quite small when you first open it, but you can enlarge it using the Control menu's Size command or the window's borders.

The dialog box shows you all documents you've viewed in the current session. Double-click one to go to it, or select it and choose the Goto button.

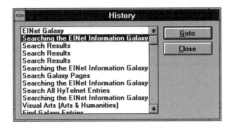

Fig. A.26
Use the History dialog box to return to documents you viewed earlier.

Saving Files

WinWeb uses a similar system to Mosaic for downloading files from the World Wide Web. When you find a link that is a connection to a file (a link that when clicked begins a file transfer), choose the **O**ptions, **L**oad to File command.

Now WinWeb is in Load to File mode. Each time you click a link, the Save As dialog box appears. (You see this box even if the link is a normal document-to-document link.) Select the directory in which you want to place the file, and the file name you want to use, and then choose the OK button. The file transfers to your hard disk.

Tip
You can use this method to load an HTML file to your hard disk. If you click a normal link, you see the Save As dialog box. When you save the document, it is saved as an ASCII HTML file that you can then modify and use as, for example, your home page.

Printing a Document

You can print from WinWeb using the same procedure you use in Mosaic. WinWeb also has a print preview function that works essentially the same way as Mosaic's.

Customizing WinWeb

You have a few ways to customize WinWeb; use the **V**iew menu to get to the tools that let you do so (perhaps the View menu needs to be renamed).

WinWeb has a tool for selecting the fonts you want to use for various types of document text. Choose **V**iew, **F**onts to see the dialog box shown in figure A.27.

Click the type of text you want to change, and the dialog box shows you how that text is currently set up. Choose the Change button to see a typical Windows Fonts dialog box, in which you can modify the font—remember that you can change font color, not just typeface.

Fig. A.27
Use the Select
Fonts dialog box
to determine how
documents are
displayed.

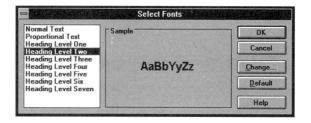

Notice also that WinWeb's Select Fonts dialog box has a Default button. Choose this button if you want to return the selected font to its default setting, which is useful if you've been goofing around with the fonts and don't like what you've done to them.

You can also change the **H**ighlight Color and **B**ackground Color by selecting these options from the **V**iew menu. The Highlight Color is the *link* color, what would be called the *anchor* color in Mosaic; this is the color of the text (or of the border around the graphic) that you click to display another document or download a file. The Background Color is the color of the WinWeb background. In both cases use the Windows Color dialog box—the one that is used by the Windows Control Panel—to select the color you want.

Tip
The more of
these items you
remove, the
more space you
have to view
your WWW
documents.

The other three options on the **V**iew menu are **T**oolbar, **S**tatus Bar, and **U**RL Display. These options turn those three items on and off. The URL Display is a line that appears below the toolbar and menu bar that shows the current document's URL, and the URL of the link to which the mouse pointer is pointing.

Another very important option is the **O**ptions, Load **I**mages command. Use this to turn the display of inline graphics on and off. If you are using WinWeb on a telephone line—through a SLIP or PPP connection—this capability is very important, because displaying all those inline graphics can take a long time.

NetCruiser

NetCruiser is a Windows program that works with the NETCOM system. NETCOM is a large Internet service provider—they created NetCruiser to give their customers an easy-to-install way to get a suite of easy-to-use Internet tools. NetCruiser only works with NETCOM—you can't buy the software and install it on other systems.

A

Appendix A

A really remarkable thing about NetCruiser is that it uses a PPP connection, yet it is as easy to install as the average Windows program. There's no need for you to worry about entering IP addresses or anything complicated like that—NetCruiser handles it all for you. All you need to enter is your name and address, the COM port you are using, the type of modem, and so on. Because the software only works with one system, the NETCOM system, it knows how to communicate with that system—there's no need for you to set up communications parameters. NetCruiser even has a command that automatically downloads and installs the latest software upgrade. On the Internet, well-designed, easy-to-use software is the exception, not the rule—and NetCruiser is a delight to work with.

What's There

After you've installed and started NetCruiser, you'll find a well-designed Windows interface with a variety of Internet tools: e-mail, newsgroups, Telnet, FTP, a Gopher client, finger, and, most importantly for us, a World Wide Web browser. To get to the browser, click the WWW button in the toolbar—it's the one with a picture of a web, of course. Or choose the **I**nternet, **W**orld Wide Web—Browser menu option. You see the screen in figure A.28.

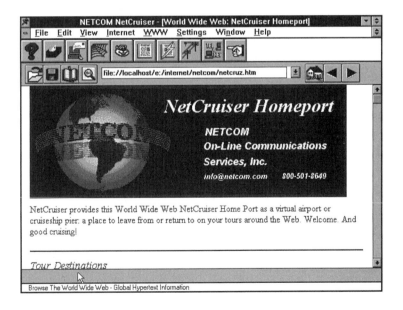

Fig. A.28
NetCruiser's World Wide Web Browser is a well-designed program that's fast and easy.

You use NetCruiser in much the same way you do Mosaic—click the links to go somewhere. But before we get into detail about working with this program, let's have a quick look at how to customize it.

Configuration Options

When you open the WWW browser, a couple of things happen to the menu bar. A new menu appears, WWW, and another option appears on the Settings menu. Choose the **S**ettings, WWW **O**ptions menu item and you see the dialog box in figure A.29.

Fig. A.29

The Options dialog box lets you set up your WWW Browser.

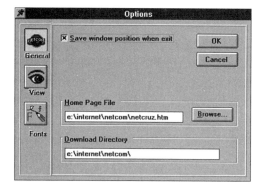

When you first open this box you see the General options. To make sure the window is the same size the next time you open the browser, choose **S**ave window position when exit. This option is useful because otherwise the window is small when it opens and you have to maximize it. You can also select the home page you want to use; by default, the home page is a file that was installed on your hard disk. Finally, you can specify the **D**ownload Directory, which is the directory in which you want to place any files downloaded during a WWW session.

Choose the View button, and the dialog box changes (see fig. A.30). Here you can define a few characteristics of the documents you are going to view. Choose the Background Color button to select the background color and the Anchor Color button to select the link colors. (Remember, in WWW-speak the hypertext links that you click to display a document are often known as *anchors*).

You can also modify how the links will look in a few other ways. You can choose Display anchor **w**ith underline to place an underline below each text link, Display anchor U**R**L to put the URL in the status bar when you point at a link, and **C**hange Cursor over anchors to turn the pointer into an arrow when it passes over the links. Clearing the Display **i**n line images check box makes sure that inline images are not transferred, which speeds up your session somewhat.

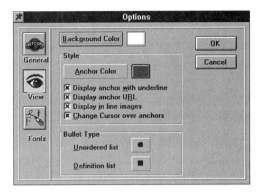

Fig. A.30
The View options
let you define
what many of
the document
elements look like.

You can also change the types of bullets used in your documents by choosing
the bullet buttons at the bottom of the dialog box. In each case, a dialog box
appears with several choices.

Choose the Fonts button to see the different fonts defined for the documents
(see fig. A.31). Each button has the name of the type of font, and even displays the name in the format that you have selected, so that you can see all
elements as they will appear in the documents. To change one, choose the
button and select the type of font you want from the Fonts dialog box that
appears.

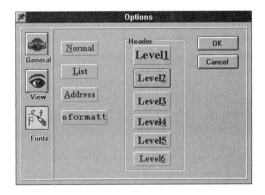

Fig. A.31
The Fonts options
let you select each
document font
type.

The NetCruiser Toolbar

When you open the WWW browser, you actually have two toolbars, the large
one under the menu bar, which lets you select the different NetCruiser modules (FTP, Telnet, WWW, and so on), and a slightly smaller one that is for the
WWW browser itself.

Tip
To make a little
more room for
your WWW ses-
sions, open the
View menu and
choose Toolbar to
remove the large
NetCruiser toolbar.

Figure A.32 shows the buttons you can find on the toolbar.

- **Open Local File.** Opens an HTML file.

- **Save to Disk.** Displays a Save As dialog box so that you can save the current document on your hard disk (as an HTML document).

- **Bookmark.** Opens the Bookmark dialog box.

- **Find.** Displays the Find dialog box, so that you can search the current document.

- **Home.** Displays the home page.

- **Back.** Goes to the previous document.

- **Forward.** Goes to the next document.

- **Stop.** This button only appears while the browser is transmitting information. Click it to cancel the transmission

Fig. A.32
The NetCruiser
toolbar.

The Menu Options

Let's take a quick look at the menu options that you can use for your WWW session (see table A.3).

Table A.3 NetCruiser's World Wide Web Menu Options	
Command	**Purpose**
File, **V**iew Text File	Lets you view a text file that you have downloaded.
File, **V**iew Graphics File	Lets you view a graphics file that you have downloaded.
File, **O**pen WWW File	Opens an HTML file on your hard disk.
File, **S**ave	Saves the current document as an HTML file on your hard disk.
Edit, **F**ind	Searches the current document for a particular word or phrase.

Command	Purpose
Edit, Find **N**ext	Repeats the search.
View, **S**ource File	Displays the HTML file so you can copy portions of it to the Clipboard.
WWW, **L**oad to Disk	Changes the browser to "download mode" so that when you click a link, a file is downloaded to your hard disk.
WWW, **B**ack	Displays the previous document.
WWW, **F**orward	Displays the next document.
WWW, **H**ome	Displays the home page.
WWW, His**t**ory	Displays the History list.
WWW, **R**eload	Reloads the current document.
WWW, Book **M**ark	Displays the Book Mark dialog box.
Settings, **W**WW Options	Lets you customize your WWW browser.

Working with Bookmarks

NetCruiser has a simple bookmark system that is adequate, but by no means great. When you want to place a bookmark, choose the **W**WW, Book **M**ark option or click on the Bookmark toolbar button. You see the Book Mark dialog box (see fig. A.33).

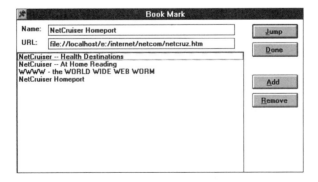

Fig. A.33
The Book Mark dialog box provides an adequate but simple bookmark system.

Choose the Add button to place the bookmark into the dialog box. To go to one of the bookmarks, choose the Jump button. You can also remove bookmarks with the Remove button and close the dialog box with the Done button. You can't edit entries; there's no way to save any changes you make in the Name and URL text boxes. You can, however, copy the URL from this box and paste it into another Windows application (highlight the text in the URL box and press Ctrl+C to copy it to the clipboard).

The History List

If you want to see where you've been in the current session, choose WWW, History. You see a very simple dialog box (see fig. A.34) in which you can double-click an entry to return to that document, or select it and choose the Jump to button. Unfortunately there's a serious problem with the History list—it displays URLs, not document titles. Which is easier to remember, "WWWW - the World Wide Web Worm" or "http://www.cs.colorado.edu/home/mcbryan/WWWW.html"?

Fig. A.34
The History dialog box provides a simple way to return to an earlier document.

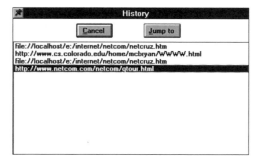

Viewing Graphics

NetCruiser's WWW browser has a couple of built-in, automatic viewers, one for text and one for graphics. Click a link that transfers a JPG file, for instance, and that file is transferred to your disk and then displayed in the Graphics viewer (see fig. A.35). You can also open the graphics and text viewers from the File menu, and load a variety of different file formats from your hard disk. You can view BMP, GIF, JPG, and XBM files. These types cover most, but not all, graphic file types you will run across (GIF and JPG are probably the most common formats used for pictures on the Web).

Fig. A.35
Graphics are displayed in NetCruiser's graphics viewer (you can find Dr. Fun's cartoons at **http:// sunsite.unc.edu/ Dave/ drfun.html**).

What Can't It Do?

A number of useful features are missing from this browser. It can't copy text from the current document or save the document as a text file (without the HTML codes that is—it can save it as an HTML file). Freeware Mosaic can't do this right now, either, but it should be able to soon, and some other commercial browsers can.

The bookmark system is very simple, also. There is no way to create menus or hotlists, and no way to export the bookmark list so that others can use it or so that you can load it from your hard disk as an HTML document. (You can't do this with the History list, either, which is a nice feature of some browsers).

Viewer support is fairly limited, too. There are built-in text and graphics viewers, but no sound support, and no way to add your own viewers. For instance, if you click "Shut up boy!" at the **http://cc.lut.fi/~mega/ simpsons.html** WWW site, NetCruiser will transfer the .AU file and put it on your hard disk—but you won't hear Homer Simpson shout at his son.

Also, although you can turn off inline images, you can't view selected images—it's all or nothing. In other words, if you are not getting inline images and want to view just one image or the images in a particular topic, you have to turn inline images back on. Other browsers, including freeware Mosaic, have commands that let you work with inline images turned off (for speed), but still view selected images.

Finding NetCruiser

If you'd like to try NetCruiser, you have to contact NETCOM. There's a $25 registration fee for the NetCruiser system (which gets you the software). Then you have to pay $19.95 a month, which gets you 40 peak hours and unlimited use at weekends and from midnight to 9 am during the week. Use more than 40 peak hours and you have to pay $2/hour. NETCOM has local telephone numbers all over the country, so you probably will not have to pay long distance rates on top of these charges. For more information about NetCruiser, contact NETCOM:

> NETCOM
> 3031 Tisch Way, 2nd Floor
> San Jose, CA 95128
> (800)353-6600
> (408)345-2600
> Fax: (408)241-9145
> E-mail: **info@netcom.com**

NetCruiser is a very nice system, and its WWW browser is pretty good, too. It's very easy to use, and very quick (because it's a PPP connection as opposed to a SLIP connection). The browser doesn't have the flexibility and features of Mosaic, however. That's probably okay for most users, but the advanced user will prefer a little more power.

Few people are going to get NetCruiser just for the WWW browser, anyway. They are going to get the product because it's a well-designed, all-in-one Internet tool, with a consistent user interface that is easy to install and to use. We need to see more of this type of tool on the Internet.

The Pipeline

The Pipeline is a unique Internet system. It's designed to be used over the phone lines, but it's not a SLIP, CSLIP, or PPP connection. It isn't a simple dial-in terminal connection. It's what The Pipeline has called *Pink SLIP,* their own packet-switching protocol.

SLIP, CSLIP, and PPP are all TCP/IP (Transmission Control Protocol/Internet Protocol) protocols. A *protocol* is a set of rules that defines how two systems can communicate; the protocol used by the Internet is TCP/IP, a packet-switching protocol. The data transmitted is broken into packets, sent, and then put back together by the system receiving the data.

The Pipeline decided to create their own system because they wanted a packet-switching terminal system. Rather than giving all their clients dial-in direct accounts—in which the user's computer becomes a host on the Internet—they wanted to use a simpler system, in which each user's computer is a terminal on The Pipeline's system. That way they wouldn't have to worry about setting up IP addresses for each user, for instance. But they still wanted to provide all the benefits of a dial-in direct account, and for that they needed packet switching.

For example, users working with packet-switching systems—whether SLIP, CSLIP, PPP, or The Pipeline—can run multiple sessions. They can download a file from an FTP site (or several files, even) at the same time they work on the World Wide Web. By creating their own packet-switching system, The Pipeline has more control over how the system works, and can actually make multiple sessions work more smoothly than with dial-in direct connections. For instance, they are adding error-correction to Pink SLIP, to make transmissions more reliable. The design of The Pipeline's user interface makes multiple sessions quite simple to start. With most TCP/IP FTP software, for instance, you'd have to open several FTP programs to run several sessions. With The Pipeline, you just double-click each file you want to download—you don't really start an FTP program (The Pipeline does it all for you in the background).

Installation and Setup of The Pipeline

The Pipeline software was designed to be used with The Pipeline service. The Pipeline is a service provider based in New York. It has three ways to connect: dial the New York number, dial a SprintNet number from almost anywhere in the United States (you'll pay extra for the connection, though), or, if you have a local service provider, dial your service provider and connect to The Pipeline using an rlogin connection. (If you use rlogin, you have to pay both your service provider and The Pipeline for connect time, but it may be less than long-distance charges.)

There's another way to use The Pipeline software, though. The Pipeline is being licensed to service providers throughout the country. You may find a local service provider that uses the software.

To get a demo of The Pipeline software, or to find out if there's a service provider in your area using the software, contact The Pipeline:

> The Pipeline
> 150 Broadway
> Suite 1710
> New York, NY 10028
> Phone: (212)267-3636
> Fax: (212)267-4380
> E-mail: **info@pipeline.com**
> Modem: (212)267-6432 (login as guest)
> Telnet, Gopher, FTP: **pipeline.com**

Note that you may be able to download The Pipeline software from the pipeline.com FTP site, though the site is often unavailable.

Once you have the software, simply run the SETUP program to install it onto your hard disk. When you first run the program you will have to enter the configuration information—the number you want to dial, the COM port you want to use, and so on. It's all fairly straightforward, though. (At the time of writing, you could not use the rlogin method for a demo session, only for access once a subscriber to The Pipeline.)

Using the Web Browser

The Pipeline is an integrated system that has all the usual Internet tools—FTP, Telnet, Internet Relay Chat, e-mail, newsgroups, and so on. But of course we are here to talk about the World Wide Web. Let's take a look at what's available, and how it works.

> **Note**
>
> At the time of writing, The Pipeline had just released a beta version of its Web software, and it lacked a number of features that will be in the final released version. The program I used when writing this chapter, and the snapshots you see here, aren't exactly the same as the version available now.

You can run the Web browser in a couple of ways. The Pipeline has, until now, been based on a Gopher menu system. The main window has a list of options that you can double-click—these options are actually Gopher menu items. But you can replace this system with the Web browser, if you wish, so that every time you open The Pipeline you are shown the browser, not the Gopher menu.

To do this, simply choose the **O**ptions, **U**se Web browser in main screen menu item. (You can go back to the Gopher menu screen at any time by choosing this option again.) You'll see something like the screen in figure A.36.

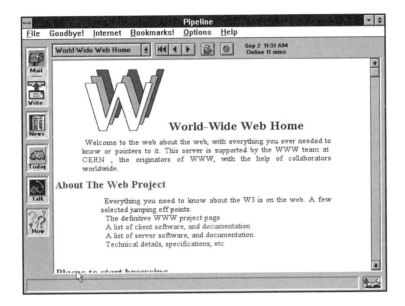

Fig. A.36
The Pipeline main screen, once you've selected the Web browser.

If you prefer to keep the Gopher main menu, and just start the Web browser occasionally, you can choose the Internet, World Wide Web option, or press Ctrl+W. The dialog box in figure A.37 appears. Enter the URL of a Web site you want to use (or select from the drop-down list box, in which you'll find URLs you used in previous sessions). When you choose the OK button, a new window opens, in which your Web session begins (see fig. A.38).

Tip
You can run multiple web sessions. Each time you choose the Internet, World Wide Web option, or press Ctrl+W, a new Web window opens. If you are in a Web window, you can click the Open URL toolbar button (see the next section, "Using the Toolbar").

Fig. A.37
This dialog box saves the URLs you've used in the past, so you can quickly select them.

Fig. A.38

The Pipeline's browser displays each page in a separate window.

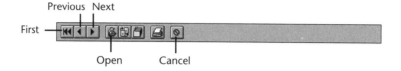

Using the Toolbar

Notice the two toolbars. The one on the left side of the main window is a way to get to the other Pipeline services—e-mail, talk, newsgroups, and so on (see fig. A.36). But the one at the top of the Web browsers contains buttons related to the web (see fig. A.39).

Fig. A.39

The Pipeline's browser displays each page in a separate window.

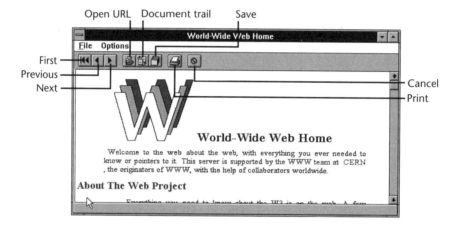

Here are descriptions of each of these buttons:

- **First.** Go to the first document you looked at in this session.

- **Previous.** Go to the previous document.

- **Next.** Go to the next document.

- **Open URL.** Open a URL.

- **Document Trail.** Displays document trail—a history list.

- **Save.** Saves the current document on your hard disk.

- **Print.** Prints the current document.

- **Cancel.** Cancels the current transfer.

Using the Document Trail

The Pipeline browser calls its history list a *document trail*. At the time of writing the feature wasn't fully implemented. However, the drop-down list box in the main window to the left of the toolbar buttons contains the document trail (refer to fig. A.36). Simply click the down arrow to see the list, and then click the document you want to return to.

Using Inline Images

As with most browsers, The Pipeline's browser lets you turn off inline images to speed up transfers. In the beta version this could only be done from a Web browser window, not the main window (though the released version will probably have the option in the main window, also). Choose Options, Expand inline images to turn the images on and off. The inline images will be replaced with asterisks in braces ([*]), and, in some cases, with Pipeline icons.

What if you want to view one of the missing inline images? Simply click the image and The Pipeline runs off and grabs it for you.

Using a Home Page

In the first released version the web browser may not have a way for you to change the home page directly—you can do so by modifying the PIPELINE.INI file, but there may not be a menu option that lets you.

Future versions will have better home page support, and may even have HTML editing tools. These will let The Pipeline's users create HTML files and place them on The Pipeline's computer, providing quick and easy Web publishing.

What Else?

When this chapter was written, some of the Web browser's features weren't working—such as the document trail, for instance. Pipeline promises that certain other features will be added before the software is released. Here's what the browser should have by the time you read this:

- **Forms support.** The WWW browser lets you enter data into HTML documents that contain interactive forms.

- **Viewers.** You can view most graphic files you find on the web and listen to most sounds by simply clicking the link. The Pipeline's built-in viewers will do the rest.

- **Video support.** This won't be available in the first release of the web browser, but will be added later.

- **Home Page.** A Pipeline home page will be created (the beta version was using the Cern home page).

How Does It Compare?

It's difficult to tell just how The Pipeline's browser will compare to Mosaic right now. It's a much simpler system, but it's also much easier to use—it has fewer features, but what there is you will find easier to work with.

Appendix B

Other Versions of Mosaic for Macintosh

While the last appendix looked at the other versions of Mosaic that are available for Windows, this appendix looks at the versions that are available for Macintosh.

So why would anyone be interested in using another version when the NCSA version is readily available? As discussed in earlier chapters, many features that you might expect to work don't. The commercial version of Mosaic from Spyglass discussed in this chapter doesn't have quite as many of the rough edges and has added some features that weren't finished in the NCSA version.

If you buy a commercial version of Mosaic, you may notice that files load faster (although the main speed limitation is still from the speed of the pipeline you have to the Internet itself; faster lines result in faster interaction), inline images display faster, and in general, all aspects of the program involve less waiting time. You also may find that a commercial version takes less memory and disk space than NCSA's.

The first wave of commercial versions of Mosaic are very similar to the NCSA versions in the way that you use them. The essential Mosaic and World Wide Web features and concepts that are covered elsewhere in this book work in essentially the same way. This chapter points out the differences so that no matter what version of Mosaic you use, you will be able to make full use of this book.

The bad news for Macintosh users is that at this time only one company, Spyglass, has developed a commercial version of Mosaic. To make matters worse, you can't even buy this version from them. However, other companies are developing Macintosh versions; they just weren't available at the time of this writing.

One other Mac program for the World Wide Web that is available now is a shareware product called MacWeb. While this isn't technically Mosaic, it serves the same purpose: it lets you cruise the Web in a graphical interface. For that reason, we cover it here too.

This chapter discusses the following:

- Enhanced NCSA Mosaic for Macintosh from Spyglass

- MacWeb from EINet

Enhanced NCSA Mosaic for Macintosh from Spyglass

You can't buy Enhanced Mosaic in a retail software store. Spyglass is only interested in licenses with at least 10,000 users; you'll probably encounter S-Mosaic if you work for a large business or attend a large university.

> **Note**
>
> Spyglass has not been consistent with the name of this product. In some places it is called Enhanced NCSA Mosaic for Macintosh from Spyglass, Spyglass Mosaic for the Mac, S-Mosaic, and in others just Spyglass Mosaic. These names are used interchangeably in this chapter. In any event, you will probably see it with other names because companies that sublicense it are likely to put their own names on it.

Another possibility of getting a Spyglass version of Mosaic is by purchasing a sublicensed one. Spyglass plans to sell (or sublicense) the product to OEMs (Original Equipment Manufacturers). If you purchase computer hardware from one of these manufacturers and it includes Mosaic, it will usually be labeled with the hardware manufacturer's name, not Spyglass.

Spyglass is also sublicensing Mosaic to other software companies. These companies refine the product and resell it. Again, you don't see the Spyglass name on these versions, because they usually bear the names of the software companies licensing them.

So while you may not see Enhanced NCSA Mosaic for sale at your local computer store, you may run across it under another name bundled with some other product you bought.

Performance Enhancements

S-Mosaic has a number of advantages over the original NCSA version. For starters, the standard 68KB Mac version takes a mere 304KB, compared to the lumbering 1.3MB bulk of NCSA Mosaic version 2.00. Beyond that, it's fast and has plenty of new features. The key elements in Spyglass's plan that have not been implemented yet are provisions for credit-card based transactions and for platform-independent document exchange.

Installing Enhanced NCSA Mosaic

Spyglass has three versions of Mosaic for the Mac: a 68KB version, a PowerMac version, and a Fat version. Functionally, these are the same; each version is optimized to run on different Mac processors.

> **Note**
>
> In case you aren't up on the technical lingo, a "fat" version of an application is one that has both 68KB and PowerMac executables tucked inside itself; it's really big. When you install this application, the installer program determines what kind of Mac you have and automatically gives you the right kind of executable without you having to worry about it.

Installation is simple. Just drag the icon for the version you want to use into a folder on your hard drive. There is also a MosaicMacHelp folder you should drag onto your hard drive (see fig. B.1).

> **Note**
>
> The version of Mosaic from Spyglass discussed here is the version licensed to other companies to resell. The resellers may make changes in their retail versions, such as adding an installer or selling the three versions (68KB, PowerMac, and Fat) separately, so don't be surprised if there are slight differences.

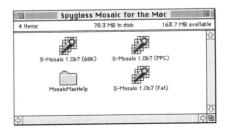

Fig. B.1

The Spyglass Mosaic for the Mac folder contains three versions of the software (for different processors) and a help folder.

B

Appendix B

After you have Mosaic copied to your hard drive, if you have a SLIP or network TCP/IP connection, all you have to do is launch your Internet connection and double-click the S-Mosaic icon. After you start Spyglass, you can connect to any Web site with the same method used in the NCSA version.

What's New in Enhanced Mosaic?

When you start Enhanced NCSA Mosaic, the first thing you'll notice is that it looks pretty much like Mosaic itself (see fig. B.2). There are, however, some important changes.

Fig. B.2
At first glance, Enhanced NCSA Mosaic looks much like NCSA Mosaic.

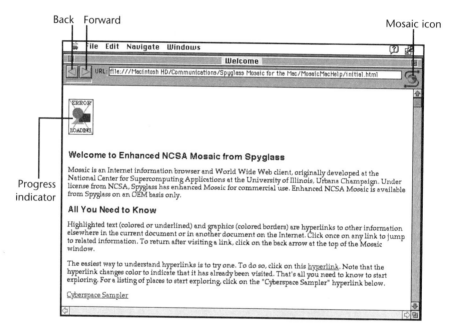

Here are some of the obvious changes:

■ There's no true toolbar, although backward and forward buttons are below the title bar.

■ The Mosaic icon is not a button—you can't click the icon to stop a transfer.

■ There's no Options menu. There are fewer options, and they are reached through the Edit menu.

■ As the pointer goes over a link, the status bar displays the URL.

- A small progress indicator has been added to the left end of the status bar. This shows how much of a document or file has been transferred.

- The drop-down history list has been removed from the status bar.

- There are lots of menu-option changes.

Enhanced NCSA Mosaic may look the same, but there are some important changes from the freeware version. Let's look at the other important changes between these two versions of Mosaic.

Copy and Save

The current version of basic Mosaic makes it difficult to save information from the current document. This will change, but Enhanced NCSA Mosaic already has the problem fixed.

In Enhanced Mosaic from Spyglass, you can copy all the text from the displayed document to the Clipboard. You can then paste it into any Mac application (a word processor, for example). You use the copy and paste feature through the usual Mac method of opening the Edit menu and choosing Copy.

> **Note**
>
> NCSA Mosaic has the copy option on the Edit menu, but the feature does not work.

There's still no way to select and copy just part of a document. It's all or nothing. There is also still no way to paste anything into Mosaic.

You also can save the document as a file. Open the File menu and choose Save As to see the Mac Save As dialog box (see fig. B.3). Enter a file name, and select the radio button for the file type you want to save it as. You can save the file as Plain Text, which means all you get is ASCII text, which is what you see on-screen. Or you can save the file as HTML; in which case you get the text *and* the HTML codes, so you can use the page at a later date (by opening the File menu and choosing Open Local).

> **Caution**
>
> Although the Save As feature may appear to work in NCSA's 2.0.6a version of Mosaic, it will crash your computer and the saved files will be unusable. This bug may be fixed in alpha 8; however, we haven't had this version long enough to be certain.

Fig. B.3
Saving a document in Spyglass Mosaic is a familiar process using the Mac Save dialog box. Be sure to save the file with HTML at the end of the name. Spyglass Mosaic doesn't seem to know what to do with the file when you open it without this.

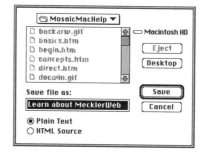

> **Note**
>
> When saving documents to a file using either the method described in this section or the method described in the next section, the saved file will not include the inline graphics in the document. Hyperlinks that use relative addresses won't work when you save the file locally.

Transferring Files

While Spyglass has tried to make Mosaic easier to use, in one way they have made it more difficult—they've hidden the command used to download files. In freeware Mosaic you open the Options menu and choose Load to Disk, and then click a link; there is no such option in Enhanced NCSA Mosaic. Instead, you must press Option and then click on the link. A Download To dialog box appears (the normal Save As dialog box) in which you can enter a file name and choose a folder. The dialog box also shows you the size of the file (see fig. B.4).

Fig. B.4
Downloading a file is as simple as saving a file. Just use the Mac Save dialog box to choose a destination and name for the file.

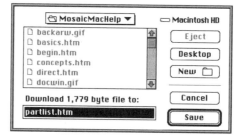

The benefit of this method is that you can't forget that Load to Disk is selected and accidentally load to disk when you wanted to load the file on-screen. You have to press Option and click for each link to load to disk.

Multiple Windows

To open another window, open the File menu and choose New Window. Then work in the new window the normal way, clicking links and so on. The other window remains open. In fact, you can open multiple windows and have several sessions working at once (see fig. B.5). This works in essentially the same way that the NCSA Mosaic does.

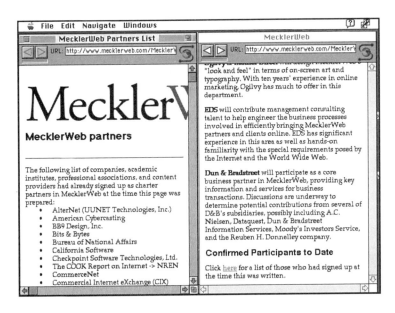

Fig. B.5
Enhanced NCSA Mosaic lets you have multiple sessions working at once. This is a great feature for serious Web cruising.

Spyglass has added a few features to help you work with these multiple windows. To arrange your open windows on-screen, open the Windows menu and choose Arrange Windows. To make any open window active, open the Windows menu and choose the name of the window (see fig. B.6).

You can control the size of any window by using the same methods used with any other Mac window.

Each session can be in a different location on the Web. When you click a link in one of the document windows, it has no effect on the sessions in the other document windows.

Tip
You also can open a new window by pressing Control and clicking a hyperlink. The document for the link opens in the new window.

Fig. B.6
All the open
Mosaic windows
are listed in this
menu.

Working with the Hotlist

Enhanced NCSA Mosaic does not let you add hotlist items to menus. Instead, it provides a Hotlist dialog box (see fig. B.7). To use this feature, open the Navigate menu and choose Hotlist.

Fig. B.7
The Hotlist dialog
box is used to find
your way back to
your favorite FTP
sites. This default
Hotlist is empty.

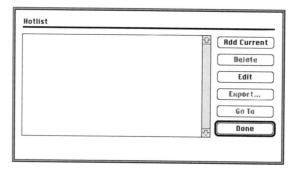

Note

While the default Hotlist in this version is empty, you can expect the licensees of Spyglass Mosaic to add some value for end-users by predefining some hotlist items for useful and interesting Web sites.

While you are traveling around on the Web, you can quickly add a document to your hotlist by opening the Navigate menu and choosing Add Current to Hotlist. Or you can open the dialog box and click the Add Current button.

When you want to return to a document that you have in your hotlist, open the dialog box and double-click the document. Or, you can select the document and click the Go To button.

The Hotlist dialog box also lets you edit entries. Select the entry you want to edit and choose the Edit button. You'll see a dialog box with the hotlist-entry title and its URL. For example, you can modify the title that appears in your hotlist, or copy the URL from the text box to paste into a word processing or e-mail document.

There's also a Delete button for removing entries from your list, and a method for creating an HTML file from your hotlist. Choose the Export button and you'll see the Export Hotlist dialog box, a typical File Save dialog box. Give the document a name, and select the directory you want to place it into, and then choose the OK button. Enhanced NCSA Mosaic not only creates the file, but also displays the file in the window, so you can immediately see what it looks like—each entry in the hotlist appears as a line in the document. Clicking the line takes you to the referenced document.

You can now use this document in the future by loading it into the window, opening the File menu, and choosing Open Local. Or you can send the file to someone else, so that they can use it in their WWW browser—it doesn't have to be Enhanced NCSA Mosaic, of course—to quickly reach the documents in your hotlist.

Using the History List

The History list is a listing of all the documents you've viewed in the current session. In Enhanced NCSA Mosaic, the History list works in much the same way as the Hotlist. In fact, it uses the same dialog box, except that the Add Current button is disabled in the History list (see fig. B.8).

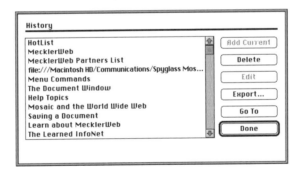

Tip

URLs for documents can change if a document gets moved to a different server or a different location on the server. If this happens to a document on your hotlist, use the Edit feature to update the URL.

B

Appendix B

Fig. B.8
The History dialog box shows all of the documents you have opened in this session.

To view the History list, open the Navigate menu and choose History. After it is open, you can use it in the same way as the Hotlist. Double-click an entry to go to that document, or select the entry and choose the Go To button.

The Edit button lets you change the entry, though you probably won't want to. However, you may want to use it to copy the URL for a particular document you've just viewed. The Export button also is handy. You can create an HTML file showing your current session. This HTML is sort of an interactive record of what you've done. The next time you want to repeat a particular "journey" over the web, you can open the HTML file (by opening the File menu and choosing Open URL), or you can send the session to someone else so they can follow your route.

Enhanced Mosaic Options

NCSA Mosaic has a menu full of options. Enhanced NCSA Mosaic, in the interest of simplicity, has reduced the number of options available. Open the Edit menu and choose Preferences to see the Preferences dialog box in figure B.9. This box is the replacement for Mosaic's Options menu.

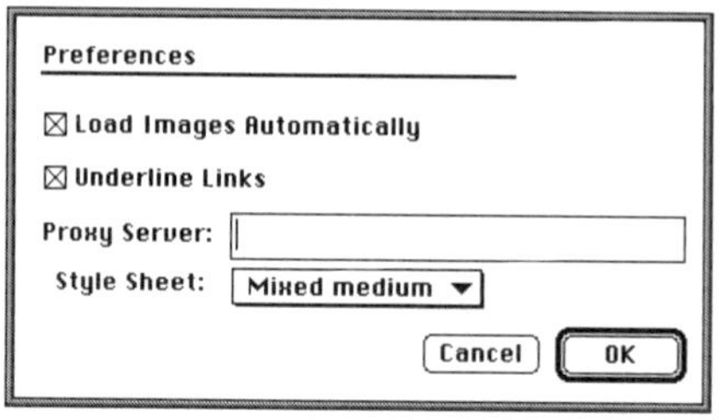

Fig. B.9

The Preferences dialog box replaces Mosaic's Options menu.

Preferences

☒ Load Images Automatically

☒ Underline Links

Proxy Server: |

Style Sheet: Mixed medium ▼

Cancel   OK

Tip

If you turned off Load Images Automatically, you can open the Navigate menu and choose Load Missing Images at any time to view the inline images in the current document.

The Load Images Automatically check box turns inline images on and off. Turn them off to increase speed. (Inline images in HTML files on your hard disk are still displayed, but images in documents that have to be transferred across the WWW aren't.)

The Underline Links check box turns on link underlining. If you leave this turned off, you are still able to see the links because they are a different color (but you can't change that color).

Finally, the Style Sheet is Enhanced NCSA Mosaic's version of Mosaic's Styles dialog (from the Options menu). Each style sheet is preconfigured with all the different fonts—headers, body text, and so on—set up correctly. Instead of creating your own style sheet by configuring each font individually, you use one of Spyglass's preconfigured setups (see fig. B.10).

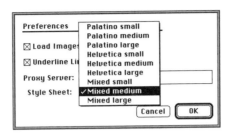

Fig. B.10
This is the list
of style sheets
that come
preconfigured
with Enhanced
Mosaic.

You might not like using the style sheets—after all, you don't have as much flexibility—but there are some advantages. You will probably find a style sheet that suits you, saving you the trouble of experimenting. And if more than one person uses the program it makes it easy to swap between different setups.

Where's the Home Page?

When the people at Spyglass first started working on Enhanced NCSA Mosaic they decided to remove the Home Page feature. They thought many companies would want to control the home page, and not allow their users to change it. But Spyglass got so many requests for home-page features that they put it back in. However, the version I saw did not have this capability.

The current version of Spyglass Enhanced NCSA Mosaic has no way to change the home page, nor does it have a Home Page command that takes you back to the home page. Rather, the home page is set up as a local HTML file, and the only way to go directly back to the home page is to choose File, New Window, which opens a new window with the initial .html file as home.

Later versions of the program will let you change the home page. There will be a text box in the Preferences dialog box and a Go Home Page menu option.

Bits and Pieces

The following are a few other changes Spyglass made to the NCSA version in their version, not necessarily significant, but worth noting:

■ To see the HTML source for the document you are viewing, open the Edit menu and choose View Source (see fig. B.11). You can select a part

B

Appendix B

of the document and press ⌘+C to copy it. You then must click OK to close the window before pasting this selection into another application.

■ To close all open windows, open the File menu and choose Close All.

Fig. B.11
The Source Window shows the raw HTML codes and text for the document you have open.

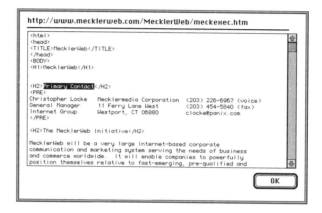

Missing Features

So what can Mosaic do that Enhanced NCSA Mosaic does *not* do? There are a few things missing from the Spyglass version:

■ There is no toolbar. Toolbars are useful, so it's a shame this is missing.

■ There's no reliable way to stop a transfer. You can't click the globe icon to do this, as you can in freeware Mosaic.

■ No way to add a menu of hotlist items—but that's because Spyglass wants the product to be simple to use. You still have the Hotlist dialog box, though.

■ None of the annotation features are included (although these features weren't working in the NCSA version until alpha 8 either!).

■ Spyglass Mosaic has less control of the specifics of styles.

Enhanced NCSA Mosaic is a solid program, with some real advantages over freeware Mosaic—in particular speed, size, and the ability to reliably save the current document. But some of the omissions are a little irritating. There should be a way to stop a transfer, for example, and to change home pages. However, for some, the smaller program size and faster operation may make up for these omissions.

MacWeb from EINet

MacWeb is a World Wide Web viewer from EINet (Enterprise Integration Network), a service provider owned by Microelectronics and Computer Technology Corporation (MCC). They have created a Web site they call EINet Galaxy, and the main Galaxy document appears as MacWeb's home page— though you can select whatever page you want as the home page, of course. And, like Mosaic, MacWeb is free for noncommercial use. There's also a Windows version, WinWeb.

Installing MacWeb

At the time of this writing, EINet had released Version 1.00 alpha2.2, a prerelease version. This version is available and you can use it, but don't be surprised if you run into bugs. When I used MacWeb, though, I found it to be pretty stable.

You can find MacWeb at the **ftp.einet.net** FTP site, in the /einet/mac/ macweb directory. Download the file macweb.latest.sea.hqx to get the latest available version. Or, if you are already working with a WWW viewer, you can get MacWeb off the World Wide Web at **http://galaxy.einet.net/ EINet/MacWeb/MacWebHome.html**. (In this document, you'll find a link currently called macweb.latest.sea.hqx. Set up your browser to download, because clicking the link causes the EINet site to send the file to your system.)

When you download the sea archive file, extract the MacWeb files to a folder you've created for MacWeb. That's it. You've installed MacWeb. Start your Internet connection, double-click the icon, and MacWeb starts. You can see the MacWeb home page in figure B.12. You see this page when you first start MacWeb.

> ### Note
>
> In the 1.00 alpha2.2 version, loading graphics is off by default. Figure B.12 shows the home page with the graphics on.

The home page file is a local file called MacWeb.html that is saved in a folder named Documents, which is in the folder where you extract MacWeb. You don't have to use this page as your home page. If you would prefer to use another—the one provided by your service provider, for instance—open the File menu and choose Preferences. The Preferences dialog box appears (see fig. B.13).

Fig. B.12
The MacWeb window, showing the default home page.

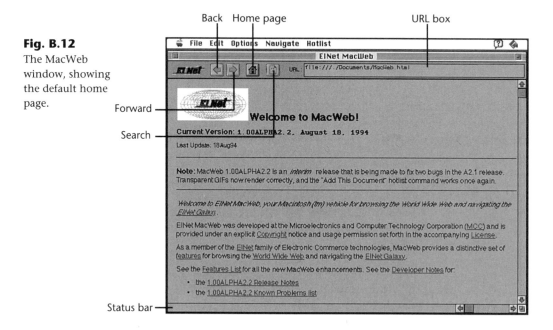

Fig. B.13
Among other options, the Preferences dialog box is where you choose the home page you see each time you start MacWeb.

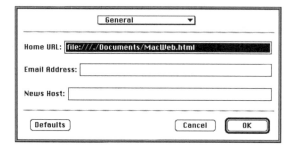

Tip
If you have already saved some document URLs in a hotlist, you can copy the URL for a page and paste it into the box for the home page.

The MacWeb Home Page is the default page, but you can enter any other URL address here.

The MacWeb Toolbar

Let's take a quick look at the MacWeb toolbar. The toolbar buttons are shown in figure B.14.

- *Backward.* Returns to the previous document (the same as Navigate, Back).

- *Forward.* Goes to the next document in the history list if you are not at the last document (the same as Navigate, Forward).

- *Home.* Displays the home page (the same as Navigate, Home).

- *Search.* Lets you search the current document (the same as Navigate, Search. However, this was not working in the alpha2.2 version I saw).

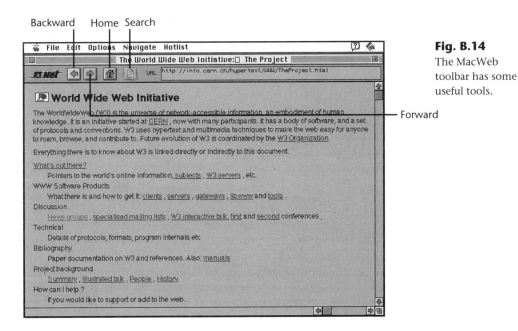

Fig. B.14
The MacWeb toolbar has some useful tools.

Using MacWeb

MacWeb is not as sophisticated as Mosaic or some of its derivatives, but for many users its simplicity more than makes up for that. It doesn't have as many options as Mosaic, but what it does have is pretty well designed. In fact, the design is so good that you should notice much faster performance. You will also find that MacWeb takes less memory to run (about 2MB is suggested with a 700KB minimum compared to a 3MB suggested and 2MB minimum for NCSA's latest release). And it requires a mere 400KB of hard disk space compared to 1.3MB for NCSA.

The basics are the same as with any WWW viewer, of course; click links to go places. When MacWeb transfers a document, it displays a small dialog box with a Cancel button inside it. You can just click the button to stop the transfer.

Let's look at the other navigational tools—you can see the menu commands in table B.1. Notice that all the navigation commands are not under the Navigate menu.

Table B.1 The Navigation Commands	
Command	**Action**
Navigate, Forward	Displays the next document
Navigate, Backward	Displays the previous document
Navigate, Home	Displays your home page
Navigate, History	Opens a submenu History List so that you can go back to a previous document
Navigate, Search	Searches the current document. You can enter a search keyword. (Does not work in the alpha2.2 version.)
Navigate, ElNet Galaxy	Opens the ElNet Galaxy Home Page
Navigate, ElNet	Opens the ElNet Home Page
Navigate, MacWeb Home Page	Opens the MacWeb Home Page
File, Open URL	Displays a dialog box that you can type a URL into. When you choose the OK button the document is displayed.
File, Reload	Reloads the current document.

Using the Hotlist

Mosaic uses a hotlist, a sort of bookmark system, to help you find your way back to documents you want to return to. MacWeb has a similar system. The current version has the hotlist as part of the menu bar.

If you are viewing a World Wide Web document that you think you'll want to return to, open the Hotlist menu and choose Add This Document. The document is immediately added to your hotlist.

When you need to go to one of the documents you've added to your hotlist, open the Hotlist menu and choose the document to go to. Figure B.15 shows this menu with items added.

Two documents added to hotlist

Fig. B.15
The hotlist with
two documents
added.

Using Multiple Hotlists

MacWeb's scheme for multiple hotlists isn't as slick as the NCSA version
(there's no way to add more than one hotlist to a menu and you can't create
hierarchical submenus), but its simplicity is nice compared to NCSA. Like the
NCSA version, you can create unlimited numbers of hotlists (the only limit is
the drive space to store them). MacWeb stores each hotlist as a separate file.
So, if you want to send a particular hotlist to a friend or colleague so that
they can easily get to the documents on your list, just give them a copy of
your hotlist file.

To start a new hotlist file, open the Hotlist menu, choose Hotlist Operations,
and then choose New.

> **Note**
>
> If you have made any changes to your currently open hotlist, you will be prompted
> to save them before you open a new one.

After choosing New, your hotlist will have no entries in it. You can now add
any new items to it as described earlier in this chapter in the section "Using
the Hotlist."

To open another Hotlist, open the Hotlist menu, choose Hotlist Operations,
and then choose Open. In the dialog box, choose the name of the hotlist you
want to open.

To save hotlists, open the Hotlist menu, choose Hotlist Operations, and then
choose Save. If the hotlist has already been named and saved, it is saved immediately. If this is the first time you are saving it (or if you open the Hotlist
menu, choose Hotlist Operations, and then choose Save As), you need to
enter a name and choose a folder for the hotlist.

When you use the Save as command, you have the option to save the hotlist
as a different file type. You can save this as a MacWeb Hotlist, a MacMosaic
Hotlist (to use with NCSA's Mosaic hotlist feature), or you can save it as an
HTML document to create a Web document that you can open (see fig. B.16).

B

Appendix B

Fig. B.16
The three format
options for saving
a hotlist.

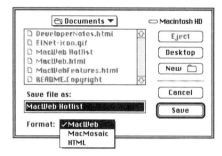

One final worthwhile feature is the ability to edit hotlists. This feature is
similar to the edit feature in NCSA Mosaic. To edit an item on the open
hotlist, follow these steps:

1. Open the Hotlist menu, choose Hotlist Operations, and then choose
Edit. The dialog box shown in figure B.17 opens.

Fig. B.17
Select the item to
edit here.

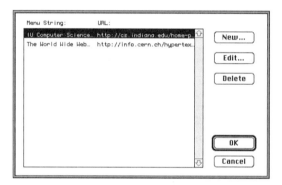

2. Click the item to edit.

3. Click the Edit Button. The dialog box shown in figure B.18 appears.

Fig. B.18
Change the name
or URL of the item
here.

4. Make any desired changes to the Menu String (what MacWeb called the
title) or the URL, and then click OK twice to close the two dialog boxes.

Sorting Your Hotlists

Here's a feature that must have been designed just for the terminally unorganized, like myself. After adding a dozen items to a hotlist, you may notice it is difficult to find a particular entry. To organize your hotlists, follow these steps:

1. Open the Hotlist menu, choose Hotlist Operations, and then choose Sort.

2. This opens another sublevel in the menu with these two options:

   By Menu String. Sorts alphabetically according to the name of the entries in the hotlist.

   By URL. Sorts alphabetically according to the document URL. The entries are still displayed by name, though.

   Choose one of these options and the currently open hotlist is sorted.

Using the History List

To access the History list, open the Navigate menu and choose History. A submenu with all the documents from this session opens (see fig. B.19). Choose the document you want to open.

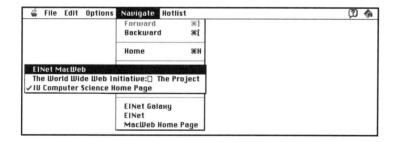

Fig. B.19
Use the History list to return to documents you viewed earlier.

Customizing MacWeb

You have a few ways to customize MacWeb; open the File menu and choose Preferences to get to the tools that let you do so. You get three sets of options here.

The first is the same dialog box where you change your home page (this dialog box was described earlier in the section "Installing MacWeb"), as shown in figure B.20.

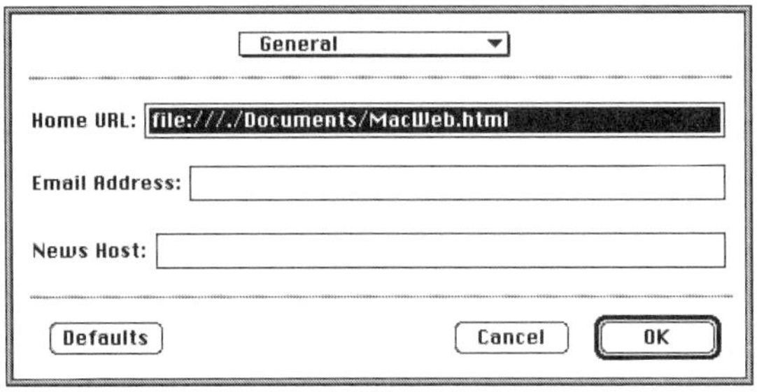

Fig. B.20
Customizing the home page, e-mail address, and newshost.

If you plan to use MacWeb for e-mail or newsreading, you should fill in the appropriate information in this dialog box.

Selecting the files/folders item from the drop-down list at the top of the dialog box changes the dialog box to the one shown in figure B.21.

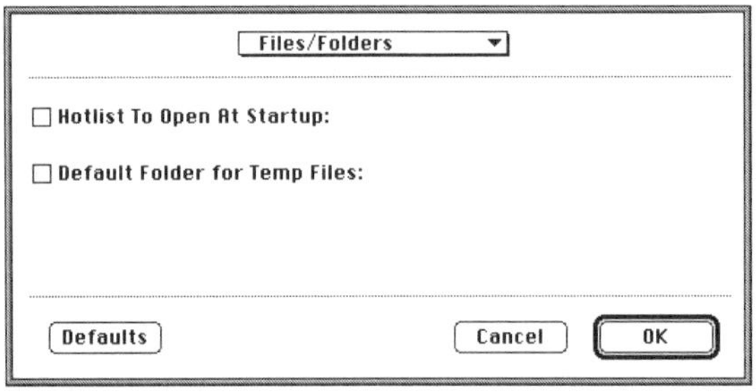

Fig. B.21
Customizing the hotlist and temp folder.

To customize the hotlist to open when MacWeb starts or the default folder for temp files (MacWeb temporarily stores files on your drive when downloading large files to view), select the appropriate check box. A standard Open dialog box appears; select the hotlist or folder you want.

Finally, if you select the Format option from the drop-down list at the top of the dialog box, the dialog box in figure B.22 appears.

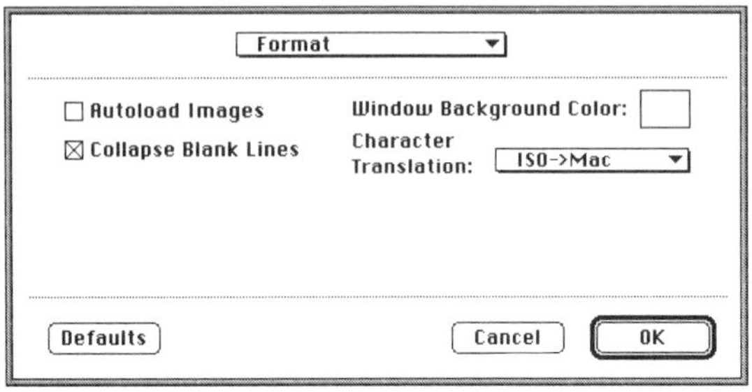

Fig. B.22
MacWeb lets you modify several Web options.

The most commonly used option on this dialog is Autoload Images. When selected, inline images are automatically loaded. If not selected, you can open the Options menu and choose Load Images to load inline images.

The other options in this dialog box are:

- Collapse Blank lines, which shrinks documents that you view so that you never have more than one empty line in a row (some people try to format documents by having five, ten, or more blank lines in a row as spacers).

- Window Background Color, which lets you select a background color for Web documents.

- Character translation, which opens a drop-down list of various character sets you can use for various foreign languages.

Font Options

MacWeb has a nice little tool for selecting the fonts to use in various types of document text. Open the Edit menu and choose Styles to see the dialog box shown in figure B.23.

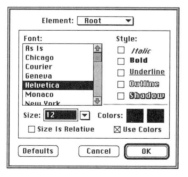

Fig. B.23
Use the Styles dialog box to determine how documents are displayed.

Click the Element drop-down list to display the types of text you can change and select the item you want to change (see fig. B.24). The dialog box shows you how that text is currently set up. Choose the new font styles you want to use, and then click OK.

Fig. B.24

Use the drop-down list of elements to choose the type of text to change.

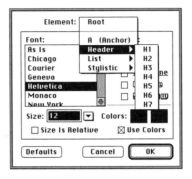

Multiple Windows

Like NCSA Mosaic, MacWeb allows multiple independent open windows. To open a new window, open the File menu, choose New or press the Option key on the keyboard, and then click a hyperlink.

Helper Applications and Suffixes

Changing the Helper applications (applications used to view images in JPEG, MGEG, or QuickTime, Stuff-It Expander, and so on) is done in essentially the same way as in NCSA. To get to these options, follow these steps:

1. Open the Options menu and choose Helpers. The dialog box shown in B.25 appears.

Fig. B.25

This shows a list of all the file types and their helper applications.

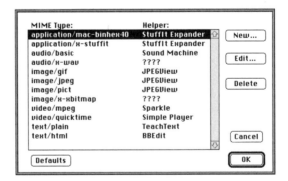

2. Select a type from the list to edit.

3. Click the Edit button. The dialog box shown in figure B.26 appears.

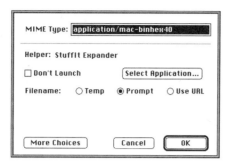

Fig. B.26
Options for the
selected helper.

4. Here you can choose a different file (MIME) type for the application, a
different application for the file type, whether to start the application
when a file of its type is downloaded, and whether to use a temporary
file name, be prompted for a file name, or use the URL as a file name
when downloading files.

5. To see even more choices, click more choices (see fig. B.27). The defaults in this dialog box depend on the file type chosen. Make any
needed changes, and then click OK.

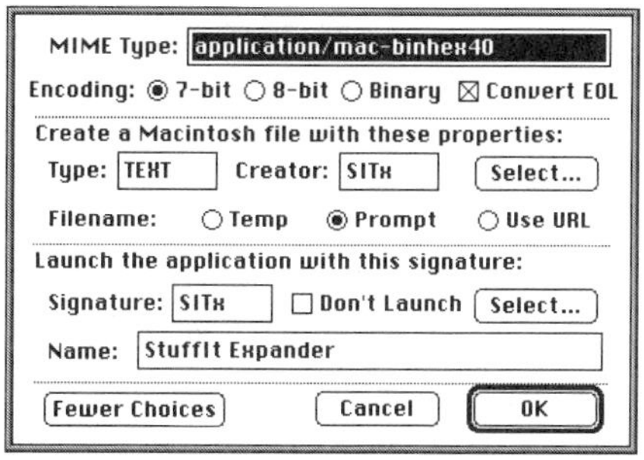

Fig. B.27
More options for
the chosen helper
application.

6. Click OK to close the dialog box and to accept the changes.

Note

To add a new type for a different type of file, click New.

The part of the file name after the period is called the *file suffix*. To change
the file suffixes, open the Edit menu and choose Suffixes (see fig. B.28). Macs
can usually identify file types, but they can't always identify files transmitted
on the Internet. These default settings should be okay for most uses, but if

B

Appendix B

you find that a particular file suffix opens an application for the wrong file type (for instance, Stuff-it opens to view a picture rather than your image viewer opening to view the picture) you may need to change the settings.

Fig. B.28

The suffixes are on the left and the file type is on the right. These types correspond to the types from the helpers dialog boxes.

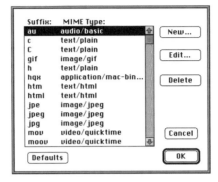

Select an entry, and then click Edit. You'll see the box shown in figure B.29.

Fig. B.29

Use this dialog to change the suffix or type.

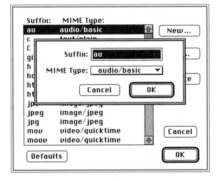

Enter the suffix in the box provided or select a file type from the MIME Type drop-down list.

Viewing the Source for a Document

MacMosaic gives you three options for viewing the underlying HTML document source. To view any of these, open the Options menu, choose View Source, and then choose Generated, Retrieved, or Retrieved+Headers. The best way to see this difference is to look at examples, as shown in figures B.30, B.31, and B.32. Your text helper application opens all these. Depending on what information beyond the basic text you need, choose the appropriate option. You can copy and paste using the commands for your text editor.

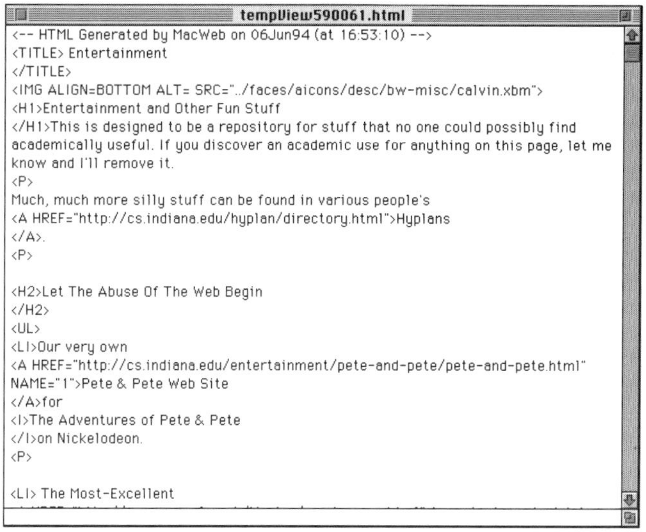

Fig. B.30
Viewing Source
Generated option.

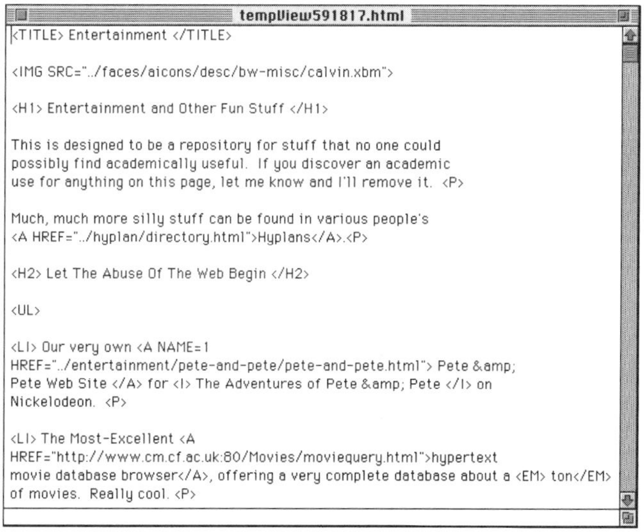

Fig. B.31
Viewing Source
Retrieved option.

B

Appendix B

Fig. B.32

Viewing Source
Retrieved+Headers
option.

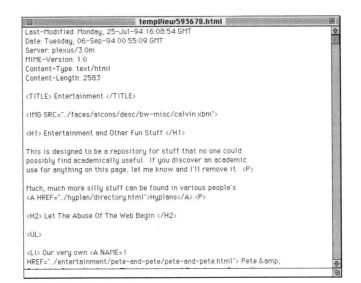

Index

Symbols

A

15 Hour Free Trial*

Internet access doesn't have to be expensive or difficult. Now you can enjoy **professional quality access** to the Internet for a **reasonable price**. We staff our network site **24 hours a day** 7 days a week 365 days a year to keep the network up and running.

We have also put together a collection of shareware programs for our Windows and Macintosh users to make getting started on the Internet a breeze. You'll get all the software you need and installation instructions when you subscribe.

Billing Options for Every User

Dial-up SLIP or PPP Internet Accounts

- Regular: $0.75 per hour with a $20.00 per month minimum.

- High Volume: $30.00 flat rate per month for up to 70 hours. $0.75 per hour for additional hours.

High   Speed   Lines

All of our modems are 14.4kbps or faster. No waiting for a slow 9600 baud connection. We also have new 28.8K V.34 modem lines for the ultimate in SLIP and PPP speed.

To Get an Account Now:

Call (317) 259-5050 or (800) 844-8649
and tell us you saw our ad in *Using the World Wide Web.*

We'll set up your account immediately and send you all the information and software you need so that you have your Internet access working with no hassles and no delays.

*Some restrictions apply. Call for details.

Easily Navigate the Vast Resources of the Internet

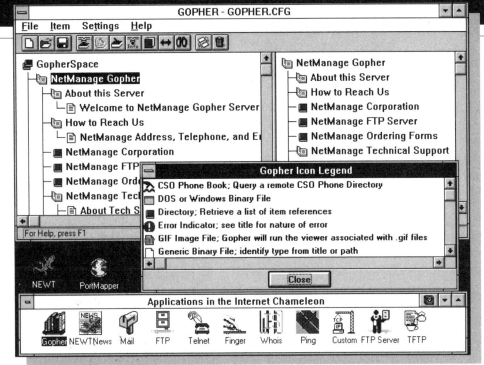

With Internet Chameleon™

Nothing makes cruising the Internet easier than Internet Chameleon. A Windows graphical user interface makes finding information resources easy. The Library of Congress, weather maps, art, history, games. Meet new friends and converse with old friends. Read the latest news as soon as it's written; or cruise through a web of computer networks with information resources so numerous that no other on-line service comes close! With Internet Chameleon, you can navigate the largest universe of information with the click of a button.

Applications Included:

Electronic Mail (SMTP, POP) with MIME and Rules, Internet News Reader, Gopher Client, File Transfer: FTP, TFTP, and FTP Server, Telnet; Utilities: Ping, Finger, WhoIs, SLIP, CSLIP, PPP and ISDN Dial-Up Connections

- More Internet access tools than any other package
- Easy to use point-and-click interface
- Dial into the Internet
- Support for SLIP, CSLIP, PPP and ISDN Internet access
- Pre-configured connections for popular Internet providers
- Easy 5 minute installation
- Native Windows installation and ease of use

MICROSOFT
WINDOWS.
COMPATIBLE

(408) 973-7171
e-mail: sales@netmanage.com
WorldWideWeb: www.netmanage.com
10725 North De Anza Blvd., Cupertino, CA 95014 USA